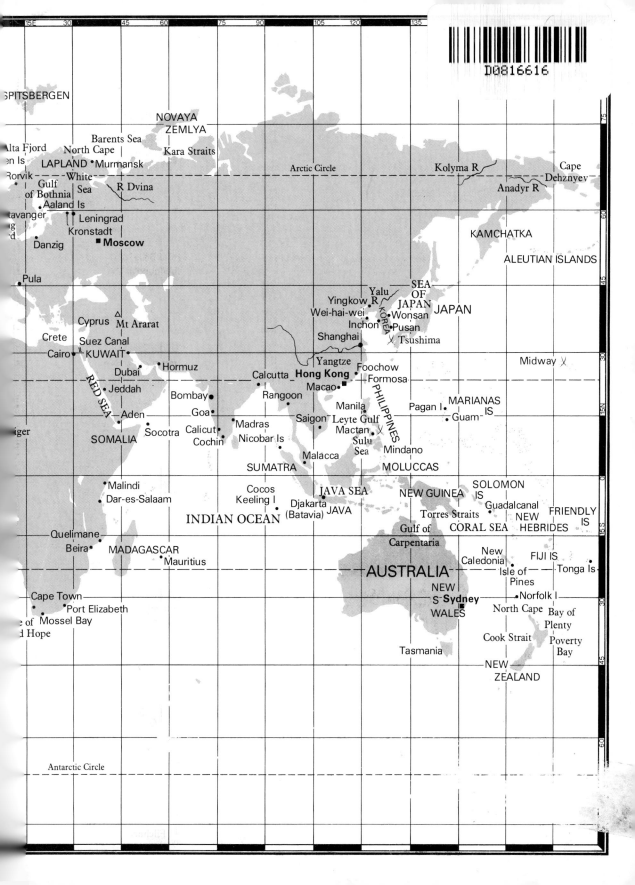

THE **GUINNESS** BOOK OF
SHIPS
AND SHIPPING
FACTS & FEATS

TOM HARTMAN

Guinness Superlatives Limited
2 Cecil Court, London Road, Enfield, Middlesex

For
Sophie and J. B.
with love

Editor: Josie A Marsden
Design and layout: Roger Daniels
Maps: Tony Garrett
First published 1983
© Tom Hartman and Guinness
Superlatives Limited 1983

Typeset in 10/11pt Plantin
by Fakenham Photosetting Ltd, Fakenham,
Norfolk. Printed and bound in Great
Britain by Butler and Tanner Ltd,
Frome, Somerset.

Guinness is a registered trademark of
Guinness Superlatives Ltd.

British Library CIP Data

Hartman, Tom
The Guinness book of ships and shipping facts and feats.
1. Ships – Directories
I. Title
623.8'2'00321   V23
ISBN 0-85112-269-8

Frontispiece **Submarines passing the**
Dreadnought. National Maritime Museum

Contents

Introduction

I hope that this book will not prove totally unworthy to stand beside its predecessors which dealt with transport by car, train and aeroplane. Whatever its shortcomings, I can only plead in justification that the field I have been asked to cover, stretching as it does over the entire timespan of recorded history, is infinitely wide and that the choice of what to include and what to leave out is such that some are bound to feel that important facts have been left out, while much which might be regarded as trivia has been included. Well, as Lincoln or Barnum didn't quite say, depending on which book of 'Facts' you look it up in, 'You can't please all the people all the time' and if I only manage to please some of the people some of the time I shall not feel that the labour was in vain.

The order in which the 'facts' are arranged also caused many headaches. Should, for instance, the loss of a submarine come under 'warfare', 'submarines' or 'disasters'? There is no easy answer and I am aware that many paragraphs could have gone in two or three different places, but I hope that the index is sufficiently comprehensive for the reader to be able to find what he wants without too much trouble. Since all the mistakes in this book are entirely my own responsibility I do not wish to embarrass the many people who have helped me in its compilation by naming them publicly. I must, however, make exceptions in the case of Chris Ware of the National Maritime Museum, who, in the very limited time available to him, checked much of the typescript and corrected numerous howlers, of Mrs Hood and Simon Davis at Lloyd's Register of Shipping, who were unfailingly helpful and patient, and of my father-in-law, for whose advice I am deeply grateful. I would also like to thank Beryl Hill and my wife, who shared the task of typing my manuscript, and last but far from least, Josie Marsden, an editor with the rare but priceless gift of making an author feel that his lonely endeavours, during the long period of gestation, are not going unnoticed.

TOM HARTMAN, LONDON

4

EXPERIMENT
— & —
EXPLORATION

Mediterranean Beginnings

Almost certainly **the first water transport used by man** was no more than a log, astride which our intrepid ancestor sat and propelled himself across a lake or river by paddling with his hands. Later he learned to hollow out the log, either by burning it or by chipping at it with a flint axe and can thus be said to have progressed from the float to the boat. Such dugout canoes are still in daily use in many parts of the world.

From the log or raft, made of several logs lashed together, man progressed to the dugout, to the skin boat, then to the boat made of planks of wood fixed together. This last transition was made in the Neolithic period (2000–1000BC).

The first artificial method of propulsion was probably a branch of wood used as a paddle, and later fashioned as such. In the East the sail came before the oar, the latter, relying as it does on the principle of the fulcrum, being a relatively sophisticated concept.

The earliest known drawings of boats are rock carvings found near Stone Age coastal settlements in Norway. Since man still lived by hunting, it is reasonable to assume that his skill as a seaman developed alongside his skill as a fisherman. Northern seamen of the time certainly ventured 20–30 miles (32–48km) offshore as is proved by the bones of deep-water fish such as cod and pollock found on a Stone Age site near Stavanger. For such expeditions they certainly used skin boats.

Though it is possible that at one time the seamen of the North were more skilled than those of the Eastern Mediterranean and the Nile Valley, certainly it was the latter who were to display the more rapid advance in nautical achievement in the pre-Christian era, and it is to them that we must turn our attention.

The Eastern Mediterranean

The development of civilization in Ancient Egypt was conditioned, geographically, by the River Nile, which is, so to speak, both the backbone and the lifeblood of the country.

As there is very little timber in Egypt **the earliest boats were made of bundles of papyrus-reed** and were essentially rafts rather than boats. They were propelled by paddles and steered with an oar.

These boats from Huanchaco, Peru, are made from bundles of reeds, as were their Ancient Egyptian ancestors. *Exeter Maritime Museum*.

Later, man learned to use the skins of animals for clothing, to make primitive shelters, or to use as a curtain in the entrance to a draughty cave. From this development evolved the 'skin boat', light craft made of skins stretched over shaped frames of basketwork. Such craft survive to this day in the Eskimo kayak, in the Welsh coracle and the Irish curragh.

Although it is likely that the sail was in use around the shores of the Persian Gulf well before 3500BC, **the first known picture of a sailing ship** is on an Egyptian vase dated to *c* 3100BC. It shows a craft with high, almost vertical ends, a pole mast and a rectangular sail.

It being impossible for the Egyptians to build boats made of long strakes of timber, they had recourse to short planks of acacia wood, probably making the transition to this form of construction at about the same time as it occurred in the North. A boat of the Twelfth Dynasty (2000–1800BC), constructed of planks laid edge to edge and joined by flat dowels and dovetail-shaped tenons, was excavated at Dahshur, 20 miles (32km) south of Cairo.

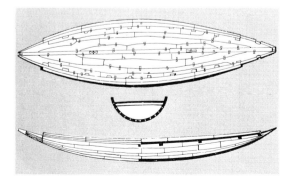

The claim of Noah to have been among the earliest shipbuilders on record must, sadly, be relegated to the realms of legend. In answer to the question 'How can one say categorically that it is not true?' several arguments have been put forward; firstly that there would not have been enough wood in the entire Tigris–Euphrates valley to build a vessel entirely of timber, as Genesis VI. 14. lays down; if the ark did exist it was more likely to have been a raft built of reeds in the manner still practised in that part of the world. Secondly, all the water in the world, together with the vapour, if reduced to water, would not cover the earth to the height of Mount Ararat. Thirdly, the collection of the animals would plainly have been impossible. Flood legends occur in the folklore of many of the world's peoples but efforts to link them together as evidence of one universal catastrophic flood are futile. To Noah, however, does go the credit for being **the first to cultivate the vine and to have drunk not wisely but too well** (Genesis IX. 21)!

The prevailing wind in Egypt blows from the north so boats can sail up-river with the wind and coast downstream on the current. Indeed, the hieroglyphic symbol for 'Go South' showed a boat with a sail, that for 'Go North' a boat without one.

By the time of the Pharoah Snefru (*c* 2920BC) voyages to Syria were made regularly, the ships being paddled north against the prevailing wind and running home before the wind with the sail hoisted on the tall bipod mast.

The first historical reference to a naval expedition dates from about 2700BC when the Pharaoh Sahu-re sent an expedition to the coast of Phoenicia to capture slaves. Although no two Greek or Roman writers accord Phoenicia the same boundaries, at one time or another it

Fragment of a relief showing one of the ships of Sahu-re's expedition to the coast of Phoenicia.

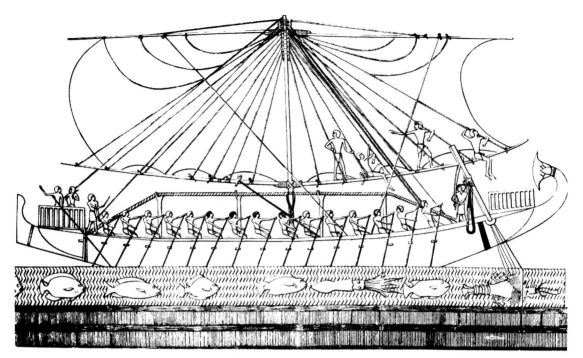

Drawing of a relief carving in the temple of Deir el Bahari at Thebes showing an Egyptian ship of Queen Hatshepsut's expedition to Punt.

covered the area roughly described by the Amanus Mountains, the Anti-Lebanon and Mount Carmel.

A relief of that date gives a clear idea of what Sahu-re's vessels were like. The hulls, which had no keel or frames, were supported fore-and-aft by a rope stretched over a series of props or Sampson's posts. The bipod mast could be lowered when the ship was under oars. On the forepost was painted the symbolic eye which has remained a feature of ship decoration to this day.

Records have also survived of the fleet of five Egyptian ships which Queen Hatshepsut sent, in about 1500BC, to the land of Punt which lay somewhere to the south of the Red Sea, possibly on the northern coast of the Republic of Somalia.

Queen Hatshepsut married her half-brother, Thutmose III, who erected many obelisks, including two misleadingly known as Cleopatra's Needles, one now in London, the other in New York.

One obelisk, 100ft (30.5m) high and weighing about 350 tons, still stands before the Temple of Amon Ra at Karnak. It is one of a pair brought down the Nile from the quarries at Karnak, and it

is estimated that this would have required a barge about 200ft (61m) long, with a beam of 80ft (24m) and an unloaded displacement of 800 tons. This was probably **the largest craft in Ancient Egypt.**

It is interesting to compare the drawing of the Punt Expedition ship with the relief of a ship of the time of Sahu-re. The bipod mast has been replaced by a single spar, the tall narrow sail by a much wider sail lashed to an adjustable boom. The shape of the hull is much the same and the truss, supported on Sampson's posts, to brace the hull against hogging, remains a feature of the design. The motive power has increased from eight to 15 oarsmen on either side. The single steering oar of the Punt ship would have made it easier to control than its predecessor.

The first picture of a naval engagement dates from the time of Rameses III, who ruled Egypt from 1198 to 1167BC. In his tomb at Medinet Habu reliefs show the Egyptians doing battle with what the inscriptions call 'the peoples of the sea', believed to be Indo-Europeans who had advanced by sea and land from Cyprus and Cilicia (Southern Turkey) down the coast of Palestine. In the reliefs the Egyptian boats are identical to those of the invaders which some historians have taken as evidence that the former, essentially a river people, modelled their seagoing craft on those of the seafaring people from the North. It seems equally possible that the sculptor never saw the enemy craft and therefore stuck to the one design with which he was familiar.

Nevertheless the reliefs show **two features which have not appeared hitherto**: the masts have cup-shaped 'tops', ancestors of the fighting tops of sailing-ship days; and the sails are 'brailed', thus enabling them to be furled without the yard being lowered.

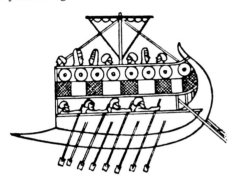

The first known depiction of a bireme, a galley with the oars arranged on two levels.

The first known pictures of biremes, on two Assyrian reliefs dating from the reign of Sennacherib (705–681 BC), probably depict part of the fleet which he had built by Phoenician prisoners and with which he destroyed the Babylonian colony in Elam, at the head of the Persian Gulf, in 694 BC. It would appear from these that the outer oarsmen sat on thwarts which projected from the hull, their oars supported by outriggers.

The first triremes, Thucydides tells us, were built in the middle of the 7th century BC. Unfortunately he does not tell us how the oars were arranged, merely saying that 'these ships were still only partially decked'. The Finnish historian and artist Björn Landström has suggested that the thwarts on which the oarsmen sat were placed 'at an angle, each running obliquely forwards and outwards from the centre-line of the vessel. Two oarsmen sat side by side on the upper bank of thwarts and only one on the lower, sitting in such a position that he could stretch his arms forward between both the oarsmen in front of him.'

Many other theories as to how the oarsmen were arranged have been advanced over the years and much academic heat has been generated, but it is possible that the argument may soon be resolved. In *The Times* of 20 August 1982 it was announced that a Greek shipowner had put up £250,000 to allow three Englishmen to build a replica of the trireme. One of the trio, Professor John Morrison, President of Wolfson College, Cambridge, said that 'the trireme was a vessel built largely of pinewood, with an oaken keel, which employed 170 oarsmen on three decks and a few footsoldiers on top'. His subsequent remarks appeared to confirm the conclusions of two American scholars, Vernard Foley and Werner Soedel, whose description of a 5th century Greek trireme was published in *The Sunday Times* on 26 April 1981: 'The hull was 115ft (35m) long by 11½ft (3.5m) wide, and made of light wood, with a dead weight of 40 tons. The crew of 170 men were seated in three tiers and were not slaves but free men who were comparatively well paid. Perfect discipline and dedication were essential, for if even one disaffected oarsman got out of rhythm the effect would be disastrous, but the men were certainly not whipped into action. The stroke was called by a chanter. They estimate the trireme's top speed at 11.5 knots, which is 1½ knots better than the average speed of a University Boat Race crew.'

The first people to design ships to attack other ships were the Phoenicians who dominated the Eastern Mediterranean from 1100 to 800 BC. They invented the ram, which was to remain part of the offensive equipment of the world's most sophisticated navies until late in the 19th century. Hitherto ships of war had been no more than floating platforms which served as a precarious battlefield for the soldiers they carried. Henceforward the ships themselves became weapons of war.

The first sea battle in recorded history was fought in 664 BC between the Corinthians and the Corcyrans, who lived on the island we know as Corfu; but **the first recorded use of the ram in a sea battle** does not occur until over 100 years later when Herodotus describes how the Carthaginians sank the Phocaean fleet at the Battle of Alalia off the coast of Corsica.

The Egyptian Pharaoh Necho (609–543 BC), son of Psamtik I and father of Psamtik II, is said by

Herodotus to have sent a Phoenician ship down the East coast of Africa in about 600BC. The intrepid sailors are reputed to have sailed westward round the Cape of Good Hope and finally to have reached Gibraltar after a journey lasting three years. Modern scholars say that such a journey would not have been impossible but add that it would have called for 'qualities of endurance and fortitude that raise it to the level of the magnificent; while the problem of preserving the fabric of the ships during three active sailing seasons must have verged on the insuperable' (PHILLIPS-BIRT, *A History of Seamanship*).

Nevertheless, the claims of Necho should not be too lightly dismissed. In the Second Book of Chronicles he is quoted as saying to Josiah, 'Forbear thee from meddling with God, who is with me, that he destroy thee not.' Josiah meddled and was destroyed.

The Phoenicians were **the most skilful navigators of their day**. 'They knew a better way of distinguishing North than by means of the Great Bear group of stars. This was by using the Little Bear, which had the advantage of appearing brighter and earlier in the night. Furthermore, the Little Bear was at that time more nearly circumpolar than the Pole star, also used by the Phoenicians; circumstances differing from those of today when the processional movement has brought the Pole star almost coincidental with the Pole, while the Bear constellations are further away from it. "By her [the Little Bear's] guidance the men of Sidon steer the straightest course," said the Greek poet Aratus in 275BC when the practice was already old.' (PHILLIPS-BIRT).

The Phocaeans, who dominated the Mediterranean after the eclipse of the Phoenicians, **were the first of the maritime Greek states to develop the penteconter**, the forerunner of the oared fighting vessels which dominated the Mediterranean for the next 2000 years. The penteconter, as its name implies, had a crew of 50; it was about 80ft (24m) long including the ram and 10ft (3m) in the beam.

While the Carthaginians were establishing themselves as the supreme power in the Western Mediterranean, thereby laying the foundations of the Punic Wars, in the Eastern Mediterranean the city states of Greece were engaged in **a series of wars** with the Persians **which have been described as the most important that occurred for the next 1000 years**. The eventual victory of the Greeks was achieved by their supremacy at sea.

The Greek victory at Salamis on 23(?) September 480BC has been called **the most important naval battle in all history**, since it was the defeat of the Persians under Xerxes which allowed the civilization of Ancient Greece to flourish and eventually to become the foundation on which so much of our own cultural heritage is based. The Persian fleet outnumbered that of the Greeks by about 800 to 380 but the Athenian commander Themistocles managed to lure the Persians into the narrow channel between the Greek mainland and the island of Salamis where they were unable to manoeuvre and superior numbers were of no avail. The battle lasted for seven hours, while hundreds of small 'land' battles were fought across the decks of the jammed vessels, but in the end the superiority of the Greek hoplite over the soldiers under Xerxes' command decided the issue. The Persians lost about 200 ships, the Greeks 40. Never again did the Persians challenge the Greeks at sea and in the following year they abandoned their attempt to conquer Greece altogether.

The longest maritime war in history, the Peloponnesian War, lasted for nearly 55 years, though some historians do not regard the period between 459 and 431BC as belonging to the war proper. Nevertheless, intermittent naval warfare between Athens and Sparta, backed by their respective allies, continued from 458BC, when the Corinthian fleet was overwhelmed by the Athenians, until 405BC when the Athenian fleet of nearly 200 vessels was completely destroyed by the Spartans at the Battle of Aegospotami.

The first man to equip his ships with missile throwers was Dionysius the Elder (*c* 430–367BC) who set himself up as tyrant of Syracuse in 405. He caused machines to be fitted to enlarged triremes which could throw sizeable rocks a distance of about 200yd (183m). From these enlarged triremes was developed the quinquereme, also first built by Dionysius. By the time of the Punic Wars (from 264BC) the quinquereme had become the standard warship in the

Mediterranean, and carried a crew of about 300 oarsmen and seamen, as well as about 100 foot-soldiers, equivalent to latter-day marines.

The first recorded instance of the use of a special assault clearance ship occurred during the Peloponnesian War at the siege of Syracuse in 413BC. The Syracusans, under command of the Spartan general, Gylippus, drove piles into the bed of the harbour, whereupon the Athenians sent down divers to saw off the submerged piles which were then winched out of the mud by a vessel specially equipped with protective screens.

The first major minesweeping operation in naval history was undertaken by Alexander the Great (356–323BC) during the siege of Tyre in 332BC. The Tyrians dropped massive boulders into the harbour to impede Alexander's ships which were lashed together in pairs to form a stable base for his seaborne assault towers. Eventually, after a siege lasting seven months, the harbour was cleared, a breach was made by sea-borne siege engines and the city fell. As an example to others, Alexander ordered the city to be levelled and the inhabitants dispersed as slaves.

The first Greek to visit and describe Western Europe was the navigator, geographer and astronomer Pytheas (300BC). Though his principal work, *On the Ocean*, is lost, something is known of his journeys through the Greek historian Polybius. Polybius himself thought that the work of Pytheas was a tissue of lies, but it is now accepted that he sailed from Massilia (Marseilles) to Gabes (Cadiz), up the coast of Brittany, to Belerium (Land's End) and then along the Channel and some distance up the east coast of England. He may also have travelled as far east as the mouth of the River Vistula on the Baltic Sea, but it is more likely that the 'amber' island which he describes is Heligoland. To the northernmost island of which he heard tell he gave the name Thule and it was through him that this name was destined to become famous in the works of Roman authors. 'The identification of Thule with Mainland in the Shetlands rests on the authority of Ptolemy. But ... in all probability Thule was Norway.' (Additional notes by M. CARY to H. TOZER's *History of Ancient Geography*.)

Pythias was **the first man to use observations** of the sun's altitude to fix the latitude of a certain place. He was also **the first Greek to observe that the movement of the tides was connected with the phases of the moon.**

The largest ship of ancient times is said to have been the tesserakonter built by Ptolemy IV (244–203BC), ironically known as Ptolemy Philopator because he murdered his father and, incidentally, his mother, brother and also his sister, having first married her. The tesserakonter is reputed to have been 430ft (131m) long, 58ft (17.7m) in the beam, and to have carried a crew of 7000 men, but it is doubtful if she ever went to sea. An equally apocryphal and, in this context, quite irrelevant story is told of Ptolemy IV. He ordered an immense number of Jews to be exposed on a plain and trodden under the feet of elephants, but by supernatural instinct, the generous animals turned their fury not on the Jews but upon the Egyptian spectators.

Carthage and Rome

The greatest power in the Mediterranean after the fall of Athens was Carthage. The First Punic War (264–242BC) was fought between Rome and Carthage to decide who should be paramount in Sicily. At the outset the Romans had no navy but, by using a captured Carthaginian quinquereme as a model, they managed to build 120 ships in 60 days.

An imaginative engraving of the grappling corvus first used at the Battle of Mylae in 260BC. *Mary Evans Picture Library.*

A Roman trireme of about 30BC. The tower is thought to be part of the background, not of the ship. *Mansell Collection.*

The first tactical use of a secret weapon in warfare occurred at the Battle of Mylae in 260BC when the Romans demonstrated the effectiveness of the 'corvus'. Confident of the superiority of the Roman legionary over his Carthaginian rival, they set out to create conditions of land warfare at sea by equipping their recently-built ships with a device which combined a gangway and a grapnel. Known as a 'corvus', or raven, it was a narrow bridge about 18ft (5.5m) long mounted on a pivot near the bow of the galley. When not in use it was held upright by ropes and pulleys. When an enemy ship approached it could be swung outboard in any direction and let down with a crash on the enemy vessel's deck where it was held fast by a spike fixed under its outer end. The legionaries then dashed across the corvus and engaged the enemy hand-to-hand. The Romans, unlike the developers of many subsequent technological innovations, had the good sense to wait until they had a considerable fleet of ships so equipped before they used them in battle, thereby winning a decisive victory.

The commander at Mylae, **Rome's first naval victory**, was Gaius Duilius. He was awarded **the first naval triumph in Roman history** and a memorial column adorned with the bronze beaks of the captured ships was erected in the Forum.

The Punic Wars were **the first in which administrative organizations were established comparable to a modern admiralty**. Special departments were set up, both by the Romans and the Carthaginians, to control their respective navies in which individual fleets sometimes numbered as many as 350 ships.

The greatest disaster which befell the Romans during the war owed more to the hand of God than to those of the Carthaginians. After the Battle of Tunes in 255BC, in which the Romans were defeated by the Spartan soldier of fortune, Xanthippus, who had come to the assistance of the Carthaginians, 5000 soldiers were rescued by the Roman fleet. Returning to Sicily, the fleet ran into a storm and 284 ships out of 364 went to the bottom, taking with them 100,000 of Rome's best soldiers, sailors and marines.

The artemon was first used, on Roman merchant ships, in about 200BC. This small square sail was carried below a spar which projected obliquely over the bow to the side of the forepost. It was used primarily as a steering aid.

The only battle in classical times between a fleet of sailing ships and an oared fleet occurred in 56BC during Caesar's campaign against the Veneti, the inhabitants of Armorica (Brittany). The opposing fleets met in the Gulf of Morbihan (Quiberon Bay) and the light Roman galleys soon found themselves at a disadvantage against the stoutly built vessels of the Veneti, with their high stems and sterns. So the Romans attached sickles to the ends of long poles and cut the halyards of the Gallic vessels, thus rendering them unable to manoeuvre. They were then able to board the enemy ships and overcome their opponents in hand-to-hand fighting.

Caesar's account of the ships of the Veneti in *De Bello Gallico Book III* is, with the Broighter model (see p. 15), the only evidence of indigenous sail in northern waters during the pre-Christian era. He describes their ships thus: 'Their keels were flatter than in our ships so that they could more easily negotiate the shallows . . . the whole of their ships were made out of oak so as to be able to stand up to any force and stress; the benches a foot high were secured with nails as thick as your thumb; the anchors were fastened with chains instead of ropes; skins and soft leathers served as sails, whether on account of the scarcity of linen and ignorance of how to use it, or more probably because they thought that linen sails would not be strong enough to stand up to the worst storms of the ocean.'

The first effective use of the 'harpago' occurred at the Battle of Naulochus in 36BC. The harpago consisted of a pole with a hook at one end and a rope at the other. The pole was shot from a catapult and the hook attached itself to the side of the enemy ship. The rope was then winched in, bringing the two vessels together to facilitate boarding. It was the invention of Marcus Vipsanius Agrippa who commanded Octavian's fleet at Naulochus where he defeated Sextus Pompey, thereby ending the war known as the War of the Second Triumvirate.

The Battle of Actium in 31BC was **the last great sea battle of the Roman Empire**. Agrippa was once again in command of Octavian's fleet and quickly overcame the fleet of Mark Antony. An interesting feature of the battle was that a reserve squadron of more than 60 vessels was commanded by Antony's wife, Cleopatra. The fact that Antony had divorced Octavian's sister, Octavia, in order to marry Cleopatra was one of the main causes of the war.

The first direct evidence we have of the seaman's use of star altitudes to discover position as opposed merely to give direction comes from the Roman poet Lucan (39–65AD): 'We do not follow any of the restless stars which move in the sky, for they deceive poor sailors. We follow no stars but one, that does not dip into the waves,

the never-setting Axis, brightest star in the twin Bears. This it is that guides our ships.'

Greek fire was apparently first used at the Battle of Cyzicus in 672AD. The invention of Greek or 'wet' fire is attributed to a Syrian architect named Callinicus who fled from his native Heliopolis to Constantinople during the reign of Constantine IV, Pogonatus (the bearded one) (648–85). Exactly what the mixture was is unknown, but one authority suggests that its unique property derived from having quicklime as an ingredient, which, when mixed with sulphur, naphtha, etc., ignited spontaneously when wet. The Byzantine navy were the first to equip their ships with bow tubes from which the deadly fire was blown by a pump. The sailors who manned the pumps were called *siphonariori*. At the Battle of Cyzicus, in the Sea of Marmara, it was used to great effect by the Byzantines to destroy the Saracen fleet which was endeavouring to blockade Constantinople.

The first ships of war that might be called the ancestors of the landing craft of the 20th century were used by Nicephorus Phocas when he captured Crete from the Saracens in 960–61AD. His transport vessels were equipped with ramps down which his cavalrymen could charge and engage the enemy at once. Nicephorus later (963) became co-regent emperor of the Eastern Roman Empire but was murdered by his nephew in 969.

Numerous representations of **Roman merchant ships** have survived, stretching over a considerable period, and from them it would appear that the basic design did not alter much throughout Rome's supremacy in and around the Mediterranean. The ships are broad in the beam, carry a mainsail, two triangular topsails and an artemon sail. The forepost curves up under the forestay, while the sternpost is usually elegantly carved in the shape of a swan's neck and head.

Lucian, writing in the middle of the 2nd century AD, gives us a vivid description of a Roman grain ship: 'What a tremendous vessel it was! 180ft (55m) long . . . and more than a quarter of this across the beam and over 44ft (13.4m) from the deck to the deepest part of the hold. . . . The stern rose in a graceful curve ending in a gilt goosehead, in harmony with the equal curve of the bow and the forepost with its picture of Isis.'

NAUTICAL DEVELOPMENT IN NORTHERN EUROPE

The Vikings

The oldest find made in Scandinavia of a boat made of wood is the Hjortspring boat, which takes its name from the farm on the Danish island of Als where it was found. It is 43ft (13.1m) long and 6ft (1.8m) on the beam and dates from about 350–300BC. It has no keel but the broad bottom plank protrudes at either end in the form of a beak. Similarly the gunwale planks project beyond the hull and are fixed to the 'beak' by vertical end-posts. Ten thwarts cross the hull at gunwale level on which were seated 20 paddlers. The hull, which was made of limewood, comprised a bottom plank, four sideplanks and two endpieces. The upper strakes overlapped the lower strakes by about ¾in (1.9cm), thus making this **the oldest known boat with overlapping strakes** and the forerunner of later clinker-built boats.

The first evidence we have of a Scandinavian boat which carried a mast and sail dates from about 600AD. It is a wooden clinker-built boat excavated at Kvalsund in Norway in 1920. It is 60ft (18.3m) long and 10½ft (3.2m) wide and

A reconstruction of the Hjortspring boat showing the projecting 'beak' and gunwale planks.

shows significant developments in the art of Scandinavian boat-building in that it had a rudimentary form of keel and a fixed side rudder, both vital steps on the road to true ocean sailing.

The two most important archaeological discoveries of Viking ships are those of the Gokstad ship in 1880 and the Oseberg ship in 1904. Both are now to be seen, fully restored, in their own museum outside Oslo. The Oseberg Ship dates from the 9th century, is 70ft (21.3m) long, 17ft (5.2m) wide and constructed entirely of oak. The ship was rowed by 30 oarsmen but had a mast which could be lowered by hinging it downwards into the stern.

The Gokstad ship dates from the 10th century and measures 76½ft (23.2m) long and 17ft (5.2m) wide. On each side are 16 holes for the oars and under the railing can be seen a narrow strip of planking where the crew hung their shields. In spite of the fact that in virtually every picture of every Viking ship in any weather on any seas the inevitable row of shields appears along the gunwale, it is probable that they were only hung there for decorative purposes when the ship was at anchor.

In 1893 Captain Magnus Anderson sailed a replica of the Gokstad ship across the Atlantic in 28 days, and was favourably impressed by the

ease with which the helmsman could control the ship with the short steering oar.

The largest ship mentioned in the Norse sagas is Canute's (*c* 994–1035) *drakkar*, which was said to have been propelled by 120 oarsmen. If one bases one's calculations on the space allotted to each oarsman in the Gokstad ship, this would make Canute's vessel 260ft (79.2m) long. Historians agree that the author of that saga was exaggerating; Björn Landström calls it 'the phantom drakkar'!

Advances in Design and Technique

The earliest evidence of sails being used in Northern Europe dates from the 1st century BC. In the National Museum in Dublin is a small gold model of a boat from Broighter, County Derry. It has eight thwarts (transverse seats) for oarsmen and a steering oar and is thought to be a representation of a skin boat. In addition it has a mast and yard showing that it could also be sailed.

The first use of the word 'starboard' in English occurs in Alfred the Great's translation of *Adversus Paganos Historiarum*, a general history of the world by the 5th century Spanish historian Paulus Crosius. Alfred's translation dates from *c* 893. 'The word refers to the mode of steering the early Teutonic ships, by means of a paddle worked over the right side of the vessel' (*OED*).

When bringing a ship into harbour the helmsman naturally tried to keep the side to which the steering oar was attached away from the quay, both to prevent the oar from being damaged and to enable him to work it until the ship came right alongside. Hence, the right side of the ship was the 'steer-board' and the left side was the side from which the ship was laden – the 'ladeboard' or 'larboard'. The latter was later supplanted by 'port', which has the same basic idea underlying it, to avoid confusion with the similar-sounding 'starboard'.

A handy mnemonic to help one remember which side is which is 'No red port left in the

The Gokstad ship, seen from the bows, in the Viking Ships Museum, Oslo, Norway.

cellar', which also tells one that the colour of the port navigation light is red. The starboard light is green.

The earliest pictures of a lateen sail occur in two Greek manuscripts dating from the end of the 9th century, although historians believe that the lateen rig dates back to the pre-Christian era and was probably of Arab origin. A narrow, triangular sail is set on a very long yard, which is made up of two or more spars bound together so as to give the ends more whip than the middle. The lateen sail is at its best when there is a beam wind beating across the ship, but is less effective than the square sail when the wind is right aft. The name is simply a corruption of the word Latin, the sail having first been seen by sailors from the North when they began voyaging to the Mediterranean.

The Seal of Elbing.

The relief on the font in Winchester Cathedral – probably the earliest known representation of a ship with a stern rudder.

The earliest known 'picture' of a ship with a stern rudder is on a relief on the font in Winchester Cathedral and is said to date from about 1180. Whether or not it is a stern rudder – the leading edge does seem to overlap the hull – and whether the date is correct are open to dispute; but, once introduced, the advantages of a stern rudder must rapidly have become apparent. The steering oar would have worked well enough in calm water but if the wind was to starboard the oar would have tended to lift clear of the water, while if the wind was to port the oar would have dug in until it was in danger of snapping.

The earliest indisputable representation of a stern rudder appears on the seal of the town of Elbing and dates from about 1242. Elbing was a member of the Hanseatic League, the federation of North German cities which, at the height of its power, exercised a monopoly, which embraced fishing as well as seaborne trade, throughout Northern Europe.

The best pictures we have of ships in the 13th century are all on seals of towns connected with the shipping industry. It can be assumed that the ships were longer and lower than they were portrayed and were distorted to fit the circular shape of the seal. The ships are not dissimilar from those of the Vikings but one or two developments should be noted: the ships have no oars; fore- and aftercastles – battlemented platforms supported on pillars – appear; in some cases – La Rochelle, Hastings – the sails have reef-points. On the seal of the town of Sandwich **appear for the first time a topcastle and a rudimentary bowsprit.**

The importance of the bowsprit was much greater than its appearance might imply. Its function was to extend the bowlines beyond the hull, thereby allowing them to support the foreleech of the sail more effectively. In such short, squat vessels with such disproportionally large sails it was vital to maintain the efficacy of bowlines and we later find a notched spar fitted below the bowsprit to allow the bowlines to be rigged according to the strength of the wind and the trim of the sail.

The Seal of Dover.

The hawsehole first makes its appearance in a relief dating from the 14th century on the tomb of St Peter Martyr in the Church of St Eustorgio in Milan. The hawsehole is the hole in the forecastle or upper deck of a ship through which the anchor cable passes. The ship still has a side-rudder, although it is known that the stern-rudder was in use in the Mediterranean during the 14th century.

It is uncertain whether the square sail ever completely disappeared from the Mediterranean, though it was certainly eclipsed by the lateen sail for nearly 1000 years. There is a painting by Giovanni de Milano which dates from 1350 and shows a vessel much like a cog which has a square sail, and a map dated 1367 shows for the first time a two-masted vessel carrying both a square and a lateen sail.

The first mention of a bonnet occurs in 1399 in a work called *Richard the Redeles*, once thought to be by William Langland: 'They bente on a bonet and bare a topte saile after ye wynde.' Bonnets were long strips of canvas laced to the foot of a sail in order to increase its area when the wind was very light and were quickly and easily removed in heavy weather.

The first seal to show fore- and aftercastles built around the endposts of a ship is that of Dover, dating from 1284. It will be noted that the steering oar is on the port side. When carving the seal in relief, the sculptor presumably forgot that starboard would become port when the seal was used to stamp an impression. The seal of Dover also shows for the first time what seems to be a proper bowsprit. There appears to be a branch of a tree attached to the end of the bowsprit: this is thought to be an indication that the ship was not belligerent.

The first known picture of a ship with ratlines is on a seal from the Hanseatic port of Danzig, dating from about 1400. Ratlines are the lengths of rope which run horizontally across the shrouds of a ship, thus forming the rungs of a rope ladder.

The earliest surviving illustration of a cog in which the fore- and aftercastles have become integral parts of the hull appears in a 14th century manuscript now in the British Museum. It shows two cogs engaged in a spirited battle.

Sea warfare in the early fourteenth century. The first picture to show the fore- and aftercastles as integrated parts of the hull.

They were *seized* (bound) to the outermost shrouds and secured to each intervening shroud with a clove hitch. In the Danzig ship a new kind of top, with sides turning outwards, first makes its appearance, and the aftercastle has by now virtually evolved into a quarterdeck.

We first hear of the carrack at about the beginning of the 15th century, but as the word continued to be used to describe the larger type of trading vessel found in both Northern and Southern Europe until the 17th century, one cannot be too specific in defining what is meant by a carrack. Douglas Phillips-Burt describes the early carrack thus: 'A ship with a Northern square mainsail and initially a mizzenmast carrying a Southern lateen, to which was soon added a small foremast carrying another square sail. Mizzen and foresail were small and had the primary function of balancing the ship and making control easier, rather than of adding effectively to propulsive power ... the three-masted ship was born and was to become the basic type of ocean-going vessel'. The carrack had a stern rudder hinged to an upright sternpost, the inner side of which was shaped to fit the hull and to continue to the keel. In the 15th century carracks varied in size from 200 to 600 tons carrying capacity but by the end of the 16th century Portuguese carracks of up to 2000 tons burden were sailing to the East Indies.

The earliest-known representation of a three-masted carrack is on an early 15th-century Spanish bowl. It has no less than six fenders which served the double purpose of protecting the hull from damage at the quayside and of reinforcing the upper part of the planking.

The spritsail, a small square sail set beneath the bowsprit, was introduced in the latter half of the 15th century. **It is first mentioned in 1446** and Columbus tells us that a spritsail was carried on the *Santa Maria* in 1492.

The first armed carrack of which evidence survives is in a picture by a Flemish artist known only by the initials 'W.A.'. It dates from about 1470 and shows a vessel carrying five guns on either side of the quarterdeck. All three masts have tops and a small gun is mounted on the mizzentop. In the foretop and the maintop a number of spears are visible.

W. A.'s 'Kraeck', or carrack, of about 1470. Note the awnings above the fore- and aftercastles.

The earliest known illustration of a topsail dates from about 1480. The topsail is set above the course, or lowest sail, and is thus the second in ascending order from the deck. Its main advantages were that, under certain conditions, it provided more continuous power than the mainsail, the breeze being more constant at 40ft (12.2m) above sea level than lower down, and that it had the effect of slightly lifting the bows and thereby easing the passage of the hull through the water.

The whipstaff first appeared around the end of the 15th century. Hitherto it had been possible for the helmsman at the tiller to see where he was going, to watch the sails and to adjust the ship's course accordingly. But as ships grew larger and new decks and castles proliferated this became impossible, so some form of remote control had to be introduced. The device adopted was the whipstaff – a wooden rod rising through one or more intervening decks with the base attached to the tiller. The top end was operated by the helmsman who could thus move the rudder a maximum of five degrees either side of the horizontal. For greater alterations of course the ship had to be trimmed with the sails.

The bonaventure mast, or bonaventure mizen, first appears in 1496. Set right at the stern of the ship, this fourth mast carried a lateen sail. By the middle of the 17th century the bonaventure mast had disappeared.

The topgallant mast was in use before the name itself. The Naval Accounts of Henry VII for 1497 tell us that the *Regent* had 'a Toppe maste above the mayne Toppe maste' and 'a sayle to the same'; but it is referred to by name in the inventory of the *Great Harry*, built in 1514. The topgallant mast came above the topmast, which itself came above the lower mast, making three divisions to the complete mast.

The Galleon *Ark Royal* 1587.

The first ship shown carrying a fore-topsail is the *Santa Catarina do Monte Sinai* in a picture in the National Maritime Museum dated 1520. Other notable features of the painting are the remarkable size of the mainsails and the fact that the wind appears to be blowing from several directions at once.

The first pictorial evidence of a gaff rig is on a Swedish vessel in 1525, but its development is generally credited to the Dutch some time before this date. The gaff rig emerged from the spritsail rig and was long known as a half-sprit. The gaff-sail is a four-sided fore-and-aft sail laced to and hoisted on the after side of a mast.

The word 'galleon' first appears in a work by the Scottish poet Sir David Lindsay (c 1490–1555) entitled *The Complaynt* and published in 1529, in which he refers to idle people being fettered in the

galleons. This reinforces the theory that the word was originally no more than a corruption of galley, but it came eventually to be applied with varying degrees of inaccuracy to a variety of 16th century ships, especially those built in Spain. Dr R. C. Anderson describes the galleon thus: 'A sailing-ship, usually four-masted – with the ordinary rig of the time, but with a hull built to some extent on galley lines, long for its beam, rather straight and flat, and with a beak-head low down like a galley's, instead of the overhanging forecastle of the ship.' A Venetian manuscript of 1550 gives the following dimensions for a galleon: 'overall length 135½ft (41.3m); length of keel 100ft (30.5m); beam 33ft (10m)', thus giving it the rough proportions of 4 (overall length): 3 (keel): 1 (beam), as against the 3:2:1 of the carrack which it gradually replaced as the principal type of trading ship. The low forecastle built within the bows made the ship much more weatherly and manoeuvrable than the carrack, whose high forecastle caught the wind and prevented her from holding her course. The development of the galleon was essentially an English achievement. Professor Michael Lewis, in his book *The Navy of Britain*, says: 'Nor is it wise to associate the type with Spain. It seems clear that far from being the earliest of sea-users to have galleons, she was actually the last.' As Robert Graves once remarked, John Masefield's 'stately Spanish galleon coming from the isthmus' [of Panama] had a most improbable 'cargo of diamonds, emeralds, amethysts, topazes and cinnamon, and gold moidores,' since cinnamon comes from Ceylon, the jewels come from India and the gold moidores were presumably on their way back to Portugal where they had been coined.

The studding sail (pronounced stuns'l) **is first mentioned** in 1549 but does not seem to have come into general use until the end of the 17th century. It was an additional sail, set only in fine weather, with the wind abaft the beam, outside the leech, or perpendicular edge, of a square sail. It was set by extending the yards with booms to which the studding sail was laced. It was used on the topsail as well as on the lower yards of the fore and main masts.

The first man to equip his ships with hammocks was Sir John Hawkins in 1586. On one of his later voyages to the West Indies he noticed that the natives on some of the remoter islands slept in hanging beds slung from trees which they called 'hammacoes', as indeed they continued to be called in the Navy until the late 18th century. Hitherto no provision had been made for the sailor's sleeping accommodation: he simply lay down on the wooden deck. As he had but one outfit of working clothes which he wore night and day throughout the voyage the notion of undressing to go to bed would in any case have been quite alien to him.

The spritsail topsail was introduced about 1600. It was a small square sail set on a short mast, known as the spritsail topmast, rising perpendicularly from the end of the bowsprit.

The first mention of a crossjack (pronounced cro'jeck) occurs in 1626 in a work by Captain John Smith (1580–1631), who is better remembered for his fortunate escape from death at the hands of the Indian Chief Powhatan through the intervention of his daughter Pocahontas. A cross-

Captain John Smith explored and mapped part of the coast of North America, to which he gave the name New England.

jack yard appears in a painting by the Dutch artist Hendrik Vroom of the *Red Lion* which was rebuilt in 1609 but doubt has been cast on the accuracy of the picture. The crossjack was a sail bent to the lower yard on the mizen mast of a square-rigged ship.

The first recorded yacht race in England took place on 1 October 1661, when Charles II, in the *Katherine*, raced the Duke of York, in the *Anne*, from Greenwich to Gravesend and back for a wager of £100. **The first British yachts** are usually said to have been the *Mary* and the *Bozan* presented to Charles II by the Dutch at the time of his restoration in 1660 but since the accounts kept at Herstmonceux Castle in Sussex for 1645 mention money 'paid for tow and nails used about my Lord's Yaught at Pemsie [Pevensey]' it would seem that Lord Dacre was at least 15 years ahead of the King.

The original yachts were small, fast, single-masted Dutch vessels called *jachts*, from the Dutch word meaning 'to hunt'. They were used for scouting, as dispatch boats and for transporting people of importance, usually on occasions when speed was the dominating factor. The word *jacht* was also loosely applied to any of the small boats of various shapes and sizes used by the Dutch for pleasure rather than for profit.

The jib, a triangular sail set before the foremast, was fitted to naval ships, in accordance with Admiralty Instructions, in about 1703; but there is evidence that the jib was in use at a much earlier date: 'They were certainly used by small craft at the end of the 16th century', (SIR JULIAN CORBETT, *The Successors of Drake*); 'In 1688 jibs were part of the ordinary stores at Woolwich and must therefore have been used in large ships before that date,' (MICHAEL OPPENHEIM, *Administration of the Royal Navy*).

The jib is spread on the jib-boom, a spar extending forward of the bowsprit.

The Galley

While the arts of navigation and shipbuilding were evolving to the North and the West, the galley, descendant of the bireme and the trireme of Ancient Greece and Rome, continued to serve as the warship of the Mediterranean. Why this unseaworthy and uneconomical craft should have survived, basically unchanged, for over 2500 years in the Mediterranean, and yet have found little favour elsewhere, is a question which deserves examination.

As a warship the galley had two distinct advantages. Firstly, it had freedom of movement: unlike the sailing ship, which can only proceed in the direction in which the wind blows it, the galley, propelled by human exertion, can go in any direction the captain might desire; so the commander of a fleet of galleys had the power to deploy his forces with precision, and became, indeed, **the first practitioner of naval tactics**. Secondly, from its earliest days it was equipped with a most effective weapon designed to destroy not just the enemy but the enemy's ships, namely the ram. Not until the introduction of the 'great gun' could the sailing ship compete in this respect. Against these advantages must be set its very considerable disadvantages.

Firstly it was, in modern jargon, highly labour-intensive. If, as has been suggested (see p. 9) the Greek trireme was manned by free, paid oarsmen, the subsequent use of slave labour cannot be disputed. The words 'galley' and 'slave' come together in one's mind as easily as 'horse' and 'power'! Throughout the centuries during which the Christian–Moslem wars raged in and around the Mediterranean each side could rely on an unfailing source of free 'oar-power' provided by prisoners taken from the other. And even when this source of supply dried up the galley survived, the French having found it a convenient method of utilizing the muscle-power of convicts and other undesirable citizens. Indeed, the French finally owned one of the largest fleets in the Mediterranean and continued to build galleys until 1720. In England, as in the Scandinavian countries, though galleys certainly appeared from time to time, they were usually manned by free men, the inexhaustible supply of slave labour which powered the great fleets of the Mediterranean being unobtainable in the North.

Secondly, the galley was designed for use in calm waters, and was therefore suited to the short, choppy seas of the Mediterranean where the wind is usually too light or too fresh for heavy sailing ships; while her great length in relation to her width, her shallow draught and low free-board ill-fitted her for the long swell of the Atlantic.

Thirdly, the galley could only stay at sea for a very short time. Even slaves, if they are to perform efficiently, have to be fed and the galley was woefully short of storage space. It has been estimated that a galley manned by 250 oarsmen could only carry enough food for three days. In other words she must always be within 36 hours rowing time of a port where she could revictual, feasible enough in the Mediterranean but hardly practical in the North Sea or on the Atlantic.

Though the basic design of the galley remained largely unaltered throughout its long history, it naturally underwent certain modifications over the years, particularly in the arrangement of the oars. Bearing in mind that the evidence on which the following suppositions are based is slender indeed, it would appear that until the middle of the 14th century the oars were still arranged in two tiers, as in the bireme of classical times. Thereafter the oars were grouped in twos or threes, with the rowers sitting side by side, one to each oar. By the 16th century it had been found more efficient to have several men, usually five

This representation of a galley confirms the accuracy of Biron's description, although there only seem to be 270 slaves.

but sometimes as many as seven, to each oar. In both the latter cases the oars rested on a long beam like an outrigger known as the apostis.

Galleys were first armed with guns during the 16th century. Initially a single large gun was laid on a pile of sandbags at the forward end of the corsia, the raised part of the hull which acted both as a gangway and as a means of strengthening the vessel fore-and-aft. Since the aim of the gun could not be adjusted either laterally or vertically its effectiveness must have been somewhat limited. Later other guns were added and a painting by Peter Brueghel the Elder (d 1569) shows a Portuguese galley of 1565 carrying seven forward guns.

Galleys carried lateen sails on one, two, or three masts, but these were only used for making passage and were always lowered when battle was joined in order to take advantage of the greater manoeuvrability afforded by the oars.

The desire to combine the galley's freedom of movement with the superior seaworthiness and firepower of the galleon led to the development of the galleass, but the compromise was not a happy one.

Though **the galleass** had more beam and

draught than the galley, she could not carry the rig of a sailing ship and her extra carrying capacity did not compensate for the loss of speed and manoeuvrability. As a gunship, too, the galleass was a failure: placed above the rowing deck, the guns made the ship top-heavy; placed below it, the line of fire was obscured by the oars. As a carrier of freight, however, the galleass proved more successful and in the Mediterranean she was widely used as such throughout the 16th and 17th centuries.

The following quotation will suffice to give some idea of the life of a galley slave in the reign of Louis XIV. It was written by Jean Biron, a French priest who was sent to the galleys in 1703 on account of his Protestant beliefs:

'A galley is a long, flat, one-decked vessel, though it hath two masts. Yet they generally make use of the oars, because they are so built as not to be able to endure a rough sea. There are five slaves to every oar, one of them a Turk, who, being generally stronger than Christians, is set at the upper end to work it with more strength. There are in all 300 slaves and 150 men – either officers, soldiers, seamen or servants . . . Instead of a bed they are allowed, sick or well, only a board a foot and a half broad . . . the fatigue of tugging at the oar is extraordinary. They must rise to draw their strokes and fall back again almost on their backs. And for fear they should fail, there is a gangboard on which are posted three Comites [boatswains] who unmercifully exercise a tough wand on any man they suspect of laziness, which being long is often felt by two or three of his innocent neighbours, who, being naked when they row, each blow imprints evident marks of the inhumanity of the executioner.'

Navigation

THE COMPASS
The invention of the compass is generally credited to the Chinese, whose historians optimistically ascribe its discovery to the year 2634BC. It was certainly in common use in the Far East by the end of the 3rd century AD. However, there being virtually no communication between the various ancient civilizations, it seems probable that an understanding of the properties of the magnetized needle developed independently in the various seafaring communities during the first thousand years AD.

In Europe the first written reference to a compass occurs in the *De Naturis Rerum* of Alexander Neckam (1157–1217) in which he says, 'Mariners on a sea voyage, when in overcast weather they have no advantage of sunlight or again if at night the heaven is overwhelmed with darkness and they have no idea towards what point of the heavens their ship is tending, place a needle above a magnet and the needle moves around in a circle until it stops and its point looks towards the northern region.' The *Encyclopaedia Britannica* makes the following comment: 'It is noteworthy that Neckam has no air of imparting a startling novelty: he merely records what had apparently become the regular practice of at least many seamen of the Catholic world.'

THE QUADRANT
The first instrument used by mariners for measuring the elevation of the sun and stars was the quadrant. It consisted of a piece of metal or wood in the shape of a quarter-circle (Latin *quadrans* – a quarter) marked in degrees round the arc, with pinhole sights at each end of one of the straight edges and a plumb-line hanging from the point where the straight edges met. To take an observation two men were required – one to hold the quadrant in a vertical plane and line up the pinhole sights on the observed body, the other to take the reading when the observer gave the word. Such quadrants were used by the Portuguese navigators who first ventured down the West African coast in the second half of the 15th century to determine the altitude of the Pole Star. Their unfamiliarity with the degrees of circular measure often led to quadrants being marked with the names of familiar landmarks, such as headlands, rivers, ports and islands, instead of degrees.

THE KAMAL
The longest-lived navigational instrument is the kamal, so named from the Arabic word for guide. It has been used by Arab sailors in the Indian Ocean for at least six centuries and a modified version can be seen in use on dhows in the Red Sea to this day. The kamal consisted of a thin rectangular board of wood attached to which was a string knotted at determined intervals. The board was held vertically at such a distance from the eye that the upper and lower edges aligned respectively with the observed body and the

Heaving the log on passage to India in the 19th century. The man on the right is holding the sandglass. *Mary Evans Picture Library.*

horizon. The string was then held taut between the teeth and the number of knots left hanging in the excess length of string gave the measure of latitude.

The earliest method of ascertaining the speed of a ship was to throw a piece of wood overboard and time it as it passed two spots a known distance apart on the side of the ship. Later a wooden quadrant, weighted so that it always floated point upward and known as a log-ship or log-chip, was attached to a logline marked off into definite lengths by knots. The number of knots run off in the time it took to empty a sandglass of either 14 or 28 seconds enabled one to calculate the speed of the ship.

THE ASTROLABE
According to Samuel Purchas (c 1575–1626), compiler of *Purchas his Pilgrimes*, **the first person to adapt the astrolabe for the use of mariners** was the German navigator and geographer, Martin Behaim (c 1459–c 1507) in about 1484. The astrolabe was probably of Greek origin (the word comes from the Greek *astron* – star, *labein* – to take) and had been used for centuries by astron-

omers. It was, for its day, a complex and sophisticated instrument. The mariner's astrolabe was a simplification of the astronomer's, consisting of a graduated brass ring, the rim of which was engraved with scales of degrees from zero to ninety, with an alidade, or sighting rule, with two pinhole sights pivoted at the centre. The astrolabe was suspended so that it hung vertically, the alidade rotated until the observed body was aligned with the pinhole sights and the altitude then read off.

The first written explanation of how to discover a ship's position in longitude by means of a chronometer occurs in Gemma Frisius's *De Principiis Astronomiae*, published in 1530, but there were no clocks which could keep sufficiently accurate time under seagoing conditions to enable seamen to turn theory into practice.

THE CROSS-STAFF
The cross-staff was first used at sea in the early 16th century, although its forerunner, **the Jacob's staff**, had been described in a treatise on trigonometry by the French–Jewish mathematician and philosopher Levi ben Gerson (1288–1344) as early as 1321. It consisted of a square-sectioned staff fitted with a sliding crosspiece. The end of the staff was held to the eye with the crosspiece vertical. The crosspiece was then moved along the staff until the lower end was on the horizon and the upper end on the star. Graduations on the top of the staff enabled the angle of the body observed to be read off directly, the half-length of the crosspiece divided by its distance along the shaft being a tangent of half the angle to be measured. Later cross-staves came

The cross-staff was an early navigational instrument for measuring the altitude of a heavenly body.

equipped with three or four crosspieces which were used in conjunction with different altitude scales engraved on the surfaces of the staff, thus enabling a bigger range of angles to be measured.

One of the greatest of the Elizabethan seamen was John Davis (*c* 1550–1605). He led three expeditions in search of the North-West Passage (1585, 1586, 1587) and gave his name to the strait which separates Greenland from North America. He commanded the *Black Dog* in the fight against the Spanish Armada in 1588 and in 1591 was taken on as pilot and navigator by Thomas Cavendish, who treacherously deserted him in the Straits of Magellan, leaving Davis alone to discover the Falkland Islands. He spent most of the rest of his life voyaging in the Far East and was finally killed by Japanese pirates in 1605.

Davis's greatest contribution to navigation was **the invention in about 1594 of the back-staff or Davis's quadrant,** a simple instrument for measuring the altitude of the sun, but an improvement on the cross-staff in that the observer stood with his back to the sun and so could take a reading without being blinded by the glare. It consisted of two concentric arcs and three vanes, the arc of the longer radius being 30° and that of the shorter 60°, thus making altogether 90°, or a quadrant. By manipulating the quadrant, the sun's light, concentrated by a pinhole into a bright spot, was brought into coincidence with the horizon, viewed through a slit. Davis's quadrant remained a vital instrument of navigation until 1731 when John Hadley (1682–1744) of London and Thomas Godfrey (1704–49) of Philadelphia simultaneously 'rediscovered' the reflecting quadrant, for it was learnt afterwards that a similar instrument had been invented by Sir Isaac Newton in 1699 but no account of it had ever been published.

The first comprehensive survey of the coast of Great Britain was made by Greenville Collins (*d* 1694) between 1681 and 1693, the task having been given to him by Samuel Pepys, then Secretary of the Admiralty. 'The scope of the work, embracing, as it does, the complete circuit of Great Britain, is very great and for one man in seven, or even in twelve years, excessive ... and entitles Collins to rank not only with the earliest, but with the best of English hydrographers.' (*Dictionary of National Biography*.)

Edmund Halley inspired Isaac Newton to write his *Principia* and published it at his own expense in 1687. *National Maritime Museum.*

The first sea voyage undertaken for purely scientific purposes was that commanded by Edmund Halley (1656–1742) in 1698–1700 in the war sloop *Paramour Pink* 'to observe variations in compass readings in the South Atlantic and to determine accurate latitudes and longitudes of his ports of call'. His *General Chart of the Variations of the Compass*, published in 1701, was **the first world chart to incorporate isogonic lines** – lines that indicate positions in the ocean having the same variations of the compass – a landmark in the history of navigation. He had already, in 1686, published his map of the world showing the distribution of prevailing winds over the oceans, **the first meteorological chart ever to be published,** but he is best remembered for the comet posthumously named after him, the return of which in 1758 he accurately predicted.

The first chronometer of sufficient reliability to enable longitude to be calculated at sea was made by John Harrison (1693–1776). In 1714 a Board of Longitude was set up which offered a prize of £20,000 to anyone who could construct such a timepiece and between 1735 and 1760 Harrison made four, the last of which well fulfilled the conditions laid down by the Board. But Harrison was only paid half the amount promised and his declining years were spent in a protracted struggle to obtain the balance due, which was finally paid to him in 1773.

OPENING UP THE OCEANS

The First Atlantic Voyagers

The claim of **St Brendan** (*c* 485–*c* 583) to have been **the first European to sail to North America** (between 565 and 573) is now firmly placed within the realm of legend, despite the brave voyage undertaken by Timothy Severin and three companions, who, in 1976–7, crossed the Atlantic in a craft said to have been a replica of the holy man's. It seems more likely that St Brendan visited the southern shore of Iceland and then sailed southward to the Azores. Nevertheless, the legend of St Brendan's voyage, the oldest version of which occurs in a manuscript of the 11th century, had such a firm hold on the imagination of medieval and later geographers that St Brendan's Island was marked on charts of the Atlantic until as late as 1759.

The Irish can, however, lay serious claim to have been **the first people to settle in Iceland**, for, though the Norwegians credit themselves with its discovery and colonization, the very same records admit that the Irish had been there before them. There is a small island off the south coast of Iceland called Vestmannaeyjar, which means Irish Island; the Norwegians always referred to the Irish as Westmen.

No one disputes the claim of the Norwegians to have been **the first to reach Greenland, the largest island in the world**. In about the year 900 one Gunnbjorn Ulfsson said he had sailed by the coast of a large and mountainous island and this is thought to be **the earliest reference to Greenland**. But it was not until 982 that Eric the Red, fleeing from a charge of murder, set sail from Iceland, rounded Cape Farewell and landed at Eriksfjord, near the present Julianehaab. Eric

Imagination was certainly not lacking in this medieval depiction of St Brendan.

returned to Iceland in 985 to try and persuade others to settle in the land which he had named Greenland, being well aware of the advantage of a promising name. In this he was successful and the population eventually grew to about 10,000.

The first European to set eyes on the continent of North America was Bjarni Herjulfsson, according to the *Book of Flatey*, a collection of Icelandic legends and true stories compiled in the 14th century. It is said that in the year 986 Herjulfsson, a Norse trader, was blown off course during a voyage to Greenland and sighted what was either Newfoundland or the coast of Labrador; but he did not land.

The first European to set foot on the continent of North America was Leif Ericsson, son of Eric the Red, who had been sent to Greenland by Olaf Tryggvason, King of Norway, to convert the settlers to Christianity. Whether his voyage was accidental or deliberate is not known. In *The Saga of Erik the Red* Leif is said to have been blown off course on his journey from Norway in the year

1000 and to have landed by accident on the shore of the country described by Bjarni Herjulfsson 14 years earlier. He named the country Vinland. In *The Tale of the Greenlanders* Leif's expedition is said to have been deliberately undertaken, as a consequence of Herjulfsson report, in 1003–4. Either way, Ericsson and his crew can still claim to have been the first Europeans to set foot on the American continent.

The first European child to be born in North America was probably Snorri, son of Thorfinn Karlsefni and his wife Gudrid, the widow of Thorstein Ericsson, brother of Leif. Karlsefni, with 160 companions, was **the first to attempt to establish a colony in North America**, but after three years he was obliged to abandon the project and return to Greenland.

Round Africa to India

The first known expedition in search of a sea route to India was led by two brothers from Genoa, Ugolino and Guido Vivaldi. In 1291 they left Genoa in two galleys and are known to have sailed down the coast of Africa to a point about level with the Canary Islands, but thereafter nothing was heard of them. Ugolino's son, Sorleone, led a number of expeditions in search of his father but in 1315 he too disappeared. Then, in 1455, a Genoese seaman called Antonio Uso di Mare, a member of Alvise de Cadamosto's first expedition to the west coast of Africa (see below), wrote a letter in which he claimed that he had met the last surviving descendant of Ugolino Vivaldi's expedition of 1291, on the River Gambia.

The first recorded landing on the Cape Verde Islands was made by the Venetian navigator Alvise de Cadamosto (c 1430–80). Prince Henry the Navigator sent him on two expeditions to explore the west coast of Africa, on the second of which, in 1456, he was driven out to sea by a storm and so discovered the Cape Verde Islands.

The first European to enter the mouth of the River Congo was the Portuguese explorer Diego Cam (fl. 1480–6). He was also the first to explore the west coast of Africa from the Equator nearly as far south as Walvis Bay. Cam set up four stone pillars engraved with the details of his voyages at various points on the West African coast, all of

which were still standing at the beginning of the 20th century. Three are now in museums, and one, though *in situ*, is in fragments.

The first European (see p. 10) **to round the Cape of Good Hope** was the Portuguese explorer Bartholomew Diaz (c 1450–1500) who, in February 1488, made landfall at Mossel Bay, about 220 miles (354km) east of what is now Cape Town. He continued to sail east until he reached the mouth of the Great Fish River, 110 miles (177km) north-east of the present Port Elizabeth. At this stage he was forced by his nervous crew to return and on the way discovered Table Mountain and the Cape of Good Hope, which he named the Cape of Storms (Cabo Tormentoso); it was later renamed by King John of Portugal (1481–95) to give it a hint of welcome. By a stroke of cruel irony Diaz was drowned in a storm off the cape which he had discovered.

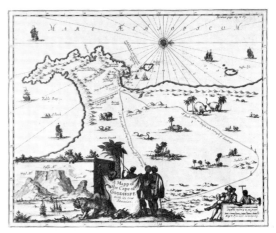

An early map of the Cape of Good Hope. The Latin word *Aethiopia* meant a country south of Egypt, hence *Mare Aethipiscopum. National Maritime Museum.*

The first man to sail from Europe to India was the Portuguese navigator Vasco da Gama (c 1460–1524). Bartholomew Diaz having discovered in 1488 that a great ocean lay to the east of the Cape of Good Hope, King Emanuel I of Portugal (1495–1521) despatched da Gama in July 1497, to follow up that discovery. He rounded the Cape of Good Hope on 22 November, had the good fortune to acquire a Gujerati pilot at Malindi and crossed the Indian Ocean to reach Calicut on 20 May 1498. But the rivalry of Arab traders, already established on the Malabar coast, made it impossible for da Gama to establish a 'factory'

CALECHVT CELEBERRI: MVM INDIÆ EMPORIVM.

and he was obliged to return to Portugal, which he reached in September 1499, after a round journey of 24,000 nautical miles. Nevertheless the expedition showed a profit of 600 per cent. Da Gama's voyage is the subject of Camoëns' epic poem, *The Lusiads*.

It should be noted that in this context the word 'factory' is not used in the sense in which we normally use it today, but in its original meaning of a place where agents (factors) carry out their business abroad.

The first man to realize the real significance of sea power and to apply it systematically was the Portuguese conqueror and explorer Alfonso Albuquerque (1453–1515), known as Alfonso the Great. It was his appreciation of the fact that sea power is founded as much upon merchant shipping and secure land bases as it is upon the fighting strength of a nation's warships that enabled him to establish Portugal as the dominant power in the Indian Ocean throughout the 16th century. He has, indeed, been described as the father of modern naval strategy.

In 1503 he set up a fort at Cochin, on the west coast of India, which was to be the foundation stone of the Portuguese empire in the East. Albuquerque was appointed Viceroy of India in 1507 and thereafter deliberately set out to gain control of all the major entrances to the Indian Ocean, setting up forts or factories at Socotra (1507), Goa (1510), Malacca (1511) and Ormuz (Hormuz) (1515). In 1513 he mounted an unsuccessful attack on the port of Aden, but subsequently **sailed on into the Red Sea, the first European ever to do so.**

An engraving of Calicut (above). *National Maritime Museum*. Vasco da Gama (below).

The Atlantic Bridge Established

The first English expedition to the West, though a failure, deserves mention; for the courage lies, not in arriving, but in setting out in the first place. William of Worcester tells us in his *Itinerary* that on 15 July 1480, John Jay the Younger left Bristol to search for the legendary island of Brasil, placed by popular tradition 70

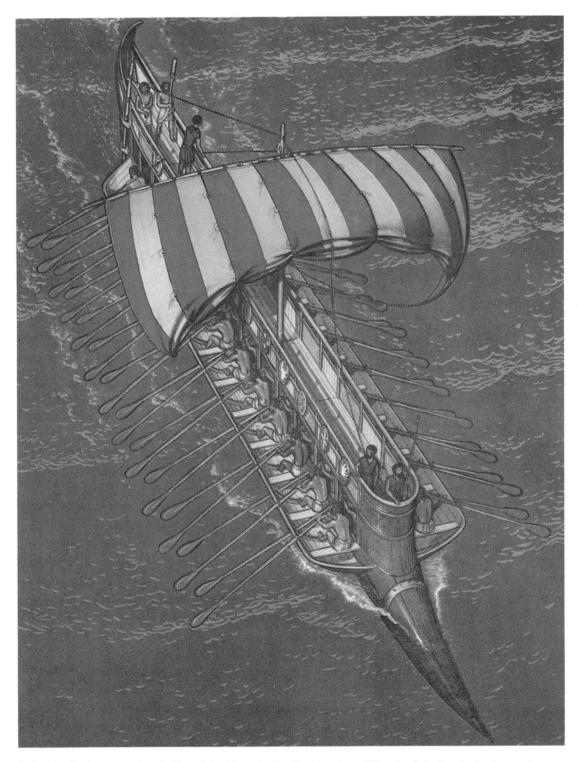

An imaginative reconstruction of a Phoenician bireme by the Finnish artist and historian Björn Landström (see p. 9).

The Oseburg ship in the Viking Ships Museum, Oslo, Norway (see p. 15).

The Spanish capture an English convoy off La Rochelle in 1372, during the Hundred Years' War: from *Froissart's Chronicles. Mary Evans Picture Library.*

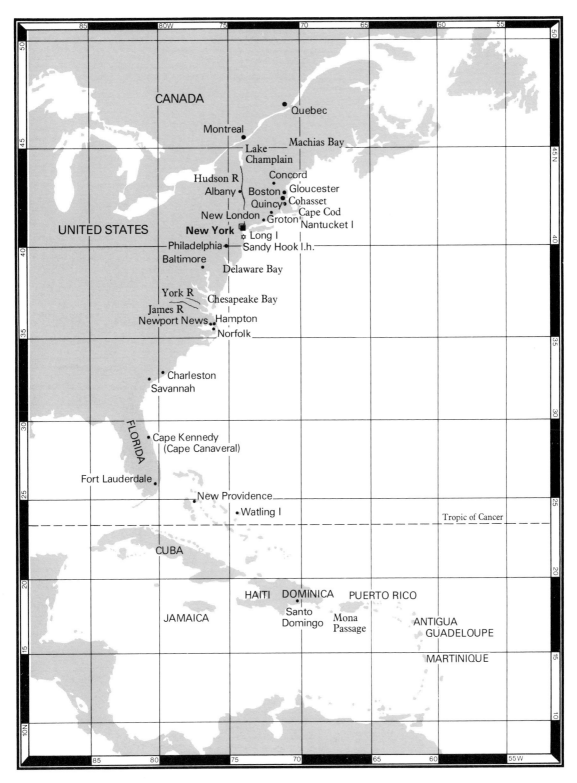

The artist who drew this picture of Colombus arriving in the New World, for an edition of his letters in 1493, had clearly never seen his ships.

that to discover America was the last thing that Columbus set out to do: what he wanted to discover was a short maritime route to the Orient. Columbus was familiar with such works as the *Imago Mundi* of Cardinal d'Ailly, the *Historia Rerum* of Pope Pius II and Marco Polo's *Book*, and from these he formed the conclusion that the Atlantic Ocean was relatively narrow; he estimated the distance from the Canary Islands to Japan at 2400 nautical miles (4445km), whereas it is in fact about 10,600 miles (19,644km). He also corresponded with the Florentine astronomer Paolo Toscanelli (1397–1482) who is reputed to have encouraged him to try to reach Asia by sailing westward. Although toying with the idea as early as 1474, it was not until 3 August 1492 that he finally set sail, having eventually secured the patronage of King Ferdinand and Queen Isabella, joint sovereigns of Spain. His fleet consisted of his flagship, the carrack *Santa Maria*, and two caravels, the *Pinta* and the *Niña*. He made landfall on 12 October on an island which he named San Salvador and which is now identified as Watling Island in the Bahamas. Columbus and his men were kindly received by the gentle Arawak natives, who he called 'Indians', convinced as he was that he had reached the East

leagues* west of Ireland. He was finally driven back by contrary winds after months of fruitless wandering.

CHRISTOPHER COLUMBUS
The first name that comes to mind when people talk of the discovery of America is that of Christopher Columbus (1451–1506) but, as we have seen, the Norsemen had actually beaten him to it by some 500 years. Nevertheless Columbus made **the first crossing of the Middle Atlantic, discovered and colonized the Bahamas and the West Indies** and was indeed the *effective* discoverer of America. But it must be remembered

* The Romans estimated the league at 1500 paces or 1.376 English miles. It was introduced into England by the Normans and was then equal to about 3 modern miles. It is now a nautical measure, the 20th part of a degree, i.e. 3 geographical miles or 3.456 statute miles. 1 nautical mile equals 1.8532km.

Christopher Columbus, known in Genoa, where he was born, as Cristofero Colombo, and in Spain as Cristobal Colón.

This ship is said to be 'of the *Santa Maria* type'. Though it differs in detail from Columbus' own description, it conveys the right impression.

Indies. He sailed on and reached Cuba on 28 October, persuading himself that this must be a peninsula reaching out from the mainland of China. He even sent a party inland to establish contact with the Emperor; instead they became **the first Europeans to see men smoking tobacco**. On 5 December he discovered Haiti, where the *Santa Maria* ran aground on a reef and had to be abandoned. He returned home in the *Niña*, reaching Spain on 15 March 1493.

Columbus made three more voyages to the Caribbean: on the second (September 1493–June 1496) he discovered Dominica, the Leeward Islands, the Virgin Islands, Puerto Rico, and Jamaica; and, in December 1493, established a settlement at Isabela on the island of Haiti, **the first European town in the New World**. On the third (May 1498–November 1500) he discovered

Trinidad and explored the coast of Venezuela, **possibly becoming the first European to set foot on the American mainland**, if one accepts that the Norsemen's Vinland was in Newfoundland. On the fourth (May 1502–November 1504) he explored the coasts of what are now Honduras, Nicaragua, Costa Rica and Panama.

Christopher Columbus was certainly **one of the greatest navigators in history** and stands second only to Magellan in the number of islands he discovered and the extent of coastline which he explored.

The *Santa Maria* must rank as **one of the most famous ships in history** but no detailed description of her has survived, so we can only guess what she was like. We do, however, know what sails she carried for Columbus himself tells us in his logbook for 24 October 1492: 'I let them set all sails, the main course with two bonnets, the fore course, the spritsail, the mizzen, the topsail and the boat's sail on the half-deck.' We also know that Columbus found the *Santa Maria* an unsatisfactory ship, 'not suited for voyages of discovery'. On his third voyage to the West Indies he emphasizes the point: 'Only smaller ships are desirable for voyages of discovery, for the ship I took with me on my first voyage was cumbersome and, because of this, was lost in the harbour at Navidad.' But when it comes to saying just how cumbersome she was, the experts fail to agree. Landström estimates her overall length at a precise 78½ft (23.9m); Phillips-Birt says she was 'believed to have been some 95ft (28.9m) overall'. Her burden is given at somewhere between 80 and 100 tons, which is to say that she was capable of carrying that quantity of tuns* of wine.

Columbus is **the first to mention the spritsail**, a small square sail set on a yard beneath the bowsprit.

Scarcely less famous than the *Santa Maria* are the *Pinta* and the *Niña*, both caravels. **The first recorded mention of a caravel** occurs in a Portuguese manuscript of 1255 and refers to fishing vessels. By the time of Columbus, the caravel had developed into two basic types – the *caravela latina* and the *caravela rotunda*, the former having lateen sails on two, and later three, masts, the latter being square-rigged on the two forward masts and lateen-rigged on the mizen. The ability

---

* 'From *c* 1688 the two spellings have been differentiated, *tun* being appropriated to the sense 'cask' and the liquid measure, and *ton* in the senses . . . which are partly measures and partly weights' *OED*.

of the lateen-rigged caravel to sail close to the wind made it suitable as a coasting vessel and such were the ships which Henry the Navigator sent on the pioneering voyages of discovery down the west coast of Africa. But the tremendous length of yard required and the need when tacking to lower the sail to bring the yard to the other side of the mast compared with the advantages of the square rig when running down wind in deep water led inevitably to a combination of the two.

The *Niña* left Portugal rigged as a *caravela latina* but, on reaching the Canary Islands, Columbus had her rerigged as a *caravela rotunda*; the *Pinta* was already square-sailed. One historian gives the overall length of the *Pinta* and the *Niña* as 58 and 56ft (17.6 and 17m) respectively, but we should bear in mind the cautionary words of Professor Samuel Morison, the American naval historian: 'We have no contemporary painting or drawing of a single ship in which Columbus sailed.' The *Niña* is thought to have been about 60 tons, meaning wine-tuns, and the *Pinta* about 70.

The *caravela rotunda* is sometimes referred to as the *caravela redonda*, the former being Latin, the latter Spanish.

The first slaves to be shipped across the Atlantic surprisingly made the crossing from west to east. Returning from his second voyage to the West Indies in March 1496, Christopher Columbus brought back 30 Indian slaves. In all Columbus shipped home about 500 Indian slaves, more than half of whom died on the journey.

The first man known to have sailed across the Atlantic from England was John Cabot (1450–98). Born Giovanni Caboto in Genoa, he came to England in 1484 and in May 1497, backed by letters patent from Henry VII, he set sail from Bristol in the *Mathew*, a three-masted trading cog of about 50 tons. On 24 June Cabot sighted either Newfoundland or Cape Breton Island, landed and took possession of it in the name of the King. On the return journey the ship passed over the Grand Banks off the coast of Newfoundland and the crew were able to catch huge quantities of cod, simply by lowering baskets into the sea. As a result Cabot is credited with having discovered the Newfoundland cod fisheries, but it now seems certain that Bristol seamen were fishing off Newfoundland some time before Cabot made his first journey. His

second expedition of five ships and 300 men set sail from Bristol in May 1498, and was never heard of again.

The significance of Cabot's achievement is that he made an independent discovery of the North American continent and laid the foundation for later British claims to discovery and colonization in that part of the world.

The first European to reach Brazil was Vicente Yañez Pinzon (c 1460–c 1524), one of three brothers who accompanied Columbus on his first voyage, Martin Alonzo (c 1440–93) commanding the *Pinta*, of which Francisco (c 1440–93) was the pilot, and Vicente Yañez commanding the *Niña*. In 1499 Vicente Yañez set sail with four caravels and reached the coast of Brazil on 26 January 1500. During this voyage he also discovered the estuary of the River Amazon. Three months later Pedro Cabral (c 1467–1530) landed in Brazil, having taken much too westerly a course en route for India, and, believing himself to be the first on the scene, claimed the country for Portugal.

The first man to sail the full length of the east coast of South America was, if he himself is to be believed, the Florentine, Amerigo Vespucci (1451–1512). Some scholars have cast doubt upon Vespucci's claims, owing to the impossible distances said to have been covered; others, however, maintain that certain conflicting documents attributed to Vespucci are forgeries. That he was no mean navigator is certainly proved by the fact that he ended his career as *piloto mayor*, or chief pilot, of Spain, of which country he had become a naturalized citizen in 1505. But **Vespucci's main claim to fame** is, of course, the fact that his friend the geographer Martin Waldseemüller (c 1470–? 1518) attached the name America to the newly discovered continent, since it was Vespucci who first established the true shape of so large a part of it.

The first man to take African slaves to the New World was Lucas Vasquez de Ayllon (c 1475–1526). Having been given a rather vague charter by the Emperor Charles V, in 1526 he landed with about 500 colonists and 100 slaves on the coast of what is now South Carolina, of which he was thus **the first European colonist**. But within a few months he and most of his company had died of fever and the colony was abandoned. Ayllon has

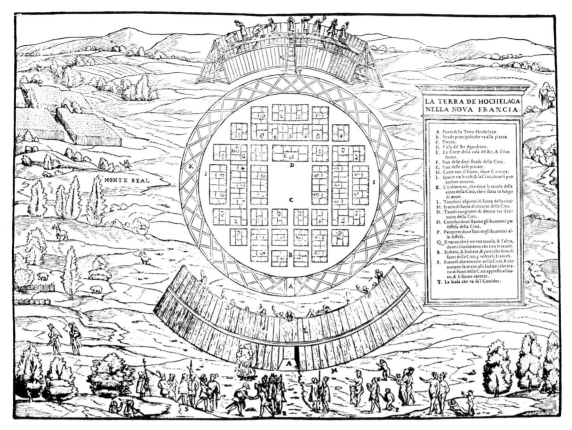

A plan of the village of Hochelaga drawn for Giambattista Ramusio's *Delle Navigazioni e Viaggi* (3 vols, 1550–69).

another claim to fame: 'On entering the river, he lost one of his ships with all its provisions, but the crew was saved. Ayllon promptly set to work to replace the lost vessel, and built himself an open boat which could be covered over at need; it had a single mast and was so planned as to admit of its being propelled by oars as well as sails. . . . It was, says Dr Shea, **the first instance of shipbuilding upon our coast**' (WOODBURY LOWERY, *The Spanish Settlements within the Present Limits of the United States*).

The first European to sail up the St Lawrence River was the French explorer Jacques Cartier (1491–1557). In 1534, when commanding an expedition to discover the North-West passage, he sailed through the Straits of Belle Isle and anchored in the river beyond. On his second journey, two years later, he sailed up the river as far as the Indian village of Hochelaga, the site of

the present city of Montreal. Though Cartier is credited with the discovery of the St Lawrence it is known that European fishermen were already using the river as an anchorage. Indeed on his first voyage a large fishing barque from La Rochelle dropped anchor close by.

The North-East Passage

The first record of the idea that it might be possible to reach China by sailing round the north of Europe and Asia dates from 1525, and in 1527 we find the geographer Robert Thorne exhorting Henry VIII to mount an expedition to seek such a route, since, 'of the four parts of the world, it seemeth three parts are discovered by other princes'. Thorne's letter to the King was even accompanied by a map.

The first attempt to find the North-East Passage, as it became known, was Sir Hugh Willoughby's (*d* 1554) ill-fated expedition which sailed from London in May 1553. The three ships became separated in a gale, but eventually Willoughby's and one other ship found shelter on the coast of Lapland, where, being quite un-equipped for the rigours of an Arctic winter, he and his men perished.

The third ship, *Edward Bonaventure*, of which the captain was Richard Chancellor (*d* 1556), having waited for a week at the arranged *rendez-vous*, sailed on to the north-east, then turned south and reached the White Sea, anchoring at last in the mouth of the River Dvina. Chancellor then travelled overland to Moscow where he was hospitably received at the court of Ivan the Ter-rible (1533–84). He sailed home in 1554 and wrote the first English account of life in Russia. He was drowned in 1556 when his ship was wrecked off the coast of Scotland.

The master of the *Edward Bonaventure* in 1553 was Stephen Borough (1525–84) whose claim to fame is that he was **the first Englishman to sight the North Cape**, as he himself then named it, and later (1556) became **the first Englishman to reach the Kara Straits**, south of Novaya Zemlya.

Many further expeditions were undertaken, but mention need only be made here of the Dutch navigator **William Barents** (*c* 1550–97) who undertook three voyages in search of the North-East passage and died in 1597 on Novaya Zemlya, where his headquarters were found in 1871 and its contents removed to The Hague. He gave his name to the **Barents Sea**.

The first explorer known to have sailed through the Bering Strait, thus proving the separation of Asia and North America, was the Russian Semyon Ivanov Dezhnyev (1605–*c* 1673). In 1648 he sailed along the north coast of eastern Siberia from the Kolyma River, rounded the north-east corner of Asia, now called Cape Dezhnyev, passed through the Bering Strait and continued south-west until he reached the mouth of the Anadyr River. His report of the expedition lay unread in the archives at Yakutsk until 1736, about eight years after Vitus Bering had explored the area and given his name to the Straits.

The first successful navigation of the North-East passage was made in 1878–9 by Pro-fessor N. A. E. Nordenskiöld (1832–1901). **Nor-denskiöld** was Finnish by birth, but an unfortu-nate remark he made in a speech in Helsinki in 1857 about Finnish hopes of being reunited with Sweden so upset the Russian Governor-General, Count von Berg, that when, in 1858, he was offered a professorship at the Academy of Science of Sweden, von Berg allowed him a passport but refused to allow him back to Finland. Eventually the ban was rescinded, prompting an English scientist to remark in 1968, 'What a fascinating man he is! The student rebel who made good, the Rudi Dutschke of his time, who ended up a by-word for stolidity and staidness.' In 1867 Nordenskiöld, in the iron steamer *Sofia*, had led the expedition that reached **the highest northern latitude (81° 42′) then attained in the eastern hemisphere**. The traverse of the North-East passage in the *Vega*, a converted whaler of 299 tons, could probably have been completed in one season had Nordenskiöld's scientific work not delayed him, for he was only 100 miles (161km) from the Bering Strait when the new ice forming in September brought the expedition to a halt.

The first ship to make the passage in one season was the small Russian ice-breaker *Sibiryakov* in 1932.

The North-West Passage

The impetus behind the search for a North-West passage, that is to say a sea-route from the Atlan-tic to the Pacific round the north of Canada, was primarily economic and may be briefly ascribed to two main causes: 1. Turkish domination of the eastern Mediterranean, culminating in the fall of Constantinople in 1453, which closed the over-land caravan routes from the Orient; 2. the Treaty of Tordesillas, drawn up by Pope Alex-ander VI in 1493, which divided all discoveries in the New World between Spain and Portugal. As a result the French, the English and the Dutch were excluded from the lucrative spice trade and were obliged to seek other routes to the East.

The credit for **the first attempt to find a North-West passage** really belongs to John Cabot (see p. 34), who was certainly inspired by the need to find an alternative route to the Orient. Indeed he was convinced that he had in fact made landfall on an island off the coast of 'Cathay'.

The first French expedition in search of a westward passage to Cathay was actually com-manded by a Florentine. Giovanni da Verrazano (1485–1528), a nobleman by birth, persuaded Francis I (1515–47) to lend him the *Dauphine*, a

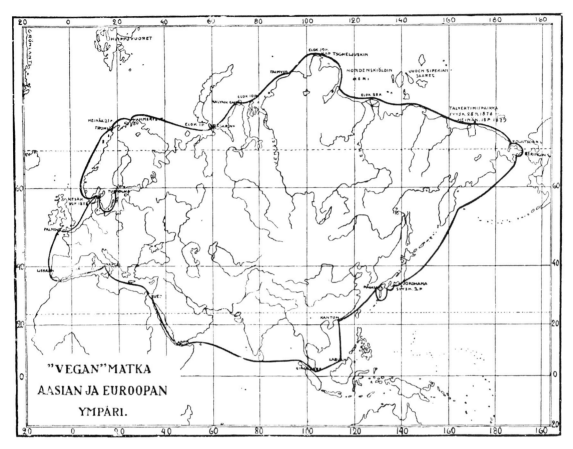

The route of the *Vega* round Europe and Asia in 1878–80
(above). Sir Martin Frobisher, who commanded the
Triumph against the Spanish Armada in 1588 (right).

ship of 100 tons, with the object of discovering for
France a new route to the Pacific. Verrazano
sailed in 1523 and explored the coast of North
America from what is now North Carolina as far
north as Labrador. On the way he became **the
first European to sail into the mouth of the
Hudson river**, or what is now New York Harbour, where his name survives in the Verrazano
Bridge and Narrows. He met a grisly death in
Guadeloupe in the West Indies in 1528 when he
was cut up and eaten by the Carbis before the eyes
of his brother, who was unable to help.

Verrazano was one of the first explorers to
grasp the fact that America was a separate continent and not an extension of Asia.

**The first Englishman to command an expedi-
tion specifically in search of the North-West
passage** was Martin Frobisher (*c* 1535–94), who

set sail from Blackwall in 1576. By this time it had been accepted by geographers and explorers alike that an entire continent lay between the Atlantic and the Pacific Oceans. Frobisher reached the bay at the southern end of Baffin Island which still bears his name and sailed up it for 150 miles (241km), but decided to turn back when five of his crew were carried off by Eskimos. He took home with him some black stone which he believed to be gold-bearing ore and thereafter his attention was diverted from the search for the North-West passage to a search for gold. He made two more voyages to Baffin Island before it was conclusively established that his gold-bearing ore was, in fact, iron pyrites.

Thereafter the search for the North-West passage becomes almost exclusively an English affair, as a glance at the names on the map will reveal. **John Davis** (see p. 25) (c 1550–1605), of the Davis Strait, made three voyages (1585, 1586, 1587) and got as far north as Baffin Bay. Next of note comes **Henry Hudson** (d 1611) who turned his attention to the North-West passage, having been frustrated in his attempts to find a North-East passage. In 1609 he sailed up the river that now bears his name as far as the present site of the town of Albany and so proved that New York Bay was not the entrance to a strait leading to a North-West passage. He set sail again in 1610 in the 55-ton *Discovery*, passed through the strait and explored the bay both of which still bear his name. He was obliged to winter in the bay and in the following year the crew mutinied and he was set adrift in a small boat with his son and eight others. Nothing was ever heard of them again. It could, however, be said that Hudson, perhaps to make amends for his disagreeable death, has been over-compensated by posterity. As the *Dictionary of National Biography* puts it, 'Though he explored further than his predecessors, Hudson actually discovered neither the bay, nor straits, nor river called after him.'

Others who left their names on the map of that inhospitable part of the world during the 17th century include William Baffin (1584–1622), who made five voyages between 1612 and 1615, Luke Foxe (1586–1636) and Thomas James (1593–1635). It was the observations of the last two which proved beyond doubt that no strait connected the Pacific Ocean with the western shore of Hudson Bay.

William Baffin first discovered the bay which bears his name in 1615. At the same time he discovered the series of straits which radiate from its head and were named by him Lancaster, Smith and Jones Sounds in honour of the patrons of his voyages. On this voyage he reached about 77° 45′ which was about 300 miles (483km) further north than John Davis had reached and was to remain unsurpassed in that sea for the next 236 years. The accuracy of Baffin's tidal and astronomical observations was remarkable and his determination of longitude at sea by lunar observation is said to have been the first of its kind on record. He was killed while serving with the East India Company in the Persian Gulf.

Though much knowledge was gained during the 18th century of the general shape of North America, little further progress was made towards finding the North-West passage. The next major advance did not come until **William Parry's expedition of 1819–20**, which sailed through Lancaster Sound, Barrow Strait and Melville Sound to Melville Island. This was the first expedition to survive the winter so far north.

It was during an expedition led by John Ross, which spent four winters in the Arctic between 1829 and 1823, that his nephew, **John Clark Ross, discovered, on 1 June 1831, the magnetic north pole.**

The final discovery of the North-West passage is usually credited to **Sir John Franklin** (1784–1847), who, sadly, did not survive to enjoy his hard-won honour. The two ships in which he set out from England, in May 1845, the *Erebus* and the *Terror*, are certainly **the best-known of all those associated with the North-West passage**, since their names were seldom out of the news for the next ten years! The ships were sighted in Baffin Bay in July 1845, and thereafter never heard of again. No less than 39 expeditions were subsequently despatched to try and discover their fate, several of them organized by Franklin's indomitable wife. On one of these expeditions **Robert McClure** (1807–73) sailed from the Pacific through the Bering Strait to the strait that now bears his name, but was forced to abandon ship in June 1853, in Mercy Bay, on the northern shore of Banks Island. McClure was rescued by an expedition led by Sir Edward Belcher (1799–1877) and thus became **the first man to complete the journey from the Pacific to the Atlantic via the Arctic route**, though his journey was made partly overland.

In 1859 Captain Leopold McClintock (1819–1907) finally discovered the diaries and log book of the Sir John Franklin expedition, the location of which entitle Franklin to the honour of being called **the discoverer of the North-West passage**.

Ironically, after so many years of British endeavour, the honour of being **the first man to navigate the North-West passage** fell to a Norwegian. Setting out from Norway in the 50-ton fishing smack *Gjøa*, with his creditors hard on his heels, **Roald Amundsen** (1872–1928) finally reached the Pacific in 1906.

One cannot escape the conclusion that, in the field of exploration, so much effort can seldom have been expended to so little advantage.

The largest ship yet to navigate the North-West passage is the 150,000-ton United States tanker *Manhattan*. She left the Delaware River on 24

Captain Sir John Franklin (left). Sir John Franklin's ship, the *Erebus*, before she was abandoned by her crew. *National Maritime Museum* (below).

August 1969, and reached Prudhoe Bay, Alaska, on 19 September, having travelled 4600 miles (7403km) in 28 days. Although the voyage proved that a feasible route exists for tankers to carry oil from Alaska's North Slope to the east coast of North America and Europe, the costs are such that an overland pipeline to an ice-free port in southern Alaska was eventually preferred. The *Manhattan* was fitted with a protective steel belt 9ft (2.74m) thick, 30ft (9.14m) deep and 670ft (204m) long and the entire testing project was reputed to have cost $39 million.

In October 1976, the *J. E. Bernier*, a Canadian Coast Guard icebreaker, completed **the first clockwise voyage around North America by a Canadian vessel in a single navigation season**. The *Bernier* sailed from Quebec City on 14 May for Victoria, British Columbia, via the Panama Canal and returned via the North-West passage, a distance of 19,000 miles (30,450km).

Into the Pacific

The first European to see the Pacific Ocean was the Spanish explorer, Vasco Nuñez de Balboa (c 1475–1517). On 1 September 1513, he set out with 190 men from Darien, the settlement he had established on the Gulf of Urabá, crossed the Isthmus of Panama, reached the Pacific Ocean and named it the 'Great South Sea'.

The first white man actually to embark upon the Pacific Ocean was Alonzo Martin, a scout sent ahead by Balboa, who reached the shores of the Gulf of San Miguel on or about 27 September 1513. Balboa himself reached the coast on the 29th when he formally took possession of the 'Great South Sea' in the name of the Spanish King.

Before returning to Darien Balboa visited the Pearl Islands which lie 25 miles (40km) offshore in the Gulf of Panama.

The first circumnavigation of the globe was achieved in the years 1519–22. A Spanish expedition of five ships, under the command of the Portuguese navigator **Ferdinand Magellan** (c 1480–1521) set sail from San Lucar de Barrameda, just north of Cadiz, on 20 September 1519. Their first landfall was Pernambuco (now Recife, in Brazil), whence they coasted south to

Port St Julian where Magellan was obliged to put down a mutiny. It is an interesting comment on the times that Magellan, who was generally regarded as a temperate and humane leader, had one insubordinate officer skinned alive and marooned two other men in the wastes of

A fanciful engraving of the *Vittoria* (top). Ferdinand Magellan, or, more properly, Fernão de Magalhães (above).

Patagonia. There he passed the winter, sailing again on 20 August and reaching the strait that has ever since borne his name on 21 October. Thirty-eight days later he emerged into the ocean which, owing to the gentleness of the weather, he named the Pacific. Ninety-eight days after that, during which time his men had suffered appallingly from starvation and scurvy, they reached what was probably the island of Guam. Magellan was killed by natives on the island of Mactan in the Philippines, whereupon command of the expedition devolved upon Juan Sebastián del Cano (*d* 1526) who arrived back in Seville at the end of July 1522, in the *Vittoria*, the only vessel to complete the journey. Of the 270 men who had set out only 31 survived to complete the first circumnavigation of the globe. One of these was Antonio Pigafetta (1491–1534) who wrote an account of the voyage for Charles V, which the King had published.

Sebastián del Cano is **probably the only mutineer in history to have been rewarded with a coat of arms and a statue.** He was one of the ringleaders of the mutiny against Magellan in Patagonia but his skill as a pilot made him too valuable to be executed. As commander of the *Vittoria*, the only ship to complete the journey, he was honoured by Charles V.

The first person to suspect and then to prove, that the constantly prevailing south winds, which made the passage up the western coast of South America so trying, did not blow further out to sea was the Spanish navigator and discoverer Juan Fernandez (*c* 1536–*c* 1604). In 1563 he proved the soundness of his theory by sailing from Callao, Peru, to Valparaiso, Chile, in 30 days and was promptly arrested on a charge of sorcery. His inquisitors, however, soon accepted his natural explanation of the marvel. During a voyage from Lima to Valdivia he discovered the islands which still bear his name, but his attempt to establish a colony there failed; only the goats remained, the descendants of which were hunted by Alexander Selkirk, **the original Robinson Crusoe,** who was marooned on the island from 1705 to 1709.

The first European to reach the Solomon Islands was the Spanish navigator Alvaro de Mendaña de Neira (1541–95) in about 1567. 'The greatest island that they discovered was according

The statue of Sebastian del Cano, in Guetaria, the town of his birth in Northern Spain.

unto the first finder called Guadalcanal, on the coast whereof they sailed 150 leagues before they could knowe whether it were an island or part of the maine land, and yet they know not perfectly what to make of it, but thinke it may be part of that continent which stretcheth to the streights of Magellan ... The discoverer of these islands named them the Isles of Salomon, to the ende that the Spaniards supposing them to bee those isles from whence Salomon fetched gold to adorne the temple at Jerusalem, might bee the more desirous to goe and inhabite the same' (*Hakluyt's Voyages XI*, p.287).

SIR FRANCIS DRAKE

The first Englishman to circumnavigate the globe was Sir Francis Drake (*c* 1540–96), possibly the most famous of all the Elizabethan seamen. Little is known of his early years, even the date of his birth being uncertain, but it is known that he was born at Crowndale, near Tavistock in Devon, and it is thought that his first lessons in seamanship were acquired in the Thames coastal trade.

In 1565 he sailed with Captain John Lovell to the Spanish Main and so distinguished himself that two years later, in 1567, he was given command of the 50-ton *Judith* on the third slave-trading voyage of his cousin, Sir John Hawkins. The voyage was not a success, the ships being attacked by the Spaniards at San Juan de Ulloa, off the coast of Mexico, only those of Hawkins and Drake returning home safely.

He spent the next few years privateering, the most celebrated of his exploits during this period being the capture in 1573 of the Spanish treasure train en route from Panama to Nombre de Dios.

Richard Hakluyt's map of the New World, drawn in 1587, nine years after Drake crossed the Pacific.

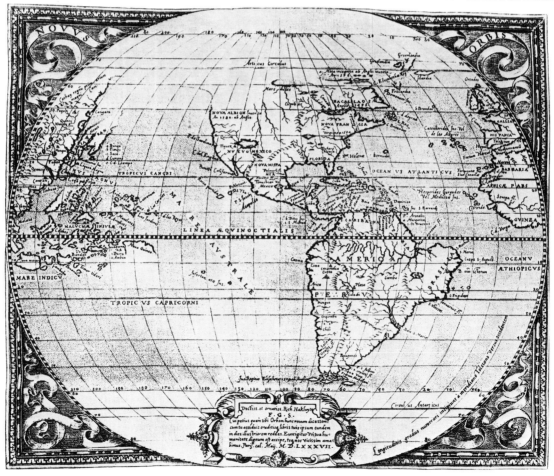

It was then that he saw the Pacific Ocean for the first time and made his famous vow to be the first 'to sail an English ship in those seas'.

His chance came in 1577 when he was appointed to command the first English expedition to circumnavigate the globe. He set sail from Plymouth on 13 December of that year with five ships and about 160 men. His own flagship was the 100-ton *Pelican*, the name of which he changed to the *Golden Hind* during the voyage in honour of Sir Christopher Hatton, a shareholder in the expedition, whose badge was a golden hind.

At Port St Julian, not far north of the straits of Magellan, Thomas Doughty, captain of one of the ships, was tried and beheaded for fomenting mutiny, close to the spot where Magellan had hanged a mutineer 50 years earlier. But the

Sir Francis Drake, variously regarded as a Protestant hero or a common pirate.

An artist's impression of Sir Francis Drake's ship, the *Golden Hind*. *National Maritime Museum.*

trouble continued and finally Drake was inspired to make what is probably **the most famous speech ever made at sea**, chiefly remembered for the following words: 'I must have the gentleman to haul and draw with the mariner and the mariner with the gentleman.... I would know him that would refuse to set his hand to a rope, but I know there is not any such here.' Two of the smaller ships were stripped and sunk at Port St Julian, the *Elizabeth* was separated from the *Golden Hind* in a storm and a small sloop was lost, leaving Drake to make the passage of the Pacific alone.

He made several successful raids on Spanish towns in South America and captured the Spanish treasure ship *Cacafuego* off Lima. He sailed as far north as latitude 48°N (Vancouver Island), then returned south and landed near San Francisco, from whence he sailed across the Pacific to the Moluccas. He eventually reached Plymouth on 26 September 1580, then sailed the *Golden Hind* round to Deptford where he was knighted by Queen Elizabeth.

His next famous exploit was the destruction, in April 1587, of the Spanish ships at Cadiz which set back the preparations for the Armada by a year and is known to history as the 'Singeing of the King of Spain's beard'. His part in the Armada itself is described elsewhere (p. 61). He died of yellow fever off Porto Bello, Panama, on 28 January 1596. 'He was,' said his contemporary John Stow, 'as famous in Europe and America as Tamburlaine in Asia and Africa.'

The second Englishman to circumnavigate the globe was Thomas Cavendish (*c* 1560–92) who had accompanied Sir Richard Grenville in 1585 on the first of the latter's voyages to encourage the development of the Virginia Colony. Cavendish sailed from Plymouth the following year with three small ships fitted out for privateering, the largest, the *Desire*, being of 140 tons. He rounded Cape Horn, had the good fortune to encounter the annual Spanish treasure ship from Manila to Acapulco off the coast of South America, and captured her after a hard six-hour fight. Returning to England via the Cape of Good Hope, he touched at St Helena, believing himself to be the first to do so, whereas the Portuguese commander Joao da Nova Castell had in fact visited the island as long ago as 1502 but had kept its existence a secret. Cavendish arrived home a few days after

Thomas Cavendish.

the defeat of the Spanish Armada. Having squandered the money he had acquired, he fitted out a second expedition, in which John Davis (see p. 38) was to be navigator. Bad weather in the Straits of Magellan caused Cavendish to lose heart and, giving the other ships the slip in the night, he turned for home and died on the way.

The first English sea atlas of the East was drawn in about 1598 by **Martin Llewellyn**, steward of St Bartholomew's Hospital, London, from 1599 until 1634, when he died and it was presented to Christ Church, Oxford, by his sons. There it lay unknown to scholars for three and a half centuries until discovered in September 1975. It is thought that Llewellyn accompanied Cornelius de Houtman on the first Dutch voyage to the East in 1595–7. The atlas consists of 16 charts each measuring 26in (66cm) by 36in (91cm). They extend from the Cape of Good Hope to the Far East, including Japan, the Philippines, the Marianas and the north-western part of New Guinea.

CAPE HORN
Though Sir Francis Drake claimed to have landed on Cape Horn, it was left to two Dutchmen, Jakob Le Maire (1585–1616) and Willem

Schouten (*d* 1618) to name it, after the town of Hoorn in Holland. Hitherto geographers had believed that the land south of the straits of Magellan was part of the great continent of Terra Australis Incognita, but Le Maire's father, Isaac, had read Drake's claim that Tierra del Fuego was an island and in June 1615, sent his son with two ships, the *Eendracht*, of 220 tons, and the *Hoorn*, of 110 tons, to see if Drake was right. On 29 January 1616, 'towards the evening we again saw land to the north-west and nor'-nor'-west of us. This was the land south of the Strait of Magellaen, which stretches away to the south. It consisted entirely of high mountains covered with snow, and ends in a sharp corner, which we called

The Death of Vitus Bering by the Dutch artist Christian Julius Lodewyck Portman (1799–1867). National Maritime Museum.

the Cape of Hoorn, and which lies in latitude 57° 48'.'

The first European to visit Alaska was the Danish explorer Vitus Bering (1680–1741). Taken into Russia's naval service in 1706, he so distinguished himself in the wars against Sweden that in 1725 Peter the Great sent him to explore the north-east coast of Asia. He crossed Siberia to Kamchatka, where he had several ships built, and in 1728 discovered the Straits that are named after him, so proving the separation of the continents of Asia and North America. In 1730 he founded the port of Petropavlorsk on the Kamchatka peninsula and in 1741 he sailed from there to discover Alaska. On the return journey his ship, the *St Peter*, was wrecked in the Aleutian Islands and there he died.

The number of islands in the Pacific discovered by **Philip Carteret** (*d* 1796) entitle him to be ranked as **one of the greatest explorers of his day**; yet, unjustly, his name is seldom remembered. In 1766 he was appointed to command the *Swallow*, which, with the *Dolphin*, commanded by Captain Samuel Wallis, was ordered to undertake a voyage of circumnavigation. The two ships were separated after passing through the Straits of Magellan and Carteret completed the voyage alone, discovering and naming en route at least 20 islands.

The first Russian to circumnavigate the globe was Admiral Adam Krusenstern (1770–1846). He served for six years in the Royal Navy (1793–99) during which time he visited America, India and China. In 1803 he was appointed by Tsar Alexander I to make a voyage to demonstrate the advantages to Russia of communication with China via Cape Horn and the Cape of Good Hope. He bought two ships in England, renamed them *Nadezhda* and *Neva* and sailed from Kronstadt in August of that year. He rounded Cape Horn, crossed the Pacific, visited Kamchatka and Japan, undertook an extended series of explorations and finally returned to Kronstadt via the Cape of Good Hope in August 1806.

Australasia

The first Europeans to set foot on Australian soil were the crew of a small Dutch vessel, the *Duyfken*, who landed on the east coast of the Gulf of Carpentaria near Cape Keerweer in 1606 and described the aborigines as 'wild, cruel, black savages ... poor and abject wretches'.

The first Englishman to leave a record of having visited Australia was the ex-buccaneer William Dampier (1652–1715). In 1688, when serving as a seaman before the mast on a privateer called the *Revenge*, he landed on the north-west coast and was equally unflattering about the natives. 'The inhabitants of this country,' he wrote in *A New Voyage around the World*, published in 1697, 'are the miserablest people in the world.'

In 1699 Dampier was appointed to command HMS *Roebuck* with orders to explore and map the 'new' continent to the south of the East Indies which he had described in his book. 'Had he,'

says Philip Gosse in *The Pirate's Who's Who*, 'taken the westward course, as he originally intended, and sailed to Australia round the Horn, it is possible that he would have made many of the discoveries for which James Cook afterwards became so famous, and by striking the east coast of Australia would very likely have antedated the civilization of that continent by 50 years. But he was persuaded, partly by his timid crew, and perhaps in some measure by his own dislike of cold temperatures, to sail by the eastward route and to double the Cape of Good Hope.... After spending some unprofitable weeks on the north coast of Australia, failing to find water or to make friends with the aboriginals, scurvy broke out among his somewhat mutinous crew, and he sailed to New Guinea, the coast of which he saw on New Year's Day, 1700.'

Dampier had the curious distinction of being navigator on the *Cinque Ports* in 1705 when Alexander Selkirk, the prototype of Robinson Crusoe, was marooned on the islands of Juan Fernandez after a violent row with the captain, Thomas Stradling, and navigator on the *Duke*, commanded by Woodes Rogers (*d* 1732), in 1709 when Selkirk was taken off the island (see p. 24).

The first European to see New Zealand was Abel Tasman (1603–59) **the greatest of the Dutch navigators**. In 1642 he was appointed by Anthony van Diemen (1593–1645), the Governor-General of the Dutch East Indies, to command an expedition to explore the 'Great South Land'. He sailed from Batavia (now Djakarta) south-west to Mauritius, then headed south and east until, on 24 November 1642, he made landfall on what he thought to be part of Australia and which he named Van Diemen's Land. It was, in fact, the island of Tasmania, to which its name was changed in 1856. He continued to sail east and after eight days sighted New Zealand, but he did not land there and sailed on in a north-easterly direction, discovered the Tonga and Fiji islands and finally returned to Batavia after a voyage lasting ten months. He thus became **the first man to circumnavigate Australia**.

In 1644 van Diemen sent him on another voyage, the purpose of which was to discover whether New Guinea was an island or was part of the Australian continent. New Guinea's insularity had in fact been established in 1606 when the Portuguese navigator Luis Vaez de Torres (d 1613) became the first to sail through the strait which separates New Guinea and Australia and which bears his name to this day. But the Spanish authorities (the kingdoms of Spain and Portugal were united in 1580 under Philip II) had for some reason kept the information to themselves and it was not until 1762 that Torres' account of his discovery came to light when the log of his voyage was found at Manila and the strait was named in his honour. Tasman, however, failed to pass through the strait and sailed south down the east coast of the Gulf of Carpentaria, then west along the north and west coasts of Australia as far south as 22°S, which he was the first to map systematically.

CAPTAIN JAMES COOK

The first man to define the eastern limits of the Australian land mass was Captain James Cook (1728–79). Though he cannot strictly be called the discoverer of Australia, it is not unreasonable to call him the first man to re-discover it. After Tasman's pioneering voyages of 1642 and 1644 the Dutch made no attempt to settle there, looking upon it solely as a wild and inhospitable coast on which their vessels crossing the Indian Ocean were too often driven by a lee wind.

Cook was certainly **one of the greatest of all English seamen**. He started his career in the merchant navy but transferred to the Royal Navy as an able seaman in 1755. His skill as a navigator won him rapid promotion and in 1757 he was promoted master (the equivalent of navigator).

During the siege of Quebec in 1759 the excellence of his survey of the St Lawrence River enabled big ships to sail up it for the first time and Cook to claim a decisive role in an event which was the key to the subsequent conquest of Canada. That and his later surveys of the coasts of Newfoundland and Nova Scotia prompted the

A drawing by Abel Tasman from his *Journal of the Voyage 1632–43*. The caption translated reads, 'Thus appears the vessel of Nova Guinea and people dwelling therein.'

Royal Society to invite him to command an expedition to Tahiti to observe the transit of the planet Venus across the face of the sun, and then to sail south in search of the supposed continent of Terra Australis Incognita which geographers still believed to exist.

He set sail from Plymouth on 25 August 1768, in the barque *Endeavour* (see below) which had been fitted out at the expense of the wealthy naturalist Sir Joseph Banks (1743–1820), who himself accompanied the expedition. They reached Tahiti on 13 April 1769, without a single man suffering from scurvy (see p. 51), observed the transit of Venus and set sail again on 13 July. They next made landfall on the east coast of New Zealand on 7 October where they were refused supplies by the Maoris of Poverty Bay, but given them by those at the Bay of Plenty – hence the names. They sailed north round North Cape, south down the west coast, through the straits that have since borne Cook's name, and round the South Island, thereby disproving the theory that New Zealand was a peninsula extending northwards from a southern continent.

Cook then sailed west across the Tasman Sea, making landfall off the south-east corner of

Australia on 21 April 1770. Following the coast north and surveying it as he went, he anchored in Botany Bay, five miles south of the present city of Sydney (see p. 50), and so named by Banks on account of the remarkable variety of the flora. Their efforts to communicate with the aborigines proved fruitless. Little groups of blacks would appear through the trees, stare at the men collecting wood or filling their watercasks, throw a spear or two and then vanish. Here died a consumptive seaman named Formby Sutherland who thus gained the distinction of being **the first white man to be buried in Australia**.

On 6 May Cook sailed north but on the night of 11 June the *Endeavour* struck a reef and only good luck and the suggestion of one of the crew to fother the ship – to drag a sail under the hull until it covered the hole – enabled them to reach the shore and run the ship aground to make the necessary repairs. Six weeks later they set sail, passed through the Torres Straits (see p. 47), reached Batavia on 10 October 1770 and England on 12 July 1771.

The *Endeavour* is **the first discovery ship of which accurate details have survived**. She started life as the *Earl of Pembroke*, carrying coal from England to Scandinavia, and her exact dimensions were carefully recorded when she was purchased and refitted for Captain Cook's first voyage. She is described as a barque of 336 tons armed with ten carriage guns and 12 swivel guns. She carried five anchors and three boats and a total complement of 94 men. The length of the keel was 81ft (24.7m), of the lower deck 97ft 8in (29.7m) and her beam was 29ft 2in (8.9m).

On his second voyage Cook became **the first navigator ever to cross the Antarctic Circle**. This second voyage has been called, without undue exaggeration, **the greatest voyage ever made**, not least because Cook returned home, after three years and 18 days, having lost only four men, three through accidents and one alone from sickness, and having travelled a distance equivalent to three times the circumference of the globe. The first voyage, though it had filled in many spaces on the map, had still not disproved the existence of Terra Australis Incognita, the great southern continent which geographers from classical times had thought must balance the land mass of the northern hemisphere. So, in July 1772, Cook set out again, this time with two ships, the *Resolution* and the *Adventure*, both, like

Captain James Cook, F.R.S. From the portrait by Nathaniel Dance R.A. in the National Maritime Museum.

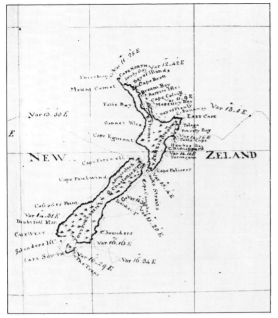

Cook's charting of New Zealand 1769–70: detail from his MS. 'Chart of the Great South Sea ... shewing the Trade and Discoveries made by the *Endeavour*...'

again separated and the *Adventure* eventually made her way back to England, Furneaux thus becoming **the first commander to complete a circumnavigation of the globe in an easterly direction.**

Cook continued south, this time reaching 71°10′ on 30 January 1774, **the farthest he was ever to get.** Having now proved conclusively that there could be no habitable continent in the South Pacific, Cook could justifiably have claimed that his job was done, but his officers agreed – he says willingly – to protract the voyage by another year. There followed a wide sweep north and then west, reaching Easter Island – not seen since its discovery by Mendaña 170 years earlier – after three and a half months out of sight of land. Subsequently he visited and charted the Marquesas Islands, the Friendly Islands, the New Hebrides, and discovered and named New Caledonia, the Isle of Pines and Norfolk Island.

Cook finally started for home from New Zealand on 10 November 1774, setting a course on latitude 55° for Cape Horn – **a route never travel-**

the *Endeavour*, converted Whitby colliers. The *Resolution*, 462 tons and 12 guns, with a crew of 118 men, was commanded by Cook; the *Adventure*, 336 tons, 10 guns and a crew of 83, by Lieutenant Tobias Furneaux. The ships' names had been changed from *Drake* and *Raleigh* in order to avoid giving offence to the Spaniards, who still regarded the Pacific as their territory, and to whom the names of Raleigh and Drake were still anathema.

Sailing south from the Cape of Good Hope, **the two ships crossed the Antarctic Circle on 17 January 1773, the first ever to do so.** On 18 January they reached latitude 67°15′ but, finding their passage blocked by solid ice, were obliged to turn back. On 8 February the ships lost contact with each other but were reunited at their pre-arranged *rendezvous* in Queen Charlotte's Sound, New Zealand, in May. After refitting, they sailed north, reaching Tahiti on 16 July, where, we are told, a swarm of naked girls, aged mostly around nine or ten, the Tahitian age of puberty, swam out through the surf and climbed on board. They sailed on to Tonga, or the Friendly Islands, as Cook named them, before heading south once again for the Antarctic. On the way the ships were

Head of a Maori. The tattoos are not mere decoration, but somewhat akin to armorial bearings.

The death of Captain Cook, Kealakekua Bay, Hawaii, 14 February 1779.

back to England. He was then to sail north up the west coast of North America in search of the Pacific end of the North-West passage. This time he was accompanied by Captain Clerke in another Whitby collier, the *Discovery*, of 229 tons. They reached Tahiti on August 1777, set out for North America in December and discovered the Hawaiian Islands en route, to which Cook gave the name Sandwich Islands in honour of the 4th Earl of Sandwich, then First Lord of the Admiralty. After a brief stay, they sailed on and sighted the North American coast on 7 March 1778. At Nootka Sound, by Vancouver Island, they carried out various repairs, then continued north and west along the coasts of Canada and South Alaska. They passed through the Aleutian Islands and on through the Bering Strait until at latitude 70°N the ice forced them to turn south. By the end of November Cook was back in the Sandwich Islands, where, after surveying the coast of Hawaii, he anchored in Kealakekua Bay on 17 January 1779. Relations with the natives, friendly enough at first, soon became strained and culminated in the theft of one of the *Discovery*'s boats. Cook proposed to take the native king hostage, but the other chiefs intervened, a scuffle ensued and Cook was stabbed in the back. It was 14 February 1779 and **the greatest seaman of his day** was dead.

The first ships to carry convicts to Australia sailed from England on 13 May 1787 under the command of Captain Arthur Phillip (1738–1814), who later became **the first Governor of Australia**. He reached Botany Bay on 18 January 1788, but thought it an unsuitable place for a penal settlement and on 26 January 1788, the British flag was hoisted at Port Jackson, a few miles to the north, thus marking the beginning of the British occupation of Australia. Phillip named the place Sydney, after Thomas Townshend, Viscount Sydney, a politician whose name is less familiar to schoolboys than that of his grandfather, 'Turnip' Townshend. The region, known to this day as New South Wales, had been named by Captain Cook because he thought that he detected a resemblance to the coastline of South Wales.

Failing health obliged Phillip to return to England in 1792, but the subsequent success of the settlement owed much to his wisdom and sense of justice.

led by any ship before – and made the crossing in five weeks, averaging a remarkable 160 miles a day. Sailing on into the South Atlantic he rediscovered South Georgia and discovered the South Sandwich Islands which he described as 'the most horrible coast in the world'. Having now circumnavigated the South Pole Cook turned north for the last time and anchored off Cape Town on 21 March 1775. The *Resolution* finally reached Portsmouth on 29 July. The 'greatest voyage ever made' was over.

Cook was to make one more voyage on which he set sail, again in the *Resolution*, on 12 July 1776. His first job was to take home to Tahiti, Omai, a native whom Furneaux had brought

Scurvy

The greatest killer at sea during the 16th, 17th and 18th centuries was scurvy, a disease which caused the death of infinitely more men than ever perished through enemy action or shipwreck. As Captain Cook is widely, though not altogether justifiably, regarded as the seaman who conquered scurvy, this is as good a place as any to consider it. Scurvy is caused by a deficiency of vitamin C (ascorbic acid) and is easily cured by a diet of fresh fruit and vegetables. It takes a minimum of six weeks on a salt diet for scurvy to manifest itself which explains why it only became a major problem when long spells at sea became customary. Columbus, for instance, had no scurvy on his voyages.

Its subsequent prevalence was hardly surprising since the official weekly scale of rations per head in the British Navy between 1622 and 1825 comprised: 7 gallons (32 litres) of beer, 2lb (0.9kg) of salt pork, 4lb (1.8kg) of salt beef, 6oz (170g) of butter, 12oz (340g) of cheese, 3 pints (1.7 litres) of oatmeal and 2 pints (1.1 litres) of dried peas – a diet which contained no vitamin C at all. The symptoms of scurvy are swollen, spongy and bleeding gums, patches on the skin which become 'as hard as wood', and an increasing sense of weakness which proceeds to total exhaustion and, ultimately, death. The response to treatment with vitamin C is immediate and dramatic.

The first man to conduct experiments into the cause and remedy of scurvy was James Lind (1716–94) who has been called the father of nautical medicine. In 1753 he published his *Treatise of the Scurvy* which urged the issue of lemon juice in the Navy as a preventive, a suggestion which it took the Admiralty 40 years to act upon, one reason for the delay being that Captain Cook himself advised against it on the grounds that it was too expensive!

The true reason for the excellent standard of health on Cook's ships was that he gave his men a great variety of food and that, in both men and supplies, his ships were the best equipped that ever sailed from England during the 18th century. Such was Cook's concern over the diet of his men that he once had two sailors flogged for refusing to eat fresh meat and himself claimed that 'few commanders have introduced more novelties as useful varieties of food and drink than I have done,' but his conquest of scurvy was, sadly, an isolated triumph and was based on his appreciation of the value of a varied diet, not on an understanding of the antiscorbutic properties of citrus fruit.

Lemon juice was made a compulsory issue in the Navy in 1795 and scurvy was soon eradicated, only to reappear in the 19th century when lime juice, which has a comparatively low ascorbic acid content, was substituted for lemon juice. This is the origin of the American and Australian slang expression 'Limey' for a Briton. It was not until 1912 when Sir Frederick Gowland Hopkins (1861–1947) published his paper on vitamins that the true cause of scurvy became known.

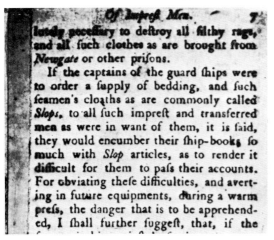

Part of a page from an essay by James Lind on the health of seamen.

The Arctic and Antarctic

The first steamship to cross the Arctic Circle was the 2306-ton wooden corvette, HMS *Challenger*, commanded by Captain (later Admiral Sir George) Nares (1831–1915) in 1874. In 1875–6 Nares led an expedition to the Arctic with HMS *Alert* and HMS *Discovery*. 'The furthest point reached by *Alert* was 82° 27′N. Lat., **the highest latitude ever attained by a ship,** and here on an exposed coast she passed the winter months' (*Annual Register*).

The first vessel specifically designed to winter in the polar pack ice was the 402-ton three-masted schooner *Fram*. Designed by the

The *Fram* in the ice.

Norwegian polar explorer **Fridtjof Nansen** (1861–1930), she was pointed at bow and stern and had sloping sides, so that the ice-floes, pressing together, should tend, not to crush, but rather to slip beneath and lift her. In 1893–6 she was used by Nansen on his long drift across the Arctic Ocean and bore the pressure of the ice perfectly. On 14 March 1895, confident that the *Fram* would continue to drift safely, Nansen set out across the ice on foot and, on 8 April, turned back from 86° 14′N., **the highest latitude then reached by man**. In 1910 the *Fram* was taken by

Roald Amundsen to the Antarctic, when he and four companions successfully reached the South Pole. Today the *Fram* can be seen in her own museum outside Oslo.

On his Antarctic expedition of 1910–11 the German explorer Wilhelm Fulchner (1877–1957) **sailed farther south than anyone before him**. He was **the first man to reach the head of the Weddell Sea** and the discoverer of Vahsel Bay, in which he anchored and landed on what he called the Weddell Barrier, but is now known as the Filchner Ice Shelf. His ship, the *Deutschland*, was a three-masted sailing ship with a 300hp auxiliary engine. It was 45 years before another ship ventured into Vahsel Bay.

On 17 August 1977, the 75,000hp Soviet nuclear icebreaker *Arktika* became **the first ship ever to break its way through the polar ice to the North Pole**. 'For the first time in the history of sea navigation, the ship crossed the massive ice cover and floated freely up toward the very top of the globe,' said Tass News Agency. Previously only three submarines had reached the Pole.

WARSHIPS
— & —
WARFARE

THE ERA
OF THE
WOODEN WARSHIP

'The wooden walls are the best walls of this kingdom.'
LORD COVENTRY, 1635.

The first English King to demand the salute in the English Channel was King John (R. 1199–1216). So long as the Norman conquerors held on to Normandy the Channel was no more than an awkward stretch of water inconveniently dividing two parts of a single estate. But when King John lost Normandy in 1204 the Channel became, as it has remained, the frontier between England and France and the setting for a series of Anglo-French naval engagements which was to stretch over the next 600 years.

The first of these took place at Damme, then up the estuary leading to Bruges, now nearly 10 miles (16km) inland. The English, under the Earl of Salisbury, anchored well offshore, rowed in in boats and destroyed the French ships, most of which were lying on the beach. Apart from the nature of the damage inflicted, the episode scarcely qualifies as a naval engagement.

The effigy of King John on his tomb in Worcester Cathedral.

The first big naval battle ever won by an English Fleet was the Battle of Dover in 1217. In 1215 a faction of English barons had invited Louis, Dauphin of France, to England to replace the unpopular King John. But the King's spirited resistance caused most of the people to come to his support in opposition to the baronial party and when John died in 1216 Louis' situation was grave. A supply fleet commanded by a notorious freebooter called Eustace the Monk set out from France in 1271 with reinforcements for Louis, but was met off Dover by an English fleet raised mostly from the Cinque Ports by Hubert de Burgh (*d* 1243), then holding Dover Castle for John's nine-year-old son, Henry III. De Burgh, who has been called '**the first Englishman to appreciate even dimly the value of sea power**', appeared at first to ignore the French fleet and to be making for Calais. but when his ships were at length to windward of the French he closed for the attack. The issue was quickly decided and most of the enemy's ships were captured. Although this is the **first recorded instance of a commander manoeuvring to take advantage of the wind**, it would be wrong to read into it any sort of concerted fleet tactics, such a sophisticated concept being far beyond the capabilities of the unwieldy ships of the time.

The greatest natural disaster ever to overtake an entire fleet left as its legacy a word which, some 660 years later, was to take on a different, if no less destructive, meaning – Kamikaze. In 1281 Kublai Khan (1216–94), founder of the Mongol dynasty in China and host for 17 years to Marco Polo, embarked upon his second invasion of Japan, the first, in 1274, having proved a failure. 4500 ships were assembled to carry an army of 156,000 men, who were met with stubborn resistance by the Japanese. A few days after the landing a violent typhoon destroyed virtually the entire fleet and the stranded Mongol army was soon defeated. To this providential storm the Japanese gave the name 'Kamikaze' – meaning 'divine wind'.

One of the most successful naval commanders of all time and certainly the most remarkable of his age was the Aragonese and Sicilian admiral Roger de Lauria (d 1305). Little is known of his early life until, in 1283, King Peter III of Aragon gave him command of his fleet in the war against the Angevins that resulted from the Sicilian Vespers, the famous uprising against the misrule of Charles of Anjou. Lauria defeated the French at Malta in June 1283, and again a year later in the Bay of Naples. In 1285 he destroyed the fleet and army of the French king, Philip III, who had invaded Catalonia by sea, in order to support his cousin of Anjou in his conflict with the Aragonese in what has been called **'one of the most brilliant campaigns in all naval history'**. Lauria realized that the French army was supported entirely by sea and that he had only to destroy the fleet to force the army to retreat. This he achieved in two remarkable engagements, one off Palamos, the other off Rosas. The defeat of the enemy was followed, as was usual in medieval naval wars, by a wholesale massacre of the enemy. As a commander Roger de Lauria was far above his contemporaries and many of his successors.

The first letter of marque was issued in England in 1293, in the reign of Edward I, though it is recorded that, in the previous reign, Henry III (1216–72) gave commissions to shipowners to attack enemy vessels on the understanding that the proceeds were surrendered to the exchequer. A letter of marque was a licence granted by the government, or in Britain later on by the Lord High Admiral on the government's behalf, to a private citizen to arm a ship and cruise in search of enemy vessels in time of war or in reprisal for damage done. It thus gave the merchant adventurer a good legal status to operate as a 'private' ship of war. Hence we get the word 'privateer'. It also fostered a condition of limited naval warfare in which the Crown frequently had a share in the profits without the bother of being concerned with the initial expenditure.

The first admiral appointed by an English king under that title was Barrau de Sescas, who, on 1 March 1295, received from Edward I a commission as admiral of the fleet of Bayonne. Later in the same year the commanders of the English fleet, Sir William Leyburn (d 1309) and Sir John de Botetourt (d 1324), were described in a royal writ as admirals (*amiraux de nostre navie Dengleterre*). **The first commission of appointment which has been found** is that of Gervase Alard, who, on 4 February 1303, was appointed Captain and Admiral of the fleet of the Cinque Ports, and of all ports as far west as Cornwall. The

King Henry III sailing home from Gascony in 1243, drawn by the historian and monk Matthew Paris (d 1259).

De reditu Regis in Angliam.

a Vascoma

Regina

Rex

title of captain is linked with that of admiral until 1344. After about 1323 the practice was to divide the coastline of England into two admiralties. The admiral of the North Fleet had under his authority ships of all ports from the mouth of the Thames to the north; the Admiral of the West Fleet those from the mouth of the Thames to the west. **The first admiral of 'all the fleets'** was John, Lord Beauchamp of Warwick, commissioned in July 1360. He died the following December (taken from *Handbook of British Chronology*).

Thomas of Lancaster, Duke of Clarence, was **the first to be commissioned as 'King's Admiral'**, on 20 February 1404/5. Sir Thomas Beaufort was **the first holder of the title 'Admiral of England'**, on 3 June 1413. **The first to bear the title Lord High Admiral** was John Holand, Earl of Huntingdon, afterwards Duke of Exeter, appointed to the rank on 2 October 1435. **The first to be styled First Lord of the Admiralty** was Prince Rupert, Duke of Cumberland, appointed 9 July 1673. (*The Complete Peerage*, Vol. II, App. D.)

Since the retirement of Lord Barham in 1806 it has been the rule (broken only in the cases of the Duke of Clarence (1827–28) and the Duke of Northumberland (1852)), that only a civilian (or, as in the case of Lord Mulgrave, 1807–12, a military man) shall be 'the ruler of the King's Navee'.

The word 'admiral' comes from the Arabic *amir-al-bahr* – commander of the sea – and was first adapted for naval use by the Sicilians. The French copied the word from the Genoese during the Crusade of St Louis (1248–54) and before the end of the 13th century it was in use in England to describe the officer in command of the Cinque Ports.

The first record of guns being carried on board ship dates from 1336 when Louis de Mâle sent ships with guns, said to have been made in Tournai, to attack Antwerp. **The first English ship known to have carried guns** was the *Christopher*. She was armed with three iron guns and a hand-gun, and was captured by the French at the Battle of Sluys in 1340, but there is no record of her guns having been used. **The first English ship in which guns were properly mounted** is traditionally said to have been the *Christopher of the Tower* in the year 1406.

It must be remembered that these guns were intended to be men-killers not ship-sinkers, though they were almost as likely to kill the men who fired them as to kill the enemy. All the early ship-guns were 'built-up', which means that the barrels were made up of a number of long iron rods with angular sides, held together by metal bands and hoops. One historian describes them thus: 'They were breech-loading. Sometimes the breech blew backwards; sometimes when the breech held, the barrel blew sideways and sometimes the ball left the barrel in the general direction of the enemy.'

The boarding party continued to be the main offensive weapon in naval warfare until late in the 16th century; 'boarding' originally meant merely 'approaching to touching distance', while 'going on board the enemy's ship' was described as 'entering'.

The maximum range of such guns was probably about 500yd (475m). It is worth noting here that 'point-blank range' does not, as is often supposed, mean 'at very close range'; it indicates the distance which a missile will travel without dropping below the horizontal plane in which the barrel of the gun lies.

The earliest known four-masted vessel in England was the *Regent*, built at Portsmouth in 1487 in the reign of Henry VII. She met her end in a battle with the French off Camaret, which stands at the entrance to Brest harbour, on 10 August 1512, when she took on Louis XII's (1498–1515) largest and most powerful ship, the *Marie la Cordelière*. The English boarded the enemy ship, whereupon a French gunner set fire to the gunpowder and, the ships being lashed together, both were burned. Every member of their crews perished in the flames. It is probable that the *Regent* was a vessel of about 600 tons, carried a crew of about 800, and was equipped with some 180 guns.

The first recorded 'cutting-out' expedition took place in 1513, the year after the loss of the *Regent*. Sir Edward Howard (1477–1513), the Lord High Admiral and brother-in-law of Sir Thomas Knyvett (*d* 1512), who had commanded the *Regent*, returned to Brest, determined upon revenge. The French prevented him from entering the harbour; but, while blockading the port, he learnt that a fleet of galleys had anchored close in shore, some distance off, and decided to attack them; but, as the ships could not get in, he determined to go in in boats. He was killed in the ensuing fight.

A 'cutting-out' action simply means entering a port or harbour, usually in ship's boats, and launching a surprise attack upon the vessels therein.

The first man to conceive the idea of cutting holes in the side of ships so that guns could be mounted on the lower deck – in other words the inventor of the broadside – was James Baker, shipwright to Henry VIII, though some say that he got the idea from a Frenchman called Descharges. Simple though it sounds, this 'discovery' was to prove **the most fundamental turning-point in the whole history of naval warfare.** Henceforward ships of war were no longer mere floating platforms used for the transportation of foot-soldiers and armed only with 'anti-personnel' guns; now they carried large guns capable of battering and sinking enemy ships from a considerable distance.

Hitherto such ordnance as fighting ships did carry had been housed in the fore- and after- (or summer-) castles. These flimsy structures, deliberately so designed in order to keep the centre of gravity as low as possible, could not possibly accommodate guns whose weight was measured in hundredweights,* even in tons. Quite apart from making the vessel hopelessly top-heavy, it would have been impossible to harness such monsters in a superstructure far too fragile to take the strain of the very violent recoil. The breech rope, which acted as a primitive shock-absorber, would simply pull out the retaining bolts from the wall and the gun would hurtle backwards through the opposite wall and topple into the sea. By putting the great guns below and cutting a 'port-hole' in the side of the ship, Baker not only invented the broadside but greatly increased the stability of the ships.

THE *MARY ROSE*

Since 11 October 1982, the nomination for **the most famous ship of the 16th century** must be awarded to the *Mary Rose*. Built in 1509, she was a 'great ship' of 600 tons, armed with 20 heavy and 60 light guns. She is said, 'on by no means perfect evidence' by cautious Professor Lewis, to have been the first ship in whose sides gun-ports were cut to receive the first 'great guns', in other words the first broadside ship. In 1512 she led an attack on the French in Brest harbour, as the flagship of the fleet. 'She picked on the French flagship, the *Grande Louise*, and opened fire with

A diagrammatic view of the wreck of the Mary Rose. *Times Newspapers Ltd.*

* Though now equal to 112lb (51kg), it was originally equivalent to 100lb (45kg), hence the name.

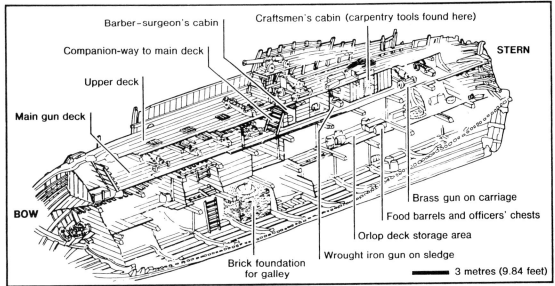

Barber-surgeon's cabin

Craftsmen's cabin (carpentry tools found here)

Companion-way to main deck

STERN

Upper deck

Main gun deck

BOW

Brass gun on carriage

Food barrels and officers' chests

Orlop deck storage area

Wrought iron gun on sledge

Brick foundation for galley

3 metres (9.84 feet)

A model of the *Mary Rose. Times Newspapers Ltd.*

her new guns. The firefight before the traditional battle between shipborne soldiers was as new a technique then as the Exocet is today, and the effect was, of its kind, as devastating' (*Sunday Telegraph*, 24 October 1982). On 19 July 1545, when going out to engage the French fleet off Portsmouth, she was swamped through the lower deck ports and sank so rapidly that nearly all of her complement of 250 soldiers and 120 mariners went down with her. In 1968 the wreck of the *Mary Rose* was found by Alexander McKee and 14 years later, 437 years after she sank, the remains of her hull were successfully raised from the sea bed. It is proposed that she be kept in dry dock next to Admiral Nelson's *Victory* at Portsmouth.

Her guns indicate that her loss occurred at a time of transition in naval gunnery, for she carried both the old wrought-iron breech-loading guns with built-up barrels and heavy muzzle-loaders cast in one piece – the new 'great guns'.

The *Henry Grâce à Dieu* was, in her day, **the largest warship in the world**. Although, as we have seen, the *Mary Rose* is said to have been the first broadside ship, to the *Great Harry*, as she was usually known, belongs the honour of being **the first English battleship**, in that she was specifically designed as a ship of war. Built for Henry VIII by his Master Shipwright, William Bond, she was launched at Erith in Kent in June 1514. She had topmasts and topgallants on the foremost of her four masts and a topmast on the bonaven-

ture, all sails on the mizen and bonaventure being lateens. She originally carried 184 guns, but this was reduced to 122 after she had been almost entirely rebuilt during the years 1536–9. The gradual transition from armed merchantman to warship can also be seen in the ship's company of 650, of whom 350 were now soldiers and 300 mariners, a ratio of 7:6 as against the *Mary Rose*'s 2:1. Nevertheless the *Great Harry* turned out to be a white elephant, not least because she was too big for most of the harbours of her day. Even as a symbol of princely magnificence she proved a failure, for when Henry went to meet Francis I in June 1520, at the Field of the Cloth of Gold he had to travel in a smaller ship because the *Great Harry* drew too much water for the harbours of Dover and Calais. In her 38 years' service she was only once in action and was eventually destroyed by fire at Woolwich in August 1553.

The size of the *Great Harry* did, however, have one lasting result. It led to **the foundation of the first permanent English dockyard** for the building and repair of ships of war. Hitherto ships had been built on temporary sites but when construction of the *Great Harry* was begun at Erith, storehouses and quarters for the shipwrights were erected and a permanent dockyard established.

The *Henry Grâce à Dieu*, from a manuscript in the Pepysian Library, Magdalene College, Cambridge.

The first sea-battle in which the English 'broadside' was fired as a tactical measure was fought against the French fleet off Shoreham on 15 August 1545. Hitherto the basic formation of sea warfare had been 'line abreast', ideally suited to the galley of which the offensive weapon was the ram. But when the means of attack was moved to the side of the ship, the tactics of naval warfare were revolutionized at a stroke, and 'line ahead' inevitably became the standard battle formation, although the change-over was far from immediate. But, once established, it was certainly made to last. At Trafalgar, and indeed at Jutland, the basic fighting formation was still 'line ahead'.

The first fire regulations on board ship occur in *Orders to be used in King's or Queen's Majesties Ships or Navy being upon the Seas in Fashion of War* which appeared in 1568. They are as crude as they are simple: 'The captain to cause two hogsheads [large casks] to be cut asunder in the midst and chained to the side: the soldiers and mariners to piss in them that they may always be full of urine to quench fire work with, and two or three pieces of old sail ready to wet in the piss; and always cast it on the fire work as need shall require.'

The greatest sea battle since Salamis was the Battle of Lepanto, fought on 7 October 1571. It was also **the last naval action fought between galleys manned by oarsmen.** Suleiman the Magnificent, Sultan of Turkey, died in 1566 at which point the Turkish Empire had reached the zenith of its power. He was succeeded by his son Selim the Sot, who, as his name implies, gave himself up to debauchery and left his generals and ministers to run the Empire. When, in 1570, they seized Cyprus from the Venetians, Pope Pius V established a Holy League of Christian nations bordering the Mediterranean to counter the Turkish threat. The allied fleet, numbering 200 ships, was commanded by Don John of Austria (1547–78), the illegitimate son of the Emperor Charles V, who at the time was only 24 years old. The Turkish fleet of 273 galleys was commanded by Ali Pasha. The only real difference between these two fleets and those which had fought in the Punic Wars nearly 2000 years earlier was that some of the Christian soldiers wore armour, a few had arquebuses and some galleys had small

A representation by an unknown artist of the Battle of Lepanto, when war at sea was still a matter of ramming and boarding. *National Maritime Museum.*

cannon mounted in the bows. Battle was joined off Cape Scropha not far from the mouth of the Gulf of Corinth and from the mêlée which ensued the Allied fleet emerged victorious. Of the Turkish fleet only 47 survived: the rest were either captured, sunk or run aground. 12,000 Christian slaves were freed from the galleys but probably as many as 10,000 went down with their ships. The Christians lost 13 galleys, 7500 men killed and 8000 wounded, among whom was Miguel Cervantes who lost the use of his left hand.

The Battle of Lepanto has been described as **the last crusade**, since it ended for ever the Turkish domination of the Eastern Mediterranean.

The idea of the gun-deck, a complete new deck running over the old cargo-deck and reserved exclusively for the guns, **is usually credited to Sir John Hawkins** (1532–95), the Treasurer (1577), and later also Comptroller (1598) of Queen Elizabeth's Navy. The cargo-deck, now right on the waterline and with no ports, was known as the 'orlop' deck (from the Dutch *overloop*: a covering) and resumed its original role of carrying stores and gear.

Probably the first gun-deck ship – that is to say a ship with a deck intended exclusively for the use of heavy artillery – was the *Revenge*. She was certainly the most famous of all Elizabethan ships and has even been called **the first sailing ship of the Line**. A Ship of the Line was a warship which carried sufficient armament to allow her to take her place in the line of battle; indeed the word 'battleship' is a contraction of 'line-of-battleship'. But as the line of battle did not evolve until the First Dutch War (1652–4) the honour must be regarded as academic. Nevertheless Professor Lewis suggests that 'it is not too much to claim for her that, could Nelson's seamen have sailed in her, though they would have discovered a hundred and one differences between her and the ship to which they were accustomed, they would have found no really radical differences'.

The *Revenge* was a ship of 441 tons, was armed with 34 guns and was launched at Deptford in 1577. She was Sir Frances Drake's flagship at the Armada and in 1590, as the flagship of Sir Richard Grenville, formed part of an expedition led by Sir Martin Frobisher sent to intercept Spanish treasure ships returning from the West Indies. In August 1591, she achieved immortality in a single-handed action off the Azores, after a

Sir Richard Grenville.

fight lasting 15 hours against overwhelming odds. When she could fight no more, Sir Richard ordered his men to sink the ship but his surviving officers persuaded him to treat for terms and he was carried aboard the Spanish Admiral's ship where he died of his wounds two days later.

The *Revenge* foundered in a storm five days after the battle, taking with her 200 Spaniards who had been put on board. Sir Francis Bacon described the incident as 'memorable even beyond credit and to the height of some heroic fable; and though it were a defeat, yet it exceeded a victory; being like the act of Sampson, that killed more men at his death than he had done in the time of all his life'.

THE DEFEAT OF THE SPANISH ARMADA

The most famous sea fight in English history was the defeat of the Spanish Armada in 1588, from which time can be dated, on the one hand, the decline of the Spanish Empire in Europe and America and on the other the beginning of Britain's mastery of the sea. For a number of reasons Philip II of Spain had decided, as early as

1583, on an invasion of England: the Spanish Netherlands were in revolt and England was actively assisting the rebels; England, under Queen Elizabeth, showed scant respect for Spain's claim to practically the entire New World – Drake, Hawkins, Cavendish and others were habitually taking Spanish treasure ships and sacking Spanish settlements in America; England was a Protestant country, whereas Philip II was the champion of Catholic Europe. These were the underlying causes. The match which lit the bonfire was the execution of Mary, Queen of Scots at Fotheringay on 18 February 1587. 'I am grieved,' Philip wrote, 'since she would have been the most suitable instrument for leading those countries [England and Scotland] back to the Catholic faith. But since God in His wisdom has ordained otherwise, He will raise up other instruments for the triumph of His cause.'

The preparation of the Enterprise of England, as Philip called it, was entrusted to the Marquis of Santa Cruz (1526–88), who had commanded a division of the Allied fleet at the Battle of Lepanto. His plans, however, were badly upset by Sir Francis Drake who, in April 1587, fell upon Cadiz harbour where, by his own estimate, he sank or captured 37 ships. Soon afterwards he captured the Portuguese carrack *San Felipe*, carrying a cargo from the East Indies valued at £114,000. **This was the greatest prize ever taken by Sir Francis Drake**. His raid on Cadiz, known to history as the Singeing of the King of Spain's beard, delayed the Enterprise by a year, during which time Santa Cruz died. In his place Philip appointed the Duke of Medina Sidonia (1550–1619) who had no naval experience but was of such exalted rank that none of the noblemen in the Armada could feel slighted by serving under him.

The great fleet, consisting of 132 ships of all sizes, finally left Lisbon on 9 May 1588, but met with such adverse conditions that it was not until 29 July that Captain Thomas Fleming of the barque *Golden Hind* was able to gain his footnote in history as **the first Englishman to sight the Armada**. Whether or not Drake was playing bowls when the news reached him and said, 'We have time enough to finish the game and beat the Spaniards, too,' is immaterial; certainly it was more than 40 years before the remark was first recorded; equally certainly it was characteristic of the man.

The English fleet was commanded by Lord Howard of Effingham, flying his flag in the new galleon, *Ark Royal*; Drake, Hawkins and Frobisher were the chief subordinate commanders. The intention of the Spaniards, however, was not so much to engage the English fleet as to join forces with the Duke of Parma, commander of the Spanish troops in the Netherlands, preparatory to the proposed invasion of England. Hence the great number of infantry soldiers carried aboard the Spanish ships. On the *Nuestra Señora del Rosario*, the *San Salvador* and the *Santa Maria del Vision*, for instance, there were 264 sailors and 861 soldiers. The relative figures for the *Triumph*, the *Ark* and the *Aid* were 550 and 300.

The Spaniards were not, of course, so optimistic as to think that they could force the passage of the channel unmolested, but, in the event, this is virtually what happened. The English had decided to fight the battle by getting to windward of the enemy and pounding his ships with their long-range 'culverins' while he was still too far away to retaliate with his shorter-range artillery.

King Philip II of Spain.

In the exercise of these intentions the English succeeded admirably. The plan failed because, at the chosen range, the shots bounced harmlessly off the thick sides of the enemy's ships.

The Spaniards, with their heavier but shorter-ranged guns, hoped to batter the English ships into immobility and then take advantage of their superiority in weight of infantry. Their plan failed because the greater agility of the English enabled them to keep their distance throughout. In the week that elapsed between the Armada

entering the Channel and its arrival off Calais, the Spaniards fired off 100,000 rounds of shot, killing one captain, about 20 seamen and inflicting no damage worth mentioning to any English ship. They themselves had three ships damaged, of which two were captured; but of these one was the result of a collision and the other of an accident with the powder. Medina Sidonia had reached Calais with his fleet virtually intact and

Chart of the Armada's course from Pine's engraving, 1739.

Model of a fifteenth-century carrack, now in the Science Museum, London (see p. 18). *Mary Evans Picture Library.*

Sir Walter Raleigh (c 1552–1618) named the north coast of Florida 'Virginia' and introduced potatoes and tobacco into England. *National Portrait Gallery.*

An artist's impression of the *Mayflower* (see p. 65). *Mary Evans Picture Library.*

A coloured engraving of the end of Admiral Brueys's flagship *L'Orient* at the Battle of the Nile, 1798 (see p. 82).

his defensive array unbroken. But his luck, like his ammunition, had now run out. Why, at this crucial stage, his liaison with Parma should have broken down, why Parma had assembled no adequate transports for his own troops and why Medina was not aware of the fact need not concern us here. The fact remains that at the crucial point of the entire enterprise Medina was on his own. The following night the Spanish fleet scattered in panic when eight fireships bore down on them 'spurting fire and their ordnance shooting, which was a horror to see'.

By dawn it was apparent to Medina that his only option lay in saving what he could from a disastrous situation. All that day Howard and Drake harried the Spaniards, closing the range sufficiently to make more effective use of their guns as the enemy's shortage of ammunition became apparent, but never giving them the opportunity to board. The soldiers remained throughout 'a useless, seasick, hungry encumbrance'.

What was left of the mighty Armada fled northwards and made its way back to Spain round the rocky shores of Scotland and Ireland. Of the 132 ships that had left Lisbon only 67 returned.

The longest and greatest sea battle ever known was over.

The first ironclad warships in history were built by the Korean admiral, Yi Sun-shin, a contemporary of Sir Francis Drake. Yi himself designed and had built two or more *Kwi-sun*, or 'tortoise boats', which were low-decked galleys covered by an armour-plated dome around which was set a ring of iron spikes to prevent boarding. The ships were fitted with heavy iron rams and armed with cannon fired from gun ports in the armour plating. Yi's two great naval victories over the Japanese at the end of the 16th century, for which the *Kwi-sun* were largely responsible, saved Korea, and possibly China, from conquest by the Japanese dictator, Hideyoshi (1536–98).

However, Yi's imaginative concept of the heavily gunned armoured warship was centuries ahead of his time and another 250 years were to elapse before the idea re-emerged.

During the reign of James I British shipping was allowed to lapse into a disgraceful state of neglect. The Crown ships lay rotting at their moorings, the King having deprived himself of the wherewithal with which to maintain them; the privateer dared not venture forth without a letter of marque (see p. 55) to protect him; the seaman, unable to find work at home, hired himself out to the Dutch; as a final humiliation, England lost control of her home waters. When the situation became too grave to be ignored any longer, the remedy can be said, with the benefit of hindsight, to have been the formation of the first direct ancestor of the modern Navy.

James I's decision in 1604 to stop issuing letters of marque was a disastrous blow to British maritime interests, automatically turning, as it did, all 'privateers' into 'pirates'. Had other countries taken the same step, all might have been well, but, as none did, the English privateer alone, deprived of his legal status, could, if caught, be hanged by the neck from his own yard-arm as a pirate.

THE PILGRIM FATHERS

The reign of James I is, however, notable for **one of the most famous voyages in history**, that of the *Mayflower* which carried the Pilgrim Fathers to the New World in 1620. A small Puritan congregation from Nottinghamshire had left England in 1607 and settled at Leyden, seeking freedom of worship among the Dutch, but the community failed to take root and the more adventurous among them resolved to emigrate to the New World. On 6 September, 35 members of the Leyden community and 66 West Countrymen set sail from Plymouth in the *Mayflower*, a vessel of 180 tons. After 63 days at sea they reached the shores of Cape Cod where they founded the town of Plymouth and thereby the colony of New England.

Thomas Clark is said to have been the mate of the *Mayflower*, but, if his tombstone tells the truth, he was 91 at the time!

PHINEAS PETT

The *Prince Royal*, designed by Phineas Pett (1570–1647) and launched in 1610, was **the first ship to have guns on three decks.** She is often described as the first three-decker but purists argue that this is incorrect as only two decks were specifically and exclusively for that purpose. The distinction is really academic as she certainly had three complete gun decks, on which she carried 56 guns. She was **the most lavishly decorated ship to date,** a contemporary account describing her as being 'most sumptuously adorned within and without, with all manner of curious carving, painting and rich gilding'.

The *Prince Royal* is **the first English ship for which it is known that a 'dockyard' model was produced.** Such models were made to show the proposed design of a projected ship.

The Pett family were **the most famous ship-builders in England during the 16th and 17th centuries,** their leadership in the field spanning four generations. Peter (*d* 1589), the founder of the 'dynasty', was master shipwright at Deptford. His son Phineas, who designed the *Prince Royal* and the *Sovereign of the Seas*, became a Commissioner of the Navy and is certainly the best remembered. Phineas had three half-brothers, a son Christopher (1628–68) and a nephew Peter (1592–1652), all of whom became master ship-wrights. Another son, Peter (1610–72), became Commissioner for the Navy at Chatham, and a grandson, Phineas (1628–78), designed the famous *Prince*.

SHIP-MONEY

Charles I was **the first King of England to propose that the whole nation,** and not merely the 'sea-shires', **should pay for a *permanent* maritime fighting force.** To this end, between 1635 and 1639, and without the consent of Parliament, he revived a tax known as 'Ship-Money' and with the proceeds built his 'Ship-Money Fleet', which succeeded in clearing the Channel of pirates and in protecting the east-coast fishing fleets from the depredations of the Dutch. But in 1641 Parliament declared the tax illegal and ship-money became the trigger which set off the English Civil War, though the contestants, for divers other reasons, were already at the tapes.

In the ensuing struggle the Ship-Money Fleet sided with Parliament and, by so doing, had a decisive effect on the outcome by preventing Charles from receiving support from his fellow monarchs in Europe.

The 'New Model Navy' created by the Commonwealth Government marked the next step in the evolution of the modern British Navy, but it is Charles II who, bestowing upon it the title of 'Royal Navy' after his restoration in 1660, has the best claim to be called the Father of the British Navy. **For the first time in her history Britain now had a permanent national maritime fighting force paid for by the nation, controlled by the Government, yet owing allegiance to the Sovereign.** There is a nice irony in the fact that the first British Navy to be called 'Royal' was the first one to which the adjective was wholly inapplicable, in so far as it was neither raised by, paid by nor controlled by the King.

SOVEREIGN OF THE SEAS

The finest ship to be built with the ship-money raised by Charles I, indeed one of the finest ships ever built, was the *Sovereign of the Seas*. Designed by Phineas Pett, the Commissioner at Chatham Dockyard, and launched there on 13 October 1637, she was **at the time the largest warship in the world and certainly the most richly decorated.** Built to specifications laid down by the King himself, her dimensions were:

A painting of Phineas Pett (1570–1647) now in the Queen's House at Greenwich. *National Portrait Gallery.*

overall length 232ft (70.7m); length of keel 127ft (38.7m); breadth 46.5ft (14.2m); draught 23½ft (7.2m); armament 105 guns. From the stern, whereon the goddess of Victory received homage from Jupiter, Neptune, Jason and Hercules, to the figurehead which depicted Edgar the Peaceful overcoming the British princes, she was covered in richly gilded carving, said to have been done from drawings by Van Dyck. It took £65,590 of Charles's ship-money to build her, at a time when a ship of 40 guns cost about £6000. Her rigging was unique in that she was **the first British warship to carry royal sails on the foremast and mainmast and a topgallant sail on the mizen.** However, she lay so deep in the water that the lowest leeside battery was virtually unusable. She was rebuilt in 1659–60, when the rig was reduced and much of the superstructure cut away, and was then renamed the *Royal Sovereign*. She played a distinguished part in many sea fights during the Dutch Wars and after, but an overturned candle put an end to her career while she was laid up at Chatham in 1696 and she went up in flames.

The *Sovereign of the Seas* was said to be the most richly decorated ship in the world. *National Maritime Museum.*

The Anglo-Dutch Wars

The three Anglo-Dutch Wars (1652–4, 1656–67, 1672–4) are unique in European history as being **the only wars in which naval forces alone were involved.** They were also **the first wars in English history which were fought for primarily economic reasons.** Thirdly, they are memorable for having witnessed **the most bitterly disputed series of battles in which the Navy has ever been involved.** All of which is understandable if one remembers that they were wars fought between two trading nations for control of the Channel and the lower latitudes of the North Sea.

The outstanding figure among England's 17th-century sea-generals – for they were not yet admirals in our sense of the word – was **Robert Blake** (1599–1657). His naval career is the more remarkable for the fact that it began when he was

Obverse and reverse of a medal commemorating Blake's victories.

already 50 years old and that his first post was as Flag Officer in joint command of England's main fleet.

Blake's skill as a naval commander was proved during the First Anglo-Dutch War (1652–4). **The outstanding tactical innovation of the First Dutch War** was the establishment of 'Line Ahead' as the normal tactical formation of British fleets. This was laid down in the first edition of *Fighting Instructions*, issued by Blake and his fellow Generals-at-Sea, Richard Deane (1610–53) and George Monck (1608–70), in 1653. It should not be assumed that the formation had not already been tried out, for it would hardly have been laid down as text-book procedure without being put to the test. Henceforward, however, it became standard practice and its efficacy was clearly demonstrated by Monck at the Battle of Scheveningen (or Texel) on 31 July 1653, in which Admiral Marten Tromp (1597–1653), one of the Netherlands' most outstanding seamen, lost his life.

Line ahead means what it says – each ship following in the wake of the one ahead. In 1665 it was laid down for the first time that the interval between each ship should be 'half a cable', or 100yd (91.1m), a cable being a tenth of a nautical mile.

Once the problem of shipping heavy ordnance had been overcome (see p. 57) it would seem too obvious to be worth pointing out that the maximum weight of fire could be brought to bear on the enemy by a fleet drawn up in line ahead firing broadside. But this crucial step in the development of naval tactics rested upon the mastery of another problem – how to control a gun's recoil in such a way that it would come to rest far enough inboard to permit fast and easy reloading.

Hitherto guns had been lashed fast to the bulkheads to inhibit recoil, which made reloading slow, difficult and dangerous. To find oneself perched precariously outboard on the muzzle of a gun clutching a heavy cannonball in a choppy sea and in the midst of a battle must have been a singularly unpleasant experience. Hence the practice evolved of a group of about five ships following each other in a circle, each in turn discharging its broadsides and then retiring to reload. Once the problem of reloading inboard by harnessing the recoil had been overcome the line ahead became possible and the firepower of a fleet potentially increased by 500 per cent.

ARTICLES OF WAR

The *Articles of War* were first issued in 1653, with the aim of providing a standard scale of punishment throughout the Navy; hitherto an offending seaman's fate had depended upon the whim and ingenuity of his captain. There were 39 articles of which 25 carried the death penalty, but in practice they were not rigorously applied in Cromwel-

General George Monck played a leading part in the restoration of Charles II and was created Duke of Albemarle in 1660. *National Maritime Museum.*

lian times. They are said to have been drawn up as a result of Blake's representations to the Commonwealth Government after his defeat by Admiral Tromp off Dungeness. In his fleet were a number of merchant ships commanded by their own masters who, seeing the English heavily outnumbered, decided to unbalance the odds a bit further. As things stood Blake himself had no power to punish them, a situation rectified by the *Articles of War*.

The earliest attempt to draw up a code of maritime law governing the rights and responsibilities of ship's captains was known as the Laws, or Judgments, of Oléron, and was enacted in 1152 by Eleanor of Aquitaine (1122–1204) who in the same year married Henry of Anjou, later Henry II of England. Taking their name from the Ile d'Oléron, off the Atlantic coast of France, they were introduced into England by Richard I in about 1190. In 1336 they were codified in the *Black Book of the Admiralty* but by the time the *Articles of War* were issued had become obsolete.

The outstanding figure in the Second Dutch War was Michael de Ruyter (1606–76), the greatest of the Dutch admirals. He it was who **inflicted upon the British Navy the greatest humiliation it has ever suffered**. After the Battle of the North Foreland (25 July 1666), in which Monck destroyed 20 of de Ruyter's ships and then sailed along the coast of Holland and burnt 120 anchored merchantmen, the Dutch were ready for peace; as, indeed, were the British, still stunned by the ravages of the Great Plague (1665–6) and the Fire of London (2–9 September 1666). Negotiations were entered into and Charles II, against Monck's advice, moored the fleet and disbanded the crews. The Dutch also made a token gesture at disarmament. Then, in June 1667, de Ruyter sailed into the Thames with a fleet of over 80 ships. They captured Sheerness, entered the Medway and sailed up to Chatham

A Dutch print published in Amsterdam in 1666 of the Battle of North Foreland in which Monck destroyed 20 of Admiral de Ruyter's ships.

where they burnt five ships and towed away the battleship *Royal Charles*. Samuel Pepys (1633–1703), visiting Chatham on 28 June, described it as 'a Dreadful Spectacle as ever any Englishmen saw, and a dishonour never to be wiped off'. Pepys was at that time Surveyor-General of the Victualling Office at the Admiralty.

The Treaty of Breda, signed on 21 July 1667, which effectively marked the end of the Second Anglo-Dutch War, shows how time alters men's ideas of what is important and what is trivial. In exchange for modifications to the Navigation Acts in favour of the Dutch, the acknowledgment of Holland's supremacy in the East Indies and the handing over of England's last nutmeg island, the tiny Pulau Run in the Moluccas, England was allowed to keep New Amsterdam and its adjacent territory, including New Jersey and Delaware, which she had taken from the Dutch in 1664. New Amsterdam was renamed New York after the Lord High Admiral, James, Duke of York, later James II.

The Battle of Solebay, which was fought on 28 May 1672, was **the first battle in the Third Anglo-Dutch War** (1672–4). Solebay, on the Suffolk coast, is today better known as Southwold. The battle was claimed as a victory by both sides, and is regarded by history as a draw. It is sometimes said that it was at the Battle of Solebay that John Churchill, later 1st Duke of Marlborough, and then serving with the 1st Company of the Guards, received his baptism of fire, but his equally distinguished descendant and biographer, Sir Winston Churchill, tells us that he took part in an action against the Dutch off the Isle of Wight on 13 March, before war had been declared. It was certainly the last action in which Edward Montagu, 1st Earl of Sandwich (1625–72) and patron of Samuel Pepys, took part. His ship, the *Royal James*, became the prey of Dutch fireships: 'With his personal officers he paced the quarter-deck until the flames drove him overboard, where he perished.'

During the Third Dutch War (1672–4) de Ruyter brought to its peak the use of fireships in naval engagements. The Dutch fireships were far more sophisticated than the British: they were carefully loaded and incorporated a fairly safe method of last-minute evacuation for their crews.

A Dutch print of 1672 of the Battle of Solebay, the first battle of the Third Anglo-Dutch war.

The first bomb ketch is said to have been built in France around 1679. Certainly the French Navy was the first to be equipped with such vessels and used them for the first time in 1682 when Admiral Abraham Duquesne (1610–88) bombarded Algiers, then the headquarters of the Barbary pirates. Bomb ketches were very stoutly constructed and their decks were supported from below by sturdy beam bridges which helped to distribute the shock of the recoil when the mortars were fired. The shot weighed about 200lb (90.7kg), compared to the 48lb (21.8kg) shot fired by the ordinary 'great guns'.

The best account of life at sea during the reign of Charles II occurs in the diary of the Rev Henry Teonge (c 1621–90) who was variously Chaplain in HM ships *Assistance* (1675–6), *Bristol* (1678–9) and *Royal Oak* (1679). Teonge was a humane and humorous man and full of original ideas: 'There are also several other countries in Africa, wherein are men and beasts of strange shapes, verefying the ancient saying: *Africa semper aliquid novi affert*: and the reason is easily given: for, there being but few watering places, and the country hott, and all manner of cattell meetinge at those places, doe many times couple with beasts of another kinde; and thence proceeds a new species, haveing part of the one and part of the other'!

The first man to formulate the policy of 'keeping his fleet in being' was Arthur Herbert, Earl of Torrington (1647–1716). In essence this simply means taking dilatory or evasive action, either while awaiting reinforcements or to avoid altogether a trial of strength. The strategy is an obvious resort for the commander of a fleet which is appreciably weaker than that of his opponent, but its executor bears the equally obvious risk of being accused of cowardice, or even treason, and this is exactly what happened to Torrington. Having commanded the fleet which brought William of Orange to England in 1688, he now found himself in 1690 in command of an Anglo-Dutch fleet off Beachy Head, while William was in Ireland dealing with the insurrection led by the exiled James II which led immediately to the Battle of the Boyne. Torrington, outnumbered 55 to 70 by the French Admiral Tourville (1642–1701), **one of the ablest seamen that France has ever produced**, decided, to use his own phrase,

to 'keep his fleet in being'. At the subsequent court-martial Torrington was acquitted, but he never again held command. The expression has long outlived the fame of its originator.

René Duguay-Trouin (1673–1736) is, after Suffren, probably **the most celebrated of all French naval heroes**. In 1689, when war broke out between France and England, he went to sea in a privateer owned by his family and displayed such courage that, in 1691, his family gave him a ship of 14 guns to command. In 1694 he was captured by the English and imprisoned in the castle at Plymouth, but he escaped, according to his own account, with the help of a pretty shopwoman and her lover. His continued successes against English and Dutch merchant ships led in 1696 to his appointment as *capitaine de frégate* in the French Navy. In 1707, off the Lizard, he captured the greater part of an English convoy of troops and munitions bound for Portugal; but his most glorious action was the capture in 1711 of Rio de Janeiro, for which he extracted a heavy ransom from the Portuguese.

THE FIGHTING INSTRUCTIONS

The *Fighting Instructions* issued over the signature of Admiral Edward Russell, later Earl of Oxford (1653–1727), in 1691, but embodying the tactical ideas of Torrington, proved to be **one of the most disastrous documents in the history of the British Navy**, for they effectively stifled the evolution of naval tactics for the next 90 years. Any commander who disregarded the *Instructions* was court-martialled and not a few senior officers were to learn that in the British Navy of the 18th century one used one's initiative at the risk of one's career. The most limiting of the *Instructions* was article 20 which laid down that 'None of the ships in the fleet shall pursue any small number of the enemy's ships till the main body be disabled or run.' As Professor Lewis says: 'No wonder a British fleet did not once inflict a whole-hearted defeat upon any enemy in any stand-up fight between the battle of Barfleur in 1692 and the Saints in 1782.' Unfortunately, it could be equally dangerous to adhere too rigidly to the *Fighting Instructions*.

The most famous as well as the most unfortunate victim of the policy of adhering too rigidly to the *Fighting Instructions* was Admiral John Byng (1704–57). By his refusal to break the sacred line of battle Byng failed to relieve the garrison of Port Mahon on the island of Minorca, which was besieged by the French; whereupon he was promptly court-martialled for failing to do his utmost to save Minorca, was found guilty and sentenced to death. He was executed by firing squad on the quarterdeck of HMS *Monarch* on 14 March 1757, the occasion being immortalized by Voltaire who remarked that in England it was found necessary to shoot an admiral from time to time *'pour encourager les autres'*.

The founder of the Russian Navy was Tsar Peter I (1672–1725), known as Peter the Great. At the time of Peter's accession in 1689 Russia's only seaboard was to the north, the shores of the Baltic being in Swedish and Polish hands and of the Black Sea in those of the Turks. So it was on the White Sea that Peter first sailed a small squadron of ships. But Peter realized that maritime power depended upon the acquisition of warm-water ports and in 1695–6 he built **the first Russian Navy** near Voronezh on the River Don. In the spring of 1696 it sailed downstream and played its part in the capture of Azov from the Turks that summer. In 1700 Peter entered into an alliance against Sweden and quietly appropriated a portion of Ingria, where in 1703, he laid the foundations of his new city of St Petersburg (now Leningrad). At nearby Kronstadt, 22 miles to the east, he built up a fleet of battleships, frigates and galleys with which he engaged the Swedes in a series of actions in which initially he was usually worsted. The most important battle in a war, however, is the last and that Peter won. The Battle of Gangut (Hanko) in 1714 was **Russia's first major naval victory** and marked the end of Swedish naval predominance in the Baltic.

Probably the only occasion on which the outcome of a naval engagement has been decided by a cargo of snuff occurred at Vigo on 12 October 1702, when Sir Thomas Hopsonn (1642–1717), second-in-command of a force under Sir George Rooke (1650–1709), attacked the French and Spanish fleets. A boom had been placed across the mouth of the harbour, through which Hopsonn, in the *Torbay*, a ship of 80 guns, managed to break, leaving a clear passage for the rest of the squadron. Then, however, the *Torbay* was set on fire by a fireship, 'but happily escaped, partly by the diligence of the officers and men,

Though a cruel and barbaric man, Peter the Great is remembered for having given Russia a recognized place among the great European powers.

but still more by the extraordinary accident of the fireship having on board a large quantity of snuff, the blast of which as she blew up extinguished the flames'. 'It so affected the crews of the French warships that many of them had to dive into the sea for relief from the pain of having inhaled the snuff.' The treasure captured at Vigo was said to have been worth over £2 million.

THE CAPTURE OF GIBRALTAR

In 1704 there occurred, almost by accident, an event which in retrospect can be seen to have been **one of the most important in British naval history**. This was the fortuitous capture of Gibraltar by Sir George Rooke. In 1700 Charles II of Spain died without direct heirs and left the throne to a grandson of Louis XIV of France. Louis immediately claimed his rights, although he had previously renounced his family's claims to the Spanish throne for ever. This led to the War of the Spanish Succession in 1702. Rooke had been sent to capture Toulon but this proved impossible and, rather than return home empty-handed, he took Gibraltar instead. It has remained in British hands ever since.

KING'S LETTER BOYS

The last person to enter the Royal Navy as a volunteer-per-order or King's Letter Boy was George Brydges Rodney (1719–92), later first Baron Rodney, in 1732. King's Letter Boys were introduced by Samuel Pepys in 1676 with the idea of encouraging the younger sons of families of gentle birth to enter the Royal Navy. The entrant was given a letter from the Crown which virtually guaranteed his promotion to commissioned rank after a specified period of training.

The greatest amount of booty ever taken on a single voyage was captured by Commodore George Anson during his circumnavigation of the globe between 1740 and 1744, a doubly remarkable feat in view of the fact that the squadron of eight ships with which he set sail from Portsmouth in September 1740, was pitifully manned, largely with raw recruits and out-pensioners from Greenwich Hospital. By June 1741, he had rounded Cape Horn and reached the island of

The *Centurion*, flagship of Commodore George Anson, engages a 'Manilla' ship. In the background is the castle of Macao. From Harris's *Voyages*.

Juan Fernandez in the Pacific, by which time only three ships, the flagship *Centurion*, the *Gloucester* and the sloop *Tryal*, remained of the squadron, and scurvy was rampant among the surviving men.

Anson's first prize was the *Nuestra Señora del Monte Carmelo*, carrying 5000lb (2268kg) of silver dollars and plate. Then, after a series of raids off the west coasts of South America and Mexico, he set sail for China, reaching Macao in November 1742, by which time only the *Centurion* and 200 men remained. There the flagship was refitted and provisioned, and, in April 1743, Anson sailed for the Philippines to lie in wait for the Spanish treasure ships en route from Acapulco to Manila. On June 20 his enterprise was rewarded when the *Nuestra Señora de Covadonga* struck her flag after an engagement lasting only 90 minutes and treasure worth more than £500,000 fell into his hands. He anchored at Spithead on 15 June 1744, having lost during the journey four men in action and over 1300 through disease. The treasure was subsequently paraded through the City of London in a procession of 32 wagons.

The system of 'rating' warships into six divisions according to the number of guns they carried was reorganized by Lord Anson during his first term as First Lord of the Admiralty (1751–6). Hitherto the rating had been as follows:

RATE	GUNS	TONS
1st	100	Over 1500
2nd	90	1000–1500
3rd	80, 90	750–1000
4th	50, 60	350–750
5th	40	200–350
6th	20	200 and under

Since any of the first four rates could fight in the line of battle this meant that the strength of the line was very variable and left the weak link in the chain as the obvious point of attack.

Anson divided his ships into two groups: battleships that stood in the line and cruisers for the performance of other duties. They were broken down as follows:

CLASS	RATE	GUNS	TONS	DECKS
Battleships	1st	100–110	2500	3
	2nd	90–100	1800	3
	3rd	70–90	1500–1800	2
Cruisers	4th	50–70	1000	2
	5th	32–50	750	1
	6th	— –32	500 and under	1

Table taken from *Admiral Lord Anson* by Captain S. W. C. Peck.

Anson's system of classification was eventually adopted by all navies and saw out the era of the broadside warships.

The exact ratio between guns and rates is shown in detail in the following table from J. J. Colledge's *Ships of the Royal Navy*:

The establishment of guns in 1677

	42PDR	32PDR	18PDR	12PDR	6PDR	3PDR
1st Rate 100	26	—	28	—	44	—
2nd Rate 90	—	26	26	—	36	2
3rd Rate 70	—	26	—	26	14	4

Ships built after 1716

	32PDR	24PDR	18PDR	12PDR	9PDR	6PDR	4PDR
1st Rate 100	28	28	—	28	—	16	—
2nd Rate 90	26	—	26	—	26	12	—
2nd Rate 80	26	—	—	26	—	30	—
3rd Rate 70	—	26	—	26	—	18	—
3rd Rate 60	—	24	—	—	26	10	—
4th Rate 50	—	—	26	—	22	6	—
5th Rate 40	—	—	—	20	—	20	—
5th Rate 30	—	—	—	—	8	20	2
6th Rate 20	—	—	—	—	—	20	—

Ships built after 1749

	42PDR	32PDR	24PDR	18PDR	12PDR	9PDR	6PDR
1st Rate 100	28	—	28	—	28	—	16
2nd Rate 90	—	26	—	26	26	—	12
3rd Rate 80	—	26	—	26	—	24	4
3rd Rate 64	—	26	—	26	—	12	—
4th Rate 58	—	—	24	—	24	—	10
4th Rate 50	—	—	22	—	22	—	6
5th Rate 44	—	—	—	20	—	24	4
6th Rate 20	—	—	—	—	—	22	—

Ships built after 1757

	42PDR	32PDR	24PDR	18PDR	12PDR	9PDR	6PDR	4PDR	3PDR
1st Rate 100	28	—	28	—	28	—	16	—	—
2nd Rate 90	—	28	—	30	30	2	—	—	—
3rd Rate 80	—	26	—	26	—	28	—	—	—
Large 74	—	28	30	—	—	16	—	—	—

Ships built after 1757 – contd

	42PDR	32PDR	24PDR	18PDR	12PDR	9PDR	6PDR	4PDR	3PDR
Small 74	—	28	—	28	—	18	—	—	—
3rd Rate 70	—	28	—	28	—	14	—	—	—
3rd Rate 64	—	—	26	—	26	—	12	—	—
4th Rate 60	—	—	26	—	26	—	8	—	—
4th Rate 50	—	—	—	22	22	—	6	—	—
5th Rate 44	—	—	—	20	—	22	2	—	—
5th Rate 36	—	—	—	—	26	—	10	—	—
5th Rate 32	—	—	—	—	26	—	6	—	—
6th Rate 28	—	—	—	—	—	24	—	—	4
6th Rate 24	—	—	—	—	—	22	—	—	2
6th Rate 20	—	—	—	—	—	20	—	—	—
Sloop 14	—	—	—	—	—	—	14	—	—
Sloop 12	—	—	—	—	—	—	—	12	—
Sloop 10	—	—	—	—	—	—	—	10	—
Sloop 8	—	—	—	—	—	—	—	—	8

After 1792

	42PDR	32PDR	24PDR	18PDR	12PDR	9PDR	6PDR	4PDR	3PDR
1st Rate 110	—	30	30	32	18	—	—	—	—
1st Rate 100	28	—	28	—	44	—	—	—	—
	—	30	28	30	12	—	—	—	—
	30	28	—	—	42	—	—	—	—
2nd Rate 98	—	28	—	28	42	—	—	—	—
	—	28	—	60	10	—	—	—	—
2nd Rate 90	—	26	—	26	38	—	—	—	—
3rd Rate 80	—	30	32	—	18	—	—	—	—
Large 74	—	28	30	—	16	—	—	—	—
Common 74	—	28	—	28	18	—	—	—	—
5th Rate 40	—	—	28	—	12	—	—	—	—
5th Rate 38	—	—	28	2	8	—	—	—	—
5th Rate 36	—	—	26	2	8	—	—	—	—
Large 32	—	—	26	—	—	6	—	—	—
Common 32	—	—	—	26	—	6	—	—	—
Sloop 18	—	—	—	—	—	18	—	—	—
Sloop 16	—	—	—	—	—	16	—	—	—

The worst administrator with whom the Royal Navy was ever burdened was often said to have been John Montagu, 4th Earl of Sandwich (1718–92). 'For corruption and incapacity Sandwich's administration is unique in the history of the British Navy. Officers were bought, stores were stolen and, worst of all, ships, unseaworthy and inadequately equipped, were sent to fight the battles of their country,' fulminates the *Encyclopaedia Britannica*. Horace Walpole, however, was more tolerant: 'The Admiralty was the favourite object of Lord Sandwich's ambition; and his passion for maritime affairs, his activity, industry, and flowing complaisance, endeared him to the profession, re-established the marine, and effaced great part of his unpopularity. No man in the Administration was so much master of business, so quick or so shrewd; and no man had so many public enemies who had so few private; for though void of principles he was void of ran-

cour, and bore with equal good humour the freedom with which his friends attacked him and the satire of his opponents,' (*Memoirs of the Reign of George III*, Vol. IV).

Lord Sandwich was responsible for the adoption of the carronade into the armament of British warships: he was **the only First Lord to keep a resident mistress at Admiralty House**; he gave his name to the sandwich, when, in 1762, he spent 24 hours at a gaming table without other food; and Captain Cook, whose three voyages of discovery he helped to promote, gave his name to the Sandwich Islands (now Hawaiian Islands) when he landed at Waimea, Kanai Island, on 20 January 1778. He is said to have died of diarrhoea.

THE AMERICAN WAR OF INDEPENDENCE

The first naval action in the American War of Independence occurred on 12 May 1775, when a party of lumbermen captured the British armed cutter *Margaretta* at Machias Bay, Maine. Increasing tension between Britain and the 13 colonies had broken into open warfare on 19 April when General Thomas Gage (1721–87) sent men from the British Garrison at Boston to capture arms from the colonists at Concord.

The first naval engagement of the war, indeed the first proper naval action in the history of the United States of America, was fought on Lake Champlain in October 1776. General Guy Carleton (1724–1808) had assembled a makeshift flotilla at the northern end of the lake and, on 11/12 October, sought out and destroyed the equally makeshift flotilla commanded by Benedict Arnold (1741–1801). Though the Americans were defeated, their purpose was achieved: Carleton's advance had been delayed for so long while he assembled his flotilla that he was forced by the oncoming winter to withdraw into Canada.

The first hero of the American Navy was John Paul Jones (1747–92). Born John Paul, the son of a gardener, in Scotland, he served in the British merchant marine from 1761 to 1773, when he killed a man in Tobago, fled to Virginia and changed his name to Jones. In 1775 he joined the Continental Navy, as the navy of the USA was

The 4th Earl of Sandwich was immortalized by John Gay as Jemmy Twitcher in *The Beggar's Opera. National Maritime Museum.*

The Battle of Lake Champlain, October 1776; the first
proper naval action in US history.

known until 1794. In 1777 he was promoted captain and appointed to command the *Ranger*, with
orders to cruise about the British Isles to 'distress'
the enemy. On the night of 22/23 April 1778, he
landed at Whitehaven, on the coast of Cumberland. Though he did little damage, the moral
effect was immense. He then crossed to Northern
Ireland where, after a one-hour fight with the
Drake off Carrickfergus, the British ship surrendered and was taken back to France where the
Ranger had the distinction of receiving **the first
national salute given to the American flag in
Europe**.

In the following year occurred **one of the most
extraordinary sea-fights in history**. Jones had
been supplied by the French with an old East
India merchant ship which he renamed the
Bonhomme Richard and converted into a man-
of-war carrying 40 guns and a crew of 380, of
whom 150 were French volunteers. In company
with four other ships, the American-built frigate
Alliance, the French frigate *Pallas*, and two
smaller French ships, all flying the American

Medal struck to commemorate the fight between the
Serapis and the *Bonhomme Richard*.

76

ensign, he sailed from L'Orient on 14 August 1779, and, on 23 September intercepted a convoy of British merchantmen from the Baltic, escorted by the *Serapis* and the *Countess of Scarborough*, off Flamborough Head, 20 miles (32km) south of Scarborough. The merchantmen made good their escape: the *Pallas*, having taken the *Countess of Scarborough* prize, played no further part in the action; the *Alliance* offered no assistance and the two smaller ships had already parted company. The *Bonhomme Richard* was therefore left to battle it out with the *Serapis* on her own. Jones manoeuvred his ship alongside and lashed her to his adversary with his own hands and thus for two hours they fought, the muzzles of their guns almost touching. All but two of the *Bonhomme Richard*'s guns were knocked out when an American grenade touched off an explosion in the *Serapis* and she was forced to surrender. However, the *Bonhomme Richard* was in even worse shape and she sank two days later, whereon Jones transferred to the *Serapis*. The exact number of killed and wounded is uncertain but in proportion to those engaged it was certainly **the bloodiest combat of its time**.

The first sea battle to be fought at night is appropriately called the Moonlight Battle and was fought off Cape St Vincent, the south-west tip of Portugal, on 16 January 1780. Admiral Rodney (1719–92) was escorting a convoy of reinforcements to Gibraltar when he sighted a Spanish fleet of 11 ships of the line commanded by Admiral Don Juan de Langara. Rodney ordered his ships to engage 'as they came up by rotation and to take the lee gage in order to prevent the enemy's retreat into their own ports'. Six enemy ships were captured, including Langara's flagship, and one was sunk.

The Moonlight Battle was also **the first engagement in which the advantage of sheathing the hulls of ships with copper was demonstrated**. Wooden ships had always been prey to the ravages of *Teredo Navalis*, a shipworm which bores long cylindrical holes in the wood, sometimes as much as 3ft (0.9m) long and 1in (2.5cm) in diameter. The first person to suggest a remedy was Sir John Hawkins, who had the

The Moonlight Battle, fought off Cape St Vincent, 16 January 1780. *National Maritime Museum.*

submerged parts of his ships' hulls covered with a layer of felt made with a mixture of hair and tar, over which was tightly nailed a sheathing of elm boards. This process, though it certainly prolonged the life of the hull, was laborious and expensive. In 1758 **a frigate was sheathed with copper below the waterline for the first time.** By the time of the Moonlight Battle in 1780 Rodney was able to report that those of his ships which were coppered were instrumental in bringing the flying enemy to close and decisive action. In 1783 copper sheathing was adopted throughout the Navy.

The most important sea battle in the American War of Independence was the inconclusive engagement fought outside Chesapeake Bay on 5 December 1781. The British Army, under Lord Cornwallis (1738–1805), was being closely invested by French and American troops at Yorktown, inside Chesapeake Bay, at the entrance to which lay 24 French ships under the command of Admiral de Grasse (1722–88). To relieve Cornwallis, Admiral Thomas Graves (1725–1802) was sent from New York with 19 ships. He encountered the French fleet emerging from the Bay against the wind and could, had he pressed home his advantage, have scored a spectacular victory. But, by his rigid adherence to the *Fighting Instructions*, he failed to seize the opportunity, and, after an inconclusive exchange of fire, in which only the leading eight ships of the British line took part, Graves returned to New York and de Grasse to Chesapeake Bay. Cornwallis, all hope of relief now gone, had no option but to surrender, which he did on 19 October 1781.

Professor Michael Lewis, in *The Navy of Britain*, sums up the outcome of Graves's action thus: '**In the whole history of sailing-warfare no rigid adherence to the line was ever more fatal than that of Thomas Graves on the afternoon of 5 September 1781.** Then, in the course of a few brief hours, he twice held the main western fleet of France in the hollow of his hand, and with it, perhaps, the issue of the whole war: possibly, even, the future of the whole world, since the existence of the United States of America was at issue too!'

The first battle for over a century in which British ships broke the ordained line-of-battle formation and indulged in a free-for-all was the Battle of the Saints, fought on 12 April 1782, between a French fleet of 29 ships under Admiral the Comte de Grasse and a British fleet of 34 ships commanded by Admiral Sir George Rodney. The battle is named after a group of small islands between Guadeloupe and Dominica in the West Indies. Disregarding all the rules, Rodney broke through the middle of the French line, splitting de Grasse's fleet into three detachments and throwing them into hopeless confusion. Five ships, including de Grasse's flagship, were taken, and Samuel Hood (1724–1816), who was second-in-command, captured two more a week later. This was **the last sea battle of the War of American Independence**.

Red-hot shot was used for the first time at the siege of Gibraltar in September 1782. The siege itself lasted from 1779 to 1783, during which time the garrison of 7000 men under the command of Sir George Eliott (1717–90) heroically endured a combined Franco/Spanish blockade and bombardment by land and sea. On 13 September 1782, the Duc de Crillon (1748–1820) launched an attack from ten floating batteries enclosed in wooden 'armour' 6ft (1.8m) thick. Red-hot cannon balls, heated on grates, were rammed home against wet wads protecting the powder and then fired at once. By noon on 14 September all ten floating batteries had either blown up or been burned to the waterline.

National Maritime Museum.

The first major sea battle of the Revolutionary War (1793–1801) between Britain and France was fought on 1 June 1794, and is known to history as 'The Glorious First of June'. It took place in the Atlantic about 400 miles (644km) west of Brest, the English fleet being commanded by Lord Howe (1750–99) and the French by Admiral Villaret de Joyeuse (1715–1812). Howe decided to put into operation a completely new manoeuvre: 'to divide the enemy at all points from to windward' and then attack from to leeward. He did not imagine that *all* his ships would get through the French line but he reckoned that he would take as many enemy ships as there were breaches in the line, and he was right: seven British ships broke the French line; seven French ships were taken. Tactically it was a great achievement; strategically it was a failure, since the convoy of grain ships which Joyeuse was escorting, bound from America to starving France, and which Howe hoped to destroy,

The painting by Mather Brown of Lord Howe, sword in hand, on the quarterdeck of the *Queen Charlotte* at the Glorious First of June. *National Maritime Museum.*

reached France in safety. At the time of the battle Howe was 69, making him **one of the oldest admirals ever to have won a victory on such a scale.**

This was **the first action for which medals were awarded to the principal officers engaged.**

The greatest French seaman of this period, indeed one of the greatest seamen of all time, was **Admiral Suffren** (1729–88). In a series of five violent actions off the east coast of India in 1782–3, in which he was matched against the British admiral Sir Edward Hughes (?1720–94), he showed himself to be a tactician of rare genius and a singularly aggressive fighter. The most amazing aspect of his operations in the Indian Ocean was that, for two years, he managed to

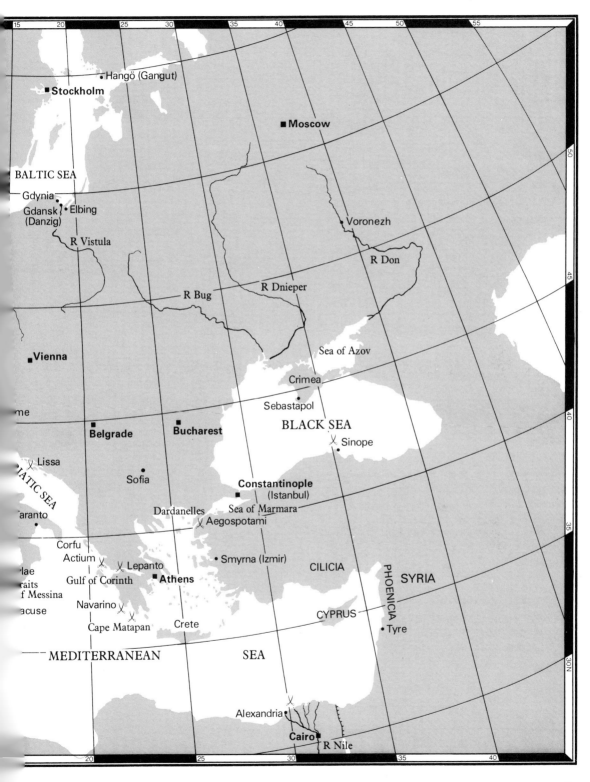

- Hangö (Gangut)
- ■ **Stockholm**

BALTIC SEA

- Gdynia
- Gdansk • Elbing
  (Danzig)
- R Vistula

■ **Moscow**

- Voronezh

R Don

R Bug   R Dnieper

Sea of Azov

- ■ **Vienna**

Crimea

me

- Sebastapol

■ **Belgrade**   ■ **Bucharest**

BLACK SEA

⚔ Sinope

⚔ Lissa

- Sofia

Constantinople
(Istanbul)

IATIC SEA

Dardanelles

Sea of Marmara

aranto

⚔ Aegospotami

- Corfu
- Actium ⚔   ⚔ Lepanto
- Gulf of Corinth   ■ **Athens**

- Smyrna (Izmir)

CILICIA

PHOENICIA   SYRIA

lae
raits
f Messina
acuse

Navarino ⚔
⚔
Cape Matapan   Crete

CYPRUS

- Tyre

MEDITERRANEAN   SEA

⚔
Alexandria •

Cairo ■
R Nile

maintain his fleet in excellent fighting order without the possession of a port in which to refit.

One of the most famous incidents in the long story of sailing-ship warfare occurred at the Battle of Cape St Vincent on 14 February 1797. A Spanish fleet of 27 ships, commanded by Admiral Don José de Cordova and bound for Brest to join the combined fleets of France and Holland, was engaged off Cape St Vincent, the south-west tip of Portugal, by a British fleet of 15 ships, commanded by Admiral Sir John Jervis (1735–1823). The Spanish fleet, when sighted by Jervis, was divided into two scattered groups and he planned to keep them apart and deal with each ship as occasion arose. But Commodore Nelson, in the *Captain*, last but two in the British line, was better able than Jervis in the *Victory* at the head of the line, to see that there was indeed a risk of the Spanish fleet reforming. So, on his own initiative, he wore out of the line and kept the gap open, engaging 7 Spanish ships with his single ship of 74 guns. Three of the enemy had over 100 guns, and one, the *Santissima Trinidad*, 130 guns, was **then the largest ship in the world**, the only four-decked man-of-war ever launched. The naval historian Oliver Warner says of this episode: 'Of the many acts of courage in Nelson's career, this was perhaps the most sublime, extraordinary – and rewarding.' Four Spanish ships were captured and ten others crippled.

The Age of Nelson

The most famous seaman of all time and England's greatest naval hero is certainly Horatio Nelson (1758–1805). Several of his major actions are mentioned elsewhere in this book but a brief summary of the main events in his life may be helpful. He was born at Burnham Thorpe, Norfolk, the son of a parson, on 24 September 1758; went to sea, aged 12, in 1771; promoted lieutenant 1777; promoted commander and given his first command, the brig *Badger*, by Admiral Sir Peter Parker (1721–1811) 1778; promoted Captain 1779; married Frances Nesbit 1787; lost his right eye at the siege of Calvi 1794; played a decisive role at Battle of Cape St Vincent 14 February 1797; Rear-Admiral 20 February 1797; failed to capture a treasure ship and lost his right arm at Santa Cruz, Canary Islands July 1797; won Battle of the Nile 1 August 1798; returned to

Horatio Nelson was created a Baron in 1798, Duke of Bronte by the King of Naples in 1800 and a Viscount in 1801.

Naples after the battle and became infatuated with Lady Hamilton; returned to London and separated from his wife 1800; Vice-Admiral 1801; won Battle of Copenhagen 2 April 1801; killed at Battle of Trafalgar 21 October 1805; accorded a public funeral and buried in St Paul's Cathedral.

The first fleet action in which Nelson was in command was the Battle of the Nile (1 August 1798). He had been sent by Lord St Vincent to seek out the French fleet which, unknown to the British, was heading for Egypt, from where Napoleon planned to launch a campaign by which he hoped eventually to topple Britain's eastern empire. Nelson guessed Napoleon's destination correctly and sailed for Egypt; but he outsailed the French and so missed them. A second attempt was successful and he found them anchored in Aboukir Bay near the mouth of the Nile. The four leading ships sailed between the French and the shore, thus subjecting them to fire from both sides. Ten French ships were captured and one blown up.

Apart from Nelson, **the best-remembered**

participant in the Battle of the Nile was a boy aged 10. The French Admiral's flagship, *L'Orient*, was commanded by Captain Casabianca (*c* 1755–98), whose son was on board with him. There are conflicting accounts of what actually happened to Casabianca and his son when the ship caught fire, but posterity may be forgiven for preferring the account given by Mrs Felicia Hemans in her emotionally overcharged poem which begins 'The boy stood on the burning deck whence all but he had fled.'

One of the most famous incidents in British naval history occurred at the Battle of Copenhagen, fought on 2 April 1801. Britain, alarmed by a pact of Armed Neutrality entered into by the Russians, Danes and Swedes, decided to act before the three could combine. A fleet was despatched under the command of Sir Hyde Parker (1739–1807), with Nelson as his second-in-command, and destroyed the Danish fleet after a battle of which Nelson said, 'I have been in a hundred and five engagements but **that of today is the most terrible of them all**'. During the battle occurred the famous incident when Nelson pretended not to have seen Parker's signal to withdraw, remarking that, as he only had one eye, he had a right to be blind sometimes.

A Danish impression of the Battle of Copenhagen, 2 April 1801. *National Maritime Museum.*

The system of signals adopted by the Admiralty in 1803, which greatly increased the range of orders which a commander could use when directing his fleet, was the work of Sir Home Riggs Popham (1762–1820). He is also remembered for having taken the Cape of Good Hope from the Dutch in 1806, in a combined operation with Sir David Baird. He then persuaded Baird that an attack on Buenos Aires would be supported by the Spanish colonists, but the latter, perversely, took the soldiers prisoner and Popham was recalled to England, court-martialled and severely reprimanded. He was the 21st child of his mother, who died in giving him birth.

War between France and Britain, halted by the Treaty of Amiens in March 1802, started again in May 1803, and Britain at once imposed a blockade on the Continent which was to last for the next two years and which inspired **the most famous quotation in the whole canon of naval history**. Alfred Thayer Mahan (1840–1914), the American historian, in his book *The Influence of Sea Power upon the French Revolution and Empire*,

83

described the effect of the blockade thus: 'The World has never seen a more impressive demonstration of the influence of sea-power upon its history. Those far distant, storm-beaten ships, upon which the Grand Army never looked, stood between it and the dominion of the world.'

The Battle of Trafalgar vies only with the Armada for the distinction of being **the most celebrated naval engagement in British history**; it was also the last major sea battle under sail except for Navarino in 1827. It marked the culmination of the long vigil kept by the British Navy through the years 1803, 1804 and much of 1805 to prevent the invasion of Britain by Napoleon. In April 1805, Admiral Pierre Villeneuve (1763–1806) eluded Nelson's blockade of Toulon, joined forces with such Spanish ships as were at Cadiz and sailed for the West Indies, with Nelson soon in hot pursuit. But Villeneuve eluded him again and returned to Europe, where he was involved in an inconclusive engagement with Sir Robert Calder (1745–1818) off Cape Finisterre, in which he lost two ships, before returning to Cadiz.

Nelson, after a brief spell in England, re-hoisted his flag on board the *Victory* on 14 September 1805, and resumed command of the fleet off the Spanish coast. Villeneuve, who knew, as Napoleon did not, that Nelson was in the offing with a fleet of 27 ships of the line, had orders to return to the Mediterranean, and these he decided to obey, smarting, as he was, under the threat of suspension for cowardice. So the two fleets, the Franco–Spanish fleet comprising 33 ships of the line, finally met off Cape Trafalgar on 21 October 1805. Nelson, his fleet divided into two lines with the strongest ships being placed at the head of each line, attacked his enemy at right-angles, himself leading the weather line in the *Victory* and Vice-Admiral Cuthbert Collingwood (1748–1810) leading the lee line in the *Royal Sovereign*.

The battle lasted five hours and resulted in what has been called '**the most decisive major naval victory in history**'. Of the 33 Franco–Spanish ships only ten remained; British Naval supremacy was firmly established and the threat of a French invasion of England finally removed. But the magnitude of the victory was clouded by the death of Nelson, who was mortally wounded by a shot from the French *Redoutable*. As the log

of the *Victory* bluntly states: 'Partial firing continued until 4.30, when a victory having been reported to the Right Honourable Lord Viscount Nelson KB and Commander-in-Chief, he then died of his wound.'

The first news of the Battle of Trafalgar was brought to England by Lieutenant John Lapenotière, an officer of French descent who was in command of the 10-gun schooner *Pickle*, one of the smallest ships at Trafalgar. Lapenotière, who was a favourite of Collingwood's, landed at Falmouth early on 5 November 1805 and arrived at the Admiralty at 1 am the following morning, a remarkable achievement considering the time of year and the state of the roads.

The most famous signal in British naval history was that sent by Nelson at the Battle of Trafalgar. The signal was actually transmitted by John Pasco (1774–1853), then Signal Lieutenant aboard *Victory*. Pasco was, in fact, partly responsible for the wording of the signal, for Nelson originally intended the signal to read 'England confides that every man will do his duty', and told Pasco to be quick about it as he had another signal to send. Pasco pointed out that it would be quicker to substitute 'expects' for 'confides', as the former was in the vocabulary whereas the latter would have to be spelt out. 'His lordship replied, in haste, and with seeming satisfaction, "That will do, Pasco, make it immediately."'

THE *VICTORY*

Few would deny that the *Victory* can properly claim to be **the most famous ship in the history of the British Navy,** not only on account of her immortal role as Nelson's flagship at Trafalgar but also because she has had the remarkable good fortune to survive to the present day. **The oldest ship on the British Naval List** can now be seen, fittingly enough, in **the oldest dry dock in the world**, No. 2 Dock at Portsmouth, where she flies the flag of the Commander-in-Chief, who still uses her to entertain distinguished visitors.

Launched at Chatham on 7 May 1765, she was the flagship of Admiral Howe at the relief of Gibraltar in 1782, of Hood at Toulon in 1793, and of Nelson at both St Vincent (1797) and Trafalgar (1805). From 1835 she was moored at Portsmouth and was allowed to fall into a sorry state of delapidation. It was not until 1921 that the

HMS *Victory*, Nelson's flagship at Trafalgar. *National Maritime Museum.*

Society for Nautical Research launched a campaign to save and restore her. Generous support was provided by Sir James Caird, the Scottish shipowner, and in July 1928, King George V unveiled a tablet recording the completion of the restoration work.

The End of an Era

The last occasion on which fireships were used by the Royal Navy was during an attack on the French fleet off La Rochelle on 11 April 1809. Lord Gambier, who commanded the fleet, was of the opinion that 'the operation of fireships is a horrible mode of warfare' but Lord Mulgrave, then First Lord of the Admiralty, retorted that 'the present was no time for professional etiquette' and sent Lord Cochrane to carry out the operation, which would have been entirely successful had not Lord Gambier been so consumed with jealousy at Cochrane's appointment that he refused to follow up the latter's initial success.

THE WAR OF 1812

The most famous ship in the history of the US Navy is the frigate USS *Constitution*, popularly known as 'Old Ironsides'. Launched at Boston in 1797, she was 204ft (62m) in length, had a displacement of 2200 tons and carried 54 guns, although her official allocation was only 44. **Her most famous action** occurred in the War of 1812 between Britain and the United States, which had its origins in the Orders in Council by which Britain had prohibited neutral ships from trading with France. On the afternoon of 19 August 1812, off Cape Race, Newfoundland, the *Constitution*, commanded by Captain Isaac Hull (1773–1843), overhauled the British frigate *Guerrière*, an old French prize-ship, commanded by Captain James Dacres (1788–1853), and destroyed her. On 29 December 1812, now under the command of Captain William Bainbridge (1774–1883), the *Constitution* encountered the British frigate *Java* off the coast of Brazil and destroyed her. On 20 February 1815, under Captain Charles Steward (1778–1869), she took two British warships, *Cyane* and *Levant*, off Madeira. She was condemned as unseaworthy in 1828 but public

The crew of the *Shannon* boarding the *Chesapeake*. Captain Lawrence, mortally wounded, cries, 'Don't give up the ship.' *National Maritime Museum.*

sentiment led to her preservation and she is still to be seen in Boston, where she started her career.

The naval side of the War of 1812 was **one of the most uneven contests in the history of warfare.** At the outset the US Navy had 14 seaworthy vessels against the Royal Navy's 1048.

The most celebrated action of the War of 1812 was the fight between the *Shannon* and the *Chesapeake* off Boston on the afternoon of 1 June 1813. The *Shannon*, a frigate which mounted 52 guns, was commanded by Captain Philip Broke (1776–1841), the *Chesapeake*, 36 guns, by Captain James Lawrence (1781–1813). In an action lasting only 12 minutes 146 Americans and 83 British were killed or wounded. Lawrence himself was killed and Broke, though wounded, took the *Chesapeake* prize and she remained on the Royal Navy list until 1819 when she was sold.

Philip Broke was **the finest gunnery officer of his day** and the *Shannon* was probably the best-drilled and most efficient ship then afloat. Among the innovations credited to Broke are 'the fitting of "dispart" sights to the guns for better aiming; scientifically graduated and notched "quoins", or wedges, for the guns, to give a horizontal-fire reference in all attitudes of the ship, even at night;

and a system of operating all the guns of a broadside in concert, involving common scales of elevation and lines of bearing cut in the deck at each gun controlled by reference to a master compass rose on deck.' (*Illustrated History of Ships* ed. E. L. CORNWELL.) A dispart sight is a sight fixed about half-way along the barrel of a gun to account for the difference between the diameters of the breech and the muzzle.

The last British sailing line-of-battle ship was the *Ganges*, launched in Bombay in 1821. When she was paid off in 1861, no other sailing ship of the line remained in commission in the Royal Navy. In 1866 she became a training ship, moored in Falmouth Bay.

The Battle of Navarino was **the last sea battle fought wholly under sail and the first in which British and French sailors had fought on the same side since the Battle of Solebay in 1672.** Public opinion had obliged the British, French and Russian Governments to support the cause of

Greece in her war of independence against the Turks and thus on 20 October 1827, the allied fleet, under Admiral Sir Edward Codrington (1770–1851), sailed into Navarino harbour, at the south-west tip of Greece, where the Turkish fleet was at anchor. The Turks were rash enough to open fire and three hours later their fleet was no more. Although the war lasted another two years, it was the Battle of Navarino which ensured the independence of Greece, as Turkey was henceforward without a principal fleet.

The action which proved to be **the final nail in the coffin of the 'Wooden Walls' era** and clearly demonstrated that they were no longer the 'best walls of any kingdom' was fought off Sinope on the Black Sea coast of Turkey on 30 November 1853. There the Russian Navy **first showed the lethal potential of naval guns** charged with explosive shells by totally demolishing a Turkish squadron of seven frigates, two corvettes, two transports and two wooden steamers in less than an hour. Explosive shells had been used for years in mortars and on bomb-ketches but conventional ships had until then used them only rarely.

The lesson taught at Sinope was reinforced in the following year at the bombardment of Sevastopol. The British and French had declared war on Russia in March 1854. During the siege of Sevastopol in the following October the British fleet bombarded the town from the sea but the attack was a failure and the ships were forced to withdraw, badly damaged, 500 men having lost their lives. One of the ships taking part was the *Arethusa*, **the last British ship to go into battle entirely under sail.** She later became a training ship for destitute boys in which role she continued to serve until 1932.

The last wooden battleship to be built for the British Navy was the *Victoria*. She was launched in 1859, carried 121 guns, and may be regarded as the ultimate development in the long tradition of 'wooden walls' from within which Britannia had ruled the waves for nigh on three centuries. By this time the supremacy of the ironclads had been firmly established but the *Victoria* was nevertheless sent to Malta in 1864 as flagship to the Mediterranean fleet on the grounds that an ironclad would be too hot and unhealthy to act as a headquarters ship!

The Battle of Sinope.

METAL
AND
MACHINERY

The first steam-propelled armoured warship was the *Demologos*, laid down by Robert Fulton in 1813 and launched the following year. She was a 38-ton vessel, powered by a single-cylinder engine driving a single paddle-wheel mounted centrally in a well. Her wooden sides, 5ft (1.5m) thick and clad with external iron plates, were, it was claimed, impenetrable by any missile of that day, but the war of 1812 came to an end before she was launched, so the claim was never put to the test. Later her name was changed to the *Fulton*, thereby causing no little confusion in subsequent works of reference. In 1829 she was accidentally blown up at her moorings off Brooklyn.

The *Diana* at Rangoon. *National Maritime Museum.*

The first steam vessels built for the Royal Navy were two paddle-wheel tugs called the *Comet* and the *Monkey*, launched in 1822, but their employment was limited to towing sailing warships out of harbour when the wind was foul. Six years later their Lordships of the Admiralty felt it 'their bounden duty to discourage to the utmost of their ability the employment of steam vessels, as they consider that the introduction of steam is calculated to strike a fatal blow at the naval supremacy of the Empire'.

The first occasion on which a steam-driven vessel took part in a naval action occurred in 1824 during the First Burmese War when the paddle-wheeler *Diana* attacked and destroyed the enemy's flotilla of warboats outside Rangoon.

The tug-of-war between the *Rattler* and the *Alecto*.

The first orthodox paddle-steamer warship was HMS *Penelope*, launched in 1829 as a 46-gun sailing frigate. In 1846 she won considerable fame in the shipping world when she was cut in two and lengthened to accommodate a 650hp engine and 600 tons of coal. In spite of her increased bulk, she managed to sail faster than before.

The Screw Propellor

'Somebody discovered the merits of the screw,' wrote Professor Michael Lewis. 'That word "somebody" is deliberate. Much ink has been spilt on the subject of who it was.' Certain it is that in 1785 Joseph Bramah (1748–1814) was granted a patent for a method of ship-propulsion by 'a wheel with inclined fans or wings,' to be fixed on a spindle at the stern of a ship, but whether it was ever tried out we do not know. Four later engineers who are variously credited with the invention of the screw propellor were: Robert Wilson (1803–82) who was awarded a silver medal for his propellor by the Scottish Society of Arts in 1832; Francis Pettit Smith (1808–74) who, we are told, invented a screw propellor for ships and constructed a model, quite independently of other experimenters, in 1836; a Frenchman, Frédéric Sauvage (1785–1857) who designed and patented an early screw propellor in 1832, 'the design of which was plagiarized by others'; and a Swedish soldier, John Ericsson (1803–89) who patented his screw propellor in 1836.

Whoever its inventor may have been, the screw propellor solved what had hitherto been **one of the greatest problems in the construction of warships** – how to combine maximum freedom of movement with maximum firepower. Sail gave an uninterrupted field of fire but only limited manoeuvrability. Oar, and, later, paddle-wheel gave increased manoeuvrability but severely obstructed the field of fire. Screw propulsion combined the advantages of both.

The first seagoing vessel to be driven by a screw propellor was the 237-ton *Archimedes*. Launched in 1839, she was initially fitted with a single-thread screw 7ft (2.13m) in diameter, which was subsequently replaced by a two-bladed screw 5ft 9in (1.75m) in diameter, turning at 139 revolutions per minute.

The Royal Navy's first iron screw steamer was built at Blackwall in 1842. At her trials in May 1843 she reached a speed of 10½ knots and was then taken over by the Admiralty, as had been agreed. Her name was then changed from *Mermaid* to *Dwarf*.

The success of the *Archimedes* persuaded the Admiralty to take a more realistic attitude to screw propulsion and resulted in **one of the strangest ship's trials ever undertaken**. In March 1845, a test of strength and speed was arranged between two steam-sloops, the propellor-driven *Rattler* of 888 tons and 200hp and the paddle-driven *Alecto* of 800 tons, also having a 200hp engine. In ordinary races the *Rattler* comfortably outpaced the *Alecto* on three occasions. The two ships were then secured stern to stern by stout cables and 'full steam ahead' was rung on both ships. After a brief struggle the *Rattler* made headway and towed the *Alecto* at a speed of 2.7 knots, conclusive proof of the superiority of screw over paddle in both speed and strength.

The Ironclad Era

The first iron warships built in Britain were two gun-boats built in 1839, not for the Royal Navy but for the East India Company. Named *Phlegethon* and *Nemesis*, they took part in the First Opium War between Great Britain and China in 1842. The *Nemesis* is said to have been **the first iron vessel in the world to carry guns** and was built by John Laird at Birkenhead.

The first iron ship of the Royal Navy was a small iron packet-ship called the *Dover*, built in 1840.

The first ship to have her machinery below the waterline was the *Princeton*, designed by John Ericsson for the US Navy in 1842. The engines, of a type originally designed by James Watt, had segment-shaped chambers in place of cylinders. The pistons were rectangles that swung on bearings as a door swings on its hinges. The piston hinge or bearing was carried outside the chamber and worked the propellor shaft by vibrating cranks and connecting rods, without the intervention of gearing. In the words of one American historian, the *Princeton* 'dictated the reconstruction of the navies of the world'.

The first truly sea-going ironclad warship in the world was the French frigate *La Gloire*, launched in 1859. Designed by Stanislas Dupuy de Lôme (1816–85), she was built of oak but was clad with a belt of iron, varying between 4 and 4¾in (10–12cm) thick, extending from the upper deck to 6ft (1.8m) below the waterline. Her length was 253ft (77.1m), beam 53ft (16.2m) and displacement 5675 tons. Her original armament consisted of thirty 36pdr smooth-bore guns, afterwards replaced by six 9.4in (23.9m) breech-loading rifled guns. There was also an oval conning tower protected by 4in (10cm) of iron armour plating.

The first true ironclad battleship was the *Warrior* laid down in June 1859, and launched in 1860. Built as a riposte to the French *La Gloire*, she was the first capital ship built throughout of iron, though she was only fitted with armour plating amidships and some 80ft (23.4m) of her hull at each end was unprotected. Her statistics were: displacement 9210 tons; length 380ft (116m); maximum speed 14½ knots: armament, twenty-six 68pdr (30.8kg) muzzle-loaders, ten 110pdr (49.9kg) and four 70pdr (31.7kg) breech loaders. In 1904 she was renamed *Vernon III* and became part of the *Vernon* torpedo school at Portsmouth. She was removed from the Navy list in 1923 and was until recently in use as an oil fuel

La Gloire, **the first true ironclad warship.** *Mansell Collection.*

The famous encounter between the *Monitor* and the *Merrimac* on 9 March 1862.

pier at Pembroke. She is now being refitted to near her original state by the Maritime Trust and it is hoped that in due course she will be on display at Portsmouth.

The first encounter in naval warfare between two ironclads occurred on 9 March 1862, during the American Civil War, which started in 1861 after the 11 southern states seceded from the Union. The action was inconclusive but nevertheless gained immortality for the two protagonists, the *Merrimac* and the *Monitor*. In 1861 the Federal Forces had abandoned the Naval dockyard at Norfolk, Virginia, burning several vessels, including the 4650-ton *Merrimac*, before they left. The Confederates, finding that she was still water-tight and her machinery in working order, raised and totally refashioned her. Above the deck a low penthouse of teak was built, to which were fastened two layers of iron plates, each 2in (5cm) thick. Inside this armoured penthouse was a battery of six 9-in (23cm), two 7-in (18cm) and two 6-in (15cm) guns, five in each broadside, firing through portholes. A heavy metal ram was fastened to the prow. The work was completed on 7 March 1862, and the following day, without any trials, she was sent out from Norfolk to attack the Union squadron blockading the estuaries of the York and James Rivers. Impervious to the enemy's cannonballs, she rammed and sank the USS *Cumberland*, then turned on the *Congress* and smashed her to pieces at a range of 200yd (183m). The USS *Minnesota* avoided a similar fate

when she ran aground and the ebb tide prevented the *Merrimac*, which drew 22ft (6.7m) of water, from reaching her. That evening she returned to Norfolk to repair superficial damage and anticipate the destruction of the rest of the United States fleet in the morning. But when morning came a strange-looking craft was seen to be guarding the *Minnesota*. Overnight the USS *Monitor* had arrived from New York. Designed by the Swedish engineer, John Ericsson, the *Monitor* was said to resemble 'a cheesebox on a raft' and has also been called **'one of the least seaworthy ships that ever ventured to sea'**. She carried two 11-in (27.9cm) guns mounted in a heavily armoured revolving turret. The hull was in two parts, an underwater body 124ft (37.8m) long, 34ft (10.4m) wide and 5¾ft (1.8m) deep, with an armoured teak hull 48ft (14.6m) longer above. The battle lasted nearly four hours during which time the *Monitor* fired 53 rounds of 135lb (61.2kg) explosive shells and scored 20 hits. The *Merrimac*, using a 68lb (30.8kg) shell, gained 23 hits. But the only conclusion reached was that contemporary projectiles were of little use against iron armour and shortly after midday they broke off the action. Both ships came to a sad end: the *Monitor* foundered off Cape Hatteras in a gale on 31 December 1862, with the loss of 16 men; the *Merrimac* was burnt by the Confederates when they evacuated Norfolk. 'The combat of the *Merrimac* and the *Monitor* made **the greatest change in sea-fighting since cannon fired by gunpowder had been mounted on ships about 400 years before'**(W. S. CHURCHILL, *History of the English-Speaking Peoples*).

Admiral David G Farragut, Member of the American Hall of Fame. *National Maritime Museum.*

The first admiral of the US Navy was David Farragut (1801–70), who ranks among **the great naval commanders of all time**, though his career was remarkably different from others who qualify for that accolade. He went to sea at the age of ten, was in action aboard the *Essex* at the age of 12 and thereafter did not hear another shot fired in anger until he was over 60, **an experience unique in the records of great sea commanders**. Though a southerner by birth, he remained loyal to the Federal Government when the Civil War started in 1861 and was put in command of the West Gulf Blockading Squadron, in which role his most important achievement was the capture of New Orleans in April 1862. He is best remembered, however, for having forced the passage into Mobile Bay on 5 August 1864. When his leading ship, the *Tecumseh*, was blown up by a mine, then known as a torpedo, the captain of the *Brooklyn* hesitated, but was urged on by Farragut in words which have gone down in naval history: '**Damn the torpedoes! Captain Drayton, go ahead!**' He returned to New York to a hero's welcome and was invested with the newly created rank of vice-admiral, the senior rank in the US Navy having

hitherto been that of rear-admiral. In 1866 the rank of admiral was created to which he was again the first to be appointed.

The first large warship designed from the start to be fitted with screw machinery was the *Agamemnon*, launched at Woolwich in 1852. She was, however, fully rigged, her screw still being regarded as an auxiliary means of propulsion. She carried the flag of Sir Edward Lyons (1790–1858) at the bombardment of Sevastopol in October 1854, and in 1858, after two abortive attempts, assisted in laying the first Atlantic cable.

The first British armoured steamers, the *Trusty*, *Thunder*, *Glatton* and *Meteor*, were commissioned in 1855, in close imitation of the French batteries. They were 173ft (52.7m) long and had armour-plating 4.3in (10.9cm) thick.

The French were the first to react to the lessons taught at Sinope and Sevastopol (see p. 87), Napoleon III (1808–73) at once ordering the construction of **Armoured Floating Batteries**, the first three of which, the *Tonnante*, the *Lave* and the *Dévastation*, were sent to the Crimea in 1855. They were clad with $4\frac{1}{2}$-in (11.4cm) iron plates fastened to a wall of 17-in (43.2cm) timber and carried 16 smooth-bore 56-pdr (25.4kg) guns and two smaller guns. Of 1600 tons displacement, they were low in the water and were only intended for use in coastal waters. Steam-driven, with a single screw, they were able to make at best four knots in tideless waters but at the bombardment of the Kinburn forts which guarded the mouths of the Rivers Bug and Dnieper, they acquitted themselves admirably. Closing to within 900–1200yd (822–1097m) of the forts they silenced the guns in four hours, while the Russian round-shot bounced harmlessly off their armour.

These were followed, a year later, by **the first four iron-hulled, armoured, steam-driven ships in the world**, the *Thunderbolt*, *Terror*, *Aetna* and *Erebus*. The last-named should not be confused with the better-known *Erebus* which sailed with the *Terror* on Sir John Franklin's last voyage to the Arctic and was abandoned in the ice in April 1845 (see p. 38). The later *Erebus* was launched in Glasgow in April 1856; the hull was built of iron and the topsides from 2ft (61cm) below the waterline up to the gunwale were clad in teak 6in (15cm) thick, which in turn was plated with iron armour 4in (10.2cm) thick. With a displacement of 1825 tons, her 1900hp engines gave her a speed of 5½ knots. She was armed with sixteen 68-pdr (31kg) guns and carried a crew of 200.

The first turret ship to be built in England was the *Rolf Krake*, designed by Captain Cowper Coles for the Danish Navy, armed with four 68-pdr (31kg) cannon and launched in 1863. Captain Cowper Phipps Coles (1819–70) was the first man to develop the idea of a seaworthy warship with low freeboard and carrying a few heavy guns in revolving, armoured turrets. The best-known ship designed by Captain Coles was the ill-fated *Captain* launched in 1869. Built of iron by Lairds of Birkenhead, she was both steam-driven and fully rigged. Unfortunately she turned out to weigh 800 tons more and to have 2ft (61cm) less freeboard than Coles had calculated. On the night of 6 September 1870, with storm sails set, she was caught in a gale in the Bay of Biscay and capsized, drowning the designer and all but 18 of the crew of 500.

Captain Cowper Coles.

THE *ALABAMA*

Of all the steamships of the 19th century, **none achieved such notoriety** as the American Confederate cruiser *Alabama*, a three-masted schooner with auxiliary steam power, built by the Laird Company at Birkenhead and still under construction when the American Civil War started in 1861. Although the British Government had issued an order of detention on 29 July 1862, her commander, Captain Raphael Semmes (1809–77), on the pretext of making a trial trip, took her down the Mersey and made for the Azores where she took on her armament and hoisted the Confederate flag. During the next two years she swept the seas of Federal shipping, taking, in all, 68 prizes, her marauding career finally ending on 19 June 1869, when she was sunk off Cherbourg by the US Sloop-of-War *Kearsage*, a screw steamer of 1031 tons. After prolonged negotiation Britain agreed to pay damages of £3.25 million to the USA in respect of damage done by the *Alabama* and two other Confederate cruisers built in Britain, in recognition of the latter's failure to observe the duties imposed by International Law upon a neutral state in time of war.

The first ship in the Royal Navy to mount an armour-plated bow battery on her main deck was the *Lord Clyde*, launched in 1864. An iron-cased steam-frigate of 7750 tons, she was one of the last armour-plated wooden ships to be built. Her engines, of the new trunk type, were the most powerful of their time but in two years they were worn out. New engines were fitted but six months later she ran aground and, when docked to have the damage inspected, it was found that her timbers were being eaten away by fungus. In 1875 she was sold out of the Service.

The first major sea battle in which ironclads fought ironclads was the Battle of Lissa in which the Austrians defeated the Italians on 20 July 1866. The battle, though of little political significance, was notable for the fact that the victorious Austrian fleet, commanded by Admiral Wilhelm von Tegetthoff (1827–71), was considerably smaller and less modern than the Italian fleet, commanded by Count Carlo Persano (1806–83). One incident, however, was to have a totally disproportionate effect on the future design of warships of all nations. During the engagement Tegetthoff's flagship, the 5000-ton *Ferdinand Max*, rammed the stationary *Re d'Italia* and made a hole of 300sq.ft (27.9m²) in the side of his victim, with the result that when the Austrian ship backed out the other sank immediately with the loss of 381 lives. Suddenly the ram, one of the oldest weapons in naval warfare, was back in fashion and, against all reason, rams continued to be fitted to all battleships and heavy cruisers until the beginning of the 20th century.

There is an interesting connection between the Battle of Lissa and the development of the **torpedo** (see p. 136). The engines of the *Ferdinand Max* had been designed and built by Robert Whitehead, and after the battle he received a telegram from Tegetthoff which read, 'Thanks to your first-class engines I was able to win the Battle of Lissa.' This public recognition of his skill as an engineer was proof enough that the Whitehead torpedo was not just the brainchild of some crackpot inventor and he took advantage of the sudden publicity to ensure that news of his weapon reached the ears of the right people.

Sadly, **the only fatal damage ever caused by British ships with the ram** was sustained by another British ship. In 1875 the 6010-ton battleship *Vanguard* was accidentally rammed and sunk, during a fog off the coast of Wicklow, by her sister-ship, the *Iron Duke*, but fortunately went down slowly enough to give all her crew time to take to the boats.

The first twin-screw ocean-going ironclad in the Royal Navy was the *Penelope*, launched in 1867. She was armed with ten 12in (30.5cm) guns.

The first sailless seagoing ironclad built for the Royal Navy was HMS *Devastation*, laid down at Portsmouth in 1869 and completed in 1873. Not only was she the first battleship to carry no sails, she was also **the first large iron ship to be built at Portsmouth**. The *Devastation* was 285ft (86.9m) long, 62.3ft (19m) in beam and had two propellors which gave her a speed of 12½ knots. She was armed with four 35-ton 12in (30.5cm) muzzle-loading guns mounted in forward and aft turrets, armour-plated to a thickness of 10–14in (25.4–35.5cm). She has been called the '**first modern battleship**' but she was also the last major war-

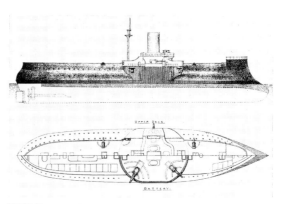

HMS *Devastation*.

ship to be fitted with trunk-type machinery. In a trunk engine the connecting rod was coupled directly to the piston, which carried a large cylindrical trunk extending through the engine covers.

In 1875 the Russians launched **the world's first circular warships**. They were described by an English Member of Parliament who witnessed the launching thus: 'The second circular ironclad was launched today at noon with great success. She was named the *Admiral Popoff* after her distinguished designer, by the express and spontaneous desire of His Majesty the Czar ... The *Novgorod* is 101ft (30.8m) in diameter and of 2491 tons; the *Admiral Popoff* is 120ft (36.6m) in diameter and of 3550 tons. The armour of the *Novgorod* is about equivalent to 13-in (33cm) plating, that of the *Admiral Popoff* to about 18in

The Russian circular battleship *Novgorod*.

(46cm). The horsepower of the former vessel is 480 nominal and of the latter 640. Each has six screw propellers, but in the latter vessel two of them are of much larger diameter than the others, and have their shafts situated lower down, so that in deep water these screws will sweep through the water much below the bottom of the vessel, while in shallow water they will be kept at rest in a position which keeps them above the keels' (E. J. REID, quoted in *The Annual Register*, 1875). They were not, however, a success.

The largest guns then mounted in a ship, not surpassed until the Japanese *Yamato* and *Musashi* were built in the Second World War, were the 100-ton 17.7in (45cm) Armstrong muzzle-loaders mounted in the Italian battleships *Duilio* and *Dandolo*, designed by Benedetto Brin (1833–98) in 1881. The guns were mounted in turrets so placed that the field of fire was virtually uninterrupted.

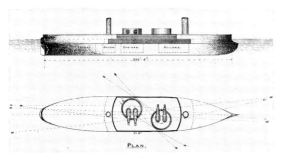

Elevation and plan of the *Duilio* and the *Dandolo* showing fields of fire.

Benedetto Brin has been called **the father of the Italian Navy**, which was established after the unification of the country in 1870. In all he was Minister of Marine for 11 years and gave to Italy a strong and efficient Navy.

Britain's answer to the *Duilio* and the *Dandolo* was the *Inflexible*, laid down in 1876 and launched in 1881. She was then **the most heavily armoured ship in the Royal Navy** as well as being **the first battleship to be fitted with under-water torpedo tubes**. Her armour was 2ft (61cm) thick, though it was restricted to a central citadel of engines and armament. She started life with two masts and a full set of sails, amounting to a spread of 18,500sq.ft (1717m²) of canvas, but these were later removed. Her vital statistics were: displacement 11,800 tons; max. speed 15 knots: length 320ft (97.5m); beam 75ft (23m); draught

26ft 4in (8m). She was armed with four 16in (41cm) muzzle-loading rifled guns, each weighing 80 tons, mounted in two turrets each of which weighed 750 tons, as well as eight 4in (10.16cm) breech-loaders, 21 anti-torpedo-boat guns and four torpedo tubes. The weight of a single discharge was 6800lb (3084kg), which was not exceeded for another 25 years.

The first Captain of the *Inflexible* was **John Arbuthnot Fisher** (1841–1920) better known as Jacky Fisher. Since he has been described as **'the greatest administrator the Navy has produced since Lord Barham'** and **'the most outstanding British admiral since Nelson'**, a brief sketch of his career is given. He entered the Navy in 1854, served in the Crimean War and in the Second Opium War of 1856–60. In 1882, as Captain of the *Inflexible*, he was present at the bombardment of Alexandria. From 1886 to 1891 he was Director of Naval Ordnance, later successively Third, Second and First Sea Lord of the Admiralty. He was largely responsible for the design of the *Dreadnought* class of battleship and it was mainly due to his efforts that Germany was confronted with a superior British fleet when war broke out in 1914. Fisher retired in 1910 but was recalled to the Admiralty in October 1914 and at once initiated a huge programme of new construction, but resigned in the following May, having fallen out with Winston Churchill, then First Lord of the Admiralty, over the latter's handling of the Dardanelles campaign.

The first British destroyer was the *Havock* (240 tons, 27 knots) built by Messrs Yarrow in 1893. The destroyer was developed to protect the major units of a fleet from attack by the fast torpedo-boat, which had been built to carry the new automobile torpedo developed by Robert Whitehead. The destroyer was originally known as the **torpedo-boat destroyer**.

The first battleship to be fitted with anti-torpedo bulges was the 14,635-ton HMS *Revenge*, completed in March 1894. In 1915 she was renamed the *Redoubtable* to release the name *Revenge* for a new battleship.

The first fleet action since Lissa and the only major fleet action of the war fought between China and Japan in 1894–5, to settle the question of predominance in Korea, was the Battle of the Yalu River. The two fleets met on 17 September 1894, near the mouth of the river and, though equally matched in numbers, the superior armoury of the Japanese won the day, during which five Chinese ships were sunk.

In February 1895, the Japanese attacked the repaired Chinese fleet at Wei-hai-wei and, though Admiral Ting and his men put up the stoutest resistance of the war, most of the Chinese fleet was destroyed, much of the damage being done by Schwartzkopff torpedoes. But the weather was bitterly cold, many men were frozen to death and several torpedo-tubes became iced up. This was the first demonstration of the effect severe weather can have on metal machined to give very close tolerances, and the last occasion on which torpedoes were fired in anger during the 19th century.

The first ship ever to be driven by a turbine engine was the appropriately named *Turbinia*, built in 1894 at Wallsend-on-Tyne. She had a displacement of 44½ tons, was 100ft (30.5m) long, 9ft (2.7m) in the beam and 3ft (0.9m) in draught. The steam turbine engine by which she was powered was the invention of Sir Charles Parsons (1854–1931).

The mechanical advantages of the steam turbine for ship propulsion were obvious. Turbines are lighter, give greater speeds and occupy less space, power for power, than reciprocating engines. There are no heat losses due to alternate cooling and heating of the working parts and there is no need for internal lubrication.

The performance of the *Turbinia*, however, was at first disappointing. She had been designed to break all existing speed records but the very high propellor speed which her engine generated resulted in excessive cavitation (the formation of voids on the blade surface) and all that she could achieve was a maximum speed of a meagre 19¾ knots.

So, in 1896, the original turbine was removed and was replaced by three parallel-flow Parsons turbines, driving separate shafts, the engines developed about 2000 shaft horse-power and there were three propellors on each shaft. By June 1897, she was ready to demonstrate her enhanced performance under the most spectacular circumstances. The occasion was Queen Victoria's Diamond Jubilee Review at Spithead, where, to the amazement of all who saw her, she steamed past the entire fleet at a speed of 34½ knots.

The first capital ship to be blown up and sunk by a mine was the *Petropavlovsk*, flagship of the Russian Admiral Makaroff (1849–1904) at the beginning of the Russo-Japanese war of 1904–5. The explosion set off 18 mines in the battleship's own magazine, whereupon she broke in two and sank within two minutes. There were no survivors.

The Battle of Tsushima, 27 May 1905, was **the first major battle fought between fleets of armoured battleships**. War between Russia and Japan had broken out in February 1904, the

A Russian warship captured at Tsushima and repaired by the Japanese.

A Russian warship passing through the Suez Canal, 1904 (see p. 99). *Mary Evans Picture Library.*

A torpedo boat of 1889, from a painting by Norman Wilkinson. *Mary Evans Picture Library.*

The French submarine *Surcouf* (see p. 140). *Mary Evans Picture Library.*

essential cause being their conflicting interests on the mainland of Asia. By August, Japan had gained complete command of the sea and in October the Russian Baltic fleet under Admiral Rozhestvensky (1848–1909) was sent to the Far East. The voyage, which must rank as **the slowest ever recorded since the days of sail**, was marked by a series of unfortunate incidents, including an attack on a British trawler fleet on the Dogger Bank, the Russians apparently thinking that they were sheltering Japanese torpedo-boats! Seven fishermen were killed and Russia nearly found herself at war with Britain. From Madagascar Rozhestvensky sent home **the most pessimistic signal any commander has ever transmitted**: 'I have not the slightest prospect,' he wired, 'of recovering command of the sea with the force under my command.' Nor was he wrong. When the Russian fleet eventually reached the Straits of Tsushima, which separate Japan from Korea, Admiral Togo (1847–1934) was waiting and, in the ensuing battle, every Russian ship was either sunk or captured. Tsushima at the time was described as **the greatest fleet action since Trafalgar**; it was also **the first major naval battle in history in which the fleets were quite independent of the strength and direction of the wind**.

The first destroyers to have oil-fired boilers were the *Tribal* class of 1905. 8-geared turbines were first used in the Admiralty 'R' class destroyers built during the First World War. They displaced 900 tons, had a maximum speed of 36 knots and were armed with three 4in (10cm) guns and four 21in (53cm) torpedoes.

The Russo-Japanese War of 1904–5 was to place beyond dispute the contention that mixed-calibre armament was now an anachronism. The rapidly increasing efficiency of the torpedo and the submarine made long-range fighting inevitable and spelt out the obvious lesson that in future the advantage would lie with the navy able to concentrate the heaviest barrage at the greatest distance. To facilitate such a concentration all the big guns must be of the same calibre – in other words the 'all-big-gun' battleship. The Japanese had realized this even before Tsushima and had actually laid down **the first-ever 'all-big-gun' battleship**, the *Aki*, before the war started, but financial difficulties resulted in subsequent modification and it was to HMS *Dreadnought* that the honour fell of being **the first of this new type of battleship to be launched**, whereupon every other battleship in the world was immediately rendered obsolete.

The *Dreadnought* was laid down in Portsmouth Dockyard on 2 October 1905, launched on 10 February 1906, and underwent her first trials on 3 October 1906. The remarkable speed of her construction was largely due to the dynamic enthusiasm of Admiral Sir John Fisher, then First Sea Lord, and it is with his name that the *Dreadnought* is for ever linked. Her ten 12in

HMS *Dreadnought. Robert Hunt Library.*

(30.5cm) guns were mounted on five turrets, three on the centre line and two on the sides. She also carried 27 small guns for repelling attacks by torpedo-boats, and five 18in (46cm) torpedo tubes. She was the first major warship to be driven by turbine machinery, giving her a maximum speed of 21 knots. She was 527ft (161m) in length, 82ft (25m) in beam and displaced 17,900 tons. Her name became synonymous with the 'all-big-gun' battleship and thereafter battleships were described as 'Dreadnoughts' or 'Pre-Dreadnoughts'.

The launching of HMS *Dreadnought* was the signal for the start of the **'Dreadnought race'** which lasted for the next 15 years and saw the major maritime powers competing with each other to build or buy more of these expensive expressions of naval might than their rivals.

*The 15-inch guns of the **Queen Elizabeth**. Robert Hunt Library.*

THE BATTLE-CRUISERS

The next child of Sir John Fisher's fertile brain was the **battle-cruiser**, though he, in fact, referred to them as fast armoured cruisers. It had become apparent that the existing armoured cruisers could no longer effectively engage enemy battleships nor take their place in the line of battle, so Fisher's answer was to achieve greater speed and firepower by cutting down on armour. The first ship of this class, the *Invincible*, had eight 12in (30cm) guns and displaced 17,400 tons, much the same as the *Dreadnought*, but her armour was only 6in (18cm) thick against the *Dreadnought*'s 11in (28cm). This, combined with the fact that she was propelled by **the most powerful engines at that time ever installed in a ship**, gave her a top speed of 26½ knots. The *Invincible* was laid down in 1906, was launched in 1907 and was ready for trials a year later. (See also pp. 104–7.)

At the time of her launching in 1910 the battle-cruiser HMS *Lion* was **the largest, fastest, and most expensive warship in the world**. She had a fully-loaded displacement of 29,680 tons, was 700ft (213m) long and 88.5ft (27m) wide, and her 70,000hp turbines gave her a maximum speed of 28 knots. She cost £2,086,458, roughly the equivalent in today's values of £550 million.

The first German battle-cruiser was the 19,400-ton *Von Der Tann*, completed in September 1910. She was also **the first German warship to be fitted with Parsons turbines and the first with four shafts**. She was hit four times at the Battle of Jutland, was interned at Scapa Flow after the First World War, was scuppered in June 1919, raised and broken up 1930-4.

The first warships ever to be subjected to aerial bombardment belonged to the Turkish Fleet. During the first Balkan War in 1913, while anchored in the Dardanelles, they were attacked by Farman bi-planes of the Royal Hellenic Navy which dropped four hand-grenades on them.

The finest series of battleships ever built were the ships of the Queen Elizabeth class. They were the *Barham*, the *Valiant*, the *Malaya*, the *Warspite* and the *Queen Elizabeth*. Their keels were laid down in 1912-13 and they were completed in 1915-16. Landstrom says of them: 'Through two world wars they were to play **a greater, longer and more important part than any other warships**.' Their eight 15in (38cm) guns fired shells which could pierce the thickest armour plating then in use and had an explosive power 50 per cent greater than any existing shell. They were **the first large warships to use only fuel oil** and their 75,000hp turbine engines gave them a speed of 24 knots. All except the *Barham*, which was sunk by German torpedoes in the Mediterranean in November 1941, survived the Second World War.

The First World War

The underlying causes of the First World War need not concern us here. Suffice it to say that the assassination of the Archduke Franz Ferdinand, heir to the Austro-Hungarian throne, by a Serbian terrorist on 28 June 1914, upset the European balance of power and by 6 August, Russia,

France and Britain were at war with Germany and Austro-Hungary. The Russian and Austrian navies were limited in strength and played only minor roles in the ensuing struggle. The comparative strength of the British, French and German Navies were as follows:

	BRITAIN	FRANCE	GERMANY
Battleships			
'Dreadnoughts'	22 (+8)*	4 (+8)	16 (+5)
'Pre-Dreadnoughts'	40	21	30
Battle-cruisers	9	—	6 (+1)
Armoured cruisers	48	25	15
Light cruisers	71 (+8)	3	33
Torpedo-boat destroyers	225 (+15)	81 (+2)	152 (+12)
Submarines	75	67	30

* +Indicates number being built.

The first naval casualty of the First World War was the German minelayer *Konigin Luise*. At 11am on 5 August the two destroyers *Lance* and *Landrail* and the new light cruiser *Amphion* sighted her off Southwold, Suffolk, having been informed by a trawler that there was a suspicious vessel 'throwing things overboard' in the vicinity. The *Konigin Luise* was sunk by gunfire before noon and her crew taken on board the *Amphion*, but not before she had planted a field of 180 mines. The following morning the *Amphion* struck one of these mines and sank so quickly that 151 men were drowned, including many of the prisoners from the *Konigin Luise*. Her commander, Captain Cecil H. Fox, survived and was later sent for by King George V and congratulated on being **the first Captain to lose his ship in the war!**

MINES AND MINESWEEPING

As the first British casualty of the war fell victim to a mine, it seems appropriate to pause here to examine the development of **the naval mine** at this stage. During the Russo-Japanese War of 1904-5 'non-controlled' mines were used successfully by both sides. **A 'non-controlled' mine** has positive buoyancy and is attached by a wire cable to a sinker on the sea-bed. It thus remains at a predetermined depth beneath the surface and explodes when hit by a ship.

The first attempts at minesweeping were made by the Japanese. A long length of stout wire, fitted with cutters and held underwater by two anchors, was towed through the minefield by two boats. The cutters sever the mine cable and the mine rises to the surface where it can be exploded or disarmed. That, at least, is the theory. The risk incurred by the vessels towing the 'sweep' needs no underlining! **'Controlled' mines** were detonated electrically by observers on the shore and were used mainly for harbour defence.

The British Admiralty, however, failed to appreciate the threat posed by the mine, 'considering it a weapon no chivalrous nation should use'. How crazy this assessment was can be appreciated by the fact that, in the next four years, German mines 'accounted for 214 British minesweepers, 46 warships (including five battleships and three cruisers), 225 auxiliaries, 259 merchant ships of 673,000 tons (84 more of 432,000 tons were damaged) and 63 fishing vessels'. (TAFFRAIL, *Swept Channels*.)

THE *EMDEN*

At the outbreak of the war the Germans had 10 major warships scattered around the world which proceeded to wage a gallant and aggressive hit-and-run campaign until sunk or blockaded. Of these **the most famous and most successful** was the 3544-ton light cruiser *Emden*. She left Pagan Island, in the Marianas, then owned by Germany, on 14 August 1914 and during September and October captured 19 British merchant ships, bombarded Madras and sank a Russian cruiser and a French destroyer. She finally surrendered to the Australian light cruiser *Sydney* on 9 November, having been driven ashore on Cocos Keeling Island. Her captain, **Karl von Müller**, won high praise for his skill, his boldness and his chivalry, and has been called **'one of the great seamen of the age'**.

The first submarine to be sunk in the First World War was the German U–15, which was rammed and cut in two by the cruiser *Birmingham* off Fair Isle, between Orkney and Shetland, on 9 August 1914.

The first important action of the war at sea and the first in which battle-cruisers were involved was the Battle of Heligoland Bight fought on 28 August 1914. The plan was to sweep the area of sea about the island of Heligoland, off the north-west coast of Germany where the Kiel Canal enters the mouth of the River Elbe, an area of great German naval activity. The action, though undoubtedly a success for the British, owed more to good luck than good planning. The Germans lost three light cruisers and a destroyer and over 1200 men killed, lost or taken prisoner. British casualties were 35 killed and 40 wounded; four ships were damaged but none lost.

The elusive *Emden. Mary Evans Picture Library.*

The first British naval loss from submarine attack was the cruiser *Pathfinder*, torpedoed by U–21 off St Abb's Head, Berwick, on 5 September 1914. She sank in four minutes with the loss of nearly all hands.

The influence of the submarine on naval warfare was emphatically **demonstrated for the first time** on 22 September 1914, when the German U–9 sank the three British armoured cruisers *Aboukir*, *Cressy* and *Hogue* in the North Sea 30 miles (48km) off Ijmuiden. 62 officers and 1397 men of the 2200 on board the three cruisers were lost. '**Never perhaps had so great a result been achieved by means so relatively small**' (CORBETT: *Naval Operations, Vol. I*).

HMS *Hogue*, sunk by *U9*, 22 September 1914. *Robert Hunt Library.*

THE VOYAGE OF THE *GOEBEN*

The incidents surrounding the voyage of the German battle-cruiser *Goeben* during the first week of the war deserve mention more because of the consequences arising therefrom than for any remarkable feat of seamanship in the event itself. '**No other single exploit of the war cast so long a shadow on the world**,' wrote the historian Barbara Tuchman, while Churchill was moved to declare that the *Goeben* carried with her 'for the peoples of the East and Middle East **more slaughter, more misery and more ruin than has ever before been borne within the compass of a ship**'.

Briefly, the events were as follows. At dawn on 4 August 1914 the *Goeben* and the light cruiser *Breslau* bombarded the Algerian ports of Bône and Philippeville in an attempt to disrupt the transport of troops to France, then headed east towards Turkey, Germany's secret ally, but were spotted at 10.35 by a superior British fleet under Admiral Sir Berkeley Milne (1855–1938). The British ultimatum to Germany did not, however, expire until midnight and the German cruisers were fast enough to elude the British and reach Messina by nightfall, where they rebunkered, Italy then being neutral. On the night of 6/7 August they slipped out of Messina and headed for the Dardanelles, eluding on the way a squadron of armoured cruisers under Rear-Admiral Trowbridge (1862–1926), patrolling the mouth of the Adriatic. They entered the Dardanelles on 10 August and undoubtedly played an important part in bringing Turkey into the war on Germany's side three months later. At the end of the war the *Goeben* was formally handed over to

the Turks, was repaired, refitted and renamed *Yavuz Sultan Selim* (Sultan Selim the Terrible). She remained for many years the principal ship of the Turkish Navy and was finally broken up in 1973, making her **the last capital ship of the First World War to be scrapped**.

The first British merchant ship to be sunk by a U-boat was the steamer *Glitra*. On 20 October 1914 she was stopped off the Norwegian coast by U–17 and, after the ship's company had been given time to lower the boats and escape, was sunk by a boarding party which opened her seacocks.

The Battle of Coronel resulted in **the first British naval defeat since the American War of 1812**. After the outbreak of war Admiral von Spee (1861–1914) was obliged to take his China Squadron of two heavy and three light cruisers across the Pacific to the coast of Chile, in consequence of British and Japanese superiority on the China station. Fearing that his intention was to reach the Atlantic and there disrupt Allied merchant shipping, the Admiralty sent an ill-assorted force under Rear-Admiral Sir Christopher Cradock (1862–1914) with orders to 'destroy the German cruisers'. The two squadrons met off Coronel, 250 miles (400km) south of Valparaiso, in the late afternoon of 1 November 1914, with the German ships to landward of the British, so that the latter were silhouetted against the setting sun while the former were scarcely visible against the dark background of the Chilean coast. Von Spee opened fire at 1900hrs; at 2000hrs Cradock's flag-ship, the armoured cruiser *Good Hope*, blew up and sank; the *Glasgow* and the *Otranto* were both damaged but managed to escape; finally at 2128hrs the light cruiser *Monmouth* was sunk. There were no survivors from the two British ships; the Germans suffered no loss of life.

Von Spee, as the British had feared, then took his squadron round Cape Horn, so the Admiralty at once despatched the battle-cruisers *Invincible* and *Inflexible* under Rear-Admiral Sir Doveton Sturdee (1859–1925) to the South Atlantic. Spee planned to destroy the wireless and coaling stations at Port Stanley on the Falkland Islands, but, arriving on 8 December, he found the British already there and, anxious to avoid damage to his ships, made off to the south-east at high speed. Sturdee set out in pursuit and destroyed the German ships at long range; von Spee went down with the armoured cruiser *Scharnhorst* at 1615hrs; at 1810hrs the armoured cruiser *Gneisenau* was sunk; at 1930hrs and 2035hrs respectively the light cruisers *Nürnberg* and *Leipzig* went down; only the light cruiser *Dresden* escaped. The British squadron suffered very few casualties but the Germans lost over 2200 men. Revenge for the defeat at Coronel had been swift and highly effec-tive. 'The Falklands had been fought out in the old style, **the last such action between surface ships by gunfire alone in the war**. Thereafter torpedoes, mines, submarines, and, to some extent, aircraft introduced complications unknown to Sturdee and Spee' (MARDER: *From the Dreadnought to Scapa Flow*). Fisher, then First Sea Lord, called the Falklands '**the only "substantial victory" of ours in the war**'.

The first offensive action by ship-borne aircraft took place on Christmas Day 1914, when three former English Channel ferries, *Engadine*, *Riviera* and *Empress*, converted into seaplane tenders and escorted by cruisers, destroyers and submarines, sailed into the Heligoland Bight and nine seaplanes set off to bomb the German Zeppelin sheds at Cuxhaven. But when the planes crossed the coastline they encountered dense fog which made it impossible to identify anything and they were obliged to drop their bombs at random. But they were seen by German warships in the Schilling roads and these took alarm and weighed anchor so rapidly that the battle-cruiser *Von der Tan* fouled another cruiser and both were

severely damaged. Owing to their prolonged search in the fog, the seaplanes were practically out of fuel and only two succeeded in getting back to their carriers. The others had to drop short in the sea. All the pilots were picked up, though one was rescued by a Dutch trawler, taken to Ijmuiden and eventually released as a ship-wrecked mariner.

The *Empress*, *Engadine* and *Riviera* were thus **the first Royal Navy aircraft carriers to be used in warfare.**

The Battle of the Dogger Bank, 24 January 1915, while a technical victory for the British, in that the Germans lost the armoured cruiser *Blücher* and 954 men, against total British casual-ties of 15 killed and 80 wounded, gave the

The battle-cruiser *Invincible*, proud hero of the Falklands, 1914. *Mary Evans Picture Library*.

Germans an unexpected reward in that it taught them a lesson which the British were only to learn at far greater expense at the Battle of Jutland in 1916. When ships were first clad in armour the range of the most powerful naval guns then in use was still not so great that their shells would follow a very high trajectory and the most vulnerable part of a ship remained its side. So that was where the heavy armour was placed. As the power of guns increased, the shells described a higher arc and descended at a steeper angle, making the deck as vulnerable as the side and necessitating the introduction of thicker and more extensive deck armour. To this was added the danger of a hit on a turret igniting waiting charges in the working chamber and the flash passing down the hoists to the ammunition chamber. This was what happened to the *Seydlitz* at Dogger Bank, and, although she managed to make good her escape, 159 men were killed in the explosion. The

Germans wasted no time in fitting anti-flash devices to the ammunition trunks of their ships, while the British were obliged to lose five good ships at Jutland in order to learn the same lesson.

After the Dogger Bank action the Grand Fleet (British) remained at Scapa Flow and the High Sea Fleet (German) at Jade Bay for the next 16 months, while the war at sea consisted mainly of the British trying to enforce a blockade on Germany and Germany trying to sink British merchant ships with mines and U-boats. This **commerce warfare** was known as the *guerre de course*, from the French term for a privateer, and was regarded by the English as not quite cricket. In 1900 Admiral Sir Arthur Wilson had called the submarine 'a damned un-English weapon' and the prejudice remained alive. Then on 4 February 1915, the Kaiser made his notorious declaration that the seas round Great Britain and Ireland were

a war zone in which all merchant ships would be sunk 'without it always being possible to avoid danger to the crews and passengers', described by the British as 'a procedure hitherto limited to savage races making no pretence at civilization as understood in Europe'.

Although the naval side of **the Gallipoli expedition** was later overshadowed by the greater fiasco of the amphibious landings, the campaign deserves mention as possibly **the most poorly mounted and ineptly controlled operation in modern British history**. Originally conceived as a purely naval undertaking, the idea was to bring aid to the Russians by forcing the Dardanelles, taking Constantinople and thereby knocking Turkey out of the war. On 19 February 1915, the British Navy bombarded the outer forts of the Dardanelles and met with little resistance, but then waited until 18 March to enter the straits. Again the forts were successfully bombarded; for the Turks, as was subsequently learnt, had run out of ammunition; on the next day they could have passed the Dardanelles unopposed. But the ships turned back and ran into a line of mines which sank two British and one French Pre-Dreadnoughts. The naval attack was called off and never renewed. This disastrous expedition, finally called off in December 1915, led to **the resignation of Admiral Fisher as First Sea Lord** and to the removal of Winston Churchill, at the time widely held responsible for its inception and its failure, from the Admiralty.

The first successful use of a decoy ship occurred on 23 June 1915. The submarine C–24 was towed, while submerged, by the armed trawler *Taranaki* to an area where U-boats were known to be hunting, in this case off Aberdeen, the submarine also being connected to the trawler by telephone. When U–40 surfaced and called on the trawler to stop, the cables were slipped, C–24 manoeuvred into position and scored a direct hit from 500yd (475m).

By far the most successful of the German armed commerce raiders of the First World War was the 4500-ton *Moewe*, commanded by Count Nikolaus zu Dohna-Schlodien. Between 29 December 1915, and 5 March 1916, she sank or captured 15 ships of a total of 65,000 tons. On her next voyage between 23 November 1916 and

22 March 1917, she sank or captured 24 ships totalling 119,600 tons. The largest and most important prize which fell to her was the 10,077-ton White Star liner *Georgic*, sunk by her 590 miles (949km) east-south-east of Cape Race on 10 December 1916.

The most famous decoy ships of the First World War were the **Q-ships,** as they came to be called in the latter part of 1916, though they were first used as early as November 1914. They were simply small merchant vessels armed with concealed guns which could be unmasked when stopped by an enemy submarine. **The first successful Q-boat** was the collier *Prince Charles* which sank the U–36 off the Orkneys on 24 July 1915. Though much romance has been attached to the exploits of the Q-ships, they were not a success. 180 vessels were equipped as such, of which 31 were sunk, the total Q-ship bag being 11 U-boats.

The tragic sinking of the *Lusitania* is mentioned elsewhere (p. 199). **The sinking of the 15,800-ton White Star liner *Arabic*** by U–24 off Ireland on 19 August 1915, caused an even greater uproar – though only 44 lives were lost, of which only 3 were American – and forced Germany to abandon unrestricted U-boat warfare as from 30 August. In future, submarine commanders were not allowed to sink passenger steamers, neutral or enemy, without saving the passengers and crew.

The only full fleet action of the First World War, the Battle of Jutland, known to the Germans as the Battle of the Skaggerak, was fought on 31 May 1916. It was **the first major naval engagement in which mines, submarines and torpedoes governed the actions of the commanders**; for though, in fact, neither of the first two played any part in the battle, the threat they posed could not be ignored. The action itself is **one of the most complicated in history**, which is scarcely surprising since some 250 ships of all types were involved. Briefly, the sequence of events was as follows: On 30 May the German High Seas Fleet under Vice-Admiral Scheer (1863–1928) put to sea, Admiral von Hipper (1863–1932), in command of the battle-cruisers, leading the way. The Grand Fleet, warned by intercepted wireless messages, at once followed suit, commanded by Admiral Sir John Jellicoe

(1859–1935), with Vice-Admiral Sir David Beatty's (1871–1936) battle-cruisers in the van. Beatty engaged Hipper early the following afternoon and the *Indefatigable* and *Queen Mary* were sunk. Beatty then saw the main High Seas Fleet approaching and turned back to join Jellicoe, pursued by Hipper. There followed a series of complex manoeuvres in which only Scheer's masterly execution of a series of 180° turns prevented him from being trapped inside a converging arc. Jellicoe did not attempt to pursue, fearing the risk from mines and submarines, though in fact the Germans had none of either on the scene. Then, half-an-hour later, Scheer suddenly reappeared in the centre of the British line and battle was renewed for some 15 minutes before Scheer turned away once more and Jellicoe did the same. But Jellicoe was now between Scheer and his home ports and in a chaotic night battle Scheer battered his way through the tail of the British fleet and made for home. By dawn Scheer was limping back to the Jade and Jellicoe realized that his quarry had escaped. **The last great fleet action in which the opponents battled it out within view of each other** was over.

The battle to decide who had been the winner was as bitterly contested as the naval battle itself, but lasted very much longer. Indeed, it still rages whenever two or three naval historians are gathered together round a table with an adequate supply of pepperpots! The bald statistics are as follows:

	BRITISH	GERMAN
Total of ships engaged	151	99
Battleships sunk	0	1
Battle-cruisers sunk	3	1
Armoured cruisers sunk	3	0
Light cruisers sunk	0	4
Destroyers sunk	8	5
Number of men at sea	60000	36000
Casualties	6097	2551

Jutland was, therefore, a German success in purely numerical terms, but it was a strategic success for the British in that the High Seas Fleet never again challenged British dominance of the North Sea.

The tragic end of the *Invincible*, sunk at Jutland, 31 May 1916. *Robert Hunt Library.*

The first submarine to be sunk by an aeroplane was the French submarine *Foucault*, sunk by an Austrian Lohner flying-boat on 15 September 1916.

One of the greatest mistakes made by the British during the First World War was their failure to introduce **the convoy system** for the protection of merchant shipping until May 1917. It was a mistake which very nearly cost the Allies the war. The general principle of merchant ships sailing in company for mutual protection against piracy is certainly older than recorded history, in which it can be traced back to the 12th century. In the 17th and 18th centuries convoys were the normal practice in time of war, indeed during the Revolutionary and Napoleonic Wars the master or owner of any ship which sailed out of convoy was liable to a fine of £100.

Why, then, were the British so dilatory in introducing this time-honoured method of safeguarding their merchant ships in the First World War? In a nutshell, the Navy were against it, and the statistical information was lacking to prove that their arguments were based on false premises. In addition, Jellicoe, who had become First Sea Lord in December 1916, maintained that the organizational problems such a system would present were insuperable. However, Commodore (later Admiral Sir Reginald) Henderson (1881–1939), after careful study of the statistics of the Ministry of Shipping, and backed by powerful support from the American Admiral William S. Sims (1858–1936) persuaded Lloyd George, then Prime Minister, that this was not the case and the system was introduced, but not

before losses of Allied and neutral shipping had reached its peak, in March that year, 1917, of 869,000 tons.

Between the Wars

At the time of her completion in 1920, the battle-cruiser HMS *Hood* was **the largest warship in the world**. She was built by John Brown & Co. on Clydebank, begun on 1 September 1916, launched on 22 August 1918, and completed on 5 March 1920. She had a displacement tonnage of 42,000 tons, an overall length of 86oft (262m), a beam of 105ft (32m) and a maximum draught of 31½ft (9.6m). Her eight 15in (38cm) guns fired a shell of nearly 2000lb (907kg) to an extreme range of 17 miles (27km). Her 144,000hp engines gave her a speed of over 31 knots. After the Battle of Jutland her design was modified to include an additional 5000 tons of armour, but all this, in the end, was still not enough. On 24 May 1941, she was sunk off Greenland by the German battleship *Bismarck*, with the loss of all but three of her crew of 1419 men.

The first battleship in the world to carry 16in (41cm) guns was the 32,720-ton Japanese *Nagato*. She was completed in 1920, survived the Second World War and was finally sunk in an atom bomb test at Bikini Atoll in July 1946.

The only British battleships to carry 16in (41cm) guns were the *Nelson* and the *Rodney*, the former completed in June 1927, the latter in

HMS *Hood*. Robert Hunt Library.

August of that year. Both displaced about 40,000 tons when fully loaded. The *Rodney* was scrapped in 1948, the *Nelson* in 1949.

The French Fantasque class of *contre-torpilleurs* (**torpedo-boat destroyers**), of which six were built in the mid-1930s, averaged 41 knots on their trials, **a record for a class of ships never equalled since.**

The term '**pocket battleship**' was coined to describe three heavily armoured cruisers built by Germany in the 1930s. Under the terms of the Treaty of Versailles Germany was prohibited from building any warship larger than 10,000 tons. Her answer was to build three miniature battle-cruisers armed with six 11in (28cm) guns firing 700lb (317kg) shells, eight 5.9in (15cm) guns and numerous anti-aircraft guns. They were **the first large men-of-war to have diesel drive only** and were capable of a cruising endurance of 20,000 miles (32,186km).

The first pocket battleship was the *Deutschland*, laid down in 1929. She was later followed by the *Admiral Scheer* and the *Admiral Graf Spee*. The *Graf Spee*, launched in June 1934, had a short career which ended when she was scuttled off Montevideo on 17 December 1939 after the action known as the Battle of the River Plate (see below). The *Deutschsland*'s name was then changed to *Lutzow* because the Germans felt that, if she too were sunk, the effect on the nation's morale of losing a ship with such a name would be disastrous. In the end she was sunk by British bombers at Swinemünde on 16 April 1945, exactly a week after her sister-ship the *Scheer* had suffered the same fate at Kiel.

The first capital ships designed to operate aircraft were the King George V class, of which five were built. Under the terms of the Treaty of Washington the first could not be laid down until 1936 and completion of the class was preceded by the outbreak of war. They had a displacement of 35,000 tons, length 745ft (227m), beam 103ft (31.4m), draught 34.5ft (10.2m) and speed of 29.5 knots. They were also **the first capital ships designed with a dual-purpose secondary armament.** Ironically, perhaps the best remembered of the five is the *Prince of Wales*, sunk by Japanese aircraft off the coast of Malaya, 10 December 1941.

The Second World War

The first shots in the Second World War were fired at 0440hrs on 1 September 1939, when the German battleship *Schleswig-Holstein* opened fire on a Polish fort in Danzig (Gdansk) harbour.

The first British ship to be sunk in the Second World War was the 13,465-ton Cunard liner *Athenia*. Bound from Liverpool to Montreal, she was torpedoed without warning by U–30 at 2100hrs on the night of 3 September 1939, when 200 miles (382km) west of the Hebrides. 112 of the 1400 people on board lost their lives, including 28 American citizens.

The first British warship to be sunk in the Second World War was the 26,500-ton aircraft carrier *Courageous*. On 17 September 1939, while cruising with four escorting destroyers in the Bristol Channel, she was torpedoed at dusk by U–29 and went down with the loss of 515 of her crew of 1260 men.

The first naval action of the Second World War was the Battle of the River Plate, fought on 13 December 1939, between the British cruisers *Exeter, Ajax* and *Achilles*, under the command of Commodore (later Admiral Sir) Henry Harwood (1888–1960), and the German pocket battleship *Admiral Graf Spee*, commanded by Captain H. Langsdorff. It was fought off the mouth of the River Plate which flows into the South Atlantic between Argentina and Uruguay. The *Exeter* carried six 8in (20cm) guns, the *Ajax* and *Achilles*

The Battle of the River Plate December 1939. *Robert Hunt Library.*

eight 6in (15cm) guns each, while the *Graf Spee* had six 11in (28cm) guns and eight 5.9in (15cm) guns and should, in theory, have been able to blow the lighter British ships out of the water. Harwood, however, manoeuvred his squadron with such skill that the *Graf Spee* was unable to concentrate her fire on any one ship, and though the *Exeter* was completely silenced and the *Achilles* and the *Ajax* were both badly damaged, after an hour and 20 minutes the *Graf Spee* turned away under cover of smoke and made for Montevideo, with the *Ajax* and the *Achilles* hard on her heels. Unable to break out and unable, under international law, to remain in a neutral port, on 17 December Langsdorff scuttled his ship on Hitler's orders and, two days later, shot himself.

The last occasion on which a ship was boarded in wartime occurred on 16 February 1940, when the 1870-ton Tribal class destroyer HMS *Cossack* entered Josing Fjord, in Norwegian territorial waters, and rescued 299 British prisoners-of-war from the 8053-ton tanker *Altmark*. These men had formed the crews of nine merchant ships which had been sunk in the South Atlantic by the *Graf Spee*, to which the *Altmark* had acted as auxiliary. After the *Spee* was scuttled off Montevideo on 17 December 1939, the *Altmark* hid in the South Atlantic for nearly two months, then made a dash for home, but was spotted by British aircraft on 14 February in Norwegian territorial waters and took refuge in Josing Fjord, where,

Above: Two Lascar seamen who were imprisoned in the *Altmark* coming ashore at Leith. *Below:* HMS *Cossack*, the Tribal-class destroyer which rescued them. Both pictures *Robert Hunt Library.*

two days later, she was boarded by men from the *Cossack*, under the command of Captain (later Admiral of the Fleet Sir Philip) Vian (1894–1968), and the prisoners released. 'A sharp hand-to-hand fight followed, in which four Germans were killed and five wounded. . . . The search began for the British prisoners. They were soon found in their hundreds, battened down, locked in store-rooms, even in an empty oil-tank. Then came the cry, "The Navy's here". The doors were broken in and the captives rushed on deck. . . . Their rescue and Captain Vian's conduct aroused a wave of enthusiasm in Britain almost equal to that which followed the sinking of the *Graf Spee*. "The Navy's here" was passed from lip to lip.' (CHURCHILL, *The Second World War*.)

The first aircraft carrier to be sunk by a surface ship was the 26,500-ton HMS *Glorious*. Surprised by the German battle-cruisers *Scharnhorst* and *Gneisenau* with all her planes on deck, she and her two escorting destroyers, *Ardent* and *Acasta*, were sunk off Norway on 8 June 1940 with the loss of 1474 officers and men of the Royal Navy and 41 of the Royal Air Force.

The first occasion in history that a fleet was destroyed by enemy aircraft was on 11 November 1940, when 21 Fairey Swordfish torpedo-bombers took off from HMS *Illustrious* and flew to Taranto where they sank one Italian battleship, caused one to be beached and put a third out of action for six months. Two British aircraft were shot down.

One of the saddest incidents in British naval history was **the destruction of the French fleet** in Oran harbour, Algeria, on 3 July 1940. By then France had been over-run by the Germans, an armistice having been signed on 22 June, and de Gaulle had escaped to England to rally the Free French. The few French ships in British ports were disarmed, those at Alexandria were disarmed by the French themselves, but the most powerful force was at Oran. Vice-Admiral Sir James Somerville (1882–1949), commanding the British squadron based at Gibraltar, presented the following ultimatum – the French ships must either join the British, sail to a British or neutral port for internment, or scuttle themselves. When the French admiral refused these demands, Somerville opened fire. Two battleships and one battle-cruiser were destroyed and 1300 French sailors were killed. It was, said Churchill, who had been Prime Minister of Great Britain since 10 May, 'a hateful decision, **the most unnatural and painful in which I have ever been concerned**'.

The first fleet engagement of the war took place off Calabria on 9 July 1940. Admiral Cunningham (1883–1963), who was then Commander-in-Chief of the British naval forces in the Mediterranean, was escorting a convoy from Malta to Alexandria when he encountered an Italian force of two battleships and 16 destroyers taking a convoy to North Africa. Cunningham interposed his fleet between the enemy and their base and, despite his inferiority in numbers, put them to flight. 'This spirited action established the ascendancy of the British Fleet in the Mediterranean and Italian prestige suffered a blow from which it never recovered' (CHURCHILL, *The Second World War*).

The biggest fleet action of the war in the Mediterranean was the Battle of Cape Matapan, fought between British and Italian fleets off the southern extremity of Greece on 28 March 1941. The Italian battleship *Vittorio Veneto* was badly damaged by torpedo aircraft, the cruisers *Zara*, *Fiume* and *Pola* and two destroyers were sunk. The British fleet suffered no loss of any kind. From now on Italian surface naval strength ceased to be a significant factor in the war.

The *Bismarck*, at the time of her completion early in 1941, was **the heaviest and most powerful battleship afloat**. She displaced 42,345 tons, carried eight 15in (38cm) and twelve 5.9in (15cm) guns and was so well constructed that Germany claimed she was unsinkable. She left Norwegian waters, in company with the cruiser *Prinz Eugen*, on 21 May 1941, and was sighted in the Denmark Strait, between Iceland and Greenland, on the 23rd. On the 24th she sank the British battle-cruiser *Hood* (see p. 108) and so badly damaged the battleship *Prince of Wales* that the latter was obliged to break off the action. However, her position was now known and the cruisers *Norfolk* and *Suffolk* continued to shadow her while other ships moved in for the kill. Then for $31\frac{1}{2}$ hours contact was lost and it was not until 1030hrs on the 26th that she was resighted by a Catalina flying boat of the Royal Air Force Coastal Command. The main body of the Home Fleet was now steaming towards the reported position of the *Bismarck*, while another force, including the battleships *Rodney* and *Ramilles*, was converging on the area. At 0847hrs on the 27th she came under fire from the *King George V* and *Rodney* and by 1015hrs her guns were silent. The British battleships, acutely short of fuel, now left the scene and the *coup de grâce* was delivered by the cruiser *Dorsetshire* who fired two torpedoes into the blazing wreck. She finally heeled over and sank at 1036hrs, after an action lasting five days and requiring the co-ordinated movement of 19 major British warships.

The most successful armed merchant raider of this, or any, war was the *Atlantis*. Launched in 1937 as the 7860-ton *Goldenfels* of the Hansa Line, in 1939 she was armed with six 5.9in (15cm) guns. Between 31 March 1940, and 22 November 1941, she steamed 102,000 miles (164,150km) in the Atlantic, Pacific and Indian Oceans, under a variety of disguises and often with Japanese assistance, during which time she captured or sank 22 ships amounting to 145,697 tons. She was finally sunk off Ascension Island by the British cruiser *Devonshire*.

The first loss suffered by the United States Navy in the Second World War occurred on 31 October 1941, five weeks before America officially declared war, when the destroyer *Reuben James* was torpedoed and sunk with heavy loss of life while escorting a convoy west of Iceland.

The shortest time taken to build a Liberty Ship was 4 days 15½ hours. Liberty Ships were mass-produced, prefabricated cargo ships of 7100 gross

HMS **Rodney. Mansell Collection.**

tonnage (10,500dwt) built under the auspices of the US Maritime Commission between 1941 and 1945 to replace tonnage sunk by enemy U-boats. Their dimensions were: length 441ft 6in (134.5m); beam 56ft 10in (17.3m). They had a speed of 11 knots and in all 2770 were built. 'The Sunderland shipbuilding firm of Joseph L. Thompson & Sons designed and built *Dorington Court* in 1939 for Court Line Ltd. of London. She was a single-screw steamer of economical design, having a cargo capacity of 10,200 tons and a service speed of 11 knots. This design was adopted for the first British wartime "emergency" ship *Empire Liberty*, and formed the prototype from which the "Liberty Ship" was evolved' (ROBIN CRAIG, *Steam Tramps and Cargo Liners*).

The only known occasion on which both hunter and hunted were sunk, each by the other, occurred off Shark Bay, Western Australia, on 19 November 1941, when the Australian cruiser *Sydney* encountered the German surface-raider *Kormoran* and the former, having been torpedoed by the latter, managed to sink her opponent by gunfire, before she herself blew up. Of the *Sydney*'s crew of over 700 none survived.

One of the most famous German warships of the Second World War was the battle-cruiser *Scharnhorst*, not to be confused with the *Scharnhorst* of the First World War (see p. 104), though both were named after General Gerhard von Scharnhorst (1755–1813) who is remembered for having reorganized the Prussian Army in 1807. In both world wars the sister ship of the *Scharnhorst* was the *Gneisenau*, named after Count August von Gneisenau (1760–1831), the distinguished Prussian soldier and Blucher's Chief of Staff at the Battle of Waterloo. The latter pair were laid down in 1934 after Hitler had given up any pretence of heeding the shipbuilding restrictions imposed upon Germany by the Treaty of Versailles. They had the following statistics: displacement 31,000 tons; length 741.5ft (226m); beam 98.5ft (30m); draught 24.6ft (7.5m); speed 32 knots; main armament nine 11in (28cm) guns.

The two sisters left Kiel on January 1941, and in the next two months sank 115,622 tons of Allied shipping in the North Atlantic before returning to harbour at Brest, where they remained blockaded for nearly a year. In January 1942, Hitler, obsessed with the idea that Britain was about to invade Norway, demanded that they be brought home, and so on 12 January, they made their famous dash up the Channel and managed, by successfully jamming British radar, to get to within 20 miles (32.2km) of Boulogne before they were spotted.

Air and sea attacks were then launched but both ships managed to reach port by the morning of 13 February. However, it was subsequently learned that both had hit mines which had damaged them so severely that the *Scharnhorst* was out of action for a year, while the *Gneisenau* was never again operational and was eventually towed to Gdynia where she was scuttled in March 1945. Nevertheless the incident caused much commotion and outcry in England at the time.

In March 1943, the *Scharnhorst*, now back in commission, sailed north to Norway and her eventual doom. In September, with the *Tirpitz* and ten destroyers, she took part in a successful raid on Spitzbergen. On 24 December she sailed out of Alta Fjord to attack an Allied convoy heading for north Russia, but was driven off by three British cruisers which drove her into the waiting

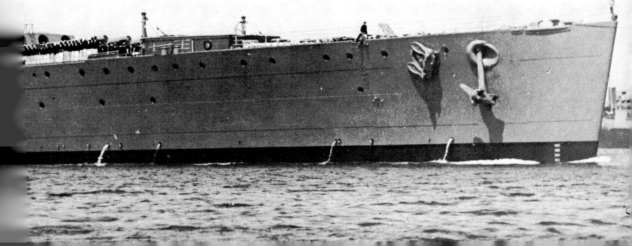

arms of Admiral Sir Bruce Fraser, later Lord Fraser of North Cape (1888–1981) in the battleship *Duke of York*. Battered by heavy gunfire, she was finally sunk by torpedoes and only 36 of her 1900-man crew were saved.

The bombardment of Spitzbergen (see above) was **the one and only occasion on which the super-battleship *Tirpitz***, sister ship to the *Bismarck*, **fired her heavy guns**. She displaced 42,500 tons, was completed in 1941 and spent her entire working life in Norwegian waters where she presented a permanent threat to the British convoys to North Russia. She was damaged several times by bombers and by mines laid by midget submarines (X-craft), and was finally sunk by the RAF on 12 November 1944.

The first X-craft was laid down in 1941 and thereafter they were used on several occasions during the war. They were perfect submarines in miniature, were towed to the target area and were then able to operate for several days on their own. The major limit to their endurance was crew fatigue, for they were quite remarkably uncomfortable.

X-craft must not be confused with **'chariots'**, which were a type of manned torpedo, and were, in fact, **first used by the Italians at the end of the First World War**. Two men in frogmen's suits rode astride the chariot which was the same size as a normal 21in (51.5cm) torpedo and was fitted with a detachable warhead which could be attached by magnets to the hull of a ship. In the Second World War the Italians were again the first to use them and called them *maiale* – hogs. They used them with considerable success against the British Mediterranean Fleet in December 1941, when three *maiale* got into Alexandria harbour and fixed time bombs under the battleships *Queen Elizabeth* and *Valiant*, causing severe damage to both.

The only ex-German destroyer commissioned by the Royal Navy was the *Nonsuch* (ex-*Z38*). She was launched at Kiel on 11 November 1941, and broken up in May 1950.

HMS *Queen Elizabeth* after she had been damaged by *maiale* in Alexandria harbour. *Robert Hunt Library.*

PEARL HARBOR

The most treacherous blow ever struck at the navy of a country while not actually at war was certainly the Japanese attack on the US Pacific Fleet at Pearl Harbor on 7 December 1941. A fleet of six Japanese aircraft carriers with supporting battleships and cruisers set sail from the Kurile Islands on 26 November under the command of Vice-Admiral Chuichi Nagumo (1887–1944) while a Japanese delegation was actually in Washington discussing US/Japanese relationships with reference to the Sino/Japanese War. They launched their bombers and fighters from a point 275 miles (442km) north of Hawaii, and within the next hour sank four US battleships and severely damaged three others. Eleven other ships were sunk or severely damaged, 3300 US personnel were killed and 1272 wounded. The United States at once declared war on Japan and President Roosevelt telephoned Mr Churchill to say, 'We are all in the same boat now.'

The Japanese used their Long Lance torpedoes for the first time at the Battle of the Java Sea on 27 February 1942. The Long Lance, with a speed of 49 knots, a range of 12½ miles (20.1km) and a warhead of 1210lb (549kg) was then the best in the world. The Allied Fleet, under the Dutch Admiral Doorman, intercepted a Japanese squadron north of Surabaya and, in two days, without loss to themselves, the Japanese sank six Allied cruisers and four destroyers.

The first sea battle ever to be fought between two fleets which never came in sight of each other was the Battle of the Coral Sea, on 7–8 May 1942, the contest being waged by aircraft operating from carriers over 100 miles (161km) apart. The American fleet was commanded by Admiral Fletcher, the Japanese by Admiral Takagi. The Japanese lost the small carrier *Shohu*; the large carrier *Shokatu* was severely damaged. The Americans lost the carrier *Lexington* and suffered some damage to the carrier *Yorktown*. As a result of these losses, Admirals Fletcher and Takagi decided almost simultaneously to withdraw from the contest, which was therefore declared a draw. It was, however, a major strategic success for the Allies because it stopped the proposed Japanese attack on Port Moresby.

The Battle of Midway was **one of the most decisive battles in naval history** in that it marked the turning point of Japanese fortunes in the Pacific. On 3 June 1942, American aircraft located a Japanese force of four fleet carriers under Admiral Nagumo, supported by a force of seven battleships and attendant cruisers and destroyers, under the Commander-in-Chief, Admiral Yamamoto (1884–1943), heading for Midway Island. Rear-Admiral Spruance (1886–1969), commanding a force of three carriers, six cruisers and nine destroyers, scored a brilliant tactical victory by attacking the enemy carriers at a time when they had all their aircraft on deck. All four Japanese carriers were sunk, making the Battle of Midway **the greatest defeat in Japanese naval history**.

The last photograph taken of the USS *Lexington* in an operational condition. *Robert Hunt Library.*

The longest series of naval battles in the Second World War was fought off Guadalcanal between August 1942, and February 1943. '**Not since the Anglo-Dutch wars had two powerful navies engaged in such a prolonged, intensive and destructive naval campaign** as that which took place for six long months around Guadalcanal. Serious mistakes were made on both sides and the honours were approximately even in skill and gallantry displayed. The margin of the

American success was their eventual superiority of numbers and of equipment, both on the surface and in the air' (DUPUY, *Encyclopaedia of Military History*).

One of the most famous ships in the US Pacific Fleet was the amazingly durable aircraft carrier *Enterprise*, affectionately known as the 'Big E'. Launched on 21 May 1938, she displaced 19,900 tons, had an overall length of 809½ft (247m), was 83ft (25m) in the beam, with a draught of 22ft (6.7m). During the Second World War she won

USS *Pennsylvania* firing on Leyte. *Robert Hunt Library.*

twenty battle stars, the US equivalent of British battle honours, was hit by Japanese *kamikaze* planes (see p. 54) on three occasions, once by a horizontal bomber and twice by dive-bombing planes. In all she was in 20 separate actions against the Japanese and was finally decommissioned in 1947.

The attack on the *Tirpitz* by X-craft on 22 September 1943, is **the most celebrated instance of the use of these four-man midget submarines.** Six midgets set out from Scotland towed by standard submarines, but only two managed to reach the target. These, however, succeeded in laying four two-ton delayed action mines beneath the *Tirpitz* and, although she escaped complete destruction, she was so seriously damaged that she never put to sea again.

The only known case in the Second World War of a U-boat captain deliberately firing on the crew of a ship he had torpedoed occurred on 13 March 1944, when *Kapitanleutnant* Eck sank the Greek ship *Peleus* off the coast of West Africa. Fearful that the floating wreckage would betray his presence to Allied air patrols, he opened fire on the survivors, but three survived, were rescued and reported the incident. After the war Eck was tried by court martial and shot.

The most successful U-boat hunter of the Second World War was Captain F. J. Walker, R.N. Anti-submarine ships under his command accounted for a total of 23 U-boats in the Atlantic.

The most successful German U-boat commander during the Second World War was Otto Kretschmer (*b* 1912), who sank a total 266,629 tons of Allied shipping in the first 18 months of the war. In March 1941, his U-boat was sunk by the British destroyer *Walker* and Kretschmer was taken prisoner and spent the rest of the war in Canada. He later became an admiral in the Federal German Navy.

D-DAY

The greatest amphibious operation in history was that launched by the Allied Forces on the beaches of Normandy on 6 June 1944, ever since known as D-Day. It involved 1213 warships and 4126 landing ships and assorted small craft carrying 176,000 troops and their equipment. This was for the assault phase alone. '**The history of warfare knows no other like undertaking from the point of view of its scale, its vast conception and its masterly execution,**' wired Stalin to Churchill.

The first ship to be hit by a Japanese suicide aircraft, known as *kamikaze*, was the Australian cruiser *Australia* on 17 October 1944. She suffered casualties but no serious damage.

The first successful *kamikaze* attack occurred on 25 October during the Battle of Leyte Gulf when five Zero aircraft sank the US escort carrier *St Lo*, and damaged the carriers *Kalinin Bay*, *Kitukin Bay* and *White Plains*. In all 34 US ships were sunk and 288 were damaged.

The greatest naval battle ever joined, in terms of the area over which it ranged and the size of the opposing forces, was the Battle of Leyte Gulf, fought between the main fleet of Japan and the US Third and Seventh Fleets on 23–26 October 1944. In all 282 warships were involved, 216 American, 2 Australian and 64 Japanese, compared with 250 at the Battle of Jutland. The engagement also saw **the largest scale destroyer attack of the Second World War, the last battleship versus battleship action and the only fleet action between a line of battleships and a line of carriers.**

TOTAL LOSSES

JAPANESE	UNITED STATES
3 battleships	1 light carrier
1 fleet carrier	2 escort carriers
3 light carriers	3 destroyers
6 heavy cruisers	1 submarine
4 light cruisers	
9 destroyers	
1 submarine	

The battle marked the end of the Japanese Navy as an effective fighting force.

The largest guns ever installed in a ship were the nine 18in (45.7cm) guns carried by the Japanese battleships *Yamato* and *Musashi*, which had a range of 27 miles (43.5km). The shells weighed 3200lb (1452kg) each. Fortunately for the Allies, both were sunk by US carrier-borne aircraft

HMS *Vanguard. Robert Hunt Library.*

before either had fired their big guns in anger. The *Musashi* was sunk off Luzon during the series of battles collectively known as Leyte Gulf after receiving 19 torpedo and 17 bomb hits on 24 October 1944. The *Yamato* was sunk on 7 April 1945, in what was to prove the last gasp of the Imperial Japanese Navy.

Post War

The largest battleship ever built by Britain was the *Vanguard*, laid down at Clydebank in October 1941, launched in 1944 and completed in April 1946. Displacing over 50,000 tons when fully laden, she had an overall length of 814ft (248m), a speed of 29½ knots and was armed with eight 15in (38cm) and sixteen 5¼in (13.3cm) guns, none of which she ever fired in anger. She was finally broken up in 1960.

At the time of her sinking in December 1949, HMS *Implacable* was **the oldest warship in the world.** She was 148 years old, having started life in 1801 as the 74-gun French warship *Duguay-*

Trouin. She was captured by the British in November 1805, and in 1855 became a training ship for boys at Devonport. In 1912 she was moved to Portsmouth as a training ship for sea-scouts. During the Second World War she was used as a depot ship but, by December 1949, her timbers had rotted beyond repair so she was taken out to sea and sunk.

The Chinese Civil War, despite the magnitude of the forces involved (the battle fought around Suchow in November 1948, involved over 1,000,000 men), aroused little interest in the West. One incident, however, because it concerned a frigate of the Royal Navy, did hit the headlines of the free world – the escape down the River Yangtse of HMS *Amethyst* during the night of 30 July 1949. On 30 April the *Amethyst*, on her way to Nanking with supplies, was badly damaged by Communist gunfire; 13 of the crew were killed, including the captain, Lieutenant-Commander B. M. Skinner, and 15 wounded. 44 more men lost their lives in unsuccessful attempts by HMS *London*, *Black Swan* and *Consort* to bring the damaged ship down river. So, all attempts to negotiate her release having failed, and repairs having been improvised by her crew,

Lieutenant-Commander J. S. Kerans, who had been put in command, decided to make a dash for it and brought her 140 miles (225km) down river to the sea, which he reached with only 9 tons of fuel remaining. 'The *Amethyst*'s passage was **a superb feat of pilotage carried out at full speed on a pitch dark night,**' said the Admiralty.

The first major commitment of naval forces after the Second World War was occasioned by the outbreak of the **Korean War** (though there was never any official declaration of war) on 25 June 1950, when North Korean Forces crossed the 38th parallel into South Korea. United Nations forces, of which the bulk were supplied by the United States, went to the aid of South Korea and the US Seventh Fleet effectively blockaded the Korean coast and gave valuable gunfire support.

One of the most remarkable and successful amphibious operations ever undertaken and one of the greatest strategic coups in history was the landing of two US divisions at Inchon on 15 September 1950. Against overwhelming logistical and geographical odds, in that a single month was allowed to prepare for an operation that would normally have taken several and that 30ft (9m) tidal variations and difficult and treacherous beaches made Inchon a highly impractical site for an amphibious landing, the US forces gained an overwhelming victory, thanks largely to the genius and determination of General Douglas MacArthur (1880–1964).

The first US warship to carry anti-aircraft guided missiles was the 13,600-ton cruiser *Boston*, re-commissioned at the Philadelphia Navy Yard on 1 November 1955. The missiles had a range of 20 miles (32.2km) and were able to 'home' on their target by a radar device.

The first major reinforcement of troops from the sea by helicopters occurred during the Anglo-French invasion of Egypt in November 1956. The aim was to regain control of the Suez Canal which President Nasser had nationalized the previous July and to this end 415 British Commandos and 23 tons of stores were landed at the mouth of the canal by carrier-based helicopters in 89 minutes. Militarily the operation was a success but was called off before its full object had been achieved on account of the hostile reaction of the United Nations.

The first British naval vessel designed to test guided missiles was HMS *Girdle Ness*, converted in 1956 from a landing craft maintenance vessel.

HMS *Amethyst* after her dramatic dash down the River Yangtse.

The ship-to-air guided missile *Seaslug* was tested from the *Girdle Ness* in 1957 with 'marked success'.

The first nuclear-powered surface fighting ship in the world and the first surface ship to be armed with a main battery of guided missiles and engined by a nuclear propulsion plant was the 14,000-ton USS *Long Beach*, launched at Quincy, Massachusetts, USA on 14 July 1959.

The first British guided missile ship was the destroyer HMS *Devonshire*, launched in June 1960, and designed to carry the Royal Navy's anti-aircraft guided weapon the *Seaslug*. She was also **the first British warship with an automatic pilot**.

The greatest war fought by the United States since 1945 started in December 1961, President Kennedy having agreed on 11 October to support the government of South Vietnam against attacks by Communist Viet Cong guerrillas. It involved no major naval engagements but saw **the first operational use of hovercraft** which were used in the Mekong Delta in June 1966.

Helicopters were first used in a naval operation during the Korean War, to help detect mines laid by the North Koreans from sampans off the coast round Wonsan. The mines were the latest Soviet type and had been laid by the North Koreans under instructions from Russian advisers.

The US Navy's first warships to be powered by gas turbines were the Asheville class of patrol gunboats which were built as a result of the Cuban missile crisis of the early 1960s. With a displacement of 235 tons fully loaded, they are capable of a speed in excess of 40 knots and carry a crew of 24 or 27 officers and men. The Asheville was the biggest class of patrol boat built for the US Navy since the Second World War.

The first large warship to be sunk by a surface-to-surface guided missile was the Israeli destroyer *Eilat*. On 21 October 1967, she was hit by three Russian-built 'Styx' anti-ship missiles fired by Egyptian Komar-class missile craft sheltering in Port Said harbour ten miles (16km) away. 'The pairing of the fast patrol boat with the anti-ship missile has had an impact as dramatic on naval planning as the introduction of the submarine in the First World War and naval aviation and aircraft carriers in the 1920s and 1930s.

'Naval historians compare the sinking of the *Eilat* with the battle between the first Ironclads

The Israeli destroyer *Eilat*, sunk by missiles on 21 October 1967. *Associated Press.*

The USS *Pueblo*, captured by North Korean patrol boats, January 1968. *Associated Press.*

during the American Civil War and General Billy Mitchell's early demonstration of the effect of airpower on battleships . . . Credit for the idea of marrying the guided missile to the fast patrol boat hull is generally attributed to Sergei Georgievich Gorshkov, Soviet Admiral of the Fleet. Realizing that the Soviet Navy was totally incapable of competing with the air power of a US Navy task force at sea, he set out to devise a quick and inexpensive threat to American aircraft carriers. The answer was **the Komar**, derived from the wooden-hulled P.6-class torpedo-boats and equipped with two SS–N–2A "Styx" missile launchers, one on each side of the aft superstructure' (ROY MCLEAVY, *Naval Fast Strike Craft and Patrol Boats*).

The 906-ton intelligence ship *Pueblo* was **the first American naval vessel to be captured at sea since the War of 1812.** On the night of 22–23 January 1968, she was escorted by four North Korean patrol boats into the port of Wonsan, the Koreans claiming that she had violated their territorial waters. The crew of 82 and the body of one man who had died were finally handed over on 23 December 1968, after the chief US negotiator at Panmunjom, Major-General Gilbert H. Woodward, signed a document constituting a formal 'admission' by the American side that the *Pueblo* had entered North Korean waters, 'solemnly apologizing' for the vessel's 'grave acts of sabotage' and giving a 'firm assurance' against any repetition of such acts. At the same time, however, General Woodward publicly repudiated this document and made it clear that he had only signed it in order to secure the release of the *Pueblo*'s crew.

THE COD WAR

The dispute between Iceland on the one hand and the United Kingdom and West Germany on the other, which came to be known as **the 'Cod War'**, arose from Iceland's unilateral decision on 1 September 1972, to extend her territorial waters from 12 to 50 miles (19–80km). A growing number of clashes between British and West German trawlers continuing to fish within the 50-mile (80km) limit and Icelandic gunboats trying to prevent this by cutting the trawlers' fishing nets and other gear led, after much pressure from the fishing ports, to the dispatch on 23 January 1973, of a fast ocean-going tug, the *Statesman*, to protect British trawlers, and on 18 March **the first live warning shots** to be used in the 'Cod War' were fired across the bows of the *Statesman* by the Icelandic gunboat *Odinn*.

The first serious accident occurred on 26 May when the Icelandic gunboat *Aegir* fired six or eight live shots which holed the British trawler *Everton* in the forecastle and below the waterline.

The first incident between a British frigate and an Icelandic gunboat occurred on 7 June when HMS *Scylla* collided with the *Aegir* off the north-west coast of Iceland: the damage was slight and there were no casualties. But the use of

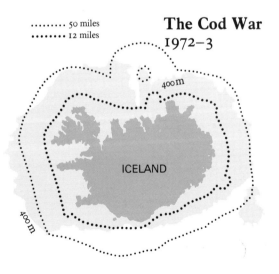

50 miles
12 miles

The Cod War
1972–3

400m

ICELAND

400m

The map shows the 12-mile fishing limit imposed by Iceland in 1958 and the 50-mile limit of 1972. The outer line marks the 400-metre isobath which limits the plankton-rich continental shelf constituting the main fishing grounds around Iceland.

frigates to protect the trawlers changed the nature of the dispute and in mid-October the two Prime Ministers, Mr Olafur Johannesson and Mr Edward Heath, reached agreement on general terms and brought the 14-month Cod War to an end.

THE FALKLANDS WAR 1982

The first missile war in history started on 2 April 1982 when 2500 Argentinian troops invaded the Falkland Islands, then defended by a garrison of 84 Royal Marines, who surrendered after three hours. The following day the Argentinians invaded Grytviken, South Georgia, where 22 marines held out for seven hours before surrendering. By 5 April no less than 20 ships had left Portsmouth, among them the aircraft carriers *Invincible* and *Hermes*, to begin what was soon to become **Britain's biggest military undertaking since the Second World War**. In command was Rear-Admiral Sandy Woodward. The naval side of the conflict is here set out chronologically:

7 April: Britain declares a 200-mile (322km) maritime exclusion zone round the Falkland Islands.

9 April: The 48,000-grt P & O cruise liner *Canberra* sails from Southampton carrying 2000 Paras and Royal Marines, also 30 nurses.

14 April: Defence Secretary John Nott warns that the Royal Navy will sink any Argentine vessel, warship or merchantman, found within 200 miles (322km) of the Falklands after midnight on 28 April.

25 April: Naval helicopters attack the Argentine submarine *Santa Fe*, a former American vessel bought in 1971, in Grytviken Harbour. Her crew run her aground and surrender. South Georgia recaptured.

2 May: 13,645-ton Argentine cruiser *General Belgrano* sunk by two wire-guided Tigerfish torpedoes fired from the nuclear submarine HMS *Conqueror*, with the loss of 368 lives. She was '**the largest ship sunk in a naval action since American attacks in the Inland Sea of Japan in 1945**' (JOHN LAFFIN, *Fight for the Falklands*). At the time of the attack she was 36 miles (58km) outside the exclusion zone.

4 May: HMS *Sheffield* hit by Exocet missile fired from an Argentine French-built Super Étendard fighter-bomber. After four and a half hours Captain 'Sam' Salt gave the order to abandon ship; she was later sunk by explosives. Twenty men lost their lives. The 3660-ton *Sheffield* was a Type 42 destroyer built by Vickers and commissioned in 1975. She cost £23.2 million. This was **the first class of ships to be equipped with the Sea Dart missile system.**

12 May: Cunard's 65,863grt *Queen Elizabeth II*, requisitioned to carry 5th Infantry Brigade (3250 men) to the South Atlantic, sails from Southampton.

15 May: Marines carry out raid on Pebble Island, supported by **'the heaviest British naval bombardment since World War II'** (LAFFIN), and destroy 11 Argentine aircraft.

20 May: UN Peace efforts break down; orders given to land.

21 May: Men of Royal Marines, 40, 42 and 45 Commandos and 2nd and 3rd Para Bns embark on landing craft from the assault ships HMS *Fearless* and *Intrepid* and land on West Falkland. 3250-ton Type 21 frigate HMS *Ardent* (completed 1977) sunk by air attack. 24 killed.

23 May: HMS *Antelope* (Type 21, completed 1975) sinks after unexploded bomb detonates. 2 killed.

25 May: HMS *Coventry* (Type 42 destroyer, completed 1978), sunk by bombs. 19 killed. *Atlantic Conveyor*, 15,000-ton container ship requisitioned from Cunard, abandoned after being hit by an Exocet. 12 killed, including Captain Ian North.

8 June: 5550-ton landing ships *Sir Tristram* and *Sir Galahad* sunk by air attack during landing at Bluff Cove. 56 killed. HMS *Plymouth* (Type 12 frigate) badly damaged by bombs. No casualties.

11 June: HMS *Glamorgan* (County Class destroyer) hit by a land-fired Exocet. 9 killed.

14 June: 'In Port Stanley at 9 o'clock p.m. Falkland time tonight, 14 June, surrendered to me all the Argentine armed forces in East and West Falkland, together with their impedimenta.... The Falkland Islands are once more under the Government desired by their inhabitants. God save the Queen. Signed J. J. Moore.'

A type-21 frigate closes in on HMS *Sheffield*, spraying water from her hoses to help fight the fire. *Press Association.*

Naval Strengths

	CHINA	FRANCE	INDIA	ITALY	JAPAN	SPAIN	SWEDEN	USSR	UK	USA
1952–3										
Fleet Aircraft Carriers	—	—	—	—	—	—	—	—	6	28
Light Fleet Aircraft Carriers	—	2	—	—	—	—	1	—	6	8
Escort & Maintenance Carriers	—	1	—	—	—	—	—	—	4	66
Battleships	—	2	—	2	—	—	—	3	5	15
Cruisers	—	5	1	3	—	6	2	14	16	74
Destroyers	7	9	3	3	—	20	6	85	93	348
Frigates, Escort Vessels	23	28	19	43	24	12	10	64	165	269
Submarines	—	12	4	—	—	6	7	370	53	200
1962–3										
Heavy Aircraft Carriers	—	—	—	—	—	—	—	—	—	10
Large Aircraft Carriers	—	—	—	—	—	—	—	—	3	24
Light Aircraft Carriers	—	4	1	—	—	—	—	—	2	5
Escort Carriers, Aircraft Carriers & Commando Carriers	—	—	—	—	—	—	—	—	2	19
Battleships	—	—	—	—	—	—	—	—	—	4
Cruisers	—	3	2	2	—	5	—	22	5	43
Leaders, Large Destroyers Frigates (DLG)	—	—	—	2	—	—	—	—	2	17
Destroyers	4	18	3	5	18	27	—	165	25	356
Destroyer Escorts & Frigates	18	37	14	17	26	11	—	275	74	339
Nuclear Submarines	—	—	—	—	—	—	—	12	1	26
Submarines	24	22	—	6	4	26	—	453	44	150
1972–3										
Large Aircraft Carriers	—	—	—	—	—	—	—	—	2	26
Light Aircraft Carriers	—	2	1	—	—	—	—	—	—	—
Escort Carriers, Helicopter Carriers, Commando Carriers	42	2	—	—	—	1	—	2	3	7
Nuclear Submarines	—	2	—	—	—	—	—	95	10	100
Conventional Submarines	—	20	4	9	13	4	22	313	24	36
Cruisers	—	2	2	3	—	1	—	27	2	23
Leaders, Large Destroyers	—	2	—	3	—	—	—	35	9	32
Destroyers	4	17	3	4	30	18	8	66	3	216
Destroyer Escorts & Frigates	20	28	24	11	14	5	5	124	66	154
1982–3										
Ballistic Missile Submarines	1 D(?)	5(1)N 1 D	—	—	—	—	—	63(3)N 16 D	4 N	37 N (7N+2res)
Cruise Missile Submarines	—	—	—	—	—	—	—	46(1)N 20 D	—	—
Fleet Submarines	2(?)	1(4)	—	—	—	—	—	58 (3+8conv)	12(4)	85 (18+3res)
Patrol Submarines	102(9)	20	8(2+2)	10	13(3+1)	8(4)	13(4)	155 (3+100res)	16	5(1res)
Aircraft Carriers	—	2(2)	1 L	1(1)	—	1 L(1)	—	3(1+1N)	2(2)L	12(3N) (2N+6res)
Cruisers	—	2	1	2	—	—	—	39(11)	4	27(6+5res)
Destroyers	12(6)	20(4+3)	3(2)	6	33(9+2)	12	3	66(+14res)	12(8)	90(2)
Frigates	16(2)	24(1+1)	24(6)	12(6)	16(2)	20(3)	—	192 (3+12res)	43(9res)	80(29)
Personnel in thousands	298	69	46	42	44	63	22	448	70	741

Figures in italics in brackets indicate vessels under construction or planned   N=nuclear   L=Light   D=Diesel
conv=being converted   res=reserves
This table is reproduced by kind permission of the Editor of *Jane's Fighting Ships*.

Aircraft Carriers

The first flight made by an aircraft from a ship took place at Hampton Roads, Virginia, on 14 November 1910. Eugène Ely, flying a 50hp Curtiss biplane, took off from an 83ft (25.3m) platform built over the bows of the 3750-ton American light cruiser *Birmingham*, touched the water and damaged his propeller but maintained control and landed at Willoughby Spit 2½ miles (4km) away.

The first aeroplane to land on a ship was also a Curtiss biplane flown by Ely. On 18 January 1911, he landed on a platform 119ft 4in (36.4m) long constructed over the stern of the 13,680-ton armoured cruiser *Pennsylvania* anchored in San Francisco Bay.

The first successful flights from and on to warships were made in 1911. During the First World War a number of warships were fitted with special platforms from which aeroplanes could take off; 'landing', however, was infrequent until HMS *Argus* became **the first proper aircraft carrier**, with a flight deck extending the whole length of the ship. Laid down in 1914 as a liner for the Italian Lloyd Sabaudo Co., she was commandeered by the Admiralty and completed as the aircraft carrier *Argus* in 1918. Her flight deck was 565ft (172m) long and she had accommodation for 20 aircraft. She was finally scrapped in 1947.

HMS *Argus*, the first proper aircraft-carrier. *Robert Hunt Library.*

The first officially recorded instance of an aeroplane taking off from a vessel of the Royal Navy occurred on 10 January 1912, when Lieutenant **Charles Samson** (1883–1931), flying a Short S.38 biplane, took off from a platform on the bows of the 17,500-ton battleship HMS *Africa* at anchor in Sheerness Harbour; but he is said to have made a secret flight from the same ship in December 1911.

Samson was also **the first man to take off from a ship under way**. During the Naval Review at Portland on 8 May 1912, he took off from the deck of the battleship HMS *Hibernia* while she was steaming at 10.5 knots.

Because the fitting of flying-off platforms on battleships prevented the main armament from being used, it was decided that seaplanes, or hydro aeroplanes as they were initially called, were better suited for work at sea, since they required only hangar and workshop space on board and cranes to lower them into and recover them from the water. The first naval vessel to be adapted for this purpose, while still under construction, was HMS *Ark Royal*, launched in 1914. She thus became **the first ship in the world to be completed as an aircraft carrier**.

In 1934 she was renamed *Pegasus* in order to release the name for a new carrier launched in 1937. The second *Ark Royal* was torpedoed and sunk by the Germans on 12 November 1941, when only 25 miles (40km) from Gibraltar.

The third, at 36,800 tons, **for many years the largest warship in the Royal Navy**, was built in the 1950s at a cost of £21.5m. She was modernized in the 1960s at a cost of a further £32.5m and

was scrapped in 1978, after 23 years' service. The fourth *Ark Royal*, launched on 2 June 1981, cost £220m, making her **the most expensive ship ever built for the Royal Navy.**

The first launching of an aeroplane by catapult from on board ship occurred on 5 November 1915, when an AB2 flying boat was catapulted from the stern of the American battleship USS *North Carolina*, anchored in Pensacola Bay, Florida, USA.

The first landing by an aeroplane on a ship under way took place on 2 August 1917, when Squadron Commander E. H. Dunning landed his Sopwith Pup on the deck of HMS *Furious*. On 7 August Dunning tried to do it again, but was killed when his aircraft was blown over the side of the ship.

The first aircraft carrier to have the superstructure and funnel offset on the starboard side of an otherwise unobstructed flight deck was HMS *Eagle*. Originally laid down as a battleship for the Chilean Navy in 1913, she was purchased by the Royal Navy and completed in 1920. Such ships became known as 'island' carriers and the basic design is still with us. The *Eagle* was sunk by a U-boat off Algiers on 11 August 1942.

The US carriers *Lexington* and *Saratoga* were **the most expensive warships of their time**. Laid down in 1920–1, they were originally intended to be battle-cruisers but, as a result of the Treaty of Washington, which, in 1922, put a stop to naval competition by stabilizing the battleship strength of the five principal maritime powers, they were converted to aircraft carriers. Launched in 1925 and completed in 1927, they were **then the largest and fastest carriers afloat.** Displacing 33,000 tons, their flight decks were 909.5ft (277m) long and 105.6ft (32.3m) wide. They could carry 90 planes and 1788 men at a top speed of 34½ knots. The main armament, intended for use against destroyers and cruisers, was eight 8in (20cm) guns. The *Lexington* was sunk by Japanese aircraft during the Battle of the Coral Sea on 8 May 1942. The *Saratoga* was destroyed in an atom-bomb test off Bikini atoll in 1946.

The first Japanese aircraft carrier to be laid down as such was the 7470-ton *Hosho*. Laid down in December 1919, and completed in 1922, she was scrapped in 1947.

The first aircraft carrier in the modern sense was the light battle-cruiser *Furious*. That is to say, she was equipped with a flight deck from which aeroplanes could take off and on which they could land. Laid down shortly after the outbreak of the First World War, in March 1917, it was decided to alter her design and she was equipped with a hangar and a flight deck on her forecastle. But the landing deck was short and was disturbed by air currents set up by the bridge and by smoke from the funnels. So between 1921 and 1925 she was rebuilt with no superstructure and the funnel suppressed so that boiler smoke and gases were discharged overside through horizontal ducts. She then had a clear flight deck 700ft (213m) by

A destroyer goes alongside HMS *Ark Royal* to take off survivors, 12 November 1941. *Robert Hunt Library.*

Top: **USS Saratoga.** *Above:* **HMS Furious**: Both pictures *Mansell Collection.*

8oft (24.4m) and displaced 22,450 tons. She had two aircraft lifts and could carry 33 aeroplanes. She had a long and adventurous life and was not finally scrapped until 1949, by which time she was **the longest-lived active carrier in the world.**

The world's first aircraft carrier to be designed as such was the 10,850-ton HMS *Hermes.* She was laid down in January 1918, and completed in July 1923. She was sunk by Japanese aircraft off Ceylon in April 1942, thus gaining the unenviable distinction of being **the first carrier in the world to be sunk by aircraft from another carrier.**

The first American aircraft carrier was the 11,050-ton USS *Langley* converted from the collier *Jupiter,* fitted with a flight deck of 534ft (163m) and completed in 1924. She was sunk by Japanese aircraft off Java in February 1942.

The first and only aircraft carrier built by France between the wars was the 25,000-ton *Bearn,* laid down as a Normandie-class battleship, converted during construction and com-

pleted in 1927. After the scrapping of the *Furious* in 1949, she became **the longest-lived carrier in the world** and was not herself finally scrapped until 1968.

The first escort carrier was HMS *Audacity,* a captured German merchant ship converted into an aircraft carrier by the addition of a wooden flight deck 46oft (140m) long, from which operated six Martlet fighters. Her brief career lasted from September 1941 until 20 December of that year when she was sunk by a U-boat while escorting a homeward-bound convoy from Gibraltar. Nevertheless, during her short life she had proved such a success that she became the model on which large numbers of vessels were built in the United States. These escort carriers, the next of which came into service late in 1942, were known by the Americans as CVEs (Carrier Vessel Escort). In the meantime flight decks were built over the hulls of oil tankers and grain ships.

These were known as merchant aircraft carriers or MAC-ships for short.

The first and only paddle aircraft carriers were the converted Great Lakes steamers *Sable* and *Wolverine* which the Americans used for deck-landing during the Second World War.

The Essex class of aircraft carriers which formed the backbone of the American wartime carrier fleet and of which 24 were built, have been described as **'the most cost-effective warships ever built'**. These 27,000-ton ships carried 82 aircraft, were capable of a speed of 33 knots, and have only recently been scrapped after 35 years of service. They first came into service in 1942.

The only aircraft carrier ever to be built in a Royal Dockyard was HMS *Terrible*, built at Devonport dockyard and launched on 30 December 1944. In December 1948, she was handed over to the Royal Australian Navy and renamed *Sydney*. In 1976 she was broken up in South Korea.

Jet aircraft took off from and landed on a British aircraft carrier for the first time in December 1945. In the early 1950s **three British inventions** did much to facilitate the handling of jet aircraft on carriers. These were 1) **the angled deck**, which allows an aircraft to go round again if it misses the arrester wire. It was first fitted to the American carrier *Antietam*. 2) **The mirror landing aid** which gives the pilot an automatic reference for his final run. It was first fitted to the British carrier *Eagle*. 3) **The steam catapult** which compensates for the jet aircraft's slow acceleration and gives it sufficient take-off speed.

USS *Forrestal* was, at the time of her launching on 11 December 1954, at Newport News, Virginia, not only the **largest warship in the world** but also **the biggest ship ever built in the United States**. She displaced 59,650 tons, was 1036ft (315.8m) long and 252ft (76.8m) broad and incorporated two British inventions added after her keel was laid down in July 1952 – the angled flight deck and the steam catapult. She was named after James Forrestal (1892–1949) who was Secretary of Defence 1947–9. Just under a year later on 8 October 1955, her sister ship the USS *Saratoga* was launched at the New York Navy Shipyard.

The *Clemenceau* was **the first aircraft carrier to be designed and built in France**. She was laid down in November 1955, launched in December 1957, and completed in November 1961. She displaced 27,300 tons, carried 40 aircraft including jets, and had a speed of 32 knots. Her sister ship, the *Foch* was completed in 1963.

In 1961 the USS *Iwo Jima* became **the first carrier specially built to take a helicopter strike force**. HMS *Albion* was converted to a Commando carrier in 1961/2.

The first nuclear-powered aircraft carrier was the USS *Enterprise*, launched at Newport News, Virginia, on 24 September 1960, and commissioned on 25 November 1961. 'Built at a cost of $444m (approx. £158m) the 85,350-ton *Enterprise* from mast-tip to keel is as tall as a 25-storey building. With her eight reactors delivering 280,000 horse-power, she is capable of out-speeding and out-distancing any conventional-powered carrier or other ship, and at a cruising speed of 20 knots she can steam more than 400,000 miles (644,000km) without refuelling.

USS *Enterprise* entering Hobart, Tasamnia, 29 October 1976. *US Navy Photo/MARS.*

HMS *Invincible*. Invincible class anti-submarine cruiser. *MARS*.

At her designed speed of 35 knots, she can cover 150,000 miles (241,000km). She is 1123ft (342m) long and at its extreme width her angled deck measures 257ft (78.3m). She has $4\frac{1}{2}$ acres (18,211m²) of flight deck. The ship will carry about 200 aircraft and have a complement of 4000 men' (*The Times*, 27 November 1961).

The first Russian aircraft carrier, the *Kiev*, was laid down in 1971, launched in 1973 and commissioned in 1976. She is of the through-deck or command cruiser type, designed to operate helicopters and V/STOL aircraft. She displaces about 36,000 tons and carries about 25 helicopters and 20 fixed-wing V/STOL aircraft.

The largest warships laid down in Britain since the Second World War* are the three light carriers of the Invincible class. They are also the **largest vessels to be driven by gas turbines** so far. The first, HMS *Invincible*, is equipped with the Sea Dart missile system and carries five Sea Harrier Vertical/Short Take-Off and Landing (V/STOL) aircraft, and ten Sea King helicopters. 'Another innovation is the "ski-jump", a device so simple as to be almost ridiculous. It is a ramp at the forward end of the flight deck to give the Sea Harrier an upward trajectory on take-off, and by assisting the aircraft's transition from jet-lift to wing-lift it adds 1500lb (680kg) to its payload. The ski-jump will take its place alongside the angled deck and the steam catapult as an invention which kept naval aviation in being by appearing at the crucial moment' (ANTHONY PRESTON, *Dreadnought to Nuclear Submarine*). She was built by Vickers and handed over to the Royal Navy on 19 March 1980.

---

* The *Hermes* was laid down on 21 June 1944, but not completed until 18 November 1959.

SUBMARINES;
TORPEDOES;
TORPEDO BOATS

The earliest surviving description of a submarine ship occurs in William Bourne's *Inventions or Devises* (1578). He describes a boat covered over with a watertight deck from which rises, through a watertight joint, a hollow tube to ventilate the inner chamber. The sides of the boat are perforated with a number of holes and covered with inner 'walls', made partly of leather, which can be moved in and out to draw into and expel water from the space in between. Such a craft could, of course, only move vertically and it is uncertain whether it was ever constructed.

The first attempt to construct a submarine that could be propelled under water is generally credited to Cornelius Drebbel (1572–1634), a Dutchman, who, sometime in the 1620s, is said to have constructed a vessel with a watertight cover propelled by 12 oars fitted closely through holes in the side. The boat was ballasted until it retained a very small degree of positive buoyancy and submerged by directing the strokes of the oars slightly upwards.

The first submarine attack took place on 6/7 September 1776. An American inventor, David Bushnell (c 1742–1824), designed and built a small, hand-operated submarine which floated upright in the water and could be submerged by admitting water to two small internal tanks. Named the *Turtle*, she carried a detachable explosive charge which could be fitted to the bottom of an enemy ship. Operated by an army sergeant named Ezra Lee, the *Turtle* drifted down the Hudson River, which was being blockaded by Lord Howe (1726–99), towards Howe's flagship the *Eagle*. Although Lee managed to get the *Turtle* under the hull of the *Eagle*, the attempt failed because Bushnell had not made allowance

for the fact that the bottoms of British warships at that time were copper-sheathed and Lee was therefore unable to attach the charge to the hull.

The first submarine to be built in France was Robert Fulton's *Nautilus*. Fulton had settled in Paris in 1797 and in 1801 he persuaded Napoleon to finance the construction of a prototype, receiving a grant of 10,000 francs. The vessel was made of copper, was 21ft (6.4m) long and 7ft (2.1m) in diameter and was fitted with a ballast tank in the lower part of the hull to enable it to dive and return to the surface. It was driven under water by a hand-cranked propellor and had a collapsible mast and sail. Though Fulton remained underwater in the *Nautilus* for four hours and successfully blew up an old schooner in Brest Harbour by attaching an explosive charge to her bottom, the French were unimpressed. So he went to England to demonstrate his machine, where he was given an equally unenthusiastic reception (see also p. 88).

Bushnell's *Turtle. Mary Evans Picture Library.*

HMS *Resolution* (see p. 143). *Crown Copyright MOD-RAF/MARS.*

Hospital ship with escort of destroyer and coastal motor-boat (see p. 145). *Robert Hunt Picture Library.*

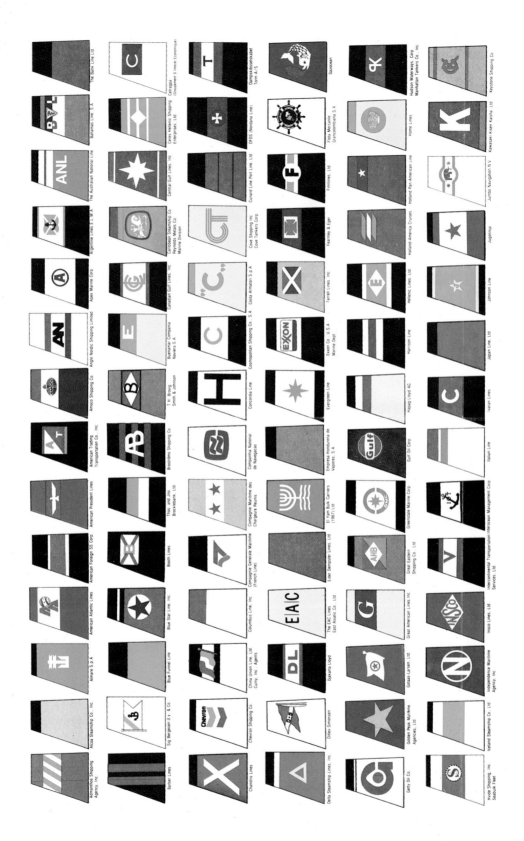

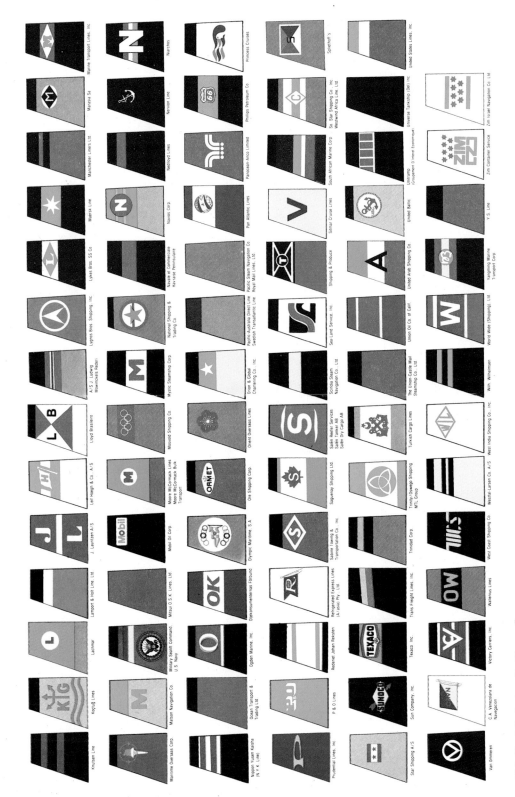

Ship Stack Insignia 1982. *Texaco Inc.*

Frederick Carter, the largest railway ferry. *CN Marine.*

Fuji Maru, the largest vehicle carrier. *Nippon Yusen Kaisha Line.*

The first escape from a sunken submarine occurred in February 1851, when the *Plongeur Marin*, built by a Bavarian engineer named Wilhelm Bauer got stuck with his crew of two on the bottom of Kiel harbour. Bauer flooded the craft until the pressure within equalled that of the sea outside and was then able to open the hatch and swim to the surface.

The first ship to be damaged in a submarine attack was the Federal ship *New Ironsides*. On 5 October 1853, at Charleston, S. Carolina, she was attacked by the Confederate submersible *David* armed with a spar torpedo and commanded by one Lieutenant Glassell. The torpedo exploded successfully and caused considerable damage to the Federal ship but the shock waves caused by the explosion sank the submersible.

These submersibles, or semi-submersibles as they are sometimes described, were later known collectively as 'Davids' on the analogy of the Confederate boy David tackling the Federal giant Goliath. They were not true submarines in that they were unable to dive, but really torpedo-boats with a steam engine and funnel, trimmed down so that only the funnel and hatchway were above water.

Hunley's 'David'. *Mary Evans Picture Library.*

One of the most advanced designs among early submarines was that of a Spaniard named Monturiol. In 1862 he built *El Ictineo* which incorporated a number of novel features. It had a double hull and ballast tanks between the hulls which could be pumped out by compressed air. It was driven by a steam engine even when submerged and the oxygen was replaced by a chemical plant.

The first submarine designed to be driven by compressed air was the *Plongeur*, built in France in 1863 by Charles Brun and Captain Bourgois, but it was not a success.

The first ship to be sunk by a submarine was the steam frigate *Housatonic*, part of the Federal squadron blockading Charleston Harbour. The attacker was a Confederate 'David' called the *H. L. Hunley*, after her designer. She was about 40ft (12.2m) long and powered by eight men turning a crankshaft which drove the propellor, while a ninth man steered. On the night of 17 February 1864, she rammed the *Housatonic* with a spar torpedo and blew a large hole in her side, causing her to sink almost at once, but once again the aggressor went down with her prey. Three years later divers sent down to examine the wreck of the *Housatonic* found the *Hunley* lying alongside her with the remains of her crew still on board.

The first man to construct a successful self-propelled torpedo was Robert Whitehead (1823–1905). 'No one man,' it was said, 'ever cost the world so much by an invention as did the late Mr Whitehead of Fiume.' It should be remembered that, before the advent of the locomotive torpedo, all submarine explosive devices were referred to as torpedoes. The name comes from that of a fish capable of giving an electric shock of 20–30 volts.

The first man to make a serious attempt at building a self-propelled torpedo was a retired Captain of the Austrian Navy called Giovanni de Luppis. Early in the 1860s he constructed *Der Küstenbrander* (the Coastal Fireship) which was made of wood, driven by a clockwork motor, and controlled from the shore by tiller-ropes attached to the rudder. When it struck its victim the gunpowder charge packed into the hull was detonated by a percussion pistol device in the bows. That, at least, was the idea, but the Austrian Navy was unimpressed, so de Luppis took his brainchild to Whitehead, then working as manager of a marine engineering firm in Fiume. Whitehead was less discouraging but saw that the device was too slow, too limited in range, too

visible and too inaccurate. The result of his deliberations on how best to solve these problems led to his being **the first man to conceive of a weapon which travelled independently beneath the surface throughout the attack.** Thus the modern torpedo was conceived, though its birth was still some way ahead.

In 1866 Whitehead was asked by the Austrian Navy to submit his invention for official trials. But, as he was well aware, it was still a very imperfect device and the Imperial Navy declined to buy the rights. By the time he had incorporated various improvements, including a balance chamber in which a pendulum connected to horizontal rudders corrected any fore-and-aft tilt, the Austrians, bled dry by the Seven Weeks War, were in no position to negotiate. Thus it came about, after successful trials completed in October 1870, that in April 1871 the British Government became **the first to acquire a non-exclusive licence to build the Whitehead torpedo.**

The Royal Laboratory at Woolwich completed its first weapon, the Mark 1* RL, early in 1872,

The earliest known Whitehead torpedo, probably the 1868 design. Note the propeller guards.

The Royal Navy's first torpedo boat, HMS *Lightning*. *Mansell Collection.*

incorporating one important modification – the introduction of contra-rotating propellors which raised the speed from 7 to 12 knots.

'The first launch built by Thornycroft and specially designed for torpedo-carrying was No. 23. She was delivered to the Norwegian Government in 1874. The length on the waterline was 55ft 6in (16.9m) and the beam 7ft 6in (2.28m). The compound surface-condensing engine developed 90ihp and gave a speed of about 14½ knots.' (The indicated horse power of an engine is greater than the output or brake horse power since some of the power generated is lost in friction. The mechanical efficiency is the brake horse power divided by the indicated horse power.) 'The armament consisted of a 9in (23cm) diameter torpedo, 13ft (3.96m) in length and arranged to be towed from a ring on the top of the funnel and to diverge about 40 degrees from the launch's own course. The torpedo was normally carried in davits from which it was dropped overboard' (K. C. BARNABY, *100 Years of Specialized Shipbuilding and Engineering*).

In 1876 **the British Admiralty ordered their first torpedo boat** from Thornycroft. This was HMS *Lightning*, afterwards renamed *T.B. No. 1*. She displaced 19 tons, was 81ft (24.7m) on the waterline, and her two-cylinder compound engine, developing 390ihp, gave her a speed of 18½ knots. Originally designed to carry spar torpedoes, she was modified in 1879 by the addition of two above-water tubes for the discharge of Whitehead torpedoes, thus becoming **the first warship in the world equipped to launch a locomotive torpedo.**

The first submarine to be fitted with an electric storage battery was the *Peral*, built in 1886 by a Spanish officer called Lieutenant Isaac Peral. It was also the first submarine to have two propellors, which were driven by two 30hp motors powered by 480 storage accumulators.

But the Spanish naval authorities refused to co-operate with Peral and by the turn of the century the French had an unchallenged lead in the development of submarines, hoping thereby to redress the imbalance of British naval supremacy without going to the vast expense of building more battleships. In 1888 they launched the *Gymnote*, designed by Dupuy de Lôme and Gustave Zédé (1825–91), **the first submarine to be fitted with horizontal rudders in the bow**, designed to overcome the tendency of submarines of that era to plunge. She was 60ft (18.3m) long and was driven by an electric motor supplied with current from 564 lead-acid accumulators.

In 1896 the French built the *Morse*, said to be 'the first self-contained submarine'. She was powered by steam when on the surface and by an electric motor when submerged, but the engine could also drive a dynamo to recharge the accumulators.

Nevertheless the man whose name was eventually **to be most closely linked with the early development of the submarine** was an Irish-American schoolmaster named John Philip Holland (1840–1914). Born in Co. Clare, he settled in Paterson, New Jersey, in 1873 and in 1875 offered his first submarine design to the US Navy

Holland's submarine at her moorings in New York. *Mary Evans Picture Library.*

Department, who rejected it. In 1877 he designed the boat which incorporated his major contribution to underwater navigation; it had horizontal rudders. Until now submarines, when submerging, had simply *sunk*. Holland's boat *dived*. In 1898, at Elizabeth, New Jersey, he launched the *Holland*, **the first submarine to be equipped with internal combustion engines for surface power and electric motors for submerged cruising**. It embodied all the design characteristics of subsequent submarines until the advent of nuclear power.

The first occasion on which a torpedo was fired in action was off the Chilean port of Ilo on 29 May 1877. The Peruvian turret ironclad *Huascar* had been stolen by a rebellious general called Nicolas de Pierola (1839–1913) and turned pirate. Rear-Admiral de Horsey, commander of the Royal Navy's Pacific Squadron, and flying his flag in HMS *Shah*, was sent to deal with the situation and found the *Huascar* at Ilo. The original report reads, '5.14 Fired Whitehead torpedo. Not seen. Port electric broadside. 400 yards.' The first torpedo fired in action had missed. The *Huascar* slipped away but surrendered to a Peruvian naval squadron at Iquique the following day.

The first phosphor-bronze torpedoes were built by the German engineering company of L. Schwartzkopff and Co. It has been suggested that plans stolen from Whitehead's office had somehow fallen into the hands of the German firm, for, apart from the fact that it was made of phosphor-bronze not steel, the Schwartzkopff torpedo was said to be 'almost an exact copy of Whitehead's'. The great advantage of phosphor-bronze was that it was immune to rust and could be kept 'in a state of perfect adjustment for many weeks', whereas the Whitehead torpedo needed stripping and cleaning after every immersion in salt water.

The earliest seagoing torpedo-boat was the 40-ton *Batoum*, built for the Russian Navy by Alfred Yarrow (1842–1932) at Poplar, with a speed of 22 knots. The Russians were then the chief advocates of the torpedo-boat and by 1884 had a fleet of 115, as many as the rest of the European navies combined. At the time France had 50 and Britain a modest 19.

The development of the torpedo-boat inevitably led to the birth of **the torpedo-boat-destroyer**, later better known simply as the destroyer. First in the field were the Spaniards who ordered the 386-ton *Destructor* from Thompson of Clydebank (later the John Brown shipyard) in 1884. She was also **the first warship to be driven by twin triple-expansion engines**, which gave her a speed of $22\frac{1}{2}$ knots.

The obvious basic requirement of a torpedo-boat-destroyer, however, was that she should be faster than the opposing torpedo-boat and in this respect the *Destructor* was soon obsolete. **The first true destroyers in the world** were HMS *Havock* and HMS *Hornet*, built by Alfred Yarrow at Poplar and launched in 1893, each with a speed of 27.3 knots. They displaced only 240 tons but carried one 3in (7.62cm) 12pdr (5.4kg) gun and three 6pdrs (1.36kg), as well as three torpedo tubes.

The *Sokol*, built by Alfred Yarrow for the Russian Navy in 1895, was **the first destroyer to achieve a speed of 30 knots.**

The first ship to be sunk by a Whitehead torpedo was the 3500-ton Chilean battleship *Blanco Encalada*, during the Chilean Civil War in 1891. The Presidential Party's two torpedo-gunboats *Almirante Lynch* and *Almirante Condell* found the Congressionalist Party's *Blanco Encalada* anchored in Caldera Bay on 23 April. The *Condell* fired three torpedoes from about 500yd (457m) but they all missed. The *Lynch* then fired one torpedo from 150yd (137m) which also missed. She closed to 40yd (37m) and fired again. One of the torpedoes found its mark, there was a tremendous explosion and in 6½ minutes the Chilean battleship had disappeared, taking with her 11 officers and 172 men.

The first woman to go down in a submarine was Clara Barton (1821–1912), the founder of the American Red Cross. She made her descent in *Holland VI* off Sag Harbour, Long Island, in July 1899.

The 'finest' epitaph on the loss of a submarine must surely be that penned by Congressman H. C. Canfield on the loss of US Submarine *S4*:

> *Entrapped inside a submarine,*
> *With death approaching on the scene,*
> *The crew compose their minds to dice,*
> *More for the Pleasure than the Vice.*

HM Submarine *No 1*, designed by J P Holland and fitted with a periscope designed by Captain R Bacon, the first Inspecting Captain of Submarines.

The first diesel-engined submarine was the French *Aigrette*, launched in 1904. The Russians followed with the *Minoga*, then the British and Americans followed suit. Not until 1912, did Germany, whence the diesel engine had originated, finally change over.

The Russians were the first to design a submarine minelayer when the *Krab* was laid down in 1908, but she was not completed until 1915, by which time the Germans had built mine-layers of their own. 'These UC-boats had six vertical wells inside the pressure hull, each containing two mines which could be dropped through hatches underneath. The mine and its sinker dropped clear, and the submarine automatically took in the equivalent weight of water as ballast to maintain itself at the correct depth. In 1916 the first British mine-laying submarine also appeared, with 20 mines in similar wells in the ballast tanks on either side' (ANTHONY PRESTON, *Dreadnought to Nuclear Submarine*).

The Royal Navy's first submarine, HM Submarine One, or Holland One as she was popularly known, was one of five ordered in 1901. She sank near the Eddystone lighthouse, south-west of Plymouth, on her way to the breaker's yard in 1913. In November 1981, she was located by Royal Navy divers and, when brought to the surface, will be put on display at the Royal Navy Submarine Museum at Gosport. The museum director, Commander Richard Compton-Hall, said, 'The Americans, the Russians, the Swedes, the Dutch, all had the same design built on licence from America but there are none still existing.'

In 1933 the Japanese produced the *Long Lance*, **an oxygen-driven torpedo**. 'Inspired by rumours that the Royal Navy was using oxygen in its torpedoes the Japanese perfected a torpedo which could run for 40,000yd (36,576m) at 36 knots. As contemporary Western torpedoes had a range of about 10,000yd (9144m) it can be seen that the *Long Lance* gave Japanese destroyers a tremendous tactical advantage. In fact, as *Long Lance* remained a secret until well into the Second World War, it can be claimed to be **the only genuine "secret weapon" of modern times**' (ANTHONY PRESTON, *Dreadnought to Nuclear Submarine*) (see also p. 115).

The first submarines to be fitted with schnorkels were built by the Dutch. When a submarine dives she can no longer use her diesel engines because these require a constant supply of oxygen. The schnorkel is a device for providing an air supply while the submarine is at periscope depth. It is simply a tube about 9in (229mm) in diameter which can be raised to the vertical when the submarine dives and down which air can be sucked into the diesel engine. When Germany invaded Holland on 10 May 1940, the 12 operational submarines then in Dutch home ports managed to escape to the British submarine base at Gosport. Three of them were fitted with schnorkels, the first operational boats in the world to be so equipped. Curiously, the Royal Navy saw no need to adopt the device, while the Germans, finding it fitted to half-completed Dutch submarines which had fallen into their hands, later fitted it to their U-boats, thus enabling them to operate safely in British coastal waters since they no longer needed to surface to recharge their batteries.

The greatest number of men to perish in a single submarine during the war was the 159 lost when the French submarine *Surcouf* was rammed by the American merchant ship *Thompson Lykes* in the Caribbean on 19 February 1942. The *Surcouf*, built in 1929, was the largest submarine in the world. She was 361ft (110m) long, 29.5ft (9m) in the beam and her surface displacement was 2880 tons. Perhaps the French were tempting fate by naming her after Robert Surcouf (1773–1827) who, we are told, 'added a spirit of chivalry to great courage and admirable seamanship', but was called 'The King of the Corsairs'.

The longest tow in submarine history is claimed by HMS *Turpin*. Having developed engine trouble in the West Indies, she was towed 5200 miles from Kingston, Jamaica, by the tug *Samsonia* to Devonport which she reached after 29½ days on 9 April 1948.

The US submarine *Pickerel* took the record in 1950 for **the longest voyage ever made by a submerged submarine**. She left Hong Kong on 15 March and surfaced in Pearl Harbor on 5 April, a distance of 5200 nautical miles (9637km) in 21 days. She was fitted with schnorkel-type underwater breathing apparatus.

The first ever submerged crossing of the Atlantic was made by HMS *Andrew* in May 1953, 'snorting' from Bermuda to the English Channel. She was also **the last submarine in the Royal Navy to carry a deck gun**. She played the role of USS *Swordfish* in the film *On the Beach*, starring Gregory Peck and Ava Gardner.

The first British submarines of post-war design were the *Explorer*, built by Vickers Armstrong and launched at Barrow-in-Furness on 5 March 1954, and the *Excalibur*, launched 25 February 1955. They were known to those who served in them as HMS *Exploder* and *Excruciator*. Additional to diesel-electric machinery they were fitted with turbine machinery for which energy was supplied by burning diesel fuel in decomposed hydrogen peroxide. With a top speed in excess of 25 knots submerged, they were then about the fastest submarines in the world.

HM Submarine *Explorer* running on the surface. *Crown Copyright (MOD-RN)/MARS.*

The world's first nuclear-powered submarine, the USS *Nautilus*, was built by the General Dynamics (Electric Boat) Corporation of Groton, Connecticut. Her keel was laid on 14 June 1952, she was launched by Mrs Eisenhower at Groton on 21 January 1954 and first commissioned for service on 30 September 1954. She was 324ft (987m) long and had a beam of 88ft (268m); displaced 4040 tons submerged and had a crew of ten officers and 95 men. Two steam turbines developing 15,000hp gave her a submerged speed of over 20 knots, the heat required to produce the

The launching of USS *Nautilus*. *US Navy Official/MARS.*

steam being provided by a nuclear reactor. In August 1958, she became **the first submarine to travel under the polar ice-cap from the Pacific to the Atlantic.** The *Nautilus* started from Pearl Harbor in Hawaii on 23 July, went under the ice off the coast of Alaska on 1 August and, after a journey of 1830 miles (2945km) under the ice, surfaced on the Greenwich meridian at 79° north on 5 August. A few days later a similar journey was made by her sister ship, the submarine *Skate*.

The USS *Seawolf* (3400 tons), launched at Groton, Connecticut, on 21 July 1955, was the US Navy's second atomic-powered submarine but **the first to have an intermediate reactor and a liquid metal coolant.** She took the record on 6 October 1958, for **the longest submerged cruise.** She began her underwater cruise at an undisclosed point in mid-Atlantic on 7 August and surfaced off New London, Connecticut, USA, on 6 October. The previous record of 31 days 5½ hr had been set up in May of that year by the nuclear submarine *Skate*.

The first submarine to be built for the US Navy from the keel upwards as a nuclear-powered guided-missile submarine was the USS *Halibut*, laid down on 11 April 1957, launched at Mane Island shipyard on 15 December 1958, and completed in late 1959.

The world's first nuclear-powered ballistic missile submarine, the USS *George Washington*, was launched by President Eisenhower at Groton, Connecticut, on 9 June 1959. She had a displacement of 5400 tons, a length of 380ft (115.8m) and cost about £35,800,000 ($100,000,000). She carried 16 vertical tubes for firing Polaris missiles, either on the surface or when submerged, these having a range of 1500 miles (2413km).

The first undersea round-the-world voyage was completed on 10 May 1960, when the US nuclear submarine *Triton* surfaced off the coast of

HMS *Dreadnought* at the North Pole. *Crown Copyright (MOD-RN)/MARS.*

USS *Triton. US Navy Official/MARS.*

Delaware after travelling 41,519 miles (66,804km) in 84 days. Her journey was known as Operation Magellan because it followed under water the route taken by Ferdinand Magellan on the first-ever voyage of circumnavigation in 1519–21. The *Triton* was commanded by Captain Edward L. Beach, author of the best-selling novel *Run Silent, Run Deep*. She was **the first atomic submarine with two nuclear reactors in her power-plant.** She was the eighth atomic submarine in the US Navy and **the largest submarine then built**, with a displacement of 5900 tons, a length of 447ft (136.2m) and a crew of 148 officers and men. She was also **the first submarine in the world to have three decks inside her hull.**

The first two ballistic missiles to be fired from underwater were launched on 20 July 1960, by the US submarine *George Washington*. These were Polaris missiles, fired from a depth of 90ft (27.4m). The missile is ejected from a launching tube by compressed inert gases which drive it above the water surface where the rocket motor ignites. The early Polaris missile had a range of 1200–1500 miles (1932–2415km).

The point on the earth's surface furthest from the sea is in Central Asia, near Lake Baikal. It is 1720 miles (2769km) from the nearest coastline. By the early 1970s the range of Polaris had increased to 2800 miles (4508km).

Britain's first nuclear submarine, the 3500-ton HMS *Dreadnought*, was launched by H.M. Queen Elizabeth II at Barrow-in-Furness, on Trafalgar Day, 21 October 1960.

A *Subroc* missile being prepared for testing. *US Navy Official/MARS.*

The first submarine-to-submarine missile was the United States' *Subroc*, which is fired from the torpedo tubes of an attack submarine. After leaving the tube the missile's solid-propellant motor ignites and the missile emerges from the water and flies as a rocket. At a pre-selected point the warhead separates and dives into the water, continuing on course to its pre-selected target controlled by an inertial guidance system.

HMS *Revenge*, Resolution-class nuclear-powered ballistic missile submarine of the Royal Navy. *Crown Copyright (MOD-RN)/MARS.*

The first nuclear submarine of all-British design was HMS *Valiant*, *Dreadnought*'s reactor having been bought from America. *Valiant* was launched at Barrow-in-Furness on 3 December 1963; she had a surface displacement of 4000 tons, a crew of 90, was 285ft (86.9m) long and 33ft 3in (10.1m) in the beam. She was commissioned on 18 July 1966.

Britain's first Polaris submarine, HMS *Resolution*, was launched by H.M. Queen Elizabeth, the Queen Mother, at Barrow-in-Furness on 16 September 1966. The *Resolution* displaced 7500 tons, carried 16 Polaris A–3 missiles with a range of 2300 nautical miles, could cruise submerged for two months and had a crew of 138. She was commissioned on 2 October 1967, and carried out **the first British test launch of a Polaris missile**, with a dummy warhead, while submerged off Cape Kennedy, Florida, on 15 February 1968.

The Exocet was the first anti-ship missile to be developed by a Western nation. In 1970 a launcher was fitted to a *Combattante* diesel-powered patrol boat in an attempt by the French navy to counter the threat of the Russian Styx anti-ship missile. The wooden-hulled *Combattante* had entered service in 1964 and was capable of 23 knots.

HOSPITAL SHIPS; TROOPSHIPS; MEDALS

Hospital Ships

The earliest recorded reference to a naval hospital ship dates from 1608 and refers to a vessel called the *Goodwill*. Two hospital ships are mentioned as having sailed with an expedition to the West Indies in 1654; but these were isolated instances and it was not until after the Restoration in 1660 that the Royal Navy regularly earmarked certain ships for use as hospital ships.

The first record of English ships being used as military hospital ships dates from 1683 when a fleet of 29 vessels sailed for Tangier, two of which, the *Unity* and the *Welcome*, were fitted out as hospital ships. 'On the evacuation of Tangier, the *Unity* sailed in October with 144 invalid soldiers and 104 women and children. During the next month the *Welcome* took off another batch of sick soldiers and families and female nurses were aboard both vessels to care for the patients' (J. H. PLUMRIDGE, *Hospital Ships and Ambulance Trains*).

The difference between naval and military hospital ships, apart from the obvious fact that the former are for sailors and the latter for soldiers, is that naval hospital ships formed a permanent part of the fleet, whereas military hospital ships were brought into use only when occasion demanded.

The first attempts to cater for the medical needs of merchant seamen and deep-sea fisherman were sparked off by a severe cholera epidemic in the early 1800s which resulted in the formation, on 8 March 1821, of the Seamen's Hospital Society. On 25 October 1821, the first patient was taken aboard the *Grampus*, a former 48-gun ship which had been loaned by the Admiralty, converted into a hospital ship and moored at Greenwich. The staff of the *Grampus* consisted of 'a superintendant, a surgeon, a steward and clerk, a boatswain and carpenter, two boatswain's mates, three male nurses, a male cook and a washerwoman'.

Ten years later the *Grampus* was replaced by the *Dreadnought*, 'a 98-gun 1st rate which had fought at Trafalgar', replaced in her turn in 1857 by HMS *Caledonia*, a 120-gun ship whose name was changed to *Dreadnought*. Then, on 13 April 1870, the seamen patients were moved from the ship to the Infirmary of the Greenwich Hospital and thus became the first inmates of the Dreadnought Seamen's Hospital, which still flourishes on the same site between the River Thames and the National Maritime Museum.

Breaking-up of the hospital ship *Dreadnought* at Chatham dockyard.

The first ships to be specifically fitted out as 'floating hospitals' to attend an army on active service were the sail-rigged steamships *Melbourne* and *Mauritius* which were sent out to China at the end of the **Second Opium War in 1860.** Plumridge describes them thus: 'The whole of the lower decks, where there was approximately 8ft (2.4m) between decks, was used for hospital purposes and each of the 125 patients had an allotment of some 230 cubic feet. Berths were provided and each had a small tray suspended above, which the patient could raise or lower, while a rope handle could be used to help him change his position in bed.

'The surgery was in the centre of the ship and was immediately beneath a skylight which provided light not only for the surgeons but also for dispensing medicines. The top of the skylight was moveable, permitting patients to be placed on the operating table direct from the main deck.'

Hospital accommodation and surgery on the Melbourne. Mary Evans Picture Library.

The international agreement respecting the succour of the wounded in time of war, known as **The Geneva Convention, was first drawn up in August 1864,** but applied only to land warfare. In October 1868, **the first principles were laid down for the adaption of the first Geneva Convention to maritime warfare.** At a Peace Convention held at The Hague in 1907 **the conditions were first laid down under which hospital ships were entitled to immunity in time of war.** It ordained that hospital ships be painted white overall with a horizontal band of green round the hull (red if the ship had been equipped by private subscription). All should have red crosses painted on their sides – fore, aft and amidships – and fly their national flag as well as the Red Cross flag. At night the hulls must be illuminated.

In 1917 the Central Powers decided to ignore the Geneva Convention and started torpedoing hospital ships. **The first British hospital ship to be torpedoed** was the *Asturias* on 21 March 1917. There were no patients on board but 43 of the

HMS *Serapis* was specially converted to take the Prince of Wales to India in 1875.

crew and staff were drowned. There is, however, evidence that hospital ships had been sunk well before the intention was made public. On 17 March 1916, the Russian hospital ship *Portugal* was torpedoed off the coast of Turkey with the loss of 85 lives, and another Russian hospital ship, the *Vpered*, was sunk on 10 July 1916.

The National Mission to Deep-Sea Fishermen was founded in 1881 by E. J. Mather, who, though primarily interested in the spiritual welfare of the men, soon realized that their physical welfare also needed attention and decided that vessels with doctors should accompany the fishing fleets to sea. It should be borne in mind that there might have then been up to 200 fishing smacks on the Dogger Bank at one time, each with a crew of four or more, accompanied by carriers who took the catch home while the trawlers went on fishing, thus giving the Mission doctor a thousand or more potential patients in a relatively confined area. **The first such vessel** to attend a fishing fleet was the *Ensign* who made her first trip in July 1882.

The first vessel to take medical aid to the cod fishermen across the Atlantic was the *Albert*, which left England on 12 June 1892, and arrived in St John's, New Brunswick on 22 July to find that the town had been destroyed by fire and spent five weeks there giving medical aid.

The first occasion on which hospital ships carried officers of the Army Dental Corps was during the brief Norway campaign from April to June 1940, when the *Aba* and *Atlantic* evacuated casualties.

Troopships

The first ships to be built specifically as troopships were the *Crocodile*, *Euphrates*, *Jumna*, *Malabar* and *Serapis*. The existing practice of using Naval ships for the transportation of troops was not ideal, owing to the ill-feeling between the Army and the Navy, summed up in the sailor's traditional order of precedence: 'A messmate before a shipmate, a shipmate before a stranger, a stranger before a dog, but a dog before a soldier.' So in 1858 it was recommended that a regular service of Government transports should be inaugurated, and, after much discussion, the five ships were built in 1866, each designed to carry a full battalion, with its supernumeraries, about 1200 men in all, at a speed of 15 knots. These ships maintained the routine Indian trooping service until 1894, when the Government decided to turn to the Merchant Service for transport. From P. & O. they chartered the *Britannia* and *Rome*, from the British India Line the *Dilwara*. These were ordinary passenger ships, converted for trooping. It was not until 1935 that **the first purpose-built troopship** appeared, also called the *Dilwara*. Until recently it was assumed that the days of the troopship were gone for good, airtrooping having taken its place. However, the *Canberra*'s role in the Falkland Islands war has shown this judgment to have been somewhat hasty.

Medals

The first naval medals were struck in the reign of Queen Elizabeth I. 'Although the Navy existed for centuries before a standing Army was established, or thought necessary in England, none of its achievements were rewarded by the presentation of medals till the reign of Queen Elizabeth.... After the defeat of the Spanish Armada, in 1588, medals in gold and silver, were struck by the English and Dutch to commemorate the event ... These medals were evidently intended to be worn from the neck ... Whether they were given specially for services against the Armada or generally as a reward to distinguished officers ... is uncertain' (W. H. LONG, *Medals of the British Navy*).

According to Long, **the first recorded instance of a medal being awarded to a specific officer** in recognition of a particular act of bravery occurred on 29 October 1649, when the Council of State ordered that Lieutenant Stephen Rose of the Commonwealth Navy and commander of the *Happy Entrance* be given a gratuity of £50, of which 40 shillings (£2) was to be in a gold medal, for having destroyed the *Antelope*, one of the best ships in Prince Rupert's royalist fleet.

The first medals to be worn with a ribbon were those presented by King George III after the 'Glorious First of June' in 1794. 'The admirals wore their medals attached to gold chains, presented to them by the King, but all other flag-officers, who subsequently received the medal, wore it suspended from the neck by a white ribbon with dark blue edges. The captains wore the medal with a smaller ribbon, and a gold buckle and swivel, between the third and fourth buttonholes of their uniform coats' (LONG).

The Naval General Service Medal was first issued in January 1849, 'Her Majesty having been graciously pleased to command that a Medal should be struck to record the services of her Fleets and Armies during the Wars commencing in 1793 and ending in 1815 and that one should be conferred on every officer, non-commissioned officer, petty officer, soldier and seaman who was present in any action, naval or military, to commemorate which Medals have been struck by

command of Her Majesty's Royal Predecessors and distributed to superior officers.' The distribution of the medal was later extended to cover naval services to the year 1840. More than 200 clasps were issued with the medal, six being the greatest number worn by any one man.

The first man ever to win the Victoria Cross (VC) was Charles David Lucas (1834–1914) when serving as Mate (equivalent today to a midshipman) on board the 6-gun steam paddle sloop HMS *Hecla* with the Baltic fleet in the summer of 1854. (It is often forgotten that the war against Russia generally known as the Crimean War also involved a naval campaign in the Baltic.) On 21 June 1854, the *Hecla* and two 16-gun paddle-steamers, *Odin* and *Valorous*, were bombarding the Russian fortress of Bomarsund in the Aland Islands, which guard the entrance to the Gulf of Bothnia, when a live shell from an enemy battery landed on the deck of the *Hecla*. All hands flung themselves on the deck with the exception of Lucas, who picked up the shell and flung it overboard, where it exploded with a great roar even before it hit the water. Lucas's Victoria Cross was gazetted in the first such list, published on 24 February 1857, and he received his medal from Queen Victoria at the first investiture on 26 June of that year.

Reverse of a Naval General Service Medal. *Spink and Son Ltd.*

The first Royal Marine to win the Victoria Cross was Corporal John Prettyjohn, RMLI, of HMS *Bellerophon*, who was responsible for repelling a Russian attack at the Battle of Inkerman on 5 November 1854.

The first man to be gazetted for the Victoria Cross was Lieutenant Cecil Buckley of HMS *Miranda* who, in May and June 1855, led what we would now call two commando raids on Russian supply depots on the shore of the Sea of Azov which caused considerable damage. His name appeared first on the list because he was alphabetically the first-named officer of the Senior Service.

The first man ever to wear the Victoria Cross was Commander Henry Raby of HMS *Wasp* who won his medal ashore at the assault on the fortress of the Redan at Sevastopol on 18 June 1855, for rescuing a wounded soldier of the 57th (West Middlesex) Regiment. He was the first to receive his medal, being the Senior Officer of the Senior Service at the first investiture, which was held in Hyde Park on 26 June 1857.

Obverse of the Sea Gallantry Medal. *Spink and Son Ltd.*

The Sea Gallantry Medal, originally known as 'The Board of Trade Medal for Saving Life' was instituted in 1855, 'for affording assistance towards the life and property in cases of shipwreck and distress at sea'. It is thus **the earliest British gallantry medal awarded to civilians** but, in this sense, it is important to note that, unlike

the Victoria Cross (extended to civilian volunteers in 1858 for services in the Mutiny) and the Albert Medal (instituted in 1866), it was not originally intended to be worn. Chief Officer James Whiteley is **the only person ever to have been awarded a bar to his Sea Gallantry Medal.** This he won while serving on SS *Urbino* on 6 February 1921.

The only naval Victoria Cross ever to forfeit his medal was Midshipman Edward St John Daniel (1837–68). It had been awarded to him for three separate acts of outstanding bravery in the Crimea in June 1855. Subsequently he took to the bottle and was severely reprimanded for being absent without leave, then court-martialled for being drunk in his cabin when he should have been on watch. For this he was awarded two years' loss of seniority. Finally he was arrested for indecently assaulting four subordinate officers, but he managed to escape, was posted as a deserter, and on 4 September 1861, became **the first man ever to forfeit the Victoria Cross.** He fled to Australia, thence to New Zealand where he died of delirium tremens. Though it is still technically possible for the forfeiture of a Victoria Cross to be ordered by Warrant, King George V made it very clear in 1920 that he strongly disapproved of the practice and it is unlikely to happen again.

The only naval Victoria Cross to be won on horseback was awarded to the inaptly-named George Chicken (*d* 1860). In 1858, during the Indian Mutiny, he was serving as a Volunteer with the Indian Naval Brigade on the strength of HMS *Calcutta*, but on 27 September he attached himself to a party of the 3rd Sikh Irregular Cavalry and, single-handed, attacked a band of 20 armed mutineers, killing five of them before he was unhorsed and rescued by four native troopers who arrived in the nick of time. Chicken's VC was gazetted on 27 April 1860, but he was drowned the following month when his schooner *Emily* was lost in the Bay of Bengal, so it is likely that he never knew of his award.

The Conspicuous Service Cross (CSC), which became the **Distinguished Service Cross** (DSC) in 1914, was instituted in June 1901. Only eight awards of the CSC were made, the first being to Midshipman T. C. Armstrong, gazetted on 22 July 1901.

The Distinguished Service Medal (DSM) was instituted in October 1914, and was awarded 4052 times with 67 first bars and two second bars during the First World War and 7132 times during the Second World War. There were 153 first bars, four second bars and one third bar, which was awarded to Temporary Petty Officer W. H. Kelly. '**One case is known of the award of two DSMs to the same man**. The *Gazette* of 12 May 1917, announced the award of the medal to Seaman James Moar, Mercantile Marine; this was in respect of services in the Mediterranean Sea on 16 February 1917. During the Second World War, Moar was awarded a second medal for services rendered on passage to North Russia, the award being announced in the *Gazette* of 6 August 1943. The award of the second medal is explicable only on grounds of inadvertence, a bar to the first medal being the appropriate award.' (P. E. ABBOTT and J. M. A. TAMPLIN, *British Gallantry Awards*).

During the First World War 1694 Distinguished Service Crosses (DSC) were awarded and 10 naval officers won it twice. During the Second World War there were 4524 awards, 434 first bars, 44 second bars and one third bar. The recipient of the third bar was Temporary Acting Commander N. E. Morley, RNVR, whose third bar was gazetted on 12 June 1945 for minesweeping operations in the Gulf of Corinth.

The first naval Victoria Cross of the First World War was won by Commander Henry Peel Ritchie (1876–1968) at Dar-es-Salaam, then the capital of German East Africa, on 28 November 1914. The Germans had supposedly surrendered but opened fire from the shore on the steam pinnace in which Ritchie had entered the harbour. Ritchie was hit eight times but the pinnace managed to get back to her mothership, the Pre-Dreadnought battleship *Goliath*, whose main 12in (30.5cm) guns were then turned on the Germans at the water's edge.

The first Victoria Cross to be awarded in the First World War (Ritchie's VC was not gazetted until 10 April 1915) was also **the first Victoria Cross ever won by a submariner**. On Friday 13 December, Lieutenant Norman Holbrook (1888–1976), commanding B.-11, an aged and obsolete submarine built by Vickers in 1905, with a crew of two officers and 15 men, forced the

Dardanelles and sank the 10,000-ton Turkish battleship *Messudiyeh*. He scored a direct hit with his starboard torpedo and she sank in about ten minutes. Holbrook's Victoria Cross was gazetted on 22 December, only nine days after the event. The crew shared a prize bounty award of £3500.

The oldest man ever to win the Victoria Cross at sea was Lieutenant Frederick Parslow, RNR, who was 59 when the ship he was commanding, HM Horse Transport *Anglo-Californian*, was attacked by a U-boat some 90 miles (145km) south-west of Queenstown, Ireland, on 4 July 1915. Though Parslow himself was killed, it was due to his skill in keeping his ship stern-on to the U-boat that his son, who was with him, was able to bring the damaged *Anglo-Californian* safely into Queenstown the next day. His son, young Fred, was awarded the Distinguished Service Cross.

John Travers Cornwell VC. *National Maritime Museum.*

The youngest member of the Royal Navy to win the Victoria Cross was Boy John Travers Cornwell who, though mortally wounded, remained at his post on board HMS *Chester* at the Battle of

Jutland on 31 May 1916. He was not quite 16½ years old at the time. For the record, the youngest boy ever to win the Victoria Cross was Hospital Apprentice Arthur Fitzgibbon who was 15 years and 3 months when he won the medal at the Taku Forts, China, on 21 August 1860.

Originally naval Victoria Crosses had a blue ribbon and military VCs a red one, but after the RAF became a separate organization in April 1918, King George V decided later that year to drop, rather than add, a colour, and since then all Victoria Crosses have had the red ribbon. **The last naval Victoria Cross to have a blue ribbon** was that awarded to Chief Petty Officer George Prowse who killed six Germans and captured another 13 at Pronville, east of Quéant, on 2 September 1918, while serving with Drake Battalion of the Royal Naval Division. He was killed at Cambrai on 27 September, a month before his citation was gazetted. **The first naval Victoria Cross to have a red ribbon** was that won by Commander Daniel Beak (1891–1967) also of Drake Battalion, for his sustained bravery over a period of four days near Bapaume in August 1918. After the war Beak, who had already won a DSO and two MCs, found civilian life 'rather tame', joined the army and had risen to the rank of Major-General when he retired in 1945.

The only member of the Royal Navy to have won the Victoria Cross in the United Kingdom, and the second of only three people ever to do so, was Acting Leading Seaman Jack Mantle, RN. On 4 July 1940, he was mortally wounded while manning his pom-pom anti-aircraft gun on HMS *Foylebank* during an attack on Portland Harbour by 12 German Stukas.

The first naval George Cross was awarded to Lieutenant Robert Armitage, RNVR, for his work in the disposal of parachute mines during September/October 1940. The award was gazetted on 27 December 1940. The George Cross was inaugurated by King George VI on 23 September 1940, for deeds of supreme gallantry 'for which purely military Honours are not normally granted'.

The first George Cross to be won at sea was that awarded to Bombardier Henry Reed for his gallantry while serving in an Anti-Aircraft battery aboard SS *Cormount*. On 21 June 1941, the ship was hit by an air-launched torpedo while sailing in convoy from Blyth to London. His citation read: 'Gunner Reed ... was badly wounded ... The Chief Officer was also badly wounded. Reed carried him from the bridge down two ladders to the deck below and placed him in a shelter near a lifeboat. Gunner Reed then died. It was afterwards found that his stomach had been ripped open by machine-gun bullets.'

TRADE
— & —
TRANSPORT

MERCHANT
SHIPS

THE HANSA LEAGUE

The first two Hansa (German: a defensive alliance) **ports** were Lübeck and Hamburg, which, in 1241, formed a league to protect themselves against pirates and robber barons. They were joined by other towns until, in the 14th and 15th centuries, about 85 cities belonged to the League, including, in England, London, Boston, York, Hull, Bristol and King's Lynn. During the 16th century the League began to disintegrate under the growing liberation of trade and by 1600 it was virtually dead.

The aptly-named cog was the ship around which the wheel of Hanseatic trade revolved and, as a result, there has grown up a tendency to call any Northern cargo-carrying vessel of this period a cog; but it should be borne in mind that Dorothy Burwash, in her study of merchant shipping of only a century later, identified as many as 43 different types of vessel plying their trade around the coast of Europe.

Nevertheless, the cog was indeed widely used for 150 years in the Baltic and North Seas and round the Atlantic coast of Europe for carrying salt fish, grain, wool, leather hides and timber for shipbuilding. Dr McGowan, in his book *Tiller and Whipstaff*, describes a cog as 'a flat-bottomed, capacious cargo ship ... often built without a keel, at other times with a simple keel-plank, from which the stem and stern posts rose sharply and in a straight line. The bottom planking was laid flush, i.e. edge to edge, the steep high sides being clinker-built from the edge of the bilge.' She had one square-rigged mast. A cog recovered from the River Weser and dated to *c* 1380 was 77ft (23.5m) in length and 23ft (7m) in the beam.

Reconstruction of a cog.

THE HULC

Towards the end of the 14th century the cog seems to have been replaced by the hulc, of which little is known, though Dr McGrail tells us, in *Rafts, Boats and Ships from Prehistoric Times to the Medieval Era*, that 'the hulc dominated northern sea commerce in the 14th century because she had been developed to have greater capacity'. The ship on the font at Winchester Cathedral, referred to earlier (p. 161) as being possibly the first representation of a stern rudder, is said to represent a hulc.

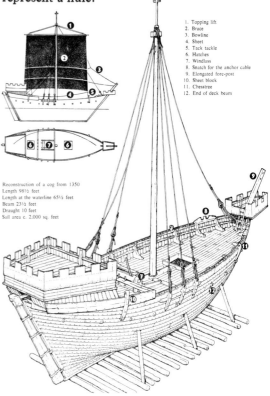

1. Topping lift
2. Brace
3. Bowline
4. Sheet
5. Tack tackle
6. Hatches
7. Windlass
8. Snatch for the anchor cable
9. Elongated fore-post
10. Sheet block
11. Chesstree
12. End of deck beam

Reconstruction of a cog from 1350
Length 98½ feet
Length at the waterline 65½ feet
Beam 23½ feet
Draught 10 feet
Sail area c. 2,000 sq. feet

THE DUTCH FLUYT

The most important merchant ship in northern waters during the 17th century was the Dutch fluyt, the first of which is said to have been built at Hoorn in 1595. The fluyt owed its success to the fact that it was admirably designed for its purpose which was to carry the maximum cargo at the minimum cost. This required a large hold, achieved, Dr McGowan says, 'by a stem and sternpost that were almost vertical, with full lines and flat floors for much of her midships length ... Her rig was kept simple ... and sails were generally smaller than those on a warship of similar size for ease of handling in order to keep the number of crew to a minimum.' Fluyts varied in size between 200 and 500 tons.

Original Arms of the East India Company.

A Dutch Fluyt.

The first fleet of the East India Company sailed from Torbay in April 1601, consisted of five ships and was commanded by Sir James Lancaster (*c* 1555–1618). He rounded the Cape of Good Hope on 1 November, visited the Nicobars, Sumatra, Java and the Moluccas and arrived back in England on 11 September 1603. The voyage had been a success and Lancaster was rewarded with a knighthood. He continued to be a director of the East India Company until his death and most of the voyages of the early Stuart period, both to India and in search of the North-West passage, were undertaken under his advice and direction. Lancaster Sound, on the north-west of Baffin Bay, was named after him by William Baffin.

The first light vessel in the world was moored in 1731 near the Nore Sands at the mouth of the River Thames. The idea is believed to have originated with an English barber called Robert Hamblin. By 1819 there were eight light vessels in the world, all off the coast of England. The Goodwin Light Vessel dates from 1795. The first was a wooden hull and the light consisted of four large candles on a cross-piece of wood. Light vessels were introduced into the United States in 1820.

The largest fleet of light vessels in the world is that of the Corporation of Trinity House, in whom 'the responsibility for erecting or laying out beacons, buoys, markers and signs of the sea' has been vested since 1565 when the first Act of Parliament relating to the Corporation was passed. Though some light vessels are self-propelled, those of Trinity House are not and must be towed from their stations for overhaul.

Edward Lloyd first began to print thrice-weekly bulletins of shipping and commercial information in 1696, but the venture, to which he gave the name *Lloyd's News*, lasted only a few months. Later he produced Ship's Lists, giving brief descriptions of ships likely to be offered for insurance. The newspaper was revived in 1734 as *Lloyd's List* and has appeared regularly ever since. Apart from the *London Gazette*, *Lloyd's List* is **the oldest newspaper now in existence**.

Lloyd's Register of Shipping, an annual publication listing and classifying every merchant ship of over 100 tons, may have first appeared in 1760 but the earliest extant volume is that for 1764–5–6. It is reverently preserved in the library of the present headquarters of Lloyd's Register at 71 Fenchurch Street, London, EC3. In it the hulls of ships were classified A, E, I, O, or U, according to the soundness or otherwise of their hulls. The classification symbol AI was used for the first time in the 1775–6 register. This is the third oldest Register to have survived.

The first steam-driven vessel to appear in *Lloyd's Register of Shipping* was the *James Watt* in 1823. She was 124ft (378m) in length, was driven by a Boulton and Watt 100hp engine and was built by John Wood of Port Glasgow. She was classed AI. By 1827 there were 81 steamers on the Register, by 1832 a round 100.

The *James Watt*, the first steam-driven vessel to be listed in *Lloyd's Register*.

'Probably the first containers ever built and to reach a ship were the brainchild of I. K. Brunel, who introduced them on the Vale of Neath railway in 1841,' says Ewan Corlett in *The Revolution in Merchant Shipping 1950–1980*. Four cubical iron boxes, each containing 2½ tons of coal, were fitted on each truck and machinery was erected at the dock to lower the boxes into the hold of the ship, but then the bottom was opened, the coal deposited and the box removed.

'Rarely can a sea-going vessel have embraced so many novel features, anticipating by several generations the rail ferry and the roll-on/roll-off ship,' says Robin Craig in *Steam Tramps and Cargo Liners* of the 277-ton *Bedlington*, built by Thomas Dunn Marshall at South Shields in 1842. In *Lloyd's Survey Report* of 22 September 1842, she was described thus: 'The vessel is fitted on the floors with rails for waggons to be run fore and aft and calculated to contain 40 waggons, fitted with a working drop to answer either side over the main hatchway which is adapted to hoist and lower by the engine that drives the propelling screws which are fitted in each run. The boilers are placed closed (sic) forward and the engines aft, leaving the entire hold amidships for the stowage of the waggons on the four railways.'

The iron auxiliary screw steamer *QED*, built in 1844 and designed to carry 340 tons of coal, was **the first vessel to be fitted with a double bottom for water ballast**.

In 1850 the steam tug *Goliath* laid the first submarine cable of any appreciable length. The *Goliath* was the **first vessel fitted with equipment specifically designed for the laying of cables**.

The most successful of the early steam screw colliers was the 486-ton *John Bowes* launched in 1852 and built by Charles Mark Palmer at Jarrow. She was 148.9ft (45.4m) long, 25.7ft (7.8m) wide, 15.6ft (4.75m) in depth and could carry 600 tons of coal. After many changes of nationality, she was sailing under Spanish colours in 1933 as the *Villa Selgas*, with a cargo of iron ore. She sprang a leak and sank off the country of her adoption with the good record of 81 years hard going. 'This notable vessel established the iron screw collier as a commercially profitable investment' says Robin Craig.

'The first ship known to be expressly built to keep navigation [routes] **open in winter** was the *Polhem*, constructed in Sweden in 1857. A

0 20 40 60   100   140 miles

0 20 40 60   100   140 km

12   10   8   6   4   2W   0   2E

ORKNEY IS

Stromness

Scapa Flow

N 58

HEBRIDES

Aberdeen

SCOTLAND
Fort William

ATLANTIC OCEAN

56

Firth of Forth

Helensburgh   Granton
Dumbarton   **Edinburgh**
Glasgow   Berwick-upon-Tweed
Firth   R Clyde   Farne I
of
Clyde   **NORTH SEA**

Bloody Foreland

Newcastle upon Tyne

N IRELAND   Portpatrick
Carrickfergus   Middlesbrough

Belfast   Whitehaven   Scarborough
Barrow-in-Furness   Flamborough Head

54

IRISH SEA   York
Hull

EIRE   Dublin   Liverpool
Birkenhead

Dun Laoghaire
Wicklow   Boston   Great
Yarmouth
King's Lynn   Lowestoft
52   Southwold

WALES

Cork
Bantry Bay   Ballycotton
Cobh (Queenstown)   **London**
Old Head of Kinsale   **Cardiff**   Avonmouth   Sheerness Margate
Fastnet Rock l.h.   BRISTOL   Chatham   Sandwich
CHANNEL   Bristol   R Medway
Southampton   Shoreham   Dover
Portsmouth   Newhaven   Hastings
Beachy Head
Devonport Plymouth
Land's End   Isle of
Falmouth   Wight
Start Point
Isles of Scilly   Lizard Point   ENGLISH CHANNEL

50

10   8   6   4   2W   0

Russian merchant named Britnoff had a small, single-screw vessel built to keep open the port of Kronstadt. This vessel had a modified bow so shaped that it broke ice by applied weight and this is the principle of most ice-breakers today. In 1871 the appropriately named *Eisbrecher I* was built in Hamburg' (R. MUNRO-SMITH, *Merchant Ship Types*).

'The petroleum industry of the world was founded in 1859 by the discovery of oil in Titusville in Pennsylvania. In 1861 **the first cargo of American oil**, in barrels, **crossed the Atlantic** from the Delaware River to London in the sailing brig *Elizabeth Watts*; the trip to the Thames took 45 days. The barrel was found to be uneconomic in use of cargo space and in 1869 a ship named *Charles* was equipped with metal tanks inside the hull.... The *Charles* ... traded for three years before catching fire and being burnt to the waterline' (R. MUNRO-SMITH, *Merchant Ship Types*).

The first vessels specially designed for the purpose of carrying oil were the *Ramsey*, an 800-ton iron-hulled sailing vessel built in the Isle of Man in 1863, and the *Atlantic* and the *Great Western*, both 416-ton iron-hulled barges built on the Tyne by John Rogerson and Co in the same year. The hold space was divided by a bulkhead along the centreline, with transverse bulkheads forming eight compartments each 20ft (6.1m) in length. There is, however, no evidence that any of them ever carried a single barrel of oil.

The first ship in which an attempt was made to use the fabric of the vessel as the actual oil-container instead of separating the tanks entirely from the shell was the 2748-ton iron steamer *Vaderland*, built in 1872 by Palmers of Newcastle for the Société Anonyme de Navigation Belge-Americaine. Unfortunately the Belgians refused to allow storage tanks to be built for the oil and the Americans refused to licence the ship to carry passengers. In addition to which, when she arrived in Philadelphia, the pumping apparatus was not complete, so the owners gladly accepted a general cargo and forgot all about the oil.

Triple-expansion engines were first fitted in a sea-going vessel in 1874 when A. C. Kirk, then manager of John Elder and Co., designed and installed such an engine in the screw-steamer *Propontis*. The three inverted cylinders were of the following diameters: high pressure 1ft 11in (58cm); intermediate 3ft 5$\frac{1}{4}$in (105cm); low pressure 5ft 2in (157cm).

Many attempts were made, with varying degrees of success, to perfect a method whereby freezing machinery could be installed and kept working within the hull of a ship at sea. **The first successful refrigerated steamer** was the *Frigorifique*, designed by a Frenchman named Tellier. In 1877 the *Frigorifique* landed a cargo of beef from the Argentine in fair condition after it had been preserved over a period of 110 days. Tellier's machinery, however, involved the use of ammonia, which could be dangerous.

The Bell-Coleman machine, in which compressed air was used to produce low temperatures was first installed in the Anchor liner *Circassia* in 1879 and proved a success.

The first cargo of frozen meat to be brought from Australia to Great Britain arrived on board the 2275-ton iron steamer *Strathleven* in 1880. She was fitted with a Bell-Coleman machine.

The first cargo of frozen meat from New Zealand to Britain was carried in the Albion Line's sailing ship *Dunedin* in 1882.

The earliest vessel recorded by *Lloyd's Register* **which used oil as fuel** was the steamer *Himalaya* in 1885. She was 'purchased by the Maharu Petroleum, Oil & Produce Co. for the express purpose of experimenting with a steam-injection

An artist's impression of the *Vaderland*.

Frigorifique, the first successful refrigerated steamer.
Mary Evans Picture Library.

type of oil burner, using a mineral oil derived from Scotch shale as fuel for her boilers. A voyage from London to Granton and back was made with one of the Society's surveyors on board. The oil was carried in barrels on deck, but from the surveyor's report it appears that the results were not satisfactory, and the installation was removed' (*Annals of Lloyd's Register*).

The first two ships in which the outer shell was actually used as the tank containing the oil were the 2307-ton *Gluckauf* built by Sir W. G. Armstrong, Mitchell & Co. on the Tyne for the German company Wilhelm Anton Reidemann in 1886 and the 1531-ton *Bakuin*, built by W. Gray & Co. of West Hartlepool in the same year.

The first vessel in which the oil was actually carried up to the underside of the weather deck was the 1436-ton *Loutsch* built by Hawthorn, Leslie & Co. of Newcastle in 1886 for the Russian Steam Navigation and Trading Co. Ltd. of Odessa. **These three were the first real 'tankers'.**

THE ISHERWOOD SYSTEM

The next vital step in the evolution of the tanker was provided by Joseph Isherwood and was later to be known as the Isherwood System. His 'plan cut right across the traditional pattern of design. It substituted longitudinal for lateral framing: that is, roughly, the ship's ribs ran fore and aft

instead of from side to side at intervals. Its application made it possible to calculate the strength of a ship's structure with a larger freedom from initial assumptions than had been possible in terms of tradition. The girders running fore and aft had the valuable effect of reinforcing the thinner plating of decks: and the system allowed considerable saving in material.' (GEORGE BLAKE, *Lloyd's Register of Shipping 1760–1960.*)

The first ship to be built according to the Isherwood System was the 4196-ton *Paul Paix*, built by R. Craggs & Sons at Middlesbrough in 1908. She was **the first ship to appear in** *Lloyd's Register* **with the notation 'Longitudinal Framing'.**

Turret deck cargo carriers were first designed and built by Messrs Duxfords in the 1890s. 'They were designed largely to reduce the tolls payable on passages through the Suez Canal, then calculated in terms of deck space. The "turret" ships ... thus took on the appearance of outsize submarines, the measurable deck space above their bulbous sides [being] little more than a series of cat-walks' (GEORGE BLAKE, *Lloyd's Register of Shipping*).

The first ship to be fitted with a combination of reciprocating engines and turbines was the *Otaki*, built by William Denny & Co. of Dumbarton for the New Zealand Shipping Co. in 1908. She had three propellors of which the two wing shafts were driven by reciprocating engines, both exhausting into the turbine driving the centre shaft. For manoeuvring and going astern only the reciprocating engines were used.

The use of oil in internal combustion engines for the purpose of propulsion owes most to the discovery by Rudolf Diesel that heavy oil could be used to produce power for heavy work in the same way as the explosion of vaporized petrol drives the pistons in a motor-car. By 1907 a large number of small craft had been fitted with internal combustion engines, but **the earliest sea-going vessel**, other than small craft, **to be fitted with heavy oil engines** was the Italian 678-ton twin-screw vessel *Romagna*, built in 1910 by Cantieri Navali Riuniti at Ancona, the engines for which were constructed by Sulzer Bros. of Winterthur.

The first ocean-going motorship to receive classification from *Lloyd's Register* was the 1179-ton *Vulcanus*, built in 1910 by the Nederlandsche Scheepsbuouw Maatschappij, Amsterdam, for the Nederlandsch-Indische Tankstoomboot Maatschappij. She was fitted with a single-screw six-cylinder 4-stroke cycle heavy oil engine of the 'Werkspoor' type.

An interesting **pioneer ship** was the 293-ton *Holzapfel I*, built by J. T. Eltringham & Co. at South Shields in 1911. She was fitted with suction gas engines using anthracite as fuel.

The first motorship built in the United Kingdom was the 5000-ton *Jutlandia* built in 1912 by Barclay Curle & Co. on the Clyde for the Danish company Aktieselskabet Det Ostasiatiske Kompagni.

The first large vessels fitted with 4-stroke cycle single-acting heavy oil engines were the sister-ships *Selandia* and *Fiona* of 5000-tons each, built in 1912 for the East Asiatic Company by Messrs Burmeister and Wain of Copenhagen.

The first cargo steamer specially designed to be powered by geared turbines was the 4016-ton steel screw steamer *Cairncross*, built by William Duxford & Sons of Sunderland in 1913. The turbines were made by Parsons Marine Steam Turbine Ltd. of Newcastle.

The world's first all-welded ship was the *Fullagar*, built by Cammell Laird & Co. of Birkenhead in 1919. She was only 150ft (45.7m) long.

The first heavy-lift ship was the *Beldis*, built in 1924 by Armstrong Whitworth for the Christen Smith Shipping Co. of Oslo, the pioneers of the heavy derrick. She had a 100-tonne capacity derrick.

The *Arcwear*, built by Short Brothers in 1933, was **the first 'arcform' ship**, a design introduced by Sir Joseph Isherwood to improve the stability, economy and efficiency of cargo ships; but it was never adopted to any notable extent.

The first roll-on/roll-off ships, now known as Ro/Ros were the Landing Ships Tank, or LSTs, built for the Royal Navy during the Second World War. However, it is interesting to note that Sir Winston Churchill had anticipated the idea by over 20 years. In a minute to the War Cabinet dated 17 July 1917, in which he puts forward a scheme for the capture of the two Frisian Islands of Borkum and Sylt, he says, 'In addition a number – say 50 – *tank-landing lighters should be provided*, *each carrying a tank or tanks* (and) fitted for wire-cutting in its bow. By means of a drawbridge or shelving bow (the tanks) would land under (their) own power' (*The Second World War*, *Vol. II p. 215*). Churchill goes on to say that this paper was only left out of *The World Crisis*, his history of the First World War, for reasons of space, otherwise the idea would certainly have been seized upon and developed by the Germans. The first LST was nicknamed the 'Winette'.

The first company to use LSTs as civilian car ferries was the Atlantic Steam Navigation Company, founded by Colonel Frank Bustard in 1946, when he bought three LSTs to run Ro/Ro services between Tilbury and Antwerp and Preston and Northern Ireland.

CONTAINERIZATION

'Perhaps the first post-war use of containers was by the United Steamship Company of Copenhagen, which built two small ships in 1950, actually called "container ships", for a door-to-door transport service via Copenhagen and other ports' (EWAN CORLETT, *The Revolution in Merchant Shipping, 1950–80*).

The breakthrough in containerization did not come until the mid-1950s, but in America Sea-

train Lines Inc, of New York had pioneered a service between New York and Houston in 1929, carrying railway wagons in cradles aboard specialized ships. The first of these was the 7648-ton *Seatrain New Orleans* and could carry 95 wagons. She was actually built on the Tyne by Swan Hunter & Wigham Richardson Ltd.

The world's first true container ship was the *Gateway City*, the brainchild of an American called Malcolm MacLean, '**the true father of containerized unitization**'. MacLean's main business was in road haulage, which is an expensive way of moving freight; so he acquired a steamship company to act as a link in his transportation chain, and, thereby, to cut costs. In 1956 he had platforms built above the tank decks of two tankers, the platforms being designed to carry 35ft (10.7m) trailer vans which could be removed from the chassis of the truck. The following year, 1957, saw the full development of the lift-on/lift-off system with the conversion of the *Gateway City*.

A reigning monarch launched a British merchant ship for the first time when Queen Elizabeth II launched the 20,000-ton passenger liner *Southern Cross* at Belfast on 17 August 1954. The *Southern Cross* represented something of a revolution in ship design since she had her propelling machinery situated aft and carried no cargo. She was designed for round-the-world service via Panama, New Zealand, Australia and South Africa, a trip scheduled to take 11 weeks.

Model of the *Kurama Maru*, the world's largest container ship.

Perhaps **the greatest impetus behind the spectacular rise in the size of oil tankers** was the closure of the Suez Canal in 1956 and the consequent necessity for all Middle East oil bound for Europe to go round the Cape of Good Hope. To keep down the cost of oil, it was necessary to build bigger tankers and in 1959 **the first 100,000-ton crude carrier** appeared – the 104,000dwt *Universe Apollo*.

Another source of economy has been the introduction of multi-purpose vessels. Until quite recently one of the characteristics of oil tankers was that they made one leg of the voyage loaded and the other in ballast. To overcome this, the oil/bulk/ore (OBO) ship was developed in the early post-war years. Such ships can carry oil on one leg and various bulk cargoes on the other, but they are expensive to build, laborious to operate on account of the cleaning required when changing cargoes, and do not have a good safety record. A development of the OBO is the PROBO, which stands for product/oil/bulk/ore, and which can carry product oil cargoes as well as crude oil and other bulk cargoes.

'**The world's first purpose-built Ro/Ro ship intended solely for deep-water operation** was the *Comet*, built by the United States Military Sea Transport Service in 1958. The main vehicle deck was equipped with a stern ramp and two side ports, ramps on either sides, with internal ramps

The *Berge Adria*, the world's largest ore carrier.

to other decks. Thus, after entering the ship, vehicles could proceed to other decks' (EWAN CORLETT).

The first merchant ship in the world to be powered entirely by gas turbines was the 8221-gwt shell tanker *Auris*. In 1949 one of her four diesel engines had been replaced by an experimental gas turbine unit and in 1955 she was stripped of all her machinery and a 5500hp gas turbine was substituted.

The world's first nuclear-powered surface ship was the Russian ice-breaker *Lenin*. She is 440ft (134m) long, displaces 16,000 tons and sailed on her maiden voyage on 15 September 1959. Her three nuclear reactors, two of which are normally used for operation and the third kept in reserve, give her a maximum speed of 18 knots. She carries a crew of 230 and two helicopters. She is said to be able to clear a channel 100ft (30.5m) wide through pack ice 8ft (2.4m) thick at a speed of between 3 and 4 knots. She can carry enough fuel to be able to cruise for a year without touching port.

The world's first nuclear-powered cargo ship, the American n.s. (nuclear-ship) *Savannah*, made her maiden voyage on 20–22 August 1962, from Yorktown, Virginia, to Savannah, Georgia. She can carry 60 passengers and 10,000 tons of cargo at 20 knots and can cruise for $3\frac{1}{2}$ years without refuelling.

The first West European nuclear vessel, the 15,000-ton ore carrier *Otto Hahn*, named after the German physicist and Nobel prize winner, was launched at Kiel on 13 June 1964.

The first commercial LNG (liquid natural gas) **carrier** was the *Methane Princess*, which docked at Canvey Island in October 1964 with 12,000 tons of LNG from Algeria. LNG boils at 161 °C so it can be appreciated that its transportation poses considerable problems, which have been overcome with remarkable success. 'Perhaps more than any other, the LNG carrier epitomizes the sheer daring and technical expertise of shipowners and naval architects in the last quarter of this century' (EWAN CORLETT).

Ships carrying butane and propane are called LPG carriers (liquid petroleum gas).

Initially **the most serious drawbacks to containerization** were the use of different sizes of container by each operator, which made interchangeability impossible, and the lack of suitable port facilities. However, in 1961 the American Standards Association adopted standard container sizes and in 1965 the International Standards Organization followed suit. The size of the standard container is 20ft (6.1m) × 8ft (2.4m), and a container ship which carries 1500 containers is said to carry 1500 TEU (twenty equivalent units).

The *Opama Maru*, built in Japan in 1965, was the **first ship to be built specifically for the purpose of carrying cars** – the first ocean-going car carrier. She could carry 1200 cars. Later came the pure car carriers (PCCs), also known as garage ships.

The first specialized container and roll-on/roll-off ferry port in Europe was opened in March 1966 at New Scandia, outside Göteborg, Sweden.

The cargo ferry *Finncarrier*, built in 1969 by Wartsila, Helsinki, was **the first vessel in the** world to be equipped with a special air-bubble system for operating in ice. Compressed air, forced through a number of holes in the lower part of the bow, combines with the water to form a lubricating film between the hull and the ice and thus reduces the friction.

The Spring of 1969 marked a turning point in the development of sea freightage when the US firm Sea-Land Service Inc., pioneers of the containerization revolution, placed orders for a fleet of 33-knot container ships. Hitherto cargo-liner speeds had shifted noticeably only twice since the Second World War, from about 15 to 17 knots in the 1950s and from 17 to 20 knots in the 1960s.

The first long-range, deep-sea-trade cellular container ship built by any shipowner was Overseas Containers Ltd's 27,000grt *Encounter Bay*, which went into service in February 1969. She was 744ft (227m) long and could carry 1500 20ft boxes at 21.5 knots. Overseas Containers Ltd. is a consortium formed by the Ocean Steamship Co., Peninsular and Oriental, the British and Commonwealth Shipping Co. and Furness Withy & Co.

The LASH freighter was conceived by LASH Systems Inc. of New Orleans, who took delivery of the first vessel, the 43,000dwt *Acadia Forest* from Japan in 1969. LASH stands for Lighter Aboard Ship and denotes a vessel equipped with its own gantry crane capable of handling and stowing on board loaded lighters which can complete the voyage from port of arrival to ultimate destination on their own bottoms.

Some trace the ancestry of the LASH freighter back to a freak called the *Connector*, built in England in about 1850. This curious vessel was built in three sections, loosely hinged together to enable the ship to ride comfortably through heavy seas with an undulating motion and also to allow the sections to be separated and loaded or discharged at separate wharves. She was not a success.

A closer ancestor was the Landing Ship Dock (LSD), another product of the Second World War. The cargo was carried in landing craft and the ship, on arrival, was flooded down by ballasting, allowing the landing craft to float out and proceed independently to the shore.

The jointed iron steamship *Connector*.

A development of the LASH ship is **the SEEBEE** in which barges are 'embarked two at a time through a stern elevator. Tugs position the barges over a submerged platform which is then raised to the required deck level where a transporter runs under each barge, jacks it up off the elevator blocks and moves it into the stowage area' (CORNWELL, *An Illustrated History of Ships*). The SEEBEE system was pioneered by the Lykes Bros. Steamship Co., of New Orleans, La., and **the first SEEBEE ship**, the 20,500grt *Doctor Lykes*, went into service in 1972.

SEEBEE barges are 29.72m × 10.67m × 3.81m and carry 847 tons. LASH barges are 18.75m × 95m × 4m and carry 370 tons.

The largest of these ships are known as Panamax; that is to say they have reached the limit at which a ship can still pass through the Panama Canal.

In 1973 **tanker size rose for the first time to around the 500,000 ton mark,** as the oil industry struggled to achieve economies by getting bigger flows through larger, simpler systems. One major snag was that in the main oil-producing area, the Persian Gulf, and in the main consumer areas, North America, Northern Europe and Japan, continental shelves prohibited the approach of ships larger than 100,000 tons in some cases, 250,000 tons in others. This led to the development of single-point mooring, which enabled a big ship to swing freely in deep water and discharge its cargo without ever coming into port at all. Though this suited the industry, being flexible, efficient and economical, it was not at all popular with adjoining communities and with environmentalists, who saw, and still see, the giant tankers as an ever present menace of pollution.

TRANSMODALITY

The process of containerization, in which the cargo is pre-stowed in boxes and slotted into the cellular holds of the ship, developed throughout the late 1960s and 1970s and roll-on/roll-off services came to involve a continuous transport process by road, rail, sea and inland waterways, to describe which the word 'transmodality' was coined. Two concepts which typified this development were LASH (lighter aboard ship) and SEEBEE land-sea bridges. Both involved ships carrying barges that originated and ended their journey by inland waterway.

World Output of Merchant Shipping since 1946

Tonnages given in gross tons. Leading shipbuilding country, tonnage built and percentage of world tonnage are shown in brackets.

YEAR	TOTAL TONNAGE			
1946	2,114,702	(United Kingdom	1,120,526	52.98)
1947	2,102,621	(United Kingdom	1,192,759	56.73)
1948	2,309,473	(United Kingdom	1,176,346	50.93)
1949	3,131,805	(United Kingdom	1,267,467	40.47)
1950	3,492,876	(United Kingdom	1,324,570	37.92)
1951	3,642,564	(United Kingdom	1,341,024	36.82)
1952	4,395,578	(United Kingdom	1,302,548	29.61)
1953	5,096,050	(United Kingdom	1,317,463	25.85)
1954	5,252,631	(United Kingdom	1,408,874	26.82)
1955	5,316,742	(United Kingdom	1,473,937	27.72)
1956	6,673,701	(Japan	1,746,429	26.17)
1957	8,501,404	(Japan	2,432,506	28.61)
1958	9,269,983	(Japan	2,066,669	22.29)
1959	8,745,704	(Japan	1,722,577	19.70)
1960	8,356,444	(Japan	1,731,656	20.72)
1961	7,940,005	(Japan	1,779,324	22.66)
1962	8,374,754	(Japan	2,183,147	26.07)
1963	8,538,513	(Japan	2,367,353	27.73)
1964	10,263,803	(Japan	4,085,190	39.80)
1965	12,215,817	(Japan	5,363,232	43.90)
1966	14,307,202	(Japan	6,685,461	46.73)
1967	15,780,111	(Japan	7,496,876	47.51)
1968	16,907,743	(Japan	8,582,970	50.77)
1969	19,315,290	(Japan	9,303,453	48.17)
1970	21,689,513	(Japan	10,475,804	48.30)
1971	24,859,701	(Japan	11,992,495	48.24)
1972	26,714,386	(Japan	12,865,851	48.16)
1973	31,520,373	(Japan	15,673,115	49.75)
1974	33,521,289	(Japan	16,894,017	50.37)
1975	34,202,514	(Japan	16,991,230	49.68)
1976	33,922,193	(Japan	15,867,828	46.78)
1977	27,531,824	(Japan	11,707,635	42.52)
1978	18,194,120	(Japan	6,307,155	34.67)
1979	14,289,369	(Japan	4,696,996	32.87)
1980	13,101,104	(Japan	6,094,142	46.52)
1981	16,931,719	(Japan	8,399,831	49.61)

Progressive Growth in the size of Merchant Ships

Table showing the largest merchant ship launched each year since 1946.

YEAR	NAME	GRT	DWT	LAUNCHED	OWNER
1946	*Willem Ruys*	23,112	4,925	Holland	Koninklijke Rotterdamsche, Lloyd NV
1947	*Kosmos III*	18,460	25,100	Sweden	A/S Kosmos, Norway
1948	*Thorshovdi*	18,361	23,250	Denmark	A/S Odd, Norway
1949	*Burgan*	17,905	28,336	USA	Afran Transport & Liberia
1950	*Augustus*	27,090	8,720	Italy	'Italia' Soc. Per Azion Dinavigazione, Genoa, Italy
1951	*United States*	51,988	—	USA	United States Lines
1952	*Kungsholm*	21,164	4,135	Netherlands	A/B Svenska Amerika Linien, Sweden
1953	*Cristoforo Colombo*	29,191	9,304	Italy	'Italia' Soc. Per Azion Dinavigazione, Genoa, Italy
1954	*Willem Barendsz II*	26,830	26,150	Netherlands	NV Nederlands Maats Voor de Walvisvaart, Amsterdam, Holland
1955	*Sinclair Petrolore*	35,477	56,089	Japan	Universe Tankships Inc., Liberia
1956	*Universe Leader*	51,400	85,515	Japan	Universe Tankships Inc., Liberia
1957	*Universe Commander*	51,398	85,618	Japan	Universe Tankships Inc., Liberia
1958	*Universe Apollo*	72,132	104,520	Japan	Universe Tankships Inc., Liberia
1959	*Oriental Giant*	43,422	70,365	Japan	Tanker Service Inc., Liberia
1960	*Universe Daphne*	72,266	115,360	Japan	Universe Tankships Inc., Liberia
1961	*Manhattan*	62,434	114,668	USA	Manhattan Tanker Co. Inc., USA
1962	*Nissho Maru*	74,396	137,134	Japan	Idemitsu Tanker KK, Tokyo
1963	*Mobil Brilliant*	58,211	97,385	Sweden	Mobil Tankers Co. (Liberia) Ltd
1964	*Yamamizu Maru*	62,195	99,655	Japan	Yamashita-Shinnihon Kissen KK, Japan
1965	*Tokyo Maru*	96,500	151,258	Japan	Tokyo Tanker KK
1966	*Idemitsu Maru*	107,957	206,106	Japan	Idemitsu Tanker KK, Japan
1967	*Megara*	105,245	206,750	Japan	Shell Tankers UK Ltd
1968	*Universe Ireland*	149,609	326,585	Japan	Bantry Transportation Co., Liberia
1969	*Universe Iran*	149,623	326,933	Japan	Bantry Transportation Co., Liberia
1970	*Berge King*	140,012	280,240	Japan	Sig. Bergesen & Co., Norway
1971	*Nisseki Maru*	184,855	372,400	Japan	Tokyo Tanker KK
1972	*Globtik Tokyo*	213,866	483,662	Japan	Norop Tankers Corp., Liberia
1973	*Globtik London*	238,207	483,960	Japan	Etra Shipping Corp., Liberia
1974	*Hemland*	190,367	372,201	Japan	Angfartygs A/B Tirfing, Sweden
1975	*Nissei Maru*	238,517	484,337	Japan	Tokyo Tanker KK
1976	*Batillus*	275,276	553,662	France	Société Maritime Shell, France
1977	*Pierre Guillaumat*	273,550	554,000	France	Cie Nationale de Navigation, France
1978	*Nanny*	245,140	499,000	Sweden	Zenit Tank AB
1979	*Prairial*	274,838	555,000	France	Compagnie Nationale de Navigation, France
1980	*Berge Pioneer*	198,554	320,000	Japan	Sig. Bergesen DY & Co., Norway
1981	*Berge Enterprise*	198,544	325,133	Japan	Sig. Bergesen DY & Co., Norway
1982	*Kazimah*	163,448	294,739	Japan	Kuwait Oil Tanker Co. S.A.K.

Largest Merchant Ships in each main cargo category

The following list shows the largest in each of the main types of merchant ship as of July 1982. Where the largest deadweight tonnage and the largest gross registered tonnage relate to different vessels, both are shown.

TYPE	NAME	GRT	DWT	FLAG	COMPLETED
Cable Ship	*Long Lines*	11,326	9,461	USA	1963
Car-Passenger Ferry	*Finlandia*	25,677	3,898	Finland	1981
			1,601 berth		
Cement Carrier	*Peleus*	21,548	42,466	Greece	1966
Chemical Tanker	*Hitra*	22,837	32,229	Norway	1961
Coal Carrier	*Elgin*	86,208	173,700	Liberia	1981
Container Ship	*Kurama Maru*	59,294	43,476	Japan	1972
			2,228 TEU*		
Dredger	*Icoa*	16,729	10,444	Venezuela	1961
Fish Cannery	*Vladivostock*	17,149	10,944	USSR	1962
Fish Carrier	*Karskoye More*	18,302	14,947	USSR	1971
Fish Factory	*Vostock*	26,400	22,110	USSR	1971
Fishing Vessel	*Soo Gong No. 51*	5,510	4,901	South Korea	1975
General Cargo	*Hoegh Clipper*	22,735	31,555	Norway	1979
General Cargo	*Hoegh Cairn*	22,735	31,555	Norway	1979
Ice Breaker	*Arktika*	18,172	4,096	USSR	1974
Lighter Carrier	*Bilderdyk*	36,974	44,799	Netherlands	1972
Liquid Nitrogen Gas Carrier	*Hoegh Gandria*	95,683	124,999	Norway	1977
Liquid Nitrogen Gas Carrier	*Rhenania*	80,946	133,000	Fed. Rep. of Germany	1981
Liquid Propane Gas Carrier	*Palace Tokyo*	64,378	99,300	Japan	1974
Liquid Propane Gas Carrier	*Esso Westernport*	54,057	100,988	Liberia	1977
Livestock Carrier	*Al Shuwaikh*	34,356	39,266	Kuwait	1967
Molasses Tanker	*Istana IV*	2,997	6,102	Indonesia	1972
Oil Tanker	*Bellamya*	275,268	553,662	France	1976
Oil Tanker	*Seawise Giant*	238,558	568,739	Liberia	1979
Ore	*Berge Brioni*	117,409	227,558	Norway	1973
Ore	*Berge Adria*	117,409	227,558	Norway	1972
Ore/Bulk/Oil	*Hitachi Venture*	70,316	264,171	Liberia	1982
Ore/Oil	*Lauderdale*	143,959	264,591	UK	1972
Ore/Oil	*World Gala*	133,748	282,462	Liberia	1973
Passenger Cargo	*Q. Elizabeth II*	67,140	15,976	UK	1969
Passenger Vessel	*Norway*	70,202	13,960	Norway	1961
Railway Ferry	*Frederick Carter*	12,221	5,339	Canada	1968
Reefer	*Fort Fleur D'Epee*	32,184	30,998	France	1980
Research Ship	*Kosmonaut Yury Gagarin*	32,291	31,300	USSR	1971
Ro/Ro Vessel	*Adm. Wm. M. Callaghan*	24,471	13,717	USA	1967
Stern Trawling Factory Ship	*Rybak Primoriya*	16,160	11,238	USSR	1980
Supply/Tender	*Raffaelio*	45,933	9,101	Iran	1965
Timber Carrier	*Hoegh Merit*	29,712	44,186	Norway	1977
Timber Carrier	*Hoegh Musketeer*	29,712	44,000	Norway	1977
Timber Carrier	*Thames Maru*	23,980	49,109	Japan	1976
Tug	*Canmar Kigoriak*	3,642	2,066	Canada	1979
Vegetable Oil Tanker	*Gogo Ranger*	12,499	21,012	Liberia	1958
Vehicle Carrier	*Fuji Maru*	36,480	37,402	Japan	1971
Wine Tanker	*Norchem*	4,555	7,339	Japan	1979

Comparative Shipbuilding Figures since 1975

	1975	1976	1977	1978	1979	1980	1981	1982
GB	1,169,516	1,500,139	1,019,695	1,133,331	691,404	427,122	212,692	434,599
USA	475,521	814,530	1,012,354	1,033,342	1,352,370	555,262	360,136	215,746
W. Germany	2,498,569	1,873,658	1,595,214	844,530	437,286	376,192	702,523	615,407
France	1,149,729	1,672,878	1,106,672	439,940	719,863	282,680	501,519	264,810
USSR	395,686	615,898	421,246	528,084	433,375	459,651	402,944	325,812
Sweden	2,187,525	2,514,948	2,311,343	1,407,017	459,644	347,509	453,031	287,319
Spain	1,592,522	1,320,220	1,813,472	821,111	630,199	394,588	779,619	557,012

World Tonnage of Merchant Ships (over 100 tons gross) since 1951

YEAR	TOTAL TONNAGE	LARGEST FLEET	SIZE OF LARGEST FLEET	YEAR	TOTAL TONNAGE	LARGEST FLEET	SIZE OF LARGEST FLEET
1951	87,254,044	United States	27,331,351	1967	182,099,644	Liberia	22,597,808
1952	90,180,359	United States	27,245,000	1968	194,152,378	Liberia	25,719,642
1953	93,351,800	United States	27,237,000	1969	211,660,893	Liberia	29,215,151
1954	97,421,526	United States	27,344,000	1970	227,489,846	Liberia	33,296,644
1955	100,568,779	United States	26,243,000	1971	247,202,634	Liberia	38,552,240
1956	105,200,361	United States	26,145,624	1972	268,340,145	Liberia	44,443,652
1957	110,264,081	United States	25,910,855	1973	289,926,686	Liberia	49,904,744
1958	118,033,731	United States	25,589,596	1974	311,322,626	Liberia	55,321,641
1959	124,935,479	United States	25,287,972	1975	342,162,363	Liberia	65,820,414
1960	129,769,500	United States	24,837,069	1976	371,999,926	Liberia	73,477,326
1961	135,915,958	United States	24,238,022	1977	393,678,369	Liberia	79,982,968
1962	139,979,813	United States	23,272,856	1978	406,001,979	Liberia	80,191,329
1963	145,836,463	United States	23,132,781	1979	413,021,426	Liberia	81,528,175
1964	152,999,621	United States	22,430,249	1980	419,910,651	Liberia	80,285,176
1965	160,391,504	United Kingdom	21,530,264	1981	420,834,813	Liberia	74,906,390
1966	171,129,833	United Kingdom	21,541,740	1982	424,741,682	Liberia	70,718,439

12 Largest Oil Tankers – July 1982

NAME	BUILT	REGISTERED	DWT	GRT	LENGTH FEET/METRES	BEAM FEET/METRES	DRAUGHT
Seawise Giant	Japan	Liberia	564,763	238,558	1504/458	209/63	80
Pierre Guillamat	France	France	555,051	274,838	1359/414	206/62	93
Prairial	France	France	554,974	274,838	1359/414	206/62	93
Bellamya	France	France	553,662	275,276	1359/414	206/62	93
Batillus	France	France	553,662	275,550	1358/413	206/62	93
Esso Atlantic	Japan	Liberia	516,893	234,638	1333/406	233/71	82
Esso Pacific	Japan	Liberia	516,423	234,626	1333/406	233/71	82
Nanny	Sweden	Sweden	491,120	245,140	1194/363	259/78	78
Nissei Maru	Japan	Japan	484,337	238,517	1242/378	203/61	91
Globtik London	Japan	Liberia	483,933	213,894	1243/378	203/61	92
Globtik Tokyo	Japan	Liberia	483,662	213,886	1243/378	203/61	92
Burmah Enterprise	Taiwan	UK	457,927	231,629	1241/378	224/68	82

Whaling

The start of modern whaling is generally dated from the 1860s when the Norwegian Svend Foyn (1809–94) developed the harpoon gun. The hunting of whales from boats can be traced back to at least the 9th century, the Basques and the Norwegians probably being the first in the field.

Before the introduction of mechanical aids whale fishing was **the most arduous, adventurous and dangerous of all forms of seafaring**. Double-ended open boats, 27–30ft (8.2–9.1m) long and 4–5ft (1.2–1.5m) broad, steered not by a rudder but by a long oar, were launched from sailing vessels when a whale was sighted and a harpoon, attached to a line of tarred hemp, two inches in circumference and 440yd (402m) long, was hurled at the whale by the harpooner standing in the bows. If the whale did not capsize the boat, it was killed with a lance or spear and brought alongside the ship for 'flensing', or stripping the blubber, which was then boiled down in the 'try-works', a brick-built structure on deck which housed iron cauldrons and furnaces and which was broken up at the end of the voyage.

It does not take much imagination to appreciate that the following quotation from Tønnessen and Johnsen's *History of Modern Whaling* is no exaggeration: 'Whaling is often considered more the province of industry than of shipping, and for this reason, in the history of seafaring generally, little mention is made of the fact that some of the finest seamanship has been displayed by crews on board tiny whale-catchers operating in the stormiest seas in the world.'

Though the credit for **the invention of the harpoon gun** is usually given to Svend Foyn, it is more accurate to say that he perfected an idea which had been around for well over 100 years. Tønnessen and Johnsen tell us that 'the English South Sea Company despatched in 1737 a whole fleet of 22 ships equipped with a freshly invented cannon for discharging harpoons, and, judging

Whaling before the days of the harpoon gun. *Mary Evans Picture Library.*

Long Lines, the largest cable ship. ***Transoceanic Cable Ship Co.***

Finlandia, the largest car-passenger ferry. ***Wärtsila/Silja Line.***

The *Seawise Giant* is the largest oil tanker and the largest ship so far built. She does not appear in the list on p. 163 as she was enlarged after launching. *C. Y. Tung Group.*

World Gala is the largest oil/ore vessel and the biggest diesel engined ship in the world. *World Wide Shipping Agency Ltd.*

by the available sources, that year probably marked **the first use of cannon in whaling**'. In 1820 the Scottish polar explorer and whaler William Scoresby (1789–1857) remarked that the harpoon gun had been 'highly improved and rendered capable of throwing a harpoon near 40 yards with effect but it has not been so generally adopted as might have been expected'.

The first person to suggest combining a shell and a harpoon in a single projectile seems to have been Sir William Congreve (1772–1828), the inventor of the Congreve rocket. Foyn perfected and patented his whale-gun in 1865, the design of which has remained unaltered, for all practical purposes, to this day.

The world's first purpose-built steam whale catcher was the *Spes et Fides*, built for Svend Foyn in Oslo in 1863. She was 94¾ft (28.9m) long, 15ft (4.6m) in the beam and had a speed of 7 knots. The whale catcher is the modern descendant of the oar-propelled whaleboat and is used solely for harpooning the whale.

A modern whale factory ship is designed to process the whales as they are caught. The dead whale is hauled aboard up a sloping ramp at the stern to the flensing deck where it is stripped of its blubber. **The first steam floating factory ship in modern whaling** was the 3643-ton *Michail*, bought in 1899 by Count Heinrich Kejzerling, a Russian/German nobleman who ran the Pacific Whale Fishing Co. She was converted during the winter of 1902–3 and received her first whale on 27 June 1903.

The first ship to be fitted with an aft slipway was the *Lancing*. Originally a British cargo liner, the 7866-ton *Flackwell* built in 1898, she was bought by the Globus Whaling Company of Norway in 1925 and converted to become the first floating factory ship with a stern slip.

The world's first diesel-driven whale catchers were built by Smith's Dock Co. Ltd., of Middlesbrough for Richard Irvin & Sons of North Shields in 1911. The engines proved so unreliable that after two years they were replaced by steam engines.

The first attempt to combine the roles of whale-catcher and factory ship occurred in 1912 with the building of the *St Ebba* for the St Abbs Whaling Co. She was equipped with tanks sufficient for 120 tons of oil, as well as two blubber cookers on deck, but the experiment was not a success.

Hovercraft

The development of the hovercraft has led to a fundamental rethinking of the tactical aspects of coastal defence in those parts of the world where conditions impose limitations upon the uses of conventional patrol boats. Hovercraft, being fully amphibious, can operate from beaches or from a mother-ship patrolling offshore. They are independent of the state of the tide and, since no part of their solid structure is immersed, they are invulnerable to acoustic, magnetic and pressure mines, and to torpedo attack.

The first man to work on the idea of an air-cushion vehicle, or what we more familiarly call a hovercraft, was the naval architect Sir John Thornycroft (1843–1928); who 'in the 1870s began to build test models to check his theory that the drag on a ship's hull could be reduced if the vessel were given a concave bottom in which air could be contained between hull and water ... (but) neither Thornycroft nor other inventors in following decades succeeded in solving the cushion-containment problem' (*Encyclopaedia Britannica*).

The first successful hovercraft was developed by Sir Christopher Cockerell whose first patent was filed on 12 December 1955. In the following year he formed a company called Hovercraft Ltd., but it was not until 7 June 1959 that the world's first practical air-cushion vehicle, the SR.NI, made its first successful flight. 'The Hovercraft, weighing about 4 tons and in the form of an oval with a major diameter of 20ft (60.96m), a width of 24ft (73.15m) and a height of 10ft (30.5m) at the central column, travelled over a concrete surface, keeping easily within the confines of a circle, which spoke well for its manoeuvrability. It was suspended about 9in (22.9cm) from the ground. A large part of the 'flying saucer' forms a buoyancy tank and an Alvis Leonides engine delivering 435hp drives a fan-bladed axial fan situated vertically in the central column. Air is drawn through this and expelled round the periphery, forming a cushion which ideally supports the machine at a height of about 15in (38.1cm). Air is also bled off to horizontal nozzles which allow the machine to be moved in any direction. In this state speeds of up to 25 knots are expected' (*The Times*, 12 June 1959).

The first crossing of the English Channel by hovercraft took place on 25 July 1959. The SR.NI. left Calais at 0449 and rounded the eastern end of the central breakwater into Dover Harbour at 0645.

The world's first regular passenger-carrying hovercraft service went into operation on 20 July 1962, when 24 paying passengers left Rhyl in North Wales on a 17-mile trip to Wallasey aboard a 60-knot Vickers Armstrong *VAJ* operated by British United Airways.

The first passenger service across the English Channel by hovercraft was inaugurated by Hoverlloyd Ltd., a company formed by Swedish-Lloyd and the Swedish American Line, on 6 April 1966.

Christopher Cockerell with his prototype hovercraft.

SCHOONERS; PACKETS; CLIPPERS

The first schooner ever constructed is said to have been built in Gloucester, Massachusetts, USA about the year 1713, by a Captain Andrew Robinson, and to have received its name from the following trivial circumstance. When the vessel went off the stocks into the water a bystander cried out, 'O, how she *scoons*!' Robinson replied, 'A *scooner* let her be'; and from that time vessels thus rigged have gone by this name. The word *scoon* is popularly used in New England to denote the act of making stones skip along the water, and is said to be of Scottish origin. For the distinguishing characteristics of a schooner see appendix p. 241.

The first advertisement announcing scheduled crossings of the North Atlantic appeared in the New York *Evening Post* on 27 October 1817. It said that the 424-ton sailing packet, the *James Monroe*, would sail from New York bound for Liverpool on 5 January 1818, that the *Couvier* would sail from Liverpool on the 1st, and that similar sailings would take place on the 1st and 5th of each succeeding month. The *James Monroe* got away punctually at 10am on 5 January, in spite of a severe snowstorm, carrying a limited cargo and eight male passengers who had paid 40 guineas (£42) each for a passage which included bedding, food and wines. The *Couvier* was delayed by the tide and did not manage to leave the Mersey until 4 January, but can still claim the distinction of being **the first scheduled transatlantic liner**. On board were a Mr and Mrs Irving and to the latter belongs the distinction of being **the first woman passenger on a transatlantic liner**. To the *Monroe* belongs the distinction of being **the first scheduled transatlantic liner to sail from New York**. Both ships were operated by a consortium which was later known as the Black Ball Line, owing to the distinguishing mark of a large black spot on the fore-topsail of its ships.

Hitherto the traveller had been obliged to take passage either on what was known as a 'regular trader'; the word 'regular' applying to the destination of the vessel but not to the time of her departure or arrival, or on a 'transient', in which case the destination, too, was subject to alteration.

These early passenger-ships were known as **packets**, an abbreviation of packet-boat, a term applied to any vessel running between two ports on a regular schedule, primarily for the purpose of carrying mail, the packets being parcels of letters, in particular parcels of State despatches from one country to another. Such vessels were also known as post-banks.

Packets later became known as **liners** because the companies who ran them owned a 'line' of steamers, hence the Cunard Line, the White Star Line etc. The word came into general use in this sense in about 1840.

The name 'clipper' was first applied to the Baltimore clippers, famous as privateers in the early wars of the United States. The word did not originally specify any particular design of ship but was loosely applied to any vessel which 'clipped' the time usually taken on passage, hence to any very fast sailing ship such as was essential to blockade gun-runners or slave traders.

Subsequently the term 'clipper' came to be applied specifically to those most romanticized ships of all time which enjoyed their brief heyday from about 1840 until 1869, when their death knell was sounded by the opening of the Suez Canal. A true clipper-ship, though impossible to define technically, was characterized by her sharp-raked stem, by the unusual ratio of five or

"STAG HOUND," 1534 Tons.
Launched, December 7th, 1850.
Estimated Cost $45,000.

"FLYING CLOUD," 1782 Tons.
Launched, April 15th, 1851.
Reported Cost $50,000.

"SOVEREIGN OF THE SEAS,"
2421 Tons.
Launched, July, 1852.
Estimated Cost $95,000.

"GREAT REPUBLIC," 4555 Tons.
(The Largest Ship in the World.)
Launched, October 4th, 1853.
Building and Outfitting Cost
Approximately $300,000.

six to one between length and breadth and by her inclined, overhanging counterstern.

No one can say with certainty that one particular ship was **the first clipper ever built**, but this has not deterred the experts from expending gallons of ink on the subject. The first claimant is the 500-ton Baltimore-built *Ann McKim*, which certainly foreshadowed many of the features that later came to characterize the clipper. Next comes the *Rainbow*, 'considered by most authors to be the first clipper'. She was built in New York in 1845 by John Willis Griffiths (1809–82). She was 154ft (47m) long at the waterline and 31½ft (9.6m) wide. The third and last contender is the *Sea Witch*, also designed by John Willis Griffiths, launched in 1846 and described by some as '**the first real clipper ship**'. She was certainly among the fastest and most beautiful of all the clippers and in 1849 established an all-time record of 74 days and 14 hours from China to New York.

The brief heyday of the clipper ships was fuelled by the coincident occurrence of three otherwise unconnected events. The first was the discovery of gold in California in 1848 which gave a great impetus to the faster, larger sailing ship, as thousands of 'prospectors' rushed out round the Horn to San Francisco. (It should be borne in mind that the first American transcontinental railway was not opened until 1869.) The second event, similar to the first, was the Australian gold rush of 1851 when thousands more hopefuls raced out to Melbourne from Europe and America. Lastly, in 1853, the British Government passed the Customs Consolidation Act which placed foreign ships on the same footing as British ships in relation to freight bound to or from Britain. Clippers were much used in the Australian wool and China tea trades, where speed was of paramount importance and this led to the famous races and the many records established.

The greatest builder of American sailing ships, some say the greatest builder of sailing ships of all time, was Donald Mackay (1810–80). In 1840 he opened a shipyard at Boston in partnership with one Enoch Train, and there he built **the fastest sailing vessels ever launched**, among the most famous of which were the *Staghound* (1850), *Flying Cloud* (1851), *Sovereign of the Seas* (1852),

Great Republic (1853) and *Lightning* (1854).

The *Lightning* disputes with several others the claim to have been **the fastest of all the clippers**. It is said that on her maiden voyage from Boston to Liverpool she made a run of 436 miles in 24 hours. Another clipper of the Black Ball Line, the *Champion of the Seas*, claimed to have covered 465 miles from noon to noon on 11/12 December 1854. Such figures, however, should not be taken too literally. Captain James Learmont, of whom it has been written that he possessed 'one great quality far more rare among ship-masters than it should have been. He set his face against dishonesty in any form,' was not impressed by such claims: 'From every angle, taking my experience in sail into account, I do not believe that *any* ship *ever* exceeded or *even reached* 400 miles in 24 hours under sail. I believe that **the best day's run (noon to noon) ever to have been made under sail** was that of the five-masted barque *Preussen*, when she made 370 miles under Captain Petersen in the South Pacific.' Alan Villiers, another writer with a long experience in sail, while anxious to stress that he does not 'doubt the integrity of those who claimed' such records, concedes that 'it is possible there was a considerable amount of guesswork in it'. For, as he points out, 'there was no means of checking them'.

Probably the fastest of them all – the five-masted barque *Preussen*.

Clipper Records

The records for complete voyages can, however, be regarded as accurate and the following list, which was compiled by the late Mr Basil Lubbock, is reprinted by kind permission of the Editor of *Lloyds' Calendar*. All vessels are British except those marked (A) American, (Ab) British-owned/American built, (G) German. 'Comp' indicates that the ship was composite-built, the term used to describe a ship planked with wood or an iron or steel frame.

DATE	VESSEL	TONS	TIME DAYS	HOURS	REMARKS
United Kingdom to Australia					
1868–9	*Thermopylæ*, comp.	948	60	0	London to Melbourne (pilot to pilot)
1870–1	*Thermopylæ*, comp.	948	60	0	London to Melbourne (pilot to pilot)
1854	*James Baines* (Ab), wood	2275	63	0	Liverpool to Melbourne
1874–5	*Ben Voirlich*, iron	1474	63	0	London to Melbourne (pilot to pilot)
1874–5	*Thermopylæ*, comp.	948	64	0	London to Melbourne (pilot to pilot)
1868	*Theophane*, iron	1525	65	0	Liverpool to Melbourne (pilot to pilot)
1875–6	*Cutty Sark*, comp.	921	64	0	Lizard to Cape Otway
1874–5	*Cutty Sark*, comp.	921	66	0	Start Point to South Cape, Tasmania
1869	*Patriarch*, iron	1339	68	0	London to Sydney (pilot to pilot)
1880–1	*Torrens*, comp.	1276	65	0	Plymouth to Adelaide
1883	*Maulesden*, iron	1500	69	0	Greenock to Maryborough
1891	*Oweenee*, steel 4-m bq.	2432	66	0	Prawle Point to Port Pirie
Europe to Australia					
1873	*Thomas Stephens*, iron	1507	66	0	Ushant to Melbourne
1896	*Wendur*, iron 4-m ship	1982	81	0	Fredrikstad to Melbourne
1933–4	*Padua* (G), steel 4-m bq.	3064	66	0	Hamburg to Wallaroo
Australia to United Kingdom					
1853	*Lightning* (Ab), wood	2090	63	0	Melbourne to Liverpool
1856	*Heather Bell*, wood	479	64	0	Melbourne to Liverpool
1869	*Patriarch*, iron	1339	68	0	Sydney to Ushant
1885	*Cutty Sark*, comp.	921	67	0	Sydney to Ushant
1887	*Cutty Sark*, comp.	921	70	0	Sydney to Channel
1887	*Cutty Sark*, comp.	921	69	0	Newcastle, N.S.W., to Channel
1894	*Swanhilda*, steel 4-m bq.	1999	66	0	Wallaroo, S.A., to Queenstown
United Kingdom to India					
1860	*Alnwick Castle*, wood	1087	67	0	Channel to Sandheads
1863	*The Tweed*, wood	1745	77	0	London to Bombay
1875	*Accrington*, iron	1831	74	0	Liverpool to Calcutta
1876	*Ailsa*, comp.	1061	76	0	Liverpool to Calcutta
1877	*Coriolanus*	1046	70	0	Channel to Calcutta
1880	*Star of Italy*, iron	1571	77	0	London to Calcutta
1883	*Glengarry*, iron	1769	76	0	Liverpool to Calcutta
1884	*Cedric the Saxon*, iron	1619	71	0	Lizard to Calcutta
1894	*Armida*, steel	1642	75	0	Liverpool to Calcutta
United Kingdom to China					
1866–7	*Ariel*, comp.	853	80	0	London to Hongkong
1898	*Muskoka*, steel 4-m bq.	2357	86	0	Cardiff to Hongkong
1898	*Metropolis*, iron 4-m bq.	1811	91	0	Cardiff to Hongkong
China to United Kingdom					
1869	*Sir Lancelot*, comp.	886	89	0	From Foochow[1]
1852	*Witch of the Wave* (A), wood	1200	90	0	From Whampoa[2]
1855	*Nightingale* (A), wood	1066	91	0	From Shanghai[2]
1869	*Thermopylæ*, comp.	948	91	0	From Foochow[1]
1871	*Titania*, comp.	879	93	0	From Foochow[1]
1873	*Hallowe'en*, iron	920	89	0	From Shanghai[2]
1874	*Hallowe'en*, iron	920	90	0	From Shanghai[2]
1875	*Hallowe'en*, iron	920	92	0	From Shanghai[2]

DATE	VESSEL	TONS	TIME DAYS	HOURS	REMARKS
China to United States					
1847–8	*Sea Witch* (A), wood	890	78	0	From Canton
1845	*Natchez* (A), wood	—	78	6	Macao to Boston
1848–9	*Sea Witch* (A), wood	890	79	0	From Canton
1847	*Sea Witch* (A), wood	890	81	0	From Canton
1852	*N. B. Palmer* (A), wood	1490	84	0	From Canton
1895	*Alcides*, steel 4-m bq.	2704	83	0	From Hongkong
Europe to West Coast of South America					
1903	*Preussen* (G), steel 5-m ship	5081	57	0	Lizard to Iquique
1904	*Eudora* (G), iron 4-m bq.	1991	57	16	Eddystone to Coquimbo
1892	*Placilla* (G), steel 4-m bq.	2845	58	0	Lizard to Valparaiso
1900	*Potosi* (G), steel 5-m bq.	4027	59	0	Dover to Valparaiso
1905	*Potosi* (G), steel 5-m bq.	4027	59	0	Isle of Wight to Valparaiso
West Coast of South America to Europe					
1903	*Potosi* (G), steel 5-m ship	4027	57	0	Iquique to Prawle Point
1900	*Pindos* (G), steel 4-m bq.	2484	61	0	Tocopilla to Dunkirk
1893	*Placilla* (G), steel 4-m bq.	2845	70	0	Iquique to Lizard
1903	*County of Angelsea*, iron bq.	1103	67	0	Pisco to Falmouth
1895	*Pamelia* (G), steel bq.	1438	68	0	Iquique to Prawle Point
1904	*Preussen* (G), steel 5-m ship	5081	61	0	Iquique to Lizard
United States to United Kingdom					
1853	*Typhoon* (A), wood	1610	13	6	Portsmouth, N.H., to Liverpool
1854	*James Baines* (Ab), wood	2275	12	6	Boston to Liverpool
1854	*Red Jacket* (Ab), wood	2035	13	1	Sandy Hook to Liverpool
1854	*Dreadnought* (A), wood	1413	13	11	New York to Liverpool
1859	*Dreadnought* (A), wood	1413	13	8	New York to Liverpool
1862	*Fidelia* (A), wood	1000	13	7	New York to Liverpool
1864	*Adelaide* (A), wood	—	12	8	New York to Liverpool
United Kingdom to United States					
1824	*Emerald* (A), wood	359	17	0	Liverpool to Boston
185?	*Fidelia* (A), wood	1000	17	6	Liverpool to New York
1855	*Mary Whitridge* (A), wood	978	14	9	Liverpool to Baltimore
1860	*Andrew Jackson* (A), wood	1676	15	0	Liverpool to New York
1892	*Howard D. Troop*, steel	2165	14	0	Greenock to New York
1892	*Procyon*, steel bq.	1122	15	0	Leith to New York
San Francisco and Puget Sound to United Kingdom or United States (East Coast)					
1891–2	*Falls of Garry*, iron 4-m bq.	2088	88	0	San Francisco to Queenstown
1891–2	*Alcinous*, iron ship	1662	93	0	San Francisco to Queenstown
1892	*Machrihanish*, iron ship	1758	91	0	Portland, Oregon, to Queenstown
1893	*Andelana*, steel 4-m ship	2579	89	0	San Francisco to Brow Head
1895	*Principality*, iron 4-m bq.	1757	95	0	Astoria to Queenstown
1895	*Susquehanna* (A), wood 4-m ship	2745	94	0	San Francisco to Queenstown
1892	*Benjamin F. Packard* (A), wood	2156	89	0	San Francisco to New York
United States (East Coast) to San Francisco					
1851	*Flying Cloud* (A), wood	1793	89	0	From New York
1854	*Flying Cloud* (A), wood	1793	89	0	From New York
1860	*Andrew Jackson* (A), wood	1676	89	0	From New York
1852	*Swordfish* (A), wood	1036	90	0	From New York
1853	*Flying Fish* (A), wood	1505	92	0	From New York
1853	*John Gilpin* (A), wood	1089	93	0	From New York
1856	*Sweepstakes* (A), wood	1735	94	0	From New York
1851	*Surprise* (A), wood	1361	96	0	From New York
1854	*Romance of the Seas* (A), wood	1782	96	0	From New York

Clipper records continued on next page.

DATE	VESSEL	TONS	TIME DAYS	HOURS	REMARKS
United Kingdom to San Francisco					
1887–8	*Merioneth*, iron	1366	96	0	Cardiff to San Francisco
1889	*Senator*, iron ship	1762	90	0	Cardiff to San Francisco
1871	*Archibald Fuller*, iron ship	700	100	0	Liverpool to San Francisco
1894	*Eudora*, steel 4-m bq.	1992	99	0	Lundy Island to San Francisco
Miscellaneous					
1852	*Swordfish* (A), wood	1036	32	9	San Francisco to Shanghai
1896	*Wendur*, iron 4-m ship	2046	29	13	Newcastle, N.S.W., to Valparaiso
1896	*Loch Torridon*, iron 4-m bq.	2081	30	2	Newcastle, N.S.W., to Valparaiso
1870	*Thermopylæ*, comp.	948	28	0	Newcastle, N.S.W., to Shanghai
1853	*Hornet* (A), wood	1426	34	0	San Francisco to Callao
1897	*Benares*, iron 4-m bq.	1721	40	0	Table Bay to New York
1897	*Foyledale*, steel	1765	25	0	Hiogo to Tacoma
1888	*British Ambassador*, iron	1794	39	0	San Francisco to Newcastle, N.S.W.
1895	*Siren*, iron	1478	28	0	Table Bay to Sydney
1894	*Drumrock*, steel 4-m bq.	3182	5	6¼	San Francisco to Tacoma
1891	*Dundee*, iron 4-m bq.	2063	31	0	Cardiff to Rio
1895	*Bangalore*, iron ship	1746	88	0	Calcutta to New York
1909	*Howard D. Troop*, steel 4-m bq.	2165	21	0	Yokohama to Astoria
1911	*Lancing*, iron 4-m ship	2764	44	0	Montevideo to New Caledonia
1899	*Glenesslin*, iron	1743	74	0	Portland, Oregon, to Algoa Bay
1894	*Lord Spencer*, iron	2675	29	0	Capetown to Newcastle, N.S.W.
1927	*Oaklands*, iron bq.	990	5	21½	Gravesend to Viborg

[1] Monsoon unfavourable.   [2] Monsoon favourable.

The largest wooden sailing ship ever built was Donald McKay's *Great Republic*, launched in 1853. Of 4555 tons, she was 325ft (99m) in length. The mainmast of the *Great Republic* was 131ft (40m) in height and 11½ft (3.5m) in circumference. The combined height of the mainmast, topmast, topgallant mast, royal mast and skysail topped by a 12ft (3.6m) pole was 288ft (87.8m). Even allowing for overlap, the built-up mast rose 200ft (61m) above the deck. Those of a suspicious turn of mind forecast an ill-starred future for the ship when the launching ceremony was performed, not with the conventional bottle of champagne, but with a bottle of mineral water. This was not, as many thought, a gesture to the women's temperance movement but because some apprentices had got hold of the champagne the night before and drunk it. However, the prophets of doom did not have long to wait. The *Great Republic* caught fire while loading in New York before her maiden voyage and was so badly damaged that it was necessary to sink her in order to save her from complete destruction. The masts were cut out and much smaller masts fitted, but even then she made the crossing from Sandy Hook to Land's End in 13 days. She met her end off Bermuda in March 1872. She was caught in a strong gale and a leak which had previously been patched became very much worse until there was 12ft (3.6m) of water in the hold and no chance of getting at the leak. The master decided to abandon ship and all hands reached Bermuda safely in the boats. As the ship was still afloat when her crew left her, there was talk of her being salvable, but she was never seen again.

The most famous of all the annual tea-clipper races occurred in 1866 when the *Fiery Cross*, *Ariel*, *Taeping* and *Serica* left Foochow on 30 May and the *Taitsing* on the 31st. The *Taeping* docked in London at 9.45pm on 6 September, the *Ariel* half-an-hour later and the *Serica* at 11.45pm. All three had sailed 16,000 miles in 99 days. The *Fiery Cross* and the *Taitsing* docked two days later.

THE *CUTTY SARK*
The most famous of all the British clipper ships, the *Cutty Sark*, survives to this day in permanent dry dock at Greenwich, London. She was designed by Hercules Linton and built at Dumbarton in 1869 for Captain Jock Willis, a Scottish shipowner known as 'Old White Hat', on account of his habit of wearing a white top hat.

Her dimensions were: length 212ft (64.6m); beam 36ft (11m); depth 21ft (6.4m); tonnage 921. In 1870 she took part in the annual tea race from China to London and made seven further voyages in the tea trade, but, with the opening of the Suez Canal, the trade was lost to steamers and from 1883 to 1895, when she was sold to the Portuguese, she made regular voyages in the Australian wool trade, for the last ten years under the captainship of Richard Woodget, her most famous commander. In 1922 she was bought by Captain Wilfred Dowman (1878–1936) for £6000, restored, and used as a training ship at Falmouth. On his death his widow presented her to the Thames Nautical Training College and she was towed to Greenhithe and continued to be used as a training ship until 1949. Her subsequent preservation was largely due to the energy and enthusiasm of Mr Frank Carr, Director of the National Maritime Museum from 1947–66.

The name 'Cutty Sark' comes from Robert Burns's poem 'Tam O'Shanter' in which a Scottish farmer is chased by a witch called Nannie who wore only 'Her cutty sark, o' Paisley harn,' which is to say 'her short shirt of coarse Paisley linen'.

The *Cutty Sark*'s most famous rival was the *Thermopylae*, who, on the three legs of her maiden voyage, broke the records for the fastest passage from London to Melbourne, Newcastle (New South Wales) to Shanghai and Foochow to Gravesend. Built by Walter Hood and Co. of Aberdeen, she was launched in 1868 and displaced 948 tons. The two ships had a famous race home from Foochow in 1872 and were lying approximately level when the *Cutty Sark* lost her rudder in a gale off the Cape of Good Hope. The *Thermopylae* was also sold to the Portuguese as a training ship but in 1907 she was declared unfit for further service, was towed out to sea and sunk by gunfire.

The last clipper built by Donald McKay was the *Glory of the Seas* (1869). Alas, the glorious days of sail were over and she was used as a cold-storage vessel by a fish company. She was finally burnt on a beach at Seattle for the value of her copper fastenings.

The record-breaking clipper *Thermopylae.*

For a brief period in 1890–1 the *France* could claim to be **the largest sailing vessel ever built in Britain.** She was a steel-hulled five-masted barque of 3784 tons; square-rigged on all her masts, she was 361ft (110m) long with a beam of 48ft 9in (14.9m) and a sail area of 49,000sq.ft (4552m²). Her most novel feature was the four steam winches to speed the handling of cargo. At Iquique in Chile she once discharged 5000 tons of coal and loaded 5500 tons of nitrate in 11 days. She was built by Henderson & Son of Glasgow for the A. D. Bordes Line. In March 1901, she was caught in a storm off the coast of South America and had eventually to be abandoned, though the crew fought the worsening leak for two months before they were finally taken off by the German four-masted barque *Hebe*.

The *Maria Rickmers*, built at Port Glasgow in 1890, was slightly larger (3822 tons) than the *France* and was very heavily rigged. She carried three skysails which added to the weight aloft far more than they were worth. On her maiden voyage she took a leisurely 82 days to reach Singapore, whereupon the owners sent the master a reprimand so severely worded that, having read it, the poor man fell dead on the spot! The mate took her up to Saigon where she took on a cargo of rice: she sailed on 14 July 1892, passed the Sunda Strait ten days later and thereafter was never seen again.

A full-rigged ship is a ship with at least three masts, all of which are square-rigged. The *Cutty Sark* was a three-masted full-rigger. The German ship *Preussen* was **the only five-masted full-rigger ever built.** She was a steel ship 433ft (132m) long with a 54ft (16.5m) beam, displacing over 11,000 tons and capable of carrying 8000 tons of cargo. Alan Villiers says, 'The *Preussen* was without a doubt **the greatest sailing ship the world has seen.'** She was built in 1902 and for eight years **she moved larger cargoes faster through the water over greater distances than they had ever been shifted under sail before.** She met her end in October 1910, when, on a foggy night in the Channel, she was in collision with the Newhaven–Dieppe steamer, was driven ashore and totally wrecked. Fortunately, no lives were lost.

The only seven-masted schooner ever built was the *Thomas W. Lawson*, constructed by the Fore River Shipbuilding Company at Quincy, Massachusetts, and launched in 1902. In excess of 5000 tons gross, her seven masts were all the same height, each consisting of a steel lower mast of 135ft (41m) and a 58ft (17.7m) pine topmast. The sails on all but the foremost mast and the mizzen were also identical, consisting of a lower sail with a gaff and boom and a topsail. Nevertheless she was worked by a crew of only 16, being equipped with steam winches for hoisting and lowering the sails. She was, however, a hybrid stranded between the ages of steam and sail and came to a disastrous end when she mysteriously turned turtle off the Scillies in 1907 with the loss of all but one of her crew.

The largest sailing ship ever built was the five-masted steel barque *France II* at 8000dwt. She was launched in 1911 at Bordeaux and operated by the Société des Navires Mixtres until 13 July 1922, when she was wrecked on a reef off the coast of New Caledonia.

STEAMERS
AND
LINERS

The Coming of Steam

The first man to formulate the idea of a steamship was probably the French physicist Denis Papin (1647–1712). 'He described a steam cylinder with a piston which was forced down by the pressure of the air when the steam under it condensed, and he believed that the piston could be used to turn the paddle wheel of a boat' (LANDSTRÖM). He certainly invented the safety valve, an essential part of his 'steam digester', a device for softening bones and the ancestor of the modern pressure cooker.

The first Englishman to entertain the idea of propelling a ship by steam-power was Thomas Savory (*c* 1650–1715) who in 1698 patented the first commercially successful steam engine, an atmospheric engine for pumping water, and later

suggested that it might be adapted for marine purposes. Nothing, however, came of the idea.

The first real step in the application of steam to marine engineering came in 1736 when a Gloucestershire inventor named Jonathan Hulls patented a form of steam tug for towing larger vessels 'It is said that this early steamer was tried by Hulls on the River Avon at Evesham. The boat was provided with a paddle-wheel at the stern. The engine was of the atmospheric type invented by Newcomen in 1710, in which a weight pulled up a piston in an iron cylinder. Steam was admitted to the underside of the piston. Then, on the steam being condensed by a jet of water, the piston was forced down and made to do useful work through suitable rods and levers.' (*Shipping*

Jonathan Hull's steam tug, from the drawing attached to his application for a patent. *Mary Evans Picture Library.*

Wonders of the World, Ed. CLARENCE WINCHESTER). His efforts aroused only derision at the time and he died destitute and broken-hearted, but to him belongs the honour of being the inventor of the steamship.

The first French paddle-steamer, the *Pyroscaphe*, was built by the Marquis Jouffroy d'Abbans (1751–1832) and launched on the River Saône at Lyons in 1783, where it plied for over a year; but further developments were halted by the French Revolution.

The first steam-powered vessel constructed in America was built either by John Fitch (1743–98) or by James Rumsey (1743–92); both laid claim to the distinction. Fitch launched his first steamboat, whose engine worked 12 vertical oars, on the Delaware River in August 1787, a second and larger one in July 1788, and a third in 1790. But his claim to have invented steam navigation was disputed by Rumsey who, in December 1787, demonstrated on the Potomac a vessel driven by streams of water forced through the stern by a steam pump, **the first instance of water-jet propulsion**.

The first successful steamboat in Britain was built by Patrick Miller (1731–1815) a Scottish banker, who, on 14 November 1788, launched a double-hulled boat, 25ft (7.6m) long, with two paddle-wheels, arranged fore and aft, fitted between the two hulls. The engine, made by William Symington (1763–1831), was in one hull and the boiler in the other. Miller's boat was constructed purely for his own pleasure and, seeking but not finding encouragement from his more successful compatriot, James Watt (1736–1819), he lost heart.

The first vessel in the world to use steam propulsion commercially was the *Charlotte Dundas*, built in 1801 by William Symington for Lord

William Symington, who built the *Charlotte Dundas*, died in poverty in London and was buried at St Botolph's Aldgate, where one may see a tablet to his memory.

Robert Fulton's steamboat, the *Clermont*, on the Hudson River.

Dundas, who wished to replace the horses used for pulling barges along the Forth and Clyde Canal. The 10hp single-cylinder engine acted directly by means of a connecting-rod on the crank of a shaft carrying a single paddle-wheel at the stern. In March 1802, she towed two 70-ton barges along the Forth and Clyde Canal for nearly 20 miles (32.3km) in six hours. She was 56ft (17m) long, 18ft (5.5m) in the beam and had a depth of 8ft (2.4m). The canal owners, however, thought that the wash from the paddles would erode the banks and the *Charlotte Dundas* was moored in a creek adjoining the waterway until she was finally broken up in 1861.

The world's first commercially successful steamboat was the *Clermont*, built by the American engineer Robert Fulton (1765–1815). Fulton had been commissioned to build a steamboat by Robert R. Livingston, US Minister to France, when he was in Paris in 1802, but the hull proved too weak to support the engine and as a result it broke in two and sank. A second boat of 66ft (20.1m) in length and 8ft (2.4m) in beam remained afloat but only achieved a speed of 4½mph (7.24kmh). Returning to the States in 1806 Fulton built the 38-ton *Clermont*, but the engine had to be made in Britain by Boulton and Watt as there were at that time no engineers in America capable of building a suitable engine. She was 133ft (40.5m) long, 18ft (5.5m) in the beam and 9ft (2.7m) deep. Between 17 and 22 August 1807, she steamed up the Hudson River from New York to Albany, a distance of nearly 150 miles (241km), in 32 hours and completed the return journey in 30 hours. This was **the first voyage of any distance ever made by a vessel under steam alone**. The *Clermont* remained in service for many years under the name *North River* and can claim to have been **the world's first pleasure steamer**.

Steam Goes to Sea

The first sea-going steamship in the world was the *Phoenix*. She was built in New York in 1808 by John Stevens (1749–1838) and was intended for service on the River Delaware, as Robert Fulton had the monopoly of steam navigation on the Hudson. This necessitated a sea voyage from New York to Philadelphia in 1809.

The first merchant steamship to be launched in Europe was the *Comet*. Built by Henry Bell

Henry Bell's *Comet*.

(1767–1830), she was launched on the Clyde in 1812 and carried passengers between Glasgow and Helensburgh, where Bell had an hotel. The *Comet* was 40ft (12.2m) long and achieved a speed of 6.7 knots. The single-cylinder engine, designed by Bell himself, developed 4hp, was 5ft (1.5m) in height and can still be seen in the Science Museum, South Kensington. In 1819 the *Comet* started a passenger run to Fort William and the following year, while returning thence, she was driven ashore and wrecked in a storm. Henry Bell had insufficient money to build another ship and died 10 years later in penury.

The first steamer to carry passengers on the Thames was the *Richmond*, which plied between London and Richmond in 1814. She was a 50-ton ship driven by a bell-crank lever engine which developed 10hp.

The first steam vessel to cross the Channel was the *Marjorie* or *Margery*. Launched at Dumbarton, on the Clyde, late in 1814, she was brought south under sail to find work on the Thames and ran for a year between Wapping Old Stairs and Gravesend, making the passage down one day and returning on the next. In 1815 she was sent out to work on the River Seine in France.

The first steam ferry on the River Mersey was the *Elizabeth* which started running between Liverpool and Runcorn in 1815.

The first steamship to cross the Atlantic was the 320-ton auxiliary wooden steamer *Savannah*, launched at New York in 1818 as a sailing ship and fitted the following year with a single-cylinder engine which drove two collapsible paddle-wheels. She left Savannah, Georgia, on 22 May 1819, and reached the Mersey on 20 June, during which time her engines had been in use for a total of only 80 hours. So, although she can claim to be the first ship fitted with an engine to cross the Atlantic, she was not the first ship to cross the Atlantic under steam alone. She returned to Savannah under sail alone and was wrecked on Long Island in 1821.

The first iron steamship was the *Aaron Manby*, built in England in 1821 for traffic on the Seine and financed by Captain Charles Napier, R.N. (1786–1860), who later became an admiral. The *Aaron Manby* was 120ft (36.6m) long and was fitted with oscillating engines of 80hp. She made her first voyage in 1822, crossing the English Channel at an average speed of between 8 and 9 knots.

The first ship fitted with an auxiliary engine to cross the Atlantic from east to west seems to have been the *Rising Star*. Built at Rotherhithe for Lord Cochrane (1775–1860) in 1820/21, she left Gravesend in October 1821, and reached Valparaiso in April 1822. We are told that she was at one time equipped with paddle-wheels and that she left England propelled by jets of water forced through apertures in the hull below the waterline, but to what extent she used her engine on the voyage is not known.

The first steamship to make the journey from England to Calcutta was the 470-ton *Enterprise*. She was 141.6ft (43m) in length, 27.8ft (8.5m) in breadth and two 60hp engines drove her paddle-wheels which were 15ft (4.6m) in diameter. She left Falmouth on 16 August 1825 and reached Table Bay on 13 October, thereby becoming **the first steamship ever seen in South African waters**. Of the 58 days spent at sea, three having been spent at Sao Tomé, she was under steam for only 35. She reached Calcutta on 7 December, having been under steam for 64 out of 103 days at sea. This was **the first long passage on which steam propulsion was used to a significant extent**.

The first iron ships to make an ocean voyage were the *Alburkah* and the *Quorra*. The two paddle-ships left Liverpool in 1832 to explore the

The paddle-steamer *Savannah*, first steamship to cross the Atlantic. *Mary Evans Picture Library.*

River Niger. On board the *Alburkah* was her designer Macgregor Laird (1808–61), who was one of only nine of the 48 Europeans to survive the expedition, the rest, apart from Richard Lander (1805–34), the leader of the expedition, having died of fever. Lander was killed by natives. The *Quorra* was 112ft (34.1m) long, 16ft(4.9m) in the beam and drew 8ft (2.4m) of water. The *Alburkah* was 70ft (21.3m) long, 13ft (3.96m) in the beam and drew 6½ft (1.98m) of water.

The first fully-fledged steamship to carry passengers between Europe and America was the *Curaçao*. A 436-ton paddle-steamer, she was built at Dover in 1826 for a firm called the American and Colonial Steam Navigation Company and named the *Calpe*. But the firm was so undercapitalized that she was sold before completion to the Dutch Navy who rechristened her. She sailed

from Rotterdam for Paramaibo in Dutch Guiana (now Surinam) on 26 April 1827, and thereafter made several round trips on that route, but it must be borne in mind that for much of the time she was under sail alone. She remained in service with the Dutch Navy until 1850 when she was broken up.

The *Curaçao*. *National Maritime Museum.*

The *Royal William* leaving Quebec for Gravesend, 1833. *Mansell Collection.*

The first steamer to cross the Atlantic from Canada to Europe was the 363-ton wooden paddle-steamer *Royal William*, built at Quebec for the Quebec and Halifax Steam Navigation Company in 1830–1. But, failing to find profitable employment for her between those towns, her owners decided to sell her in Europe and she set sail from Quebec on 5 August 1833. Her clearance papers make quaint reading:

'*Royal William*, 363 tons, 33 men, John McDougall, master. Bound to London. British. Cargo: 253 chaldrons (320 tons) of coal, a box of stuffed birds and six spars, produce of this Province. One box and one trunk, household furniture and a harp. All British, and seven passengers'!

She reached Gravesend on 12 September, having proceeded under steam for three days out of every four, it being necessary on the fourth to clear the boilers of salt, the steam being derived from salt water. In 1834 she was sold to the Spanish Government who renamed her *Ysabel Segunda*, and in 1836 she became **the first steam-driven warship to fire a gun in action**.

The first steamer to go round the Cape of Good Hope to Australia was the 143-ton *Sophia Jane*, which had started life in 1828 running between London and Gravesend. She reached Cape Town on 15 March 1831 where her master, Captain Biddulph, tried to sell her, but he failed to find a buyer, so sailed on to Sydney and into history as the master of **the first steamship to be seen in Australian waters**.

The first iron ship to be seen in America was the paddle-steamer *John Randolph*, built by John Laird (1805–74) at Birkenhead in 1834 for a customer in Savannah, Georgia.

The Development of the Passenger Liner

The first regular steamship service across the North Atlantic was inaugurated on 28 March 1838, when the 703-ton steamer *Sirius* left London, bound for New York, via Cork. She had been chartered from the St George Steam Packet Company by the British and American Steam Navigation Company, the construction of whose own *British Queen* had been delayed and whose directors were determined to make a transatlantic crossing before the *Great Western*, then nearing completion. The *Sirius* left Cork on 4 April and reached New York on the 23rd, having covered a distance of 2961 miles in 18 days and 10 hours, at an average speed of 6.7 knots, by which time her supply of coal was virtually exhausted. The invention by Samuel Hall (1781–1863) in 1834 of surface condensers which produced fresh distilled water meant that the boilers did not have to be cleaned out every three or four days, and thus enabled the *Sirius* to make **the first undisputed Atlantic crossing entirely under steam**, but it did significantly increase her coal consumption. She made two round trips to New York before she was returned to her owners and was eventually wrecked off Ballycotton, Co. Cork, in 1847. She was **the first iron ship to have been officially classed at Lloyds**.

The *Sirius* earned the distinction of making the first steam-powered crossing of the Atlantic by

The arrival of the *Sirius* in New York, 23 April 1838. *Mansell Collection.*

The famous *Great Western* steaming out of Bristol. *National Maritime Museum.*

only a few hours, for later that day, 23 April 1838, the *Great Western* secured alongside Pike Street Wharf, having covered the 3223 miles from Avonmouth in 15 days 10½ hours at an average speed of 8.2 knots. Designed by Isambard Kingdom Brunel for the Great Western Steam Ship Company, she was **the first steamer built specifically for the North Atlantic run, and the first**

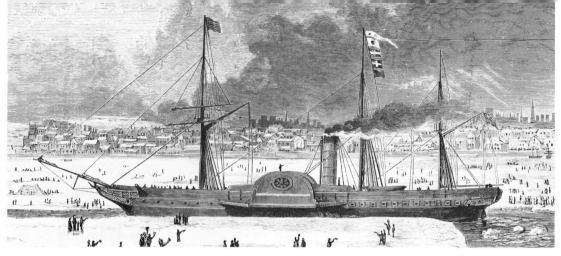

The first Cunard steamer, the *Britannia*, at Halifax, Nova Scotia.

to ply regularly across the Atlantic, running between Bristol and New York, and later Liverpool and New York, until the end of 1846. Built of wood by Patterson and Mercer of Bristol, she was 236ft (71.9m) long, had a beam of 35ft (10.7m) and a tonnage of 1340. She could carry 148 passengers but on her maiden voyage attracted only seven! On that occasion she carried coal from four different collieries in order to establish which was the best 'steaming' coal. She was broken up in 1856.

The first steamer to have a hull divided into watertight compartments by bulkheads was the City of Dublin Steam Packet Company's 617-ton wooden paddle-steamer *Royal William*, not to be confused with the Canadian steamer of the same name. She was launched in 1838, made three round trips between Liverpool and New York, and thereafter worked the Liverpool–Dun Laoghaire run until she was scrapped in 1888.

The first overseas mail contract ever awarded to a commercial shipping company was given to the Peninsular Steam Navigation Company in 1837 to carry the mails to Spain and Portugal. Since this was a crucial step in the development of a firm that was later to become, and still remains, one of the most famous of all British Shipping companies, it is worth briefly stating a few background facts. In 1815 Brodie McGhie Willcox set up as a shipping broker in Lime Street, London. Of his origins little is known, except that he was born in Ostend of English and Scottish parents. In the same year he engaged as his clerk Arthur Anderson who came from the Shetland Islands and had served in the Navy during the Napoleonic Wars. In 1822 Anderson was taken into partnership and the firm became known as

Willcox and Anderson. Initially they acted as agents for the owners of small sailing vessels trading between England and the Spanish Peninsular, first chartering their own sailing ship in 1826. In 1834 they chartered their first steamer, the 206-ton *William Fawcett*, from the Dublin and London Steam Packet Co. and until 1840 Willcox and Anderson traded as the Peninsular Steam Navigation Company in which year the company was given a contract to carry mail to Egypt and India and added the word Oriental to its title. As P. & O. the company has been affectionately known ever since.

The most successful of the early North Atlantic mail companies was the Cunard Line. In 1838 Samuel Cunard (1787–1865) of Halifax, Nova Scotia, secured from the British Admiralty* the contract to carry mail to North America, on the strength of which in 1839 he formed the British & North American Royal Mail Steam Packet Co. in partnership with the shipowners George Burns (1795–1890) of Glasgow and David MacIver of Liverpool.

The Company's first four ships were wooden paddle-wheel steamers, all built on the Clyde – the *Britannia*, the best known of the four, the *Caledonia*, *Arcadia* and *Columbia*. They were almost identical in size and engine-power, being 207ft (63m) in length, 34½ft (10.5m) in beam, 22½ft (6.8m) in depth, with a tonnage of 1154 They could carry 115 cabin passengers and 225 tons of cargo. Their average speed was about 8½

---

* The Admiralty was responsible for the carriage of overseas mails from 1823 until 1860 when it reverted to the Post Office.

knots. The *Britannia* was launched in February 1840, and sailed from the Mersey on 4 July of that year, reaching Boston after a passage of 14 days, 8 hours.

The Royal Mail Steam Packet Company Ltd., formed to carry mail to the West Indies, was incorporated by Royal Charter in 1839, and so ranks with Cunard and P. & O. as **the oldest of Britain's great steamship companies**. The mail service was inaugurated in 1842 with a fleet of 14 paddle-steamers specially built for the company. In 1851 the company became the first to institute mail communication with Brazil, the service being extended to the Argentine in 1889.

The first iron steamship to round the Cape was the East India Company's 700-ton frigate *Nemesis* which reached Cape Town on 1 July 1840. She later aroused panic among the notorious Chinese pirates whose junks were no match for her.

The first non-British steamship service on the North Atlantic was run by the Belgian Government which bought the 2000-ton wooden paddle-steamer *British Queen* from the British & American Steam Navigation Company in 1841. The venture was a commercial failure and the *British Queen* was scrapped in 1844.

The first P. & O. ship built for service in Indian waters was the 2017-ton *Hindostan*, a two-funnelled, wooden, barquentine-rigged paddler, built to the design of C. W. Williams, a director of P. & O. She was 216ft (66m) long and 36ft (10.9m) in the beam. Her Fawcett side-lever engines developed 320hp and she achieved 10.21 knots on trials. Her interior departed from tradition in having cabins amidships, gangways insulating passengers from the heat and sea noises along the ship's sides. She carried 102 passengers and 50 passengers' servants. She left Southampton on 24 September 1842, bound for Calcutta, whence she entered the service to Suez that linked with the overland route through Egypt. She was sunk on 5 October 1864, by the great Calcutta cyclone which drove nearly 200 ships ashore.

P. & O. was **the first shipping company to enter the cruising business**. An advertisement in the *Illustrated London News* for 20 June 1844, announces 'a six-weeks Tour by steam to Athens, Smyrna, and Constantinople, with the option of visiting en route Vigo, Oporto, Lisbon, Cadiz and Gibraltar. The Peninsular and Oriental Steam Navigation's well-known splendid steamship IBERIA will start from Blackwall on Monday, August 5th for the above ports.' P. & O. were also early starters in the Public Relations game, for they offered a free passage on the *Iberia* to the novelist William Thackeray, and his account of the journey was published under the title *Notes of a Journey from Cornhill to Cairo* in 1846 and begins with a fulsome dedication to Captain Samuel Lewis, the captain of the *Iberia*.

The honour of being **the first steam troopship** belongs to the P. & O. Line's 533-ton paddle-steamer *Lady Mary Wood*. Built in 1842, she was sent out to the East in 1845 to start a service between Ceylon, Singapore and Hong Kong. In 1848 a rebellion broke out in Ceylon; the *Lady Mary Wood* was despatched to Madras and returned with sufficient troops to quell the revolt. She also has a small niche in literary history for in August of 1844 William Thackeray travelled on board her from Southampton to Gibraltar, a journey of which he wrote as follows:

'I have a regard for every man on board that ship, from the captain down to the crew – down even to the cook, with tattooed arms, sweating among the saucepans in the galley, who used (with a touching affection) to send us locks of his hair in the soup.'

The *Great Britain*, designed by Isambard Kingdom Brunel, was **the first large, ocean-going ship to be built of iron**. She was also **the first**

Brunel's splendid, six-masted *Great Britain*, now back in Bristol. *National Maritime Museum*.

screw-fitted steamer to cross the Atlantic, and at 3448 tons was **the largest ship in the world when she was launched in 1843.** She was 322ft (98m) in length with a beam of 51ft (15.5m). She had six masts named Monday/Saturday and her hull was constructed of overlapping iron plates 6ft (1.8m) by 2ft 6in (76cm)). She left the Mersey on 26 July 1845, on her first Atlantic crossing, which she made in 14 days 21 hours at an average speed of 9½ knots. She spent her latter years on the Australian run and had the honour to take **the first English cricket team to Australia.** For 5 years she was used as a coal-hulk in the Falkland Islands, but is now back in Bristol being restored as a monument to her creator, I. K. Brunel.

The American transatlantic sailing packets were so successful that little attention was paid to the development of steam power in the United States and it was not until 1845, 26 years after the *Savannah*'s voyage, that **a second US-built steamer crossed the Atlantic.** This was the 400-ton wooden auxiliary screw *Marmora*, built in the United States for the Turkish Government. She docked at Liverpool on 25 September 1845, after a voyage of 23½ days, only 10 days ahead of the 750-ton auxiliary *Massachusetts*, the first US-built and -owned steamer to make the crossing since the *Savannah*. The *Massachusetts* was fitted with a propellor which could be lifted out of the water when she was under sail.

The Sarah Sands. National Maritime Museum.

The first French Company to operate a North Atlantic steamship service was the Transatlantic General Steam Packet Company, colloquially known as Heroult and De Handel, to whom, in May 1847, the French Government chartered four wooden paddle-frigates, named *Union*, *Philadelphia*, *Missouri* and *New York*, each of 1100 tons. But the service was so bad that the French residents of New York organized a protest meeting and the company was wound up in 1848. It was to be another eight years before a second French steamship line was established on the North Atlantic.

The first United States company to operate a transatlantic steamer service was the Ocean Steam Navigation Company, the first of whose ships, the 1640-ton wooden paddle-steamer *Washington* left New York on 1 June 1847, and reached Southampton on 15 June. The Company's only other vessel was the 1743-ton *Hermann*, named after the German national hero who defeated three Roman legions in AD 9, since the Company was largely supported by German money and operated a service between New York and Bremen; but it failed to make money and was wound up in 1857.

One of the earliest ocean-going screw steamers and **the second largest iron ship then built** was the 1400-ton *Sarah Sands*. She was built in 1847 by James Hodgson of Liverpool, chartered to the American-owned Red Cross Line and made a

number of crossings between Liverpool and New York in 17–21 days. She had by far the most varied career of any of the early screw steamers, including an incident well known to military historians when she caught fire off Mauritius in November 1857, while carrying troops to Calcutta and was only saved by the efforts of the soldiers, who fought the blaze for 16 hours.

The first serious challenge to Cunard's supremacy of the North Atlantic came from the American Collins Line, named after its owner, Edward Knight Collins, who, in 1847, secured a contract from the United States Government to provide a regular mail service of 20 trips a year between New York and Liverpool in return for an annual subsidy of $385,000. Collins' ships were remarkable for the lavishness of their accommodation. Two of his vessels, the *Atlantic* and the *Arctic*, both 276ft (84.7m) in length and 45ft (13.7m) in beam, were **the largest steamships that had been built up to that time**. The *Atlantic* was rammed in a fog by the French steamer *Vesta* and sank with a loss of life variously estimated at from 278 to 322 and in 1856 another Collins steamer, the *Pacific*, sailed from Liverpool and was never heard of again. The government subsidy was withdrawn and the line failed.

The Hamburg American Line, the full name of which was the Hamburg Amerikanische Paketfahrt Aktien Gesellschaft, more commonly abbreviated to 'Hapag', was founded on 27 May 1847. The company's transatlantic service was inaugurated in 1848 by the 700-ton sailing ship *Deutschland*, but it was not until 1856 when the 2131-ton Clyde-built steamer *Borussia* inaugurated the company's North Atlantic steamship service that Hapag became, and remained, a serious contender for the North Atlantic passenger trade. The later history of Hapag is as much the story of Albert Ballin (1857–1918), a Hamburg Jew who joined the company in 1886 and in due course became **one of the greatest personalities the shipping world has ever known.**

The last wooden-hulled vessel built for the Cunard fleet was the 2402-ton *Arabia*, built in 1852 by Robert Steele & Son of Greenock. Her twin side-lever engines, which had cylinders 8ft 7in (2.6m) in diameter, developed 3250hp and gave her a speed of about 15 knots.

The first steamship line to operate between Great Britain and South Africa was the General Screw Steam Shipping Co. Ltd. In 1850 the Company was awarded the Cape mail contract, by which it undertook to provide a monthly service for the sum of £30,750 per annum, the passage in either direction to occupy no more than 35 days, a daunting schedule considering that the average duration of passage between England and the Cape was then reckoned at about 60 days.

The first South African mail steamer was the 445-ton iron auxiliary screw steamship *Bosphorus*, which left Plymouth on 18 December 1850, and reached Table Bay on 27 January 1851, five days over the contract time, but nevertheless a record.

In May 1852, the General Screw Company secured an extension of its mail contract embracing Ceylon, Madras and Calcutta. The run was inaugurated by the 1752-ton *Queen of the South* with accommodation for 130 passengers who were doubtless relieved to learn that 'the bilge pump has been so arranged that an attack of pirates may be repelled with scalding waters from the boilers'! The *Queen of the South* reached Cape Town in July 1852, and, proceeding eastwards, was **then the largest screw steamer to have rounded the Cape of Good Hope**. But the days of the Screw Company were numbered. Most of its ships were requisitioned as troop-carriers on the outbreak of the Crimean War in 1854 and the Company was wound up early in 1857.

The first Italian steamer to cross the North Atlantic was the 828-ton iron paddle-steamer *Sicilia*, built on the Clyde in 1853. She left Palermo on on 2 June 1854 and reached New York 18 days later.

The first Italian ocean-going steamship company was Transatlantica, founded in Genoa in 1852. Its first two steamers, the 1665-ton *Vittorio Emanuele* and *Conte di Cavour*, were completed in England in 1855 and then chartered to the French Government for use as transports during the Crimean War. The first transatlantic sailing left Genoa for Rio de Janiero on 28 October 1856.

The first steamer to be fitted with a compound engine was the 764-ton iron screw steamer

Brandon, built by Randolph & Elder for the London & Limerick Steamship Company and completed in 1854. In a simple single-acting engine the steam expands in the cylinder and pushes the piston the full length of its stroke. The steam is then let off through a condenser to be turned back into water, the piston returning to its position for the next stroke by a vacuum caused by condensation. In the compound engine the expanded steam, which is capable of 1700 times the expansion of its volume in water, is not let off into the condenser after its partial expansion but conducted into a second larger cylinder and the expansion lifts the next cylinder. This double use of the steam made for exceptional economy in coal-consumption and Noel Bonsor in *North Atlantic Seaway* says, 'The *Brandon* was the first steamer of all to have what was undoubtedly one of the most epoch-making improvements in the long history of marine propulsion.'

The *Brandon* left Southampton for New York on 17 August 1854 but only made one Atlantic crossing, being requisitioned by the British Government on her return as a Crimean War transport. It was not until 1870 that **a second ship with compound engines appeared on the North Atlantic**, when the National Lines' 2200-ton *Holland*, originally built in 1858, was converted.

The *Persia* regained the Atlantic record for Cunard in July 1856.

In a book which sets out to record such superlatives as the best, the fastest or the first, it is not often that one can use the somewhat subjective superlative 'worst', but it is a fact that, after the demise of the General Screw Company, the Cape mail contract was awarded to the Lindsay Line, the house flag of which bore the initials of its owner W. S. Lindsay. So bad was the performance of his ships, and so primitive the passenger accommodation that it was soon said the 'W.S.L.' stood for '**Worst Steamship Line**'. The contract lasted only from August 1856, to September 1857.

Cunard's first iron-hulled ship was the 3300-ton *Persia*, built by Robert Napier & Sons of Glasgow and delivered in January 1856. In July of that year she regained the Atlantic record for Cunard, making the crossing to New York in 9 days, 1 hour, 45 minutes, at an average speed of 13.82 knots.

In 1856 the mail contract for Australia, which P. & O. had held since 1852, was awarded to a new and inexperienced company, the European and Australian Royal Mail Co., which, for a time had to charter ships from P. & O. and other lines in order to fulfil its contract. But in 1857 the line took delivery of the 2902-ton iron screw steamer *Australasian* and her sister the 2956-ton *Tasmanian*, which were, **at that time, the most powerful screw steamers afloat**, able to main-

tain a steady 11 knots under steam alone, and providing accommodation for 200 first and 60 second-class passengers.

The first shipping line to incorporate the name 'Lloyd' in its title was the German company Norddeutscher Lloyd which received its charter in the Bremen Senate on 8 December 1856. Since then the name has been used by shipping lines all over the world and in this context has come to mean 'shipping company'. The reason is as follows. In the late 17th century a Welshman named Edward Lloyd (d 1726) opened a coffee house in Tower Street, London, which he later moved to Lombard Street. It became the meeting place of those concerned with shipbroking and marine insurance and Lloyd himself collected shipping information from the docks for the benefit and interest of his customers. From this emerged the association of marine underwriters known to this day as Lloyd's. It also became the leading international authority on the specification of ships in relation to their strength and capacity – hence the expression 'A1 at Lloyd's', meaning that a ship was classified as first-class in every respect in *Lloyd's Register*, which is published annually. (A1 is now reserved for ships trading in sheltered waters.) (See also p. 154.)

In 1856 the Compagnie Transatlantique Belge claimed that its steamer *Belgique* was classified 'A1' at Lloyd's when this was not the case and was duly reprimanded. The ships of Norddeutscher Lloyd having been built in Britain under Lloyd's supervision, the directors decided to add the word to their title to indicate the soundness of their fleet and their example has since been followed by numerous non-British shipping companies.

The first man to realize the paying power of the emigrant was William Inman (1825–81) who founded the Inman Line in 1857. Hitherto steerage passengers, as those unable to afford a cabin were classed, travelled in conditions of appalling squalor and discomfort. Steerage accommodation consisted of a large space below deck lined with two or three tiers of open-sided, open-fronted wooden bunks. Lavatories, when provided, were usually on deck, but during bad weather steerage passengers were battened down in their quarters and the smell of vomit and excrement became indescribable. Sometimes passengers were

A Norddeutscher Lloyd announcement of transatlantic sailings, 1879. *Roger Daniels.*

expected to bring their own food which they could cook on a large stove on deck; other ships undertook to provide food but there was seldom enough, and in the scramble to get what there was the weakest usually went to the wall. 'The *George Canning*,' said the *New York Times* in 1853, 'has two kinds of water for her passengers – fit, drinkable water for the Captain, the cabin passengers and the crew; and bilge-water, or water taken from the ocean, for the emigrants.' In such conditions over 7 million people crossed the Atlantic in the first three-quarters of the 19th century.

In 1849 Inman bought the *City of Glasgow* for Richardson Bros. of Liverpool, of which firm he was then a partner. She was 227ft (69m) in length, 33ft (10m) in beam, and 25ft (7.6m) in depth, and was equipped with a two-bladed screw driven by engines of 350hp. She had accommodation for 52 first-class passengers, 85 second-class and 400 steerage. For eight guineas (£8.40) the emigrant

Steerage passengers on a transatlantic liner. *Mary Evans Picture Library.*

got a numbered berth and a plain but adequate bill of fare comprising porridge, beef, fish and plum pudding on Sundays.

The *City of Glasgow* has been called **the true prototype of the modern ocean steamship**, the first really successful screw steamer on the North Atlantic. She was also **the first steamship to sail from the Clyde to North America.**

In September 1857 the contract for carrying mail to South Africa was awarded to the Union Steam Ship Company Ltd., which had started life in 1853 as the Union Steam Collier Company, the original object of which was to carry coal for ships bound for Australia and the Far East to bunkers in Australia. But the Company's ships were requisitioned as transports during the Crimean War and thereafter it diverted its attention from coal to freight. On 15 September 1857, the 526-ton *Dane* left Southampton carrying the Cape mails, light freight and either four or six passengers – the records vary. On 29 October 1857, the *Dane* reached the Cape and **the flag of the Union Line was seen there for the first time.**

THE *GREAT EASTERN*

The *Great Eastern* built by Isambard Kingdom Brunel and launched in 1858 with a gross tonnage of 18,914, was the **largest ship of her time**. She had a length of 692ft (211m) along her upper deck and a beam of 120ft (36.6m) across her paddle-boxes. The cargo load was 6000 tons, in addition to 10,000 tons of coal in the bunkers. She was built of iron with an inner skin from the keel to the waterline, and was thus double-hulled, the space between the two hulls being used to contain water-ballast. She had six masts which carried a spread of 6500sq.yd (5435m²) of canvas and was fitted with both paddles and screw. The paddle-wheels were 56ft (17m) in diameter and each weighed 90 tons. The propellor had a diameter of 24ft (7.3m) and weighed 36 tons. Her speed, using both screw and paddles, attained 15 knots.

She was built on an even keel on the bank of the Thames, and was launched sideways into the river, an undertaking which proved so fraught with difficulties that it added £120,000 to the cost of the ship.

The *Great Eastern* was an unlucky ship and ended her working life laying cables across the Atlantic, a sad end for a vessel so proudly con-

ceived. When she was broken up in 1887 it is said, though there is no solid evidence to support the story, that she had carried a corpse on board throughout her career. On opening the double bottom of her hull the shipbreakers were reputed to have discovered a skeleton in one of the compartments. It was that of an unfortunate riveter who had somehow got trapped while the ship was being built.

The first steamer to be built specially and exclusively for the Cape mail service was the Union Line's 1055-ton *Cambrian*, launched in 1860. She was also the first Union liner to exceed 1000 tons. She was 245ft (74.7m) long, 30ft (9.1m) wide, and carried 64 first- and 40 second-class passengers. She ran regularly in the mail service for 11 years, was then sold to a French company and finally foundered in the Bay of Biscay in 1882.

For nearly half a century the South African shipping world was dominated by **Sir Donald Currie** (1825–1909). Born at Greenock and educated in Belfast, he started his career with the Cunard Line but in 1862 formed the Castle Line of sailing

Chain drums and checking gear used at the sideways launch of the *Great Eastern*, then still called the *Leviathan*.

ships operating between Liverpool and Calcutta. In 1872 he started the Castle Line of steamships operating between England and Cape Town, after 1876 dividing the government mail contract with the Union Line. In 1900 the two lines were amalgamated to form the Union-Castle Mail Steamship Company. In 1912 the company was acquired by Lord Kylsant and became part of the Royal Mail Shipping Group, but became independent again after the collapse of Royal Mail in 1931. It is now part of the British and Commonwealth Shipping Group.

The last paddle-steamer built for Cunard was the 3871-ton iron-hulled *Scotia*, laid down in 1862 and launched in 1864. She had two cylinders of 100in (254cm) diameter and 12ft (3.6m) stroke, producing 4000hp and driving paddle-wheels 40ft (12.2m) in diameter to give a speed of 14 knots. She had accommodation for 573 first-class passengers.

The first ocean-going twin-screw vessel was the 1504-ton steamer *Ruahine* belonging to the Panama, New Zealand and Australia Royal Mail Company, which, in 1866, started a service across the Pacific from Panama to Sydney and Wellington. No one knows why she was so designed.

The White Star Line's *Oceanic* has been called **the originator of the modern type of fast ocean liner.** The White Star Line was the popular name of the Oceanic Steam Navigation Co. Ltd., which emerged from the failure of the Aberdeen White Star Line in 1867 when the goodwill and house flag of that company were acquired by Thomas H. Ismay (1837–99). The *Oceanic*, built by Harland and Wolff at Belfast, was 420ft (128m) in length, 41ft (12.5m) in breadth and 31ft (9.4m), in depth with a tonnage of 3707. She was launched in 1871 and at once rendered all other Atlantic liners obsolete. Her accommodation incorporated many innovations, including running water in the cabins, electric bells, steam-heating and adjustable oil-lamps. But perhaps the most revolutionary feature of her design was the placing of the first-class saloon and the best cabins amidships instead of aft where they had traditionally been sited since the days of sail, the advantage of such a position having been turned to a positive disadvantage with the advent of screw propulsion and the consequent noise and motion aft.

The largest wooden merchant steamers ever built were the *America* (4454 tons), *Japan* (4351 tons), *Great Republic* (3881 tons) and *China* (3836 tons) for the Pacific Mail Steamship Company for a monthly service between San Francisco and Hong Kong. First to enter service, in May 1867, was the *Great Republic*, built by Henry Steers of Greenpoint, Long Island, and not to be confused with the earlier *Great Republic* (see p. 176). These four marked the end of the era of ocean-going wooden paddle-steamers. The *America* was destroyed by fire in 1872; the *Japan* met the same fate in 1874; the *Great Republic* was wrecked in 1879 and the *China* was withdrawn from service in the same year.

The first company to run a service of first-class screw steamers between London and New York was the London and New York Steamship Company, inaugurated when their 2058-ton *Cella*

sailed from the Thames on 1 September 1863. But the Company had overestimated the demand for such a service and the London–New York run was never a success.

The first regular steamship service between the Mediterranean and New York was inaugurated when the Anchor Line's 1039-ton *Tyrian* sailed from Naples on 30 October 1869. Hitherto the Line had brought Italian emigrants to Glasgow for trans-shipment to New York but the continued growth in this traffic persuaded Company to institute direct sailings from the Mediterranean to New York.

The first twin-screw transatlantic liner was the 3200-ton *Washington*. Built by Scott & Company of Greenock for the Compagnie Générale Trans-atlantique in 1863, she was converted by Robert Napier of Glasgow to twin screw in 1868. Her sister ship, the *Lafayette*, was converted shortly afterwards.

The first British merchant steamer to pass through the Suez Canal was the Anchor Line's *Dido*, after its formal opening by the Khedive Ismail Pasha on 17 November 1869. Begun on 25 April 1859, the Suez Canal owes its existence to the drive and inspiration of the French diplomat Ferdinand de Lesseps (1805–94). His association with the projected Panama Canal was less fortu-

The Suez Canal is 103 miles long, of which 21 miles are in lakes. The average time of transit is 15 hours.

The Inman Atlantic steamship *City of Berlin*.

nate and he and his son were both sentenced to imprisonment for misappropriation of funds, but the sentences were never carried out. The Panama Canal was finally built by the US Corps of Army Engineers between 1908 and 1914.

The first ship built for any North Atlantic company designed from the outset to be fitted with compound engines was the Guion Line's 3700-ton *Wisconsin*, who left Liverpool on her maiden voyage on 6 July 1870.

The first Norwegian steamship company on the North Atlantic was the Norse American Line whose 1935-ton screw steamer *St Olaf* left Newcastle-on-Tyne for Bergen and New York in June 1871; but it was soon apparent that there was insufficient demand for the service which was withdrawn in 1876.

The first of Donald Currie's Castle steamers was the 2341-ton *Dover Castle*, launched on 25 January 1872; but she was never seen at the Cape. For her maiden voyage she was chartered by the Pacific Line to take a sailing to the west coast of South America. Homeward bound from Callao, Peru, she caught fire, managed to reach Coquimbo, Chile, and was there scuttled.

The first of the 'Castle' steamers actually to be

seen in Table Bay was the 2446-ton *Walmer Castle*; she left Bordeaux on 10 September 1872, and reached Cape Town on 4 October.

The first ship to be fitted with electric light was the 4585-ton French liner *Amérique*, owned by the Compagnie Générale Transatlantique. In 1876, after a series of unfortunate mishaps, the Company announced the *Amérique* had been fitted with 'the lighthouse and electric light' to minimize the risk of collision. It was, however, for external use only.

The first ship to be fitted with internal electric lighting was the 5491-ton Inman liner *City of Berlin* which, in 1879, was fitted with six arc-lamps in the dining saloon and engine/boiler rooms.

The first steel-hulled (as opposed to iron-hulled) **vessel in the P. & O. fleet,** indeed one of the very first steel-built ocean liners, was the 3372-ton screw steamer *Ravenna*, completed in 1880 by William Denny & Co. for the company's Australian and Eastern services. She and her sister-ships, *Rohilla* and *Rosetta*, both built of iron, were the last liners built for P. & O. with the first-class accommodation aft over the screw. It being the company's stated policy not to carry steerage passengers, accommodation was only provided for 102 first-class and 32 second-class passengers, the latter mainly comprising the staff and servants of the former.

The first British-registered merchant ship fitted throughout with 'Edison's Incandescent electric light' was the 1003-ton *Tarawera*, delivered to the Union Steamship Company of New Zealand in 1882.

The first vessel to be fitted with a triple-expansion engine was the 3684-ton *Aberdeen*, completed for the Aberdeen Line in 1882. The triple-expansion engine was a development of the compound engine, in which, by the addition of a third cylinder, the steam was used three times instead of twice. The *Aberdeen* proved so successful that she finished the run to Australia with coal to spare in her bunkers.

The first ship to cross the Atlantic in less than a week was the Guion Line's 6950-ton *Alaska*, which sailed from New York to Cobh in 6 days 22 hours in June 1882. She was the first ship to be nicknamed *'The Greyhound of the Atlantic'*.

Guion Line advertisement. *Mary Evans Picture Library.*

The first liner to be fitted with interior plumbing was the 6283-ton *Normandie*, built at Barrow in 1883 for the Compagnie Générale Transatlantique.

The first twin-screw steamer in the Union fleet and the most famous of all the pre-Union amalgamation steamships was the 6844-ton *Scot*. She left Southampton on her maiden voyage on 25 July 1891, and reached Table Bay on 10 August, beating the previous best time by over a day and establishing a record which was only broken by the motor liner *Stirling Castle* in 1936. She was withdrawn from service in 1903 and ended her days as the *Vasco Nuñez de Balboa* of the Spanish Mail Steamship Line. A curious episode in her career was the suicide of the Jewish financier Barney Barnato who had lost a fortune in the Kaffir mining share boom in 1895, of which he himself had been the chief manipulator. In June 1897, he jumped overboard from the *Scot* and was drowned.

The last Atlantic liner to be equipped with sails was the 9047-ton *La Touraine*, belonging to the Compagnie Générale Transatlantique and launched in 1891. She is also remembered as one of the Atlantic's most beautiful liners, though C. R. Vernon Gibbs confidently states that 'opinion is unanimous that no more beautiful steamship [than the *City of Rome*] ever crossed the Atlantic' (*Passenger Liners of the Western Ocean*).

The first North Atlantic liner to be built to Admiralty specifications for rapid conversion into an armed merchant cruiser in time of war was the White Star Line's 9984-ton *Teutonic*. She held the Atlantic Blue Riband from August 1891, until October 1892, having crossed from Queenstown (Cobh) in Southern Ireland to Sandy Hook at an average speed of 20.35 knots.

The paddle-steamer continued to be used in cross-channel and coastal passenger trades until well after the turn of the century. The last two paddle-steamers built for service across the English Channel were *Le Nord* and *Le Pas de Calais*, completed for the French Chemin de Fer du Nord by the Ateliers et Chantiers de la Loire in 1898. They were, curiously, the only cross-channel paddle-steamers ever built in France.

The first German liner to take the Atlantic Blue Riband was Norddeutscher Lloyd's 14,350-ton *Kaiser Wilhelm der Grosse*, which crossed from Sandy Hook to the Needles in November 1897, at an average speed of 22.35 knots. On her third voyage, in March 1898, she took the westbound record at a speed of 22.29 knots. For two years she ranked as **the world's largest ship** and in February 1900, she was fitted with **one of the earliest radio sets ever used at sea**. Its range was only 25 miles and its use was limited to reporting arrival.

A bedroom on the White Star Line's *Teutonic. Mansell Collection.*

The Anchor Line's *City of Rome*, claimed to be the most handsome of them all. *National Maritime Museum.*

The earliest ocean newspaper was a modest sheet rather grandly entitled *The Transatlantic Times*. In November 1899, Signor Marconi left New York on board the American Line's 11,600-ton twin-screw *St Paul*, whereon he assembled a wireless receiver with which he managed to pick up six short messages broadcast from The Needles, Isle of Wight, 60–70 miles (96–112km) away, which were then published in *The Transatlantic Times*, the price of which was one dollar.

The Brief Heyday of the Luxury Liner

The first liner to exceed the *Great Eastern* in length, at 686ft (209m), was the 17,274-ton *Oceanic*, built by Harland & Wolff for the White Star line and launched in 1899. She was not a record-breaker, averaging only 19½ knots on her maiden voyage but her first-class accommodation was outstanding and she remained **the most luxurious ship on the Atlantic** for a considerable period. 'She had lavatories of "costly marble", and resembled "a Hotel Cecil afloat". The Hotel Cecil was then the grandest in London' (TERRY COLEMAN, *The Liners*). Following the outbreak of the First World War she became an auxiliary cruiser and was wrecked on the Shetlands in September 1914.

The largest ship in the world at the time of her completion was the 20,904-ton White Star liner *Celtic*, delivered by Harland & Wolff in July 1901. She represented a totally new conception in the development of transatlantic travel – the combination of spacious comfort and economy of operation. She averaged a modest 16½ knots, against the *Oceanic*'s 19½, but her fuel consumption was only 260 tons a day, against *Oceanic*'s 400. She could carry 347 first-class, 160 second-class and 2350 third-class passengers, the last in considerably greater comfort than was usual at the time. She proved so popular that all the major North Atlantic lines soon began building similar ships.

The first vessel to carry wireless equipment which enabled her to keep in touch with both sides of the Atlantic simultaneously was the 12,950-ton Cunarder *Lucania*, launched in 1893. She and her sister-ship *Campania*, were **then the two largest ships in the world**. She held the Blue Riband from August 1894 until March 1898, but it was not until 1903 that her epoch-making wireless equipment was fitted.

The *Campania*, named after a region of southern Italy.

In 1903 Owen Philipps (1863–1937) became chairman of the Royal Mail Steam Packet Co. and acquired the Pacific Line in 1910, the Union-Castle in 1912, the shipbuilders Harland & Wolff in 1924 and the White Star Line in 1927, thus making Royal Mail the centrepiece of what was **then the largest shipping group in the world**. But Philipps, who had been created Lord Kylsant in 1923, overreached himself and the group collapsed; the parent company was liquidated and in 1932 Royal Mail Lines was formed in its place. Since 1965 it has been part of the Furness Withy Group. In 1931 Lord Kylsant was sent to prison for a year for publishing a false prospectus.

The first turbine steamer on the North Atlantic was the 10,635-ton *Victorian*, built for the Allan Line by Workman, Clark & Co. of Belfast and launched in 1905. In July 1920, she carried out **the first extensive wireless telephony tests at sea,** transmitting messages over a distance of 600 miles (965km).

The first Cunard liner to be fitted with turbines was the 19,524-ton *Carmania*, which entered service on the Liverpool/New York run in December 1905. On the outbreak of the First World War she was taken over by the Royal Navy and on 14 September 1914, became the **only armed merchant cruiser to sink a similar antagonist in an armed gun duel** when she sank the 18,700-ton *Cap Trafalgar*, built in 1913 for the Hamburg–South American Line, off Trinidad.

The *Carmania* sinking the *Cap Trafalgar*, 14 September 1914. *Roger Daniels.*

The *Lusitania*, built for Cunard by John Brown on Clydebank, launched in June 1906, and completed in September 1907, was, at 30,396 tons **then the largest vessel in the world**. She was also **the first quadruple-screw steamer, the first steamer to exceed 30,000 tons and the first British four-funnelled steamer**. On her second voyage in October 1907, she took the Atlantic Blue Riband in both directions at an average speed, westbound, of 23.99 and, eastbound, of 23.61 knots.

She is best remembered, however, for her tragic end and the consequences thereof. On 7 May 1915, she was torpedoed without warning by the German submarine U–20 off the Old Head of Kinsale, Co. Cork, and sank within 22 minutes, with the loss of 1198 lives, of whom 124 were American citizens. At that time the United States was still a neutral country and the sinking of the *Lusitania* had considerable influence on her decision to enter the First World War.

The longest holder of the Atlantic Blue Riband was the *Mauretania*, sister-ship of the *Lusitania*, and described by C. R. Gibbs-Smith as having **'won for herself a place gained by no other steamship in history**. She remained as honoured in old age as in youth and was affectionately referred to as "The Grand Old Lady of the Atlantic".' She took the eastbound record in November 1907 and held it for the next 22 years; she first took the westbound record in May 1908, lost it to the *Lusitania* the following year, but regained it in September 1909 and then held it until July 1929. In all she made 269 double crossings of the Atlantic and was finally broken up at Rosyth in April 1935.

Another in the long list of **largest ships in the world at the time of launching** was the White Star's 45,324-ton *Olympic*, launched in October 1910, and extensively rebuilt in 1912 after the sinking of the *Titanic*, when her tonnage was increased to 46,359. She was soon overtaken, however, by the launching in June 1913, of Hapag's 51,969-ton *Imperator*, which, after the First World War, became the Cunard liner *Berengaria*, whereafter the *Olympic* had to content herself with being **the largest British-built steamer** and **the largest triple-screw steamer**, while her sister ship the *Homeric* claimed to be **the longest twin-screw steamer**.

The first English merchant ship to be equipped with a radio direction-finder to aid navigation by cross-bearings was the *Mauretania* in 1911.

The first notable instance of wireless telegraphy being used to summon assistance at sea occurred on 23 January 1909, when the 15,400-ton White Star liner *Republic* was rammed in a fog off Nantucket by the Lloyd Italiano 5000-ton twin-screw *Florida*. Five liners came to the aid of the *Republic* and she was taken in tow by the *Baltic*, to which her passengers and crew were transferred, but she sank before reaching port. She was the largest ship lost at sea prior to the *Titanic*. The *Florida*, despite badly damaged bows, reached New York and was repaired within a month.

The first Cape mail steamer to be fitted with equipment for wireless telegraphy was the 13,361-ton *Balmoral Castle*, launched in 1910.

The first ship with diesel engines to run on the North Atlantic was the 4600-ton twin-screw motor ship *California*, owned by the Scandinavian–American Line. She left Copenhagen on her maiden voyage on 9 October 1913, bound for New York via Oslo and Boston.

The first Union-Castle liners specially designed for service between London and East Africa via the Suez Canal were the 11,423-ton *Llandovery Castle* and her sister the 11,293-ton *Llanstephan Castle*. Both were launched in 1914 and were the first Union-Castle steamers to be built after the Company was acquired by the Royal Mail group.

The sinking of the *Llandovery Castle* by a German U-boat on 27 June 1918, is generally regarded as **one of the worst atrocities of the First World War**. She was employed on the Canadian run as a hospital ship and was displaying the usual Red Cross lights when she was torpedoed without warning 114 miles (183km) west of the Fastnet Rock by the German submarine U-86, which then proceeded to ram or sink by gunfire those boats which had got away. Only one lifeboat escaped, its 24 occupants being the sole survivors of the 258 people on board.

The first transatlantic motor passenger liner was the Swedish–American Line's 17,993-ton

Gripsholm, launched in 1925. 'Protagonists of the diesel engine claimed a number of advantages including a considerably better power/weight ratio and reduced manning requirements when compared with steam plant of comparable output. On the other hand diesel fuel was more expensive than furnace fuel oils but against this could be set the greater economy of the internal combustion engine and a reduction in the space devoted to bunkers' (JOHN M. MABER, *Channel Packets and Ocean Liners*).

The largest motor liner ever built, and the only one to be fitted with quadruple screws, was the 32,650-ton *Augustus* of the Italian Navigazione Generale Italiana. She was launched in 1926 and made one voyage to South America before entering North Atlantic service on the Genoa–Naples–New York run. In 1943 she was converted to an aircraft carrier and renamed *Sparviero*. She was scuttled by the Germans at Genoa in 1945 but was refloated and finally scrapped in 1951.

The first motorship on the South African mail run and the first Cape liner to exceed 20,000 tons was the 20,063-ton *Carnarvon Castle*, launched in 1926.

The *Mauretania* finally lost the Blue Riband to Norddeutscher Lloyd's 51,650-ton *Bremen*, which was launched on 16 August 1928 and easily took the record in both directions on her maiden voyage in July 1929. The *Bremen*, and her sister-ship, the 49,750-ton *Europa*, were **the first of the modern express liners designed to be fast enough to cross the Atlantic, refuel, load passengers and stores and be ready for the return voyage within a single week**. The *Bremen* was burnt out in an air-raid in Bremerhaven in March 1941, and subsequently broken up. The *Europa* survived the Second World War but was taken over by the USA in 1945 and made two voyages as an American transport; she was then awarded to France and reappeared on the North Atlantic in 1950 as the Compagnie Générale Transatlantique's *Liberté*, remaining in service until 1962.

The first motor passenger liner to circumnavigate Africa was the 11,951-ton *Llangibby Castle*, launched in 1929.

Though *Peleus* is the largest cement carrier in GRT, *Pytheus* is larger in DWT. *Golden Union Shipping Company SA.*

The *Flying Cloud*, one of Donald Mackay's famous clippers; from a painting by Peter Wood.

The Ocean Steam Navigation Company's paddle-steamer *Washington* (see p. 188). *Roger Daniels.*

The *Great Eastern* (see p. 192). *Mary Evans Picture Library.*

The only Italian liner ever to hold the Blue Riband was the 51,000-ton *Rex* of the Italia Line. She made her record-breaking crossing in August

Cable announcing the record run of the *Rex*. *Roger Daniels.*

A view from the top of the Rockefeller Building of the *Normandie* arriving in New York. *Mansell Collection.*

1933, when she steamed from Tarifa, the southernmost tip of Spain, to Ambrose in 4 days, 13 hours, 58 minutes at an average speed of 28.92 knots. She never won the eastbound record. On 9 September 1944, she was bombed and sunk by British aircraft at Capodistria (then an Italian port, now Yugoslavian and called Koper) and later scrapped.

The only French liner to hold the Blue Riband was the 79,300-ton *Normandie* of the Compagnie Générale Transatlantique, generally known as the French Line in Britain and the United States. On her maiden voyage from Le Havre in May 1935, she broke the existing record easily with an average westbound speed of 29.98 knots and 30.35 knots on the return journey. Between then and 1938 she shared the record with the *Queen Mary*. In 1936 her tonnage was increased to 82,799, making her **the first steamer to exceed 80,000 tons**. She was gutted by fire in New York harbour in February 1942, and, though eventually refloated, was scrapped in 1946.

QUEEN MARY

The most famous of all the transatlantic liners
and, for a brief time, another in the long list of
'largest ships in the world' was Cunard's 80,774-
ton *Queen Mary*. Her keel was laid down on 27
December 1930, but, owing to the depression,
work was halted a year later. The British
Government offered to lend £3 million at favourable rates on condition that Cunard amalgamated
with the White Star Line. There being no alternative, the proposal was accepted and work was
resumed in April 1934. The French had been
quicker to realize that ships of such magnitude
required substantial state aid and thus the *Normandie*, though laid down a month after the
Queen Mary, was finished a year ahead of her
rival. French wags referred to the *Normandie* as
'*la dette flottante*'. The *Queen Mary* was launched
on 26 September 1934, and sailed from Southampton on her maiden voyage on 27 May 1936,
but did not take the Blue Riband until her sixth
crossing in August of that year. She lost it to the
Normandie in 1937, regained it in 1938 and then
held it until 1952. During the Second World War
she was sent to Sydney, Australia, where she was
fitted out as a troopship with a carrying capacity
of some 8200 soldiers. Though she was never
herself attacked by enemy submarines or aircraft,
she had the misfortune to sink one of her own

escorting force, the anti-aircraft cruiser *Curaçao*,
off Bloody Foreland, Co. Donegal, on 2 October
1942. For reasons which have never been fully
explained, the *Curaçao* crossed the bows of the
Queen Mary and 50ft (152m) was sliced clean off
the stern of the cruiser which sank at once. The
rest stayed afloat for 20 minutes, but 338 of the
439 men aboard were lost. The *Queen Mary*
suffered no more damage than a badly twisted
stem. She went back into service after the war but
was sold in 1967 and remains afloat as a museum,
hotel ship and convention centre at Long Beach,
California.

The anti-aircraft cruiser *Curaçao*, later sunk by the *Queen
Mary*. *Roger Daniels*.

The picture below shows what it takes to equip a luxury
floating hotel. *Roger Daniels*.

QUEEN ELIZABETH

The *Queen Elizabeth*, at 83,673 tons, was at the time of her launching the largest liner in the world. She was laid down in December 1936 and launched in September 1938; but the Second World War broke out before she was completed and in November 1940, she was sent to Singapore to be fitted out as a troopship, in which role she was employed between 1941 and 1946. Her measurements were: overall length 1031ft (314m), breadth 118ft (36m). After the war she was refitted and made her first sailing as a passenger liner in October 1946. In April 1968 she was sold to a syndicate of Philadelphia businessmen for £3,230,000, but it was later announced that Cunard would have a $1,000,000 interest in the Elizabeth Corporation which would operate the ship as a hotel, museum and convention centre off Port Everglades, Florida. She left New York on her final passenger-carrying voyage on 30

The *Queen Elizabeth* arriving at New York at the outbreak of the Second World War. Behind are the *Queen Mary* and the *Normandie*. Roger Daniels.

October 1968, and on 29 November left Southampton for Fort Lauderdale, Florida. On 16 March 1969, Cunard resumed control of the *Queen Elizabeth*, following the failure of the Elizabeth Corporation Syndicate, and entered into a new agreement with a new US company, The Queen Ltd, in which Cunard had no interest. Although she was seen by over 1,000,000 visitors, the new company also became insolvent and in 1971 sold her to Mr C. Y. Tung, a Hong Kong shipping magnate, for £1,200,000. She sailed for that port in February 1971, where it was intended to convert her into the *Seawise University*; but on 9 January 1972, she was completely destroyed by a fire started, in the words of the official inquiry, 'by a person or persons unknown'.

Harold Hales (1868–1942) presented the Hales Trophy for the Blue Riband of the Atlantic in 1935. *Roger Daniels.*

The *France* and the *United States* at Le Havre. *Roger Daniels.*

The first major passenger liner to be fitted with stabilizers was the 24,215-ton P. & O. liner *Chusan*, launched in June 1949. They were 12ft (3.66m) × 6ft 6in (1.98m) and could damp a 40° roll down to 4°.

The largest liner ever built in the Netherlands is the Holland–America Line's 38,645-ton *Rotterdam*. When she sailed into New York harbour on 11 September 1959, she passed the spot where exactly 350 years earlier to the day Henry Hudson had anchored his carvel *Halve Mean*.

The last liner to hold the Blue Riband also achieved the distinction of **beating the previous best time by the biggest margin on record.** The 53,329-ton *United States* of the United States

Line was laid down on 8 February 1950, launched on 23 June 1951, and sailed from New York on her maiden voyage on 3 July 1952. In the next 11 days she took 3.9 knots off the eastbound record and 3.52 off the westbound, having made the crossings at average speeds of 35.59 and 34.51 knots.

But the *United States* was born too late. **In 1958 the number of people who crossed the Atlantic by air exceeded for the first time the number who made the crossing by sea.** The era of the scheduled transatlantic passenger service was over.

The world's longest merchant ship, when she was launched in 1960, was the 66,000-ton French-built liner *France*, owned by the Com-

pagnie Générale Transatlantique. At 1035ft (315m) she was 4ft (1.2m) longer than the *Queen Elizabeth*.

QUEEN ELIZABETH II

The Cunard Steam-Ship Company's passenger liner *Queen Elizabeth II* (65,863 tons) was launched on 20 September 1967 by Her Majesty the Queen at John Brown's Clydebank yard. She is 963ft (293.5m) long, has a beam of 105ft (32m) and a draught of 32½ft (9.9m), enabling her to pass through both the Suez and Panama canals. The liner's name was kept a secret until the moment of launching. After numerous teething troubles, she left Southampton on her maiden transatlantic voyage on 2 May 1969 and reached New York on 7 May where she was given a rous-

ing welcome, Mayor Lindsay designating the day as Queen Elizabeth II Day.

In the winter of 1970–1 **the North Atlantic was without any regular passenger services at all for the first time since 1838,** the owners of the remaining liners preferring the more lucrative winter cruise market, and the modern traveller preferring to cross the Atlantic by jet in 7hrs, or less than half that by *Concorde*.

The days of the great Atlantic liners were finally over and, even when the oil runs out, will certainly never come back in any form recognizable to those who enjoyed the luxury and social uplift of first-class travel across the North Atlantic in the years before and soon after the Second World War.

Record Passages *The Blue Riband of the North Atlantic*

WESTBOUND

YEAR	STEAMER	FLAG	LINE	FROM	TO	NAUTICAL MILES	TIME DAY	HR	MIN	SPEED (KNOTS)
1838 (Apr)	Sirius	Brit.	B. & A.	Cork	New York	2961	18	10	0	6.7
1838 (Apr)	Great Western	Brit.	GW	Avonmouth	New York	3223	15	10	30	8.7
1839	Great Western	Brit.	GW	Avonmouth	New York	3053	13	6	0	9.6
1841 (Jun)	Columbia	Brit.	Cunard	Liverpool	Halifax	2534	10	19	0	9.78
1848	Europa	Brit.	Cunard	Liverpool	New York	3047	11	3	0	11.52
1850 (May)	Asia	Brit.	Cunard	Liverpool	Halifax	2534	8	17	0	12.12
1850 (Sep)	Pacific	US	Collins	Liverpool	New York	3050	10	4	0	12.5
1851 (Aug)	Baltic	US	Collins	Liverpool	New York	3054	9	18	0	13.05
1861 (Jun)	Adriatic	Brit.	Galway	Galway	St John's, N.F.	1677	5	2	0	13.75
1866 (Jul)	Scotia	Brit.	Cunard	Queenstown	New York	2851	8	4	35	14.51
1872 (May)	Adriatic	Brit.	W. Star	Queenstown	New York	2778	7	23	17	14.52
1875 (Sep)	City of Berlin	Brit.	Inman	Queenstown	New York	2829	7	18	2	15.21
1876 (Nov)	Britannic	Brit.	W. Star	Queenstown	New York	2795	7	13	11	15.43
1877 (Apr)	Germanic	Brit.	W. Star	Queenstown	New York	2830	7	11	37	15.76
1882 (Apr)	Alaska	Brit.	Guion	Queenstown	New York	2803	7	6	43	16.04
1883 (Apr)	Alaska	Brit.	Guion	Queenstown	New York	2775	6	23	48	16.54
1884 (May)	America	Brit.	National	Queenstown	New York	2805	6	15	22	17.6
1884 (Aug)	Oregon	Brit.	Cunard	Queenstown	Sandy Hook	2792	6	9	42	18.16
1885 (May)	Etruria	Brit.	Cunard	Queenstown	Sandy Hook	2821	6	5	31	18.87
1887 (May)	Umbria	Brit.	Cunard	Queenstown	Sandy Hook	2810	6	4	42	18.90
1888 (May)	Etruria	Brit.	Cunard	Queenstown	Sandy Hook	2855	6	1	55	19.57
1889 (May)	City of Paris	Brit.	I. & I.	Queenstown	Sandy Hook	2855	5	23	7	19.95
1889 (Sep)	City of Paris	Brit.	I. & I.	Queenstown	Sandy Hook	2788	5	19	18	20.01
1891 (Aug)	Teutonic	Brit.	W. Star	Queenstown	Sandy Hook	2778	5	16	31	20.35
1892 (Oct)	City of Paris	Brit.	I. & I.	Queenstown	Sandy Hook	2782	5	14	24	20.70
1893 (Oct)	Lucania	Brit.	Cunard	Queenstown	Sandy Hook	2775	5	13	45	20.75
1894 (Aug)	Campania	Brit.	Cunard	Queenstown	Sandy Hook	2783	5	9	29	21.49
1894 (Aug)	Lucania	Brit.	Cunard	Queenstown	Sandy Hook	2787	5	8	38	21.66
1894 (Sep)	Lucania	Brit.	Cunard	Queenstown	Sandy Hook	2782	5	7	48	21.75
1894 (Oct)	Lucania	Brit.	Cunard	Queenstown	Sandy Hook	2779	5	7	23	21.81
1898 (Mar)	K. W. der Grosse	Ger.	NDL	Needles	Sandy Hook	3120	5	20	0	22.29
1900 (Jul)	Deutschland	Ger.	'Hapag'	Eddystone	Sandy Hook	3044	5	15	46	22.42
1900 (Aug)	Deutschland	Ger.	'Hapag'	Cherbourg	Sandy Hook	3050	5	12	29	23.02
1901 (Jul)	Deutschland	Ger.	'Hapag'	Cherbourg	Sandy Hook	3141	5	16	12	23.06
1902 (Sep)	Kronprinz Wilhelm	Ger.	NDL	Cherbourg	Sandy Hook	3047	5	11	57	23.09
1904	Kaiser Wilhelm II	Ger.	NDL	Cherbourg	Sandy Hook	3068	5	12	44	23.12
1907 (Oct)	Lusitania	Brit.	Cunard	Queenstown	Ambrose	2780	4	19	52	23.99
1908 (May)	Mauretania	Brit.	Cunard	Queenstown	Ambrose	2889	4	20	15	24.86
1908 (Jul)	Lusitania	Brit.	Cunard	Queenstown	Ambrose	2776	4	15	0	25.01
1909	Lusitania	Brit.	Cunard	Daunts Rock	Sandy Hook	2784	4	11	42	25.85
1909 (Sep)	Mauretania	Brit.	Cunard	Daunts Rock	Sandy Hook	2784	4	10	51	26.06
1929 (Jul)	Bremen	Ger.	NDL	Cherbourg	Ambrose	3164	4	17	42	27.83
1930	Europa	Ger.	NDL	Cherbourg	Ambrose	3157	4	17	6	27.91
1933	Bremen	Ger.	NDL	Cherbourg	Ambrose	3199	4	16	15	28.51
1933	Rex	It.	Italia	Gibraltar	Ambrose	3181	4	13	58	28.92
1935 (May)	Normandie	Fr.	CGT	Bishops Rock	Ambrose	2971	4	3	2	29.98
1936 (Aug)	Queen Mary	Brit.	C-WS	Bishops Rock	Ambrose	2907	4	0	27	30.14
1937 (Jul)	Normandie	Fr.	CGT	Bishops Rock	Ambrose	2906	3	23	2	30.58
1938 (Aug)	Queen Mary	Brit.	C-WS	Bishops Rock	Ambrose	2907	3	21	48	30.99
1952 (Jul)	United States	US	USL	Bishops Rock	Ambrose	2906	3	12	12	34.51

The Record Passages were compiled by Mr Nicholas Bonsor and are here reprinted with his kind permission.

Record Passages *The Blue Riband of the North Atlantic*

EASTBOUND

YEAR	STEAMER	FLAG	LINE	FROM	TO	NAUTICAL MILES	TIME DAY	HR	MIN	SPEED (KNOTS)
1838 (May)	*Sirius*	Brit.	B. & A.	New York	Falmouth	2988	18	0	0	6.92
1838 (May)	*Great Western*	Brit.	GW	New York	Avonmouth	3050	14	17	30	8.6
1840 (Aug)	*Britannia*	Brit.	Cunard	Halifax	Liverpool	2573	10	0	0	10.72
1842 (Jun)	*Columbia*	Brit.	Cunard	Halifax	Liverpool	2534	9	17	0	10.87
1843 (May)	*Hibernia*	Brit.	Cunard	Halifax	Liverpool	2524	9	10	0	11.17
1847 (Jul)	*Hibernia*	Brit.	Cunard	Halifax	Liverpool	2524	9	1	30	11.60
1849 (Jul)	*Canada*	Brit.	Cunard	Boston	Liverpool	2911	9	22	0	12.23
1850 (Jul)	*Atlantic*	US	Collins	New York	Liverpool	3053	10	8	20	12.29
1850 (Oct)	*Asia*	Brit.	Cunard	New York	Liverpool	3053	10	7	0	12.36
1851 (May)	*Pacific*	US	Collins	New York	Liverpool	3078	9	20	30	13.01
1852	*Arctic*	US	Collins	New York	Liverpool	3082	9	17	15	13.21
1856 (May)	*Persia*	Brit.	Cunard	New York	Liverpool	3068	9	12	7	13.49
1856 (Jun)	*Persia*	Brit.	Cunard	New York	Liverpool	3068	9	8	40	13.66
1856 (Aug)	*Persia*	Brit.	Cunard	New York Sandy Hook	Liverpool Bell Buoy	3068 3046	9 8	5 23	0 30	13.88 14.13
1863 (Dec)	*Scotia*	Brit.	Cunard	New York	Queenstown	2731	8	3	0	14.02
1869 (Jul)	*Russia*	Brit.	Cunard	New York	Queenstown	2731	8	0	30	14.19
1869 (Dec)	*City of Brussels*	Brit.	Inman	New York	Queenstown	2786	7	22	0	14.66
1873 (Jan)	*Baltic*	Brit.	W. Star	New York	Queenstown	2840	7	20	9	15.09
1875 (Oct)	*City of Berlin*	Brit.	Inman	New York	Queenstown	2820	7	15	28	15.37
1876 (Feb)	*Germanic*	Brit.	W. Star	New York	Queenstown	2894	7	15	17	15.79
1876 (Dec)	*Britannic*	Brit.	W. Star	New York	Queenstown	2882	7	12	47	15.94
1879 (Jul)	*Arizona*	Brit.	Guion	New York	Queenstown	2810	7	8	11	15.96
1882 (Jun)	*Alaska*	Brit.	Guion	New York	Queenstown	2791	6	22	0	16.80
1882 (Sep)	*Alaska*	Brit.	Guion	New York	Queenstown	2800	6	18	38	17.17
1884 (Apr)	*Oregon*	Brit.	Guion	New York	Queenstown	2815	6	16	57	17.48
1884 (Jun)	*America*	Brit.	National	New York	Queenstown	2815	6	14	8	17.80
1884 (Aug)	*Oregon*	Brit.	Cunard	Sandy Hook	Queenstown	2853	6	11	9	18.39
1887 (Mar)	*Etruria*	Brit.	Cunard	Sandy Hook	Queenstown	2890	6	4	36	19.45
1889 (May)	*City of Paris*	Brit.	I. & I.	Sandy Hook	Queenstown	2894	6	0	29	20.02
1892 (Aug)	*City of New York*	Brit.	I. & I.	Sandy Hook	Queenstown	2814	5	19	57	20.11
1893 (May)	*Campania*	Brit.	Cunard	Sandy Hook	Queenstown	2899	5	17	27	21.09
1894 (May)	*Lucania*	Brit.	Cunard	Sandy Hook	Queenstown	2823	5	8	38	21.95
1897 (Nov)	*K. W. der Grosse*	Ger.	NDL	Sandy Hook	Needles	3099	5	18	40	22.35
1900 (Jul)	*Deutschland*	Ger.	'Hapag'	Sandy Hook	Eddystone	3085	5	14	6	22.46
1900 (Aug)	*K. W. der Grosse*	Ger.	NDL	Sandy Hook	Cherbourg	3184	5	19	44	22.89
1900 (Sep)	*Deutschland*	Ger.	'Hapag'	Sandy Hook	Eddystone	2982	5	7	38	23.36
1901 (Jun)	*Deutschland*	Ger.	'Hapag'	Sandy Hook	Eddystone	3083	5	11	51	23.38
1901 (Jul)	*Deutschland*	Ger.	'Hapag'	Sandy Hook	Eddystone	3099	5	11	5	23.51
1906	*Kaiser Wilhelm II*	Ger.	NDL	Sandy Hook	Eddystone	3024	5	8	16	23.58
1907 (Oct)	*Lusitania*	Brit.	Cunard	Ambrose	Queenstown	2807	4	22	53	23.61
1907 (Nov)	*Mauretania*	Brit.	Cunard	Ambrose	Queenstown	2807	4	22	29	23.69
1908 (Mar)	*Mauretania*	Brit.	Cunard	Ambrose	Queenstown	2932	5	0	5	24.42
1909 (Feb)	*Mauretania*	Brit.	Cunard	Ambrose	Queenstown	2933	4	20	2	25.28
1909 (Mar)	*Mauretania*	Brit.	Cunard	Ambrose	Queenstown	2934	4	18	35	25.61
1909 (May)	*Mauretania*	Brit.	Cunard	Ambrose	Queenstown	2934	4	18	11	25.70
1909 (Jun)	*Mauretania*	Brit.	Cunard	Ambrose	Queenstown	2933	4	17	21	25.88
1924 (Aug)	*Mauretania*	Brit.	Cunard	Ambrose	Cherbourg	3008	4	19	0	26.16
1929 (Jul)	*Bremen*	Ger.	NDL	Ambrose	Eddystone	3084	4	14	30	27.92
1935 (Jun)	*Normandie*	Fr.	CGT	Ambrose	Bishops Rock	3015	4	3	28	30.31
1936 (Aug)	*Queen Mary*	Brit.	C-WS	Ambrose	Bishops Rock	2939	3	23	57	30.63
1937 (Mar)	*Normandie*	Fr.	CGT	Ambrose	Bishops Rock	2978	4	0	6	30.99
1937 (Aug)	*Normandie*	Fr.	CGT	Ambrose	Bishops Rock	2936	3	22	7	31.20
1938 (Aug)	*Queen Mary*	Brit.	C-WS	Ambrose	Bishops Rock	2938	3	20	42	31.69
1952 (Jul)	*United States*	US	USL	Ambrose	Bishops Rock	2942	3	10	40	35.59

'Firsts' and 'Lasts' *Relating to North Atlantic Steamships and Motor Vessels*

First crossing	1819 *Savannah* (US)
First crossing Savannah–Liverpool . . .	1819 *Savannah* (US)
First crossing from Canada	1833 *Royal William* (Canadian)
First crossing Quebec–Pictou–Cowes–London . .	1833 *Royal William* (Canadian)
First crossing by steamer built as such . .	1833 *Royal William* (Canadian)
First line to start operations	1838 British & American S.N. Co. (Brit.)
First westbound crossing	1838 *Sirius* (Brit.)
First crossing to New York . . .	1838 *Sirius* (Brit.)
First crossing London–New York . . .	1838 *Sirius* (Brit.)
First crossing Cork–New York . . .	1838 *Sirius* (Brit.)
First surface condensers	1838 *Sirius* (Brit.)
First crossing by steamer built for North Atlantic . .	1838 *Great Western* (Brit.)
First crossing Bristol–New York . . .	1838 *Great Western* (Brit.)
First crossing Liverpool–New York . . .	1838 *Royal William* (Brit.)
First watertight bulkheads . . .	1838 *Royal William* (Brit.)
First two-funnelled steamer . . .	1838 *Liverpool* (Brit.)
First bathrooms	1838 *Liverpool* (Brit.)
First crossing Portsmouth–New York . .	1839 *British Queen* (Brit.)
First mail steamer	1840 *Britannia* (Brit.)
First Cunarder	1840 *Britannia* (Brit.)
First crossing to Canada . . .	1840 *Britannia* (Brit.)
First crossing Liverpool–Halifax . . .	1840 *Britannia* (Brit.)
First crossing to Boston . . .	1840 *Britannia* (Brit.)
First crossing Liverpool–Boston . . .	1840 *Britannia* (Brit.)
First disaster	1841 *President* (Brit.)
First Belgian steamer	1842 *British Queen*
First crossing Antwerp–New York . . .	1842 *British Queen*
First crossing Southampton–New York . .	1842 *British Queen*
First iron steamer	1845 *Great Britain* (Brit.)
First screw steamer	1845 *Great Britain* (Brit.)
First steamer with six masts	1845 *Great Britain* (Brit.)
First steamer offering 'whole state-rooms' for one passenger .	1845 *Great Britain* (Brit.)
First US steamer since *Savannah* . . .	1845 *Massachusetts*
First US screw steamer	1845 *Massachusetts*
First wooden screw steamer . . .	1845 *Massachusetts*
First US line	1847 Ocean S.N. Co
First steamer of first US line . . .	1847 *Washington*
First crossing New York–Bremen . . .	1847 *Washington*
First French line	1847 Heroult & de Handel
First French steamer	1847 *Union*
First crossing Cherbourg–New York . . .	1847 *Union*
First crossing Havre–New York . . .	1847 *New York* (Fr.)
First crossing Glasgow–New York . . .	1850 *City of Glasgow* (Brit.)
First Collins Line steamer . . .	1850 *Atlantic* (US)
First straight stem	1850 *Atlantic* (US)
First steam heating	1850 *Atlantic* (US)
First crossing Galway–New York . . .	1850 *Viceroy* (Brit.)
First German steamer	1850 *Helena Sloman*
First crossing Hamburg–New York . . .	1850 *Helena Sloman*
First US line New York–Southampton–Havre . .	1850 New York & Havre S.N. Co.
First steamer of first US line New York–Southampton–Havre	1850 *Franklin*
First Inman Line steamer . . .	1850 *City of Glasgow* (Brit.)
First crossing Liverpool–Philadelphia . .	1850 *City of Glasgow* (Brit.)
First screw Cunarder	1852 *Andes* (Brit.)
Last wooden Cunarder	1853 *Arabia* (Brit.)
First line to St Lawrence River . . .	1853 Canadian S.N. Co. (Brit.)
First crossing Liverpool–Quebec–Montreal . .	1853 *Genova* (Brit.)
First crossing Liverpool–Portland (Maine) . .	1853 *Sarah Sands* (Brit.)
First German steamer Bremen–New York . .	1853 *Hansa*

'Firsts' and 'Lasts' Relating to North Atlantic Steamships and Motor Vessels

First Italian steamer	1854 *Sicilia*
First crossing Palermo–New York . . .	1854 *Sicilia*
First British steamer Southampton–New York . .	1854 *Indiana*
First compound engines	1854 *Brandon* (Brit.)
First Allan Line steamer	1854 *Canadian* (Brit.)
First two-funnelled screw steamer . . .	1854 *Canadian* (Brit.)
First four-funnelled steamer . . .	1855 *Ericsson* (US)
First iron paddle-steamer	1856 *Persia* (Brit.)
First Hamburg-American steamer . . .	1856 *Borussia* (Ger.)
First crossing Liverpool–St John's, N.F. . .	1856 *Propontis* (Brit.)
First line to Newfoundland . . .	1856 Liverpool, Newfoundland & Halifax S.N. Co. (Brit.)
First crossing London–Quebec–Montreal . .	1857 *United Service* (Brit.)
First crossing Glasgow–Quebec–Montreal . .	1857 *Clyde* (Brit.)
Last (and largest) wooden paddle-steamer . .	1857 *Adriatic* (US)
First line Galway–New York . . .	1858 Atlantic S.N. Co. (Brit.)
First Norddeutscher Lloyd steamer . . .	1858 *Bremen* (Ger.)
First crossing Liverpool–New York via Queenstown .	1859 *City of Baltimore* (Brit.)
First Cunard crossing Liverpool–New York via Queenstown	1859 *Canada* (Brit.)
First steamer to exceed 18,000 tons . . .	1860 *Great Eastern* (Brit.)
First steamer 680ft (207m) (b.p.) long . .	1860 *Great Eastern* (Brit.)
First five-funnelled steamer . . .	1860 *Great Eastern* (Brit.)
First iron steamer with straight stem . .	1860 *Great Eastern* (Brit.)
First (and only) paddle-cum-screw steamer . .	1860 *Great Eastern* (Brit.)
First Cunard screw mail steamer . . .	1860 *Australasian* (Brit.)
First Cunard screw mail steamer (to be built as such) .	1862 *China* (Brit.)
Last Cunard paddle-steamer . . .	1862 *Scotia* (Brit.)
First (and only) paddle-steamer to make more than 1 R/V to R. St Lawrence	1863 *America* (Brit.)
First CGT (French Line) steamer . . .	1864 *Washington*
First sailing to St John, N.B. . . .	1865 *Britannia* (Brit.)
First sailing Glasgow–St John, N.B.. . .	1865 *Britannia* (Brit.)
First (and only) line running a fleet of wooden screw steamers	1865 Baltimore & Liverpool S.S. Co. (US)
Last paddle-steamer	1866 *Napoléon III* (Fr.)
First US iron screw steamer . . .	1866 *Mississippi*
Last wooden screw steamer . . .	1867 *Ontario* (US)
First steam steering gear . . .	1867 *Great Eastern* (Brit.)
Last crossing by Cunard wooden paddle-steamer .	1867 *Africa* (Brit.)
First twin-screw steamer . . .	1868 *Washington* (Fr.)
First steamer built with steam steering gear . .	1869 *City of Brussels* (Brit.)
First iron steamer to be lengthened . .	1869 *City of Washington* (Brit.)
First compound engines . . .	1870 *Holland* (Brit.)
First steamer built with compound engines . .	1870 *Batavia* (Brit.)
First compound engines in steamer designed for N. Atlantic.	1870 *Wisconsin* (Brit.)
First White Star steamer . . .	1871 *Oceanic* (Brit.)
First amidships dining saloon . . .	1871 *Oceanic* (Brit.)
First Norwegian line . . .	1871 Norse American Line
First Norwegian steamer . . .	1871 *St Olaf*
First gas lighting	1872 *Adriatic* (Brit.)
Last crossing by paddle-steamer . . .	1876 *Scotia* (Brit.)
First electric light (external only) . .	1876 *Amérique* (Fr.)
First Italian line	1877 I. & V. Florio
First electric light (internal). . .	1879 *City of Berlin* (Brit.)
First British steamer with electric light . .	1879 *City of Berlin* (Brit.)
First steel steamer	1880 *Buenos Ayrean* (Brit.)
First steel steamer on New York route . .	1880 *Assyrian Monarch* (Brit.)
First bilge keels	1881 *Parisian* (Brit.)
First three-funnelled steamer . . .	1881 *City of Rome* (Brit.)
First steamer lighted throughout by electricity .	1881 *Servia* (Brit.)
First twin-screw steamer, built as such . .	1883 *Ludgate Hill* (Brit.)

'Firsts' and 'Lasts' Relating to North Atlantic Steamships and Motor Vessels

First triple-expansion engines	1884 *Martello* (Brit.)
First passenger liner with triple-expansion engines . .	1886 *Aller* (Ger.)
First British passenger liner with triple-expansion engines .	1887 *Lake Ontario*
First forced draught	1887 *Ohio* (US)
First express twin-screw steamer . . .	1888 *City of New York* (Brit.)
First steamer to exceed 10,000 tons . . .	1888 *City of New York* (Brit.)
First quadruple-expansion engines . . .	1888 *Phoenician* (Brit.)
First steamer built with quadruple-expansion engines .	1893 *Southwark* (Brit.)
First *'en suite'* rooms	1893 *Campania* (Brit.)
First single berth cabins, built as such . .	1893 *Campania* (Brit.)
First four-funnelled steamer . . .	1897 *Kaiser Wilhelm der Grosse* (Ger.)
First German 'Blue Riband' holder . . .	1897 *Kaiser Wilhelm der Grosse* (Ger.)
First remote-controlled watertight doors . .	1897 *Kaiser Wilhelm der Grosse* (Ger.)
First ship-to-shore wireless telegraphy . .	1899 *St Paul* (US)
First ocean newspaper	1899 *St Paul* (US)
First steamer to exceed *Great Eastern* in length . .	1899 *Oceanic* (Brit.)
First steamer to exceed *Great Eastern* in tonnage . .	1901 *Celtic* (Brit.)
First steamer to exceed 20,000 tons . . .	1901 *Celtic* (Brit.)
First permanent wireless set . . .	1901 *Lake Champlain* (Brit.)
First steam turbines	1905 *Victorian* (Brit.)
First triple-screw steamer . . .	1905 *Victorian* (Brit.)
First *à la carte* restaurant . . .	1905 *Amerika* (Ger.)
First 'cabin' steamer to be built as such . .	1906 *Cassandra* (Brit.)
First 'Empress' steamer . . .	1906 *Empress of Britain* (Brit.)
First quadruple-screw steamer . . .	1907 *Lusitania* (Brit.)
First steamer to exceed 30,000 tons . . .	1907 *Lusitania* (Brit.)
First British four-funnelled steamer . . .	1908 *Lusitania* (Brit.)
First combination of reciprocating engines and turbines .	1909 *Laurentic* (Brit.)
First steamer to exceed 40,000 tons . . .	1911 *Olympic* (Brit.)
First steamer to exceed 50,000 tons . . .	1913 *Imperator* (Ger.)
First motor ship (cargo) . . .	1913 *California* (Dan.)
First British motor ship (cargo) . . .	1914 *Mississippi*
Last four-funnelled steamer	1914 *Aquitania* (Brit.)
First geared turbines	1914 *Transylvania*
First passenger motor ship . . .	1925 *Gripsholm* (Swed.)
First gravity lifeboats	1927 *Île de France* (Fr.)
First H. & C. in all cabins of three-class ship . .	1928 *Duchess of Bedford* (Brit.)
First steamer to exceed 80,000 tons . . .	1935 *Normandie* (Fr.)
First British steamer to exceed 80,000 tons . .	1936 *Queen Mary*
Last four-funnelled steamer in service . .	1949 *Aquitania* (Brit.)
Last three-funnelled steamers in service . .	{ —— *Queen Mary* (Brit.) { —— *Empress of Scotland* (Brit.)

DISTRESS
— & —
DISASTER

ROBINSON CRUSOE

The most famous of all castaways is certainly Alexander Selkirk (1676–1721) who owes this distinction to the fact that his experiences inspired Daniel Defoe to write *Robinson Crusoe*. In 1703 Selkirk shipped as sailing master on board the *Cinque Ports*; he quarrelled with the captain, Thomas Stradling, and asked to be put ashore in October 1704 on Màs a Tierra, one of the Juan Fernandez islets, about 500 miles (805km) off the coast of Chile and then uninhabited. He was taken off in October 1709, by Captain Woodes Rogers who brought him back to London and subsequently published a detailed account of his adventures, as also did Richard Steele of *Tatler* and *Spectator* fame. It is unlikely that Selkirk and Defoe ever met. (See also William Dampier, p. 46.)

PETER SERRANO

A less well-known castaway was Peter Serrano, a Spaniard who bequeathed his name to a barren rock in the middle of the Caribbean, on which he lived, off cockles, shrimps and turtles, for nearly four years. His ingenuity deserves a mention, for Quiller-Couch in his *Story of the Sea* has this to say of him: 'His clothes wore out. Always fertile in resource, he hit on the expedient of going without any, and lived naked for three years and eight months'! Apparently he was eventually rescued and, on his return home to Spain, was presented to Charles V in recognition of his resourcefulness.

JOHN O'BRIEN

Maritime history abounds with stories of sailors being miraculously snatched from apparently certain death but there can be few with a record to equal that of the Hon John O'Brien. His first brush with death occurred off the coast of India when his ship was wrecked with the loss of all hands except himself and four sailors. The next ship on which he embarked foundered off the Cape of Good Hope and he alone of the ship's crew managed to get safely to shore. There he was befriended by the Dutch Governor who procured for him a cabin on a homeward-bound East Indiaman. At the very last moment, however, he generously agreed to transfer to another ship which was leaving the same day, in order to provide more space for a Dutchman travelling home from the East Indies with a large family. Twenty-four hours later he saw with his own eyes the ship which he had so recently left founder in a gale. There were no survivors.

In July 1747, our hero found himself aboard the *Dartmouth*, a ship of 50 guns, when she engaged the *Glorioso*, a Spanish man-of-war of 70 guns. The action came to an abrupt end when the *Dartmouth*'s magazine ignited and she blew up. Of her crew of 300, only 14 were saved, one of these being O'Brien who was picked up insensible on the top of a floating gun-carriage, having been blown through a port by the force of the explosion. It is said that, when introduced to the Captain of the ship by which he had been rescued, he at once apologized for his appearance, saying, 'Sir, you must excuse the unfitness of my dress to come aboard a strange ship, but, really, I left my own with so much precipitation that I had not time to put on better.'

THE FLYING DUTCHMAN

One of the most famous of all nautical legends is that of the Flying Dutchman. There are several variations on the theme, but the following seems to be the most usually accepted version. A Dutch captain, Philip Vanderdecker, homeward bound from Batavia, persists in trying to round the Cape of Good Hope in spite of a violent storm and the protests of passengers and crew. Eventually a spectre, said to be The Almighty, appears on deck, but the Captain utters a curse and is condemned to sail round the Cape for ever, unable to make a port. The appearance of the Flying Dutchman is said by sailors to be a sign of imminent disaster. The legend, variously adapted, forms the basis of Wagner's opera *Der Fliegender Hollander*, of Captain Marryat's novel *The Phantom Ship* and of Sir Walter Scott's poem *Rokeby*:

> *Then 'mid the war of sea and sky,*
> *Top and top-gallant hoisted high,*
> *Full-spread and crowded every sail,*
> *The Daemon-frigate braves the gale;*
> *And well the doomed spectators know*
> *The harbinger of wreck and woe.*
>
> Canto II, XI.

THE MUTINY ON THE *BOUNTY*

The most famous mutiny in the history of seafaring is undoubtedly that which took place on board HMS *Bounty* on 28 April 1789, though it has to be said that the embers of the story have in recent years been kept glowing by strong draughts of publicity from the cinema industry. The *Bounty*, a naval vessel commanded by **Lieutenant William Bligh** (1754–1817) sailed from Spithead on 23 December 1787, bound for Tahiti whence it was proposed to take a cargo of breadfruit seedlings to the West Indies to provide a cheap source of food for the slaves working on the sugar plantations. The *Bounty* reached Tahiti on 25 October 1788, having crossed the South Atlantic after failing to round Cape Horn, and spent the next five months there waiting for the breadfruit seedlings to mature sufficiently to be planted in pots. They eventually sailed on 4 April 1789 and 24 days later, off the Friendly (Tonga) Islands, the crew, led by Fletcher Christian (1764–93), mutinied and turned Bligh and the few who were loyal to him adrift in the ship's launch. 'The story of the *Bounty* mutiny,' says Alan Moorehead in *The Fatal Impact*, 'has become so addled by popular myth that it is generally forgotten that it was caused, not so much by the authoritarian character of Captain Bligh, as by the undermining of his men's discipline during their long stay on Tahiti.... No

large group of Europeans had remained so long on the island before, and the attachments formed by the *Bounty*'s crew were something more than those of a sailor's spree. Every man had his girl, and when they came to sail away many of them found the loss of their companions quite unendurable.'

After an epic voyage of 3600 miles (5793km) Bligh reached Timor on 20 August, by which time seven of the 18 men with him had died. The rest eventually reached England in 1790, and in 1792 Bligh returned to the Pacific in the *Providence* and successfully carried out the breadfruit project.

In March 1791, the *Pandora* arrived in Tahiti in search of the mutineers. Fourteen were captured, of whom four were drowned when the ship was wrecked on the Great Barrier Reef. Of the ten who returned to England and were court-martialled, three were hanged and four acquitted. The other nine mutineers, including Fletcher Christian, had sailed to Pitcairn Island 1400 miles (2253km) south-east of Tahiti, discovered by Captain Carteret in the sloop *Swallow* in 1767 and named after the midshipman who sighted it, where the sole survivor, John Adams, was found when the American ship *Topaz* called at the island

From a watercolour of the Bounty by Gregory Robinson. National Maritime Museum.

in May 1809. The story of the *Bounty* is not altogether without a happy ending, for Adams, at least, was allowed to remain on the island and live out his days in peace. He died there in 1829.

In 1805 Bligh was appointed Governor of New South Wales, but he fell out with his deputy and from 1808 to 1810, when he returned to England, was under virtual house arrest. He was promoted rear-admiral in 1811 and vice-admiral in 1814. His tomb can be seen in the graveyard of St Mary's Church, Lambeth, a coincidentally appropriate resting place in that he shares it with the naturalist John Tradescant, for it was Bligh, who by planting the first apple tree in Australia, indirectly gave us the Granny Smith apple.

HMS *GUARDIAN*

The last voyage of HMS *Guardian*, a 44-gun ship bound for Sydney in 1789 carrying convicts, stores and cattle, and commanded by Lieutenant Edward Riou (c 1758–1801), has been described as **'an achievement which had few parallels in naval annals'**. On 24 December the *Guardian* encountered an iceberg from which Riou determined to replenish his water, but the ship struck a

hidden part of the berg and appeared to be sinking. Next day he put as many of her crew as possible into the boats and told them to make for the Cape of Good Hope, some 1200 miles (1931km) to the north-west. After nine days they were picked up by a French merchant ship and landed safely at the Cape. Riou, meanwhile, overcame the state of his ship, the violence of the weather and the evil temper of the convicts and sighted the Cape on 21 February 1790. The *Guardian* was run on to the beach and became a complete wreck. Riou was killed after leading a squadron of frigates at the Battle of Copenhagen.

'The bloodiest mutiny that ever occurred in a ship of the Royal Navy' took place on board HMS *Hermione* in September 1797, when she was giving chase to a Yankee schooner from Newport, Rhode Island, in the Mona Passage between Santo Domingo and Puerto Rico. A tropical storm blew up and the Captain, one Hugh Pigot, sent the topmen aloft to take in canvas, and called to them that he would flog the last man down. Two of them, in their hurry to avoid the promised flogging, lost their hold and fell to their deaths, whereupon Pigot shouted, 'Throw the lubbers overboard.' That night the men killed Pigot and most of the officers and sailed the vessel to Venezuela, but in October 1799, she was recaptured and during the following ten years 24 of her men were hunted down, court-martialled and hanged at the yardarm.

The oddest ingredients of any shipwreck must surely be those that perished with the wooden paddle-steamer *Royal Tar* on 25 October 1836. She had been chartered to carry 'Dexter's Locomotive Museum and Burgess' Collection of Serpents and Birds from St John, New Brunswick, to Maine, as well as an elephant, two lions, a tiger, two camels, several horses and a large number of smaller animals'. In addition to the animals there were the circus personnel, which included a full brass band, as well as private passengers and crew, making 93 in all. The crew inadvertently set fire to the ship by lighting a fire under the boilers when they were empty, and in the ensuing panic 32 people and most of the animals lost their lives.

The first passenger steamship to founder on the transatlantic run was the British and American

Captain Edward Riou. *National Maritime Museum.*

The paddle-steamer *Royal Tar*, whose careless crew burnt a menagerie.

Steam Navigation Co's 1863-ton paddle-steamship *President*. She left New York on 11 March 1841, bound for Liverpool with 136 people on board. She was never heard of again. Many weeks later a bottle was washed ashore which contained the brief message, '*President* sinking fast'. It had been written by the Irish comedian Tyrone Power (1797–1841), great-grandfather of the cinema actor Tyrone Power (1914–58). Her loss resulted in the liquidation of the British and American Steam Navigation Co.

The 11 survivors of the British sailing ship *Rebecca* must be **among the very few survivors of a shipwreck ever to have been rescued by a dog.** The ship was driven ashore on a desolate part of the north-west coast of Tasmania on 29 April 1853, and 20 of her complement of 31 were drowned. The remainder were at the point of death from privation and exhaustion when they met a dog, to whose neck they tied a message. The dog took the message to his master, one Mr Burgess, who at once organized a rescue party.

The only ship known to have made a journey of 1000 miles (1609km) without any crew at all was the *Resolute*, which performed this remarkable feat in 1854–5. The ship was part of an expedi-

tion, commanded by Sir Edward Belcher, which left England in 1852 to search for Sir John Franklin who had disappeared with 129 officers and men and his two ships, the *Erebus* and the *Terror*, when seeking the elusive North-West Passage in 1845. The *Resolute* was abandoned, stuck fast in the ice, in May 1854, at the western end of Barrow Strait. She was next seen, 474 days later, by the commander of an American whaler named Buddington. She had shipped a little water but was otherwise in excellent condition. She had presumably drifted through Barrow Strait, Lancaster Sound and Baffin Bay.

Much of the misery suffered by the British troops in the Crimea in the winter of 1854–5 was caused by the **loss of the steamship *Prince*** which was wrecked in the famous storm of 14 November 1854, and went down with 143 officers and men and a cargo which comprised 'the whole of the winter clothing for the army – 40,000 uniforms, with undergarments, socks and gloves; a huge consignment of shot and shell and all the medical stores – the latter having been loaded with the usual negligence of the time beneath the ammunition so that it was impossible to reach it when the ship called at Scutari [where the hospital was] on her voyage out' (HOCKING, *Dictionary of Disasters at Sea*). Also lost in the storm were the British ships *Resolute*, *Kenilworth*, *Rip van Winkle*, *Panola*, *Wild Wave* and the American ships *Progress* and *Wanderer*, with a further loss of 340 lives.

The only recorded shipwreck of which a pig was the sole survivor was that of the Union Company's 739-ton *Athens*. Caught in a gale in Table Bay on 16 May 1865, she broke her moorings and, to avoid being driven inshore, put out to sea. Engulfed by mountainous seas, she was swept on to the rocks near Moville Point and was smashed to bits. All 29 people on board were drowned. The pig alone was washed up alive from the wreck.

THE *MARY CELESTE*

The story of the *Mary Celeste* is **one of the most famous mysteries in the annals of the sea** and scarcely needs retelling. The facts, as known, are as follows: A hermaphrodite brig of 282 tons, she was launched in Nova Scotia in 1861 as the *Amazon* and in 1868 was registered under the United States flag as the *Mary Celeste*. On 7 November 1872, she sailed from New York bound for Genoa with a cargo of 1701 barrels of crude alcohol, under the command of Captain Benjamin Briggs, who had on board his wife and two-year-old daughter, and a crew of seven. On 5 December 1872, she was sighted by the brigantine *Dei Gratia* (Captain Morehouse) 590 miles (950km) west of Gibraltar. It being clear that she was in distress, the mate and one seaman of the *Dei Gratia* boarded her and found her abandoned, her only boat gone and the remains of the boat's painter dangling over the stern. Innumerable theories have been put forward as to what had occurred but no one has produced an answer which satisfies *all* the pundits. The mate and two seamen from the *Dei Gratia* sailed her into Gibraltar and Captain Morehouse received a salvage award of £1700. During the next 13 years the *Mary Celeste* had no less than 17 owners and in the end was purposely wrecked on 3 January 1885, on a reef off Haiti in order to make a false insurance claim.

The *Victoria* capsizing. *Mary Evans Picture Library*.

When the *Royal Adelaide*, an iron sailing ship of 1320 tons bound from London to Sydney, New South Wales, was driven ashore on Chesil Beach, Dorset, on the night of 25 November 1875, she broke up immediately and hundreds of cases of spirits were washed from her holds on to the shore. The wreck was watched by thousands of people, **20 of whom were dead by morning from excess of drinking**. Of the 67 passengers and crew on board the *Royal Adelaide*, six were drowned.

The worst disaster that ever occurred on the River Thames took place on 3 September 1878, when the 251-ton river steamship *Princess Alice*, carrying some 900 'excursionists' from London to Gravesend collided with the 1376-ton collier *Bywell Castle* about a mile (1.6km) below Woolwich. 640 people were drowned, including Captain Grinstead of the *Princess Alice*. The *Annual Register*'s account of the catastrophe is almost too purple to be convincing: **'One of the most fearful disasters of modern times . . . a scene which has had no parallel on the river** . . . the river for a hundred yards was full of drowning people screaming in anguish and praying for help.'

The *Bywell Castle* colliding with the *Princess Alice*. Mary Evans Picture Library.

The worst disaster ever to overtake the Royal Navy in peacetime occurred on 22 June 1893, when HMS *Victoria* was rammed and sunk by HMS *Camperdown* during fleet manoeuvres off Tripoli in the Mediterranean. The *Victoria*, launched in 1887, carried two of the heaviest guns ever designed for the Royal Navy. They weighed 111 tons each and were so heavy that their muzzles drooped under the weight and it was considered unsafe to fire them with full charges. At the time of the fatal collision she was the flagship of Vice-Admiral Sir George Tryon (1832–93), Commander-in-Chief of the Mediterranean Fleet, and he it was who ordered the two ships, each heading her own half of the Fleet in a practice evolution, to turn in upon one another, though it was plain for all to see that there was not enough room for them to complete the manoeuvre without colliding. The inevitable happened and 359 men, including Tryon himself, were drowned.

Tryon had been the first commander of the *Warrior*, **the first ironclad battleship in the world** (see p. 90), and has been described as the first British admiral of the Victorian era to prepare the navy for war. It was largely thanks to the foundations he laid that, 20 years after his death, **the British Navy was indisputably the best in the world.**

Another unusual shipwreck was that of the 3961-ton steamship *Ventnor* which ran on to a reef south of Cape Egmont, New Zealand, on 27 October 1902. She was carrying 499 coffins containing the bodies of Chinamen who had died in New Zealand and were being taken home by the Chong Shing Tong Society. Nine aged Chinese 'body attendants' were drowned with the crew of 31.

The disappearance of the Blue Anchor Line's 9339-ton cargo liner SS *Waratah* on 27 July 1909, ranks with the *Mary Celeste* as **one of the great mysteries of the sea.** She was built in 1908 by Barclay, Curle & Co., was employed on the

Australian run by way of the Cape, and was bound from Sydney to London on her second voyage when the disaster occurred. On Sunday 25 July 1909, she put in at Durban and left again on the 26th. At 6am on the 27th she exchanged signals with the *Clan MacIntyre*, also bound for England, and the ships remained in sight of each other for about three hours. At 9.30am the *Waratah*, being the faster ship, was lost to view by the *Clan MacIntyre* and was never seen again. There were 211 people on board, of whom 119 were crew. Numerous ships were sent to search the area but found no clue to the fate of the *Waratah*, whose loss proved disastrous to the Blue Anchor Line, which was then bought by P. & O.

THE SINKING OF THE *TITANIC*

The *Titanic* was, **at the time of her launching the world's largest ship,** but it is not her size which gives her an immortal and tragic place in the annals of the sea. Built by Harland and Wolff of Belfast, the 46,328-ton White Star liner left Southampton on her maiden voyage on 10 April 1912. She was 882ft (269m) long, had a double bottom, was subdivided by 15 transverse bulkheads, and had a maximum speed of 25 knots. She carried 1316 passengers and a crew of 891, with Captain Edward Smith in command. In the public mind she was labelled 'unsinkable'. At 2340hrs on 14 April she was 300 miles (483km) south-east of Newfoundland when she hit an iceberg which sliced a 300-foot-long (91m) gash in her starboard bow. She sank at 0240hrs on the 15th with the loss of 1502 lives. There were 705 survivors, mostly women and children. Captain Smith went down with his ship, but among the survivors was Mr Bruce Ismay, managing director of the White Star line. Lengthy inquiries were held on both sides of the Atlantic into the cause of the disaster, but these did nothing to stem the tide

This prophetic cartoon was published in 1887, 25 years before the *Titanic* sank. *Mary Evans Picture Library.*

"EVERY ATTENTION GIVEN TO THE COMFORT AND SAFETY OF OUR PASSENGERS."

NEPTUNE.—You ought to go slower, my friend; there are many dangers about you!
TRANS-ATLANTIC CAPTAIN OF THE PERIOD.—Can't help it; I'm bound to make the fastest trip on record, and don't you forget it!

of acrimony and recrimination which it had pro-voked, for it was widely held that the second- and third-class passengers had been discriminated against in the allocation of places in the lifeboats. The reason why the *Titanic* carried lifeboats for less than half her complement of passengers and crew was, quite simply, that the Board of Trade's current regulations required no more. Soon after, these regulations, and those of other countries, were amended to ensure that all ships carried boats or life-rafts sufficient for their entire com-plement. An International Ice Patrol was also established to keep a watch on ice in the North-West Atlantic and to broadcast warnings to ship-ping. So perhaps those 1500 lives were not entirely wasted.

The shipping disaster which wreaked the great-est havoc ashore was probably that which occurred in the harbour at Halifax, Nova Scotia, on 6 December 1917, when the 3121-ton French steamship *Mont Blanc* collided with the 5043-ton Norwegian steamship *Imo*, the former being loaded with 5000 tons of high explosive. The massive explosion which followed 'broke win-dows at Truro, 60 miles (96km) distant, and damaged every building in Halifax. A square mile (2.59km²) at Richmond in the north end was demolished and part of Dartmouth was destroyed, with property damage of $35,000,000. A tidal wave broke moorings of ships, drowned those near shore and ruined the waterfront. 1630 people were killed, several thousand injured, and the blizzard that followed found thousands living in tents or windowless houses' (*Encyclopaedia Canadiana*).

The task of recovering the gold and silver amounting to £1,054,000 in value from the sun-ken P. & O. liner *Egypt* marked **the beginning of a new era in the science of undersea salvage**. The 7941-ton *Egypt* sank off Ushant when she was struck in thick fog on 19 May 1922, by the French steamship *Seine*. From 1923 to 1928 various companies searched unsuccessfully for the wreck, which was eventually found in June 1929, in 360 feet (110m) of water by the Italian Society for Marine Recovery. 'The patent diving suit carried on board the Italian salvage ship, *Artiglio*, enabled a diver to descend to this great depth in perfect safety and later to recover nearly all the specie.'

One of the major pile-ups in naval history occurred on 8 September 1923, when a flotilla of US destroyers was steaming in line ahead in dense fog off the coast of California. The commanders believed themselves to be 8 miles (12.9km) out to sea, wherein they erred grievously. In fact they were close to shore, north-west of Santa Barbara. The destroyer *Delphy*, which was leading, struck the rocks at full speed and her propellor, which was still revolving, struck the *Young* and capsized her. The *Chauncey*, which followed, came into collision with the wreckage and the four remain-ing destroyers, the *Fuller*, *Nicholas*, *Woodburg* and *S. P. Lee* ran on to the reef without having time to reduce speed. Amazingly only 22 men lost their lives, but all seven destroyers, lying along the coast at intervals of roughly 250ft (76m), were total wrecks.

The 6630-ton Ben Line cargo ship *Benlomond* left Cape Town for Paramaibo in Dutch Guiana on 10 November 1942. On the 23rd she was torpedoed and sank in a few minutes. 'Of the 24 British and 23 Chinese who formed her crew only one man, a Chinese steward named Poon Lim, survived the disaster. This man swam to a raft on which he existed for 133 days, living partly upon the pro-visions stowed on the raft and partly on fish and seagulls which he occasionally caught. He was eventually picked up by a Brazilian negro fisher-man after having been about four months adrift.... The experience of the Chinese sailor is **one of the most remarkable in the records of survival after shipwreck**' (HOCKING).

One of the worst maritime disasters in modern history occurred in China in December 1948, during the Chinese Civil War. 6000 people, mostly Chinese Government troops, were killed during the evacuation of the Manchurian port of Yingkow when the boilers of the ship they had just boarded blew up, setting off the ammunition. On the same day between 2000 and 3000 people were killed when the 2100-ton steamer *Kiang Ya*, crowded with refugees from the Civil War, blew up in the East China Sea about 50 miles (80km) from Shanghai. About 1000 people were rescued but neither the exact death toll nor the cause of the disaster were ever established.

'One of the most dramatic episodes in post-war maritime history began on 26 December 1951, when the US passenger-freighter *Flying Enterprise* (a former Liberty ship of 6711 tons gross) of the Isbrandtsen Line developed a heavy list about 500 miles (805km) west of S. W. Ireland while on a voyage from Hamburg to New York ... On 29 December, when the vessel's list had increased to 60°, Captain Kurt Carlsen, her master, ordered the crew and ten passengers to jump into the sea to be picked up by other United States and British ships which had arrived in response to radio calls, but himself refused to abandon ship, on which he remained alone' (*Keesing's Contemporary Archives*). On 4 January K. R. Dancy, mate of the British tug *Turmoil*, leaped aboard and on 5 January the tug took the freighter in tow. On 9 January, however, the tow parted and on 10 January the *Flying Enterprise* sank about 40 miles (64km) from Falmouth, Captain Carlsen and Mr Dancy having been taken off by the *Turmoil* shortly beforehand. Carlsen was later awarded the Lloyd's Silver Medal and was appointed an officer of the Danish Order of Dannebrog.

'The worst disaster in the history of transatlantic maritime navigation for many years' occurred just before midnight on 25 July 1956, when the Italian Line's 29,083-ton liner *Andrea Doria* collided with the Swedish-American Line's 12,644-ton motorship *Stockholm* in dense fog about 45 miles (72.4km) south-east of Nantucket Island. 52 people lost their lives. The *Stockholm*'s bows struck the Italian liner just below the navigating bridge amidships, causing immediate flooding of one of the 11 watertight compart-

The elegant but ill-fated liner *Andrea Doria*. Roger Daniels.

ments into which the hull was divided. She at once took on a heavy list, which increased as water came in through the portholes, and finally sank at 10.00am on 26 July. The collision involved British maritime underwriters in the heaviest total loss then experienced and a payment exceeding £4 million.

The loss of the West German training barque *Pamir* (3103grt), which foundered on the night of 21 September 1957, about 600 miles (965km) south-west of the Azores, with the loss of 80 of her crew of 86, caused widespread grief throughout West Germany. Built by Blohm und Voss in 1905 for the Hamburg firm of Ferdinand Laeisz, the four-masted steel barque *Pamir* was acquired in the early 1930s by the Finnish sailing ship owner, Captain Gustav Erikson. In 1951 she and her sister ship *Passat* were bought, 'largely for sentimental reasons', by Herr Schliewen, a Lübeck shipowner, who had them fitted with auxiliary oil engines. In 1954 they were taken over by the Pamir-Passat foundation and completely overhauled and refitted by Blohm und Voss.

The worst submarine disaster ever to occur in peacetime happened on 10 April 1963, when the 3700-ton US nuclear submarine *Thresher* failed to surface while carrying out deep-diving tests in the Atlantic 220 miles (354km) east of Cape Cod, Massachusetts. 112 officers and ratings and 17 civilian technicians were on board. In October 1964, the US Navy announced that the bathyscaphe *Trieste II* had managed to obtain pictures of large sections of the *Thresher*'s hull, lying at a depth of 6400ft (2560m), but the cause of the tragedy was never determined.

Before the loss of the *Thresher*, **the world's worst peacetime submarine disaster** was that of the *Thetis* which failed to surface when carrying out trials in Liverpool Bay off Lancashire on 1 June 1939. Though she was soon located, all efforts to raise her proved unsuccessful and, owing to a defect in the escape apparatus, only four of the 103 men on board got out alive.

She was eventually salved in April 1940, was renamed *Thunderbolt* and was sunk by the Italian corvette *Cicogna* north of Sicily on 13 March 1943.

THE *TORREY CANYON* DISASTER
The biggest oil pollution problem ever to threaten Britain arose when the 61,263grt Liberian-registered oil tanker *Torrey Canyon* (118,285dwt) owned by the Barracuda Tanker Corporation of Bermuda, a subsidiary of the Union Oil Co. of California, ran aground on the Seven Stones reef off Land's End on 18 March 1967. She was on a single-voyage charter to the British Petroleum Co., bound for Milford Haven from the Persian Gulf with a cargo of 117,000 tons of Kuwait oil. She had an Italian crew of 36. The *Torrey Canyon* was built at Newport News, Virginia, USA, in 1959 as a 60,000-ton tanker with an overall length of 810ft (247m). In 1965 she underwent structural alterations in Nagasaki, Japan, which increased her length to 975ft (297m) and her carrying capacity to 118,000 tons.

Thousands of tons of oil were soon pouring from the stricken ship, presenting a threat of oil pollution 'on a scale which had no precedent anywhere in the world'. By 21 March some 30,000 gallons (136,000 litres) had spilled into the sea and the first deposits reached the Cornish coast 8 miles (12.9km) south-west of Penzance on 24 March. On the 26th the *Torrey Canyon* broke her back while a Dutch salvage tug was trying to pull her off the reef, and thousands more tons of oil gushed into the sea. By March 27 more than 100 miles (161km) of the Cornish coast was polluted.

On 28 March the Fleet Air Arm and the RAF started bombing the wreck, the idea behind which was not to sink and destroy the *Torrey Canyon* but 'to open up what remained in the cargo tanks and burn the oil in them'. By 31 March she was thought to be free of oil and on 5 April the Royal Navy called off its operations. Meanwhile daily patrols had been maintained by

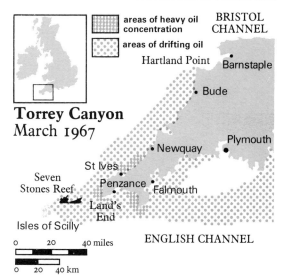

areas of heavy oil concentration
areas of drifting oil

Torrey Canyon
March 1967

BRISTOL CHANNEL
Hartland Point
Barnstaple
Bude
Plymouth
Newquay
St Ives
Seven Stones Reef
Penzance
Falmouth
Land's End
Isles of Scilly
ENGLISH CHANNEL

0   20   40 miles
0   20   40 km

an armada of over 50 naval vessels and fishing boats, spraying the oil slick with more than 30,000 gallons (136,000 litres) of detergent a day. A leading Dutch ornithologist came to Cornwall to advise on the de-oiling of seabirds. His name was Dr I. M. Kwak.

The Liberian Government, in its inquiry into the disaster, placed the blame squarely on the master, Captain Pastrengo Rugiati, because 'he alone had made the decision to go between the Isle of Scilly and the Seven Stones; he had not consulted his officers or given them advance notice of his intention, and he did not portray sound judgment or exercise the practice of good seamanship'.

THE DISAPPEARANCE OF A NUCLEAR ATTACK SUBMARINE
On 27 May 1968, the 3075-ton US nuclear attack submarine *Scorpion*, with a crew of 99 officers and men, was reported overdue. On 5 June she was presumed 'lost in the depths of the Atlantic' with all on board.

THE DISAPPEARANCE OF THE *TOTEM*
The British submarine *Totem* was launched on 28 September 1943. On 10 November 1967, she was commissioned into the Israeli Navy and renamed *Dakar*. On 26 January 1968, she was lost in the Eastern Mediterranean while on passage from Britain to Haifa. The reason for her disappearance was never discovered but an Indian tribe had once presented the submarine with a totem pole and it was said that if ever she sailed

The totem pole is now in the Submarine Museum at HMS *Dolphin*, the Royal Navy's Submarine Base at Gosport.

without it she would never return. On this occasion it was left behind and is now in the Submarine Museum at HMS *Dolphin*, Gosport.

THE COLLISION OF A DESTROYER AND AN AIRCRAFT CARRIER

On 3 June 1969 the 2200-ton US destroyer *Frank E. Evans* was cut in two, in a collision in the South China Sea, about 650 miles (1046km) south-west of Manila, by the 20,000-ton Australian aircraft carrier *Melbourne*. The bow section of the *Evans* sank within a few minutes, with the loss of 74 lives. There were 198 survivors from the aft end of the *Evans*, which was taken in tow by the *Melbourne*, on board which no casualties occurred. (The disaster was the second of its kind in which the *Melbourne* had been involved, the first being on 10 February 1964, when the *Melbourne* was in collision off the coast of New South Wales with the Australian destroyer *Voyager*, 82 of the latter's crew being killed.)

At the subsequent board of inquiry, Lieut.

Ronald Ramsey, who had been on the bridge of the *Evans* at the time of the collision, was sentenced to the loss of '1000 numbers'. Each man serving in the US Navy accumulates so many 'numbers', on which is based his promotion. This, apparently, was the lightest possible sentence on such a charge.

The largest ship ever shipwrecked was the 227,556-ton supertanker *Berge Istra*. She was owned by the Norwegian company, Sig Bergesen D.Y. of Oslo, was *en route* from Brazil to Japan with a cargo of 188,000 tons of iron ore and was last heard of on 29 December 1975. On 18 January the only two survivors were rescued by a Japanese fishing vessel 700 miles (1126km) south-east of Mindanao, about 400 miles (644km) from the ship's last reported position. They said that the ship had been blown apart by three explosions. At Lloyd's on 19 January 1976, the Lutine Bell was rung to confirm that the underwriters accepted the loss. Ship and cargo were insured in all for some £13,500,000.

The Lutine Bell is the ship's bell of HMS *Lutine*, a French warship captured and recommissioned by the British. 'On 9 October 1799, she left Yarmouth for Holland with bullion and specie to the value of some £500,000. The same night she was wrecked on a sandbank off the Zuyder Zee with the loss of every soul on board save one, who died as soon as he was rescued. . . . In 1858 some £50,000 was salvaged as well as the *Lutine*'s bell and rudder. . . . The latter was made into the official chair for Lloyd's chairman and a secretary's desk. The bell was hung at Lloyd's and is rung once whenever a total wreck is reported, and twice for an overdue ship' (BREWER).

The most serious oil pollution incident the world had then seen happened when the fully laden Liberian-registered supertanker *Amoco Cadiz* was forced on to the rocks off Portsall, on the Brittany coast of France, 35 miles (86.3km) east of Roscoff, on 16 March 1978. The *Amoco Cadiz* was en route from the Persian Gulf to Rotterdam when her steering gear failed and she called the ocean-going tug, *Pacific* to her aid, but the *Pacific* was unable to tow the tanker into safer waters, and she was blown towards the shallows and went on the rocks. Between then and 31 March 230,000 tons of crude oil were spilled into

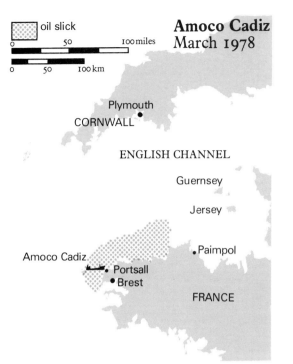

oil slick

0   50   100 miles

0   50   100 km

Amoco Cadiz
March 1978

Plymouth
CORNWALL

ENGLISH CHANNEL

Guernsey

Jersey

Paimpol

Amoco Cadiz

Portsall
Brest

FRANCE

Triumphant smiles after recovery of *Edinburgh* gold.
Wharton Williams Taylor.

the sea. A subsequent board of investigation blamed the ship's master, Captain Pasquale Bardari, for 'inexcusable delay' in calling for tug assistance and accused him of 'lamentable reluctance' to assume responsibility for dealing with the tanker's predicament, but commended him and a British safety expert, Mr L. Maynard, for courage in staying aboard the tanker after the rest of the crew had been lifted off. When the *Torrey Canyon* ran aground in March 1967, about 60,000 tons of oil were spilt.

The worst oil pollution disaster ever recorded did not, however, involve shipping. On 3 June 1979, a blow-out occurred at the Ixtoc I exploratory oil well in the Bay of Campeche, Mexico. By 14 October, when the flow of oil was partially contained by a steel funnel which was placed over the spout, about 340,000 tons of oil had poured into the sea. This compares with about 12,000 tons which escaped during the blow-out in Phillips Petroleum's Ekofisk Field in the North Sea which occurred in April 1977. At the time of going to press no reliable estimates were available of the extent of the oil slick reported in the Persian Gulf in April 1983.

Another major oil spill, in mid-1979, was described by Lloyd's of London as 'our biggest

marine loss, possibly amounting to $85,000,000'. On 19 July, two tankers, the 128,394-ton *Atlantic Empress* bound for Beaumont, Texas, with a cargo of naphthalene from the Persian Gulf, and the 92,081-ton *Aegean Captain* taking crude oil from Bonaire, Netherlands Antilles, to Singapore, collided off Tobago. The *Atlantic Empress* sank and the *Aegean Captain* was towed to Curaçao for repairs. 27 seamen lost their lives.

'The most successful diving operation ever carried out' was how Wharton Williams, the Aberdeen-based diving company, described the recovery of £45 million in Russian gold bars from the British cruiser HMS *Edinburgh* lying in 800ft (244cm) of water in the Barents Sea 170 miles (273km) north of Murmansk. Ninety per cent of the treasure, nearly 5½ tons, was recovered. HMS *Edinburgh* was sunk by German torpedoes in 1942 as she carried the gold from Russia in payment for armaments supplied by the Allies during the Second World War. The salvors kept 45 per cent of the recovered gold and the balance was equally divided between the United Kingdom and Soviet Governments.

Loss of Life at Sea

The following list is compiled from the *Dictionary of Disasters at Sea During the Age of Steam 1824–1962* by Charles Hocking FLA. It shows the 34 disasters which have led to the greatest loss of life at sea or on board ship wherein the event has not been directly caused by enemy action.

NAME OF SHIP	TYPE	OWNER	TONNAGE	DATE OF LAUNCHING	PLACE AND DATE OF ACCIDENT	NATURE OF ACCIDENT	NO. OF LIVES LOST	NO. OF SURVIVORS
Sultana	paddle-steamer	—	1719	1863	Mississippi River, USA 21 Apr 1865	boilers exploded	1653	741
Titanic	liner	White Star Line	46329	1912	400 miles (644km) SSW of Cape Race, Newfoundland 14 Apr 1912	in collision with an iceberg	1503	711
Empress of Ireland	liner	Canadian Pacific Railway Co.	14191	1906	mouth of the St Lawrence River, Canada 29 May 1914	in collision with the Norwegian collier *Storstadt*	1014	463
General Slocum	paddle-steamer	Knickerbocker Steamboat Co.	1248	1891	Hudson River New York, USA 15 Jun 1904	caught fire	957	426
Leffort	line-of-battleship	Russian Navy	—	—	Gulf of Finland 23 Sep 1857	foundered in storm	826	0
Eastland	excursion steamer	Eastland Navigation Co.	1961	1903	Chicago River, USA 24 Jul 1915	turned turtle	812	*c* 1700
Bulwark	battleship	Royal Navy	15000	1902	Sheerness, Kent, UK 15 Nov 1914	blew up	738	12
Vanguard	battleship	Royal Navy	19250	1909	Scapa Flow, Orkney Is. 9 Jul 1917	blew up	668	2
Princess Alice	river steamer	London Steamboat Co.	251	1865	River Thames below Woolwich 3 Sep 1878	in collision with a collier	640	200
Mendi	steamship	British & African S.N. Co.	4230	1905	English Channel 20 Feb 1917	in collision with the liner *Douro*	636	258
Ertogul	wooden frigate	Turkish Navy	2344	1863	off South coast of Japan 18 Sep 1890	sunk in gale	584	69
Atlantic	liner	White Star Line	3707	1871	off Halifax, Nova Scotia 1 Apr 1873	ran aground	560	371
La Bourgogne	liner	Compagnie Générale Transatlantique	7395	1885	off Newfoundland 4 Jul 1898	in collision with British ship *Cromartyshire*	546	165
Utopia	liner	Anchor Line	2731	1874	Bay of Gibraltar 17 Mar 1891	in collision with British battleship *Anson*	533	347
Neiri Shevket	line-of-battleship	Turkish Navy	—	—	off Constantinople, Turkey 23 Oct 1850	blew up	*c* 516	206
Kawachi	battleship	Japanese Navy	21420	1910	Tokuyama Bay, Japan 12 Jul 1918	blew up	500+	*c* 340
Captain	turret ironclad	Royal Navy	4272	1870	Bay of Biscay 7 Sep 1870	capsized	483	18

NAME OF SHIP	TYPE	OWNER	TONNAGE	DATE OF LAUNCHING	PLACE AND DATE OF ACCIDENT	NATURE OF ACCIDENT	NO. OF LIVES LOST	NO. OF SURVIVORS
City of Glasgow	screw steamship	Inman Line	1610	1850	N. Atlantic after 1 Mar 1854	lost without trace	480	0
Cospatrick	emigrant clipper	Shaw, Savill & Co.	1220	1856	300 miles (482km) S.W. of the Cape of Good Hope, S. Africa 17 Nov 1874	caught fire	472	3
Afrique	liner	Chargeurs-Réunis	5404	1907	off La Rochelle, France 11/12 Jan 1920	swept on to rocks after engine trouble	553	32
Austria	liner	Hamburg-America Line	2383	1857	N. Atlantic 13 Sep 1858	caught fire	471	67
Royal Charter	auxiliary sailing ship	Liverpool & Australian Steam Navigation Co.	2719	1854	off Anglesey, UK 25/26 Oct 1859	driven ashore in storm	459	39
Principe de Asturias	liner	Pinillos, Izquierdo & Co. Spain	8371	1914	off the coast of Brazil 5 Mar 1916	ran aground in fog	445	143
Birkenhead	troopship	British Government	1400	1845	50 miles (80km) W. of Cape Town, S. Africa 26 Feb 1852	struck uncharted rock	445	193
Sirio	liner	Navigazione Generale Italiana	2401	1883	off Cartagena, Spain 4 Aug 1906	ran on the rocks	442	380
Central America	mail steamship	G. Law & Co.	*c* 1200	1852	Gulf of Mexico 11 Sep 1857	sprang a leak and sank	427	160
Cataraqui	emigrant ship	—	*c* 400	*c* 1840	Bass Strait, Australia 4 Aug 1846	driven ashore in gale	414	9
Lady Nugent	chartered troopship	Sir George Hodgkinson	642	*c* 1840	Bay of Bengal May 1845	lost without trace	409	0
Natal	armoured cruiser	Royal Navy	13500	1907	Cromarty Harbour, Scotland 30 Dec 1915	blew up	405	299
Hsin Wah	steamship	China Merchants Steam Navigation Co.	1940	1921	Wanglan Island off Hong Kong 16 Jan 1929	ran aground	401	28
Pomona	emigrant ship	Howland & Frothingham N.Y.	1181	1856	Blackwater Bank off Co. Wexford, Eire 28 Apr 1859	ran aground	388	23
Eurydice	training frigate	Royal Navy	921	1843	off Ventnor, I.O.W. 24 Mar 1877	foundered in freak storm	366	2
Victoria	battleship	Royal Navy	10740	1887	off Beirut, E. Mediterranean	rammed by HMS *Camperdown*	358	284
Annie Jane	emigrant ship	Holderness	1294	1853	off the Hebrides 28 Sep 1853	smashed by huge wave	348	102

Loss of Life Through Enemy Action

The following list does not pretend to be comprehensive, since figures are not available for many warships sunk by enemy action, particularly Japanese warships lost in the Pacific in the Second World War. It simply shows the 30 warships which went down through enemy action with the greatest loss of life as recorded in CHARLES HOCKING'S *Dictionary of Disasters at Sea*.

NAME OF SHIP	TYPE	NATIONALITY	TONNAGE	DATE OF LAUNCHING	PLACE AND DATE OF SINKING	HOW LOST	NO. OF LIVES LOST	NO. OF SURVIVORS
Lancastria	liner/troopship	British	16243	1922	off St Nazaire, France 17 Jun 1940	bombed	2833	2477
Neptunia/Oceania	liner/troopship	Italian	19475/19507	1932/1933	Mediterranean, N. of Tripoli 18 Sep 1941	over 5000 troops were drowned when the two transports were torpedoed and sunk by the British submarine *Upholder*		
Laconia	liner/troopship	British	19695	1922	500 miles (805km) S. of Cape Palmas, Liberia 12 Sep 1942	torpedoed	2276	975
Bismarck	battleship	German	35000	1939	North Atlantic 27 May 1941	shelled and torpedoed by Royal Navy	c 2000	c 100
Kow Shing	chartered troopship	Chinese	2134	1883	off N. Korea 20 Jul 1894	torpedoed by Japanese cruiser *Naniwa*	c 1455	45
Scharnhorst	battleship	German	26000	1936	60 miles (96km) N.E. of North Cape, Norway 26 Dec 1943	shelled and torpedoed by Royal Navy	1425	36
Hood	battlecruiser	British	42100	1919	between Iceland and Greenland 23 May 1941	sunk by the *Bismarck*	1338	3
Queen Mary	battlecruiser	British	28000	1913	North Sea 31 May 1916	sunk during Battle of Jutland	1266	9
Lusitania	passenger liner	British	30396	1907	off Co. Cork, Eire 7 May 1915	torpedoed by German submarine *U-20*	1198	761
Rohna	chartered troopship	British	8602	1926	Mediterranean 26 Nov 1943	sunk by German bombers	c 1170	c 830
Royal Edward	chartered troopship	Canadian	11117	1906	Adriatic Sea 13 Aug 1915	torpedoed by German submarine *U-15*	c 1086	c 500
Invincible	battlecruiser	British	17250	1908	North Sea 31 May 1916	sunk during Battle of Jutland	1020	6
Indefatigable	battlecruiser	British	18750	1909	North Sea 31 May 1916	sunk during Battle of Jutland	1010	2
Tirpitz	battleship	German	42500	1940	Tromsö Fjord, Norway 12 Nov 1944	sunk by 32 RAF Lancaster bombers	c 1000	85
Bretagne	battleship	French	22189	1913	Oran harbour, Algeria 3 Jul 1940	blown up by a squadron of aircraft of the Fleet Air Arm after refusing to surrender	970	221
Defence	armoured cruiser	British	14600	1907	North Sea 31 May 1916	Battle of Jutland	903	0

NAME OF SHIP	TYPE	NATIONALITY	TONNAGE	DATE OF LAUNCHING	PLACE AND DATE OF SINKING	HOW LOST	NO. OF LIVES LOST	NO. OF SURVIVORS
Good Hope	armoured cruiser	British	14100	1901	off the Chilean coast 1 Nov 1914	sunk by the *Scharnhorst* at the Battle of Coronel	900	0
Blucher	armoured cruiser	German	15500	1908	North Sea 24 Jan 1915	sunk during Battle of Dogger Bank	870	260
Black Prince	armoured cruiser	British	13550	1904	North Sea 31 May 1916	sunk at Battle of Jutland	852	0
Bahia Laura/ Donau	steamships	German	8561/ 2931	1918 1939	off Norway 30 Aug 1941	sunk by a British torpedo	some 1700 German troops were lost in the two ships	
Barham	battleship	British	31000	1914	off Egypt 25 Nov 1941	torpedoed	848	*c* 300
Pommern	battleship	German	12997	1905	North Sea 1 Jun 1916	sunk at Battle of Jutland. (She was the only battleship on either side sunk at Jutland)	840	0
Imperator Alexander III	battleship	Russian	13516	1904	Strait of Korea 27 May 1905	sunk at Battle of Tsu-Shima	836	4
Borodino	battleship	Russian	13516	—	Strait of Korea 27 May 1905	sunk at Battle of Tsu-Shima	829	1
Royal Oak	battleship	British	29150	1914	Scapa Flow 14 Oct 1939	torpedoed by a German submarine	810	424
Leopoldville	troopship	Belgian	11509	1929	off Cherbourg, France 24 Dec 1944	explosion caused by mine or torpedo	808	*c* 1390
Neptune	cruiser	British	7175	1933	off Tripoli, Libya 19 Dec 1941	struck a mine	766	0
Arandora Star	troopship	British	15501	1927	off Co. Donegal, N. Ireland 2 Jul 1940	torpedoed by German U-boat	761 (of whom 613 were German or Italian internees)	847
Gloucester	cruiser	British	9600	1937	off Island of Milos, Aegean Sea 22 May 1941	hit by a bomb	736	69
Christian VIII	wooden line-of-battleship	Danish	—	—	off the east coast of Schleswig, Germany 5 Apr 1849	caught fire under bombardment and blew up	*c* 700	*c* 400

Loss of Life at Sea

The following list shows the marine disasters which resulted in the greatest loss of life annually since 1949:

1949: 28 January. South-east of Shanghai. More than 600 Chinese were missing and presumed dead when a collier and a passenger and freight liner, carrying war refugees, collided and sank.

1950: 19 June. Red Sea, south of Suez. The cargo ship *Indian Enterprise*, carrying a load of explosives, blew up. 73 of the 74 persons aboard died.

1951: 16 April. 16 miles (26km) north of Alderney, Channel Islands. The British submarine *Affray* failed to surface after a diving exercise. 75 officers and men lost their lives.

1952: 26 April. The US aircraft carrier *Wasp* collided with the minesweeper *Hobson* during night exercises in the Atlantic. The *Hobson* sank with the loss of 176 men, including the captain: 61 were rescued by *Wasp*.

1953: 9 January. 248 people were drowned when a South Korean passenger ship sank in a storm off Pusan, South Korea. 31 January. The British motor vessel *Princess Victoria* (2694grt) sank during a storm in the Irish Sea with the loss of 128 lives.

1954: 27 May. An explosion aboard the 41,000-ton US carrier *Bennington*, off Rhode Island, USA, killed 103 people and injured 118.

1955: 11 May. The Japanese ferryboat *Shima Maru* sank off Tokyo after a collision in fog. 135 people were drowned and 60 more were missing.

1956: 12 January. A 135-ton ferryboat caught fire and sank off the south coast of Korea with a loss of 65 lives.

1957: 15 July. 270 people lost their lives when a Soviet ship sank in a storm in the Caspian Sea.

1958: 1 March. The 148-ton Turkish ferry *Uskudar* foundered in a sudden storm in the Sea of Marmara with the loss of over 300 lives.

1959: 30 January. The Danish motor-vessel *Hans Hedtoft* (2875grt) hit an iceberg off Cape Farewell, Greenland, and sank with the loss of all 94 people on board.

1960: 14 December. About 50 people were reported missing after a Greek and a Yugoslav tanker collided and caught fire in the Bosphorus.

1961: 8 April. The British India Steam Navigation's 5030-ton liner *Dara* caught fire after an explosion between decks outside the port of Dubai in the Persian Gulf. 238 people were either drowned or burned to death.

9 July. The 2037-ton Portuguese motorship *Save* caught fire when she ran aground off the coast of Mozambique between Beira and Quelmaine. 259 lives were lost.

1962: 21 October. The Norwegian motor vessel *Sanct Svithun* of 2172 tons, ran aground near the entrance to the port of Rorbik, north Norway. 41 people were drowned.

1963: 22 December. The Greek cruise liner *Lakonia* (20,314 tons) caught fire 180 miles (290km) north of Madeira. 128 people were killed and 908 were saved. The burned-out hulk was taken in tow for Gibraltar by salvage vessels but sank in a gale on 29 December, when 250 miles (402km) from port.

1964: 10 February. 82 men were lost when the Australian destroyer *Voyager* collided with the aircraft carrier *Melbourne* off the coast of New South Wales. See also p. 224.

1965: 13 November. 89 people were drowned or burned to death when the cruise ship *Yarmouth Castle* caught fire off New Providence, Bahamas.

1966: 8 December. At least 264 people died when the 8922-ton Greek ferryship *Heraklion* sank on a voyage from Crete to Piraeus. The accident occurred when a refrigerator truck broke loose in heavy seas and smashed the loading hatch, causing the car deck to flood.

1967: 29 July. Fire broke out aboard the 75,900-ton aircraft carrier USS *Forrestal* off North Vietnam after an explosion on the flight deck. 134 of the crew were killed and 100 injured. 60 aircraft were destroyed.

1968: 11 October. Between 300 and 500 people died when the Philippine ferryboat *Dumagnete* foundered off Mindanao Island in the Sulu Sea. Many were eaten by sharks.

1969: 21 June. A barge transporting Portuguese troops off Beira, Mozambique, sank and 108 of the 150 men on board were drowned.

1970: 15 December. 259 people died when a South Korean ferryboat capsized in the Korea Strait off Pusan. Only 12 people were found clinging to the wreckage. The disaster was blamed on unbalanced cargo.

1971: 6 August. About 400 Iranians trying to enter Kuwait illegally were drowned when the two motorboats in which they had crossed the Persian Gulf capsized off the port of Abdulla, south-east of Kuwait. About 100 swam ashore and were arrested.

1972: 11 May. The 7113-ton British cargo liner *Royston Grange* collided with the Liberian oil tanker *Tien Chee* in dense fog in the River Plate estuary. All 74 people aboard the *Royston Grange* died; 10 died and 32 were saved from the *Tien Chee*.

1973: 21 February. Over 200 people were drowned when the Japanese freighter *Bombay Maru* collided with a ferryboat in the Rangoon River, Burma.

1974: It was reported from Istanbul on 26 September that a Kashin-class Soviet guided missile destroyer had blown up and sunk in the Black Sea two weeks earlier. An American guided missile destroyer of comparable size has a crew of about 350 men.

1975: 3 August. 500 people were believed to have been drowned when two triple-deck excursion ferries collided and sank on the Hsi River near Canton, China.

1976: 25 December. 150 pilgrims, returning from the sacred shrines of Mecca and Medina, died when the Egyptian passenger ship *Patria* caught fire and sank 50 miles (80km) from Jeddah in the Red Sea.

1977: 17 January. 46 US sailors and marines were killed in Barcelona harbour, Spain, when the 56-ft (17m) launch which was taking them back to the helicopter-carrier *Guam* collided with the 380-ton Spanish coastal freighter *Urela* and turned turtle.

1978: 22 November. A boat loaded with Vietnamese refugees was forced back to sea by the Malaysian police off Trengganu, on the east coast of Malaysia; it sank and 200 were drowned. On 2 December another 143 Vietnamese refugees died in the same manner.

1979: 8 January. 50 people were killed when the French oil tanker *Betelgeuse*, owned by the Total Oil Co., exploded while unloading at Bantry Bay, Eire.

1980: 22 April. 96 people were drowned when the inter-island ferry *Don Juan* was in collision with an oil tanker off the Island of Mindanao, Philippines.

1981: 25 January. 374 people were drowned when an Indonesian passenger ship, the *Tampomas II*, caught fire and sank in the Java Sea.

Lifeboats

The Chinese claim to have been **the first nation to have had an organized rescue service**, and, while due allowance must be made for the tendency of that race to lay claim to a wide variety of unsubstantiated 'firsts', it is certain that lifeboats were stationed on the Yangtse River, upstream from Shanghai, in the middle of the 18th century.

The first man to build a craft with the properties of a lifeboat was a Frenchman called de Bernières who, in 1775, designed and tested a self-righting vessel, but it was not specifically intended for rescue work. The credit for producing **the first craft specially *adapted* for saving life at sea** belongs to Lionel Lukin (1742–1834) who patented what he called an 'unimmergible' boat in 1785. **The first boat actually designed for saving life at sea** was the *Original*, built by Henry Greathead (1757–1816) of South Shields and launched in 1790. She remained in service for 40 years.

The first man to organize a lifeboat service round the coast of Great Britain was Sir William Hillary (1771–1847), the founder of the National Institution for the Preservation of Life from Shipwreck in 1824, 30 years later to become the Royal National Lifeboat Institution (R.N.L.I.). In August 1940, the crew of the Margate lifeboat rescued a pilot who had baled out of his blazing Spitfire over the Channel. He was Richard Hillary (1919–43), great-great-great-great nephew of Sir William Hillary and author of *The Last Enemy*.

GRACE DARLING

One name is imperishably linked with the heroism implicit in the work of rescue at sea – that of Grace Darling (1815–42). The incident which brought her undying fame has been told so often that it merits only the briefest mention. On 7 September 1838, the steamer *Forfarshire* was wrecked off the Farne Islands. Grace and her father, William, the keeper of the Longstone lighthouse, rowed a mile to the wreck in their coble and rescued 11 of the survivors. Public reaction to Grace's exploit was little short of hysterical, much to the bewilderment of Mr Darling

A marble bust of Grace Darling.

who regarded the incident as all part of the night's work and in whose log were recorded many such rescues. Grace enjoyed her fame for four brief years, dying of consumption at the age of 27. The coble in which she achieved immortality is still preserved at Bamburgh, Northumberland. It is an open rowing-boat, 21ft (6.4m) long and 6ft (1.8m) wide.

The worst tragedy in the history of the R.N.L.I. occurred on the night of 9 December 1886, when the barque *Mexico* went aground near the mouth of the River Ribble off the Lancashire coast. The Southport lifeboat was launched and managed to reach the stricken ship but then capsized and 13 of her crew of 15 were drowned. The St Anne's lifeboat had also put to sea and was found the following morning bottom-up on the beach. There were no survivors. The Lytham lifeboat eventually managed to take off the *Mexico*'s crew of 12, all of whom had lashed themselves to the rigging. On that fateful night, 27 lifeboatmen were drowned, leaving behind 16 widows and 50 orphans.

The first steam-powered lifeboat, the *Duke of Northumberland*, was launched in 1890 and remained in service for 33 years, during which time she rescued 295 people. In all, six steam lifeboats were built for the R.N.L.I., the last being withdrawn from service in 1928.

The first petrol engine was installed in an existing lifeboat in 1904. The first lifeboat specifically designed as a motor lifeboat went into service in 1908 at Stromness in Orkney.

The work of the R.N.L.I. has undergone a fundamental change in the last 30 years, as more and more people turn to the sea for recreation. Originally established to help the professional seaman, it is now the yachtsman, the water-skier, the pedalo enthusiast and the swimmer to whose aid the lifeboatman is most frequently called. Adapting to this change of role, the R.N.L.I. introduced **the inshore lifeboat,** an inflatable dinghy about 15ft (4.6m) long, powered by an outboard motor. The first of these came into service in 1963.

The first provision for shipwrecked mariners in North America took the form of shelters built by the Humane Society of Massachusetts to provide a refuge for those fortunate enough to reach the shore, after the loss of their ship, many sailors having previously died from exposure on uninhabited stretches of coast. One can't help thinking that an unusually generous measure of good fortune must have been required not only to survive a shipwreck but also to find a refuge conveniently at hand when swept ashore on a dark and stormy night.

The first lifeboat station in North America was established at Cohasset, just south of Boston, in 1807.

The biggest mouthful in the world of sea-rescue services is almost certainly the Dutch *Koninklijke Zuid-Hollandsche Maatschappij tot Redding van Schipbrenkelingen*, closely followed by its sister organization, the *Koninklijke Noord-en-Zuid-Hollandsche Redding-Maatschappij*. Both were founded in November 1824, and, fortunately for those in peril on the sea, both answer to their initials.

ODD FACTS

The first recorded occasion on which a flag was flown at half-mast at sea was on 22 July 1612, on board the *Heartsease*, after her master, Captain James Hall, had been killed by an Eskimo on the west coast of Greenland. The log of her sister-ship the *Patience* records that 'when the *Heartsease* joined the *Patience* her flag was hanging down and her ensign was over the poop which signified the death of someone on board'. Clements Markham, in his biography of the navigator John Davis, says, 'There can be no doubt that this was an act of vengeance by one whose relation had been killed or kidnapped by Hall ... for the Eskimos made no attempt to harm anyone else.'

Rum was first issued as an official ration in the Royal Navy some time after the capture of Jamaica in 1655. In 1740 Admiral Vernon decreed that it should be diluted with water. Prior to that each man had a minimum of a neat half-pint daily. Vernon's nickname was 'Old Grog' on account of the grogram cloak he wore and the sobriquet was thereafter transferred to the drink. By Nelson's day the daily ration was one gill of rum and three of water, later reduced to half a gill of rum to one and a half of water. It was finally abolished by Sir Michael Le Fanu in 1970, which action, combined with the colour of his hair, earned him the nickname 'Dry Ginger'.

The first man to construct a double-hulled ship was Sir William Petty (1623–87). The diarist John Evelyn describes it thus: 'The vessel was flat-bottomed, of exceeding use to put into shallow ports, and ride over small depths of water. It consisted of two distinct keeles, crampt together with huge timbers, so as a violent stream ran between them. It bore a monstrous broad sail.'

Pepys tells us, further, that the ship 'is about 30 tons in burden, and carries 30 men with good accommodation. . . . This also carries ten guns of five tons weight.' The *Experiment*, as the ship was called, was launched in Dublin on 22 December 1662 and in the following July won a race against the Dublin Packet from Dublin to Holyhead by the comfortable margin of three hours.

The first recorded instance of 'flogging round the fleet' occurred in 1698 when two petty officers of the *Mary* were found guilty of conniving at a mutiny. They were sentenced 'to receive six lashes alongside every ship in sea pay between Gillingham and Rochester'. In 1712 four seamen of the *Sorlings* were sentenced 'to be carried with a halter about their necks and to receive at the side of each of H.M. ships of war now riding in the Downs ten lashes each with a cat-o'-nine-tails on their bare backs'.

The distinguished naval historian Peter Kemp describes a flogging round the fleet thus: 'A capstan bar was set up in the stern sheets of a pinnace and the wretched man, bare to the waist, had his hands lashed to the bar above his head and his feet secure to a thwart. As he came alongside each ship, the lower deck was cleared so that all men on board would witness his punishment ... the ship's own boatswain's mates descended into the pinnace to administer the required number of lashes. No boatswain's mate gave more than six lashes for fear that his arm might weaken.'

The cat-o'-nine-tails was made of nine lengths of cord with three knots in each. It was popularly supposed to have had nine tails because a flogging by 'a trinity of trinities' would be more sacred and more efficacious.

The Naval Discipline Act of 1866 limited the

punishment to 48 lashes. In 1879 the use of the cat was 'suspended' though it was never formally abolished, as it was in the Army in 1881.

The Marine Society was founded in 1756 by Jonas Hanway (1712–86) with the twofold aim of keeping up a supply of seamen for the Navy and of rescuing destitute boys from the streets of London. So successful were its operations that within six years 5451 boys and 4787 landsmen volunteers had been fitted out by the Society. **'Hanway was the first Londoner, it is said, to carry an umbrella** and he lived to triumph over all the hackney coachmen who tried to hoot and hustle him down.'

The first record of 'Compo' rations being used in the Navy was in 1756 when a Mr Dubois invented a cube from which broth could be made. **The first supplier** of these cubes was an aptly-named apothecary in Plymouth called Mr Cook-worthy.

Haslar, the naval hospital at Gosport was, when completed in 1762, not only **the largest naval hospital in the world but also the largest brick building in Europe**. In 1758 James Lind (1716–94) was appointed first physician in charge of the hospital, a post he held for the remainder of his life. Lind is often referred to as **'the founder of naval hygiene in England'**. In 1753 he published *A Treatise on Scurvy*, the outcome of the experiments he undertook while surgeon on board HMS *Salisbury* in 1746, **the first controlled dietary experiments in history**. Sadly, it was not until 1795, 40 years and many thousands of unnecessary deaths after Lind's 'conclusive evidence of its worth', that the issue of lemon juice as a specific against scurvy was officially adopted in the Royal Navy (see also p. 51).

'The first iron boat was a 12ft (3.66m) long pleasure craft launched on the River Foss in Yorkshire on 20 May 1777. Apart from the fact that she was able to carry 15 passengers and was light enough to be carried by two men, nothing is known about the boat or its builder. The foregoing facts were recorded in a contemporary issue of the *Gentleman's Magazine* 10 years before John "Iron Mad" Wilkinson (1728–1808) built his 70ft (21.3m) barge the *Trial*, which hitherto has been generally acknowledged as the world's first iron boat.' (PATRICK ROBERTSON, *The Shell Book of Firsts*).

Wilkinson's iron barge was launched on 6 July 1787 and on the 14th he wrote to a friend, 'Yesterday week my Iron Boat was launched. It answers all my expectations and has convinced the unbelievers who were 999 in a thousand. It will be a nine days' wonder and then be like Columbus's egg.' (If anyone can explain what is the significance of Columbus's egg the author would be most grateful.)

In the early 19th century **insanity in the Royal Navy was seven times the national average**. The distinguished surgeon Sir Gilbert Blane (1749–1834), who did much to improve sanitary conditions in the Navy, suggested that this was due to head injuries caused by men constantly bumping their heads in the confined space between decks, which they naturally did more frequently when drunk!

The last recorded instance of a pigtail being worn in the Navy was in 1823. No one knows for sure why the pigtail became a popular style of hairdressing in the Navy, though it has been suggested that it may have been because it afforded some protection against a sword-blow aimed at the back of the neck. In China it was worn as a sign of servitude, the Mongols having imposed upon the Chinese the obligation of wearing their hair in a pigtail when they conquered the country in about 1660.

The sailor who is recorded as **having taken part in more sea battles than any other** is Admiral Sir Edward Berry (1768–1831), who was in eight major fleet actions, as well as many minor engagements. He also received three gold medals, a record equalled only by Lord Collingwood.

A LOAD OF TRIPE

Admiral George Dundas (*d* 1820) struck a bet with some friends that he 'and one other' would consume 16lb (7.26kg) of tripe at a single sitting. With all the bets taken, a time and place were appointed and the officers gathered round to watch the Homeric feat. Despite his fondness for tripe, Dundas laid down his knife and fork after the first 2 or 3lb (0.9 or 1.4kg); whereupon his friends led in a large bear, who quickly polished off the remainder. There were loud protests and a

The *Rosetta* and her sister ships *Rohilla* and *Ravenna* were the first steel-hulled vessels built for **P. & O.** and the last to have their first-class accommodation aft over the screw (see p. 195). *Peninsular and Oriental Steam Navigation Company.*

P. & O.'s *Iberia* was in the pleasure cruise business by 1844 (see p. 187). *Peninsular and Oriental Steam Navigation Company.*

The *Chusan* was the first major passenger liner to be fitted with stabilizers (p. 206). *Peninsular and Oriental Steam Navigation Company.*

The *QE II* (see p. 207). *Cunard Line.*

committee of officers met to decide whether or not the wager had been won. They solemnly decided that 'and one other' satisfactorily covered the bear and that the terms had been fulfilled. (*A Dictionary of British Ships and Seamen*.)

The longest-serving officer in the Royal Navy was Admiral of the Fleet Sir Provo Wallis (1791–1892). His obituary in *The Times* explains how this came about: 'His father had influence enough to get him rated on the books of the *Oiseau* as an able-bodied seaman when he was a child of four years old. Wallis did not actually go to sea until 1804 when he became midshipman on board the *Cleopatra* ... On account of the long and distinguished services of Sir Provo Wallis it had been decided that his name should be retained on the active list as long as he lived. The consequence was that from his being rated as an A.B. on board the *Oiseau* in 1795 to his decease in 1892 his name must have been enrolled on the books of the Navy for 97 years.'

The only ex-Field Marshal to have been drowned rounding Cape Horn was Johann Orth. The Archduke Johann Salvator was a member of the Austrian Royal Family who fell in love with an actress called Milli Stubel, but his request to marry her was refused by the Emperor, so he renounced his title, was relieved of his rank, changed his name to Johann Orth, married his Milli, moved to England and bought a three-masted iron sailing ship of 1428 tons called the *St Margaret*. He and Milli sailed for La Plata, Argentina, on 26 March 1896, left the River Plate on 12 July and were never seen again. The Emperor was so upset that he sent a cruiser to South America to search for the missing vessel, but all to no avail.

EDWARD LYON BERTHON

One of the most fertile of British inventors was Edward Lyon Berthon (1813–99), to whom several original ideas of maritime interest can be credited. His early experiments in the application of the screw propellor to steam propulsion led to **the development**, in 1835, **of a two-bladed propellor** which was ridiculed by the Admiralty who said that 'the screw was a pretty toy which never would and never could propel a ship'. Three years later Francis Smith patented an identical propellor and Berthon at first thought that he had copied a discarded sketch of his in the

patent office. But it transpired that both had reached the same results through similar but independent experiments. His next invention, known as **Berthon's log**, was a device for measuring the speed of a ship. In the simplest terms, the suction produced by the water streaming past the end of a pipe projected below a ship is registered on a mercury column above. Next came an instrument for showing the trim of a ship at any moment – that is to say how much and in which direction the keel was out of the horizontal, and another for indicating the number of degrees through which the ship rolled. His last and most celebrated invention was '**Berthon's folding boat**', the idea of which first occurred to him after the wreck of the steamer *Orion* off Portpatrick harbour in 1850, in which 60 people were drowned. ('The passengers,' says the *Annual Register*, 'were of an unusually superior rank.') Again he was discouraged by the Admiralty and it was not until 1873 that the encouragement of Samuel Plimsoll led to the Admiralty placing an order worth £15,000 for Berthon's boats. Some were used by General Gordon when he was besieged at Khartoum and they are still widely used to this day.

THE ROYAL YACHT *BRITANNIA*

The Royal yacht *Britannia* was launched by Her Majesty the Queen at Clydebank on 16 April 1953. She has a displacement of 3990 tons, an overall length of 413ft (125.9m) and a complement of 22 officers and 225 ratings. She is designed to be converted into a hospital ship in time of war. On 30 June 1953, the Admiralty announced that the Royal Navy College, Dartmouth, which had hitherto borne the ship's name HMS *Britannia* would in future be known as the Britannia Royal Naval College, Dartmouth, and would bear the ship's name HMS *Dartmouth*, the change being made necessary by the naming of the new Royal yacht *Britannia*.

The longest serving member of the survey ship *Hecate* was Leading Seacat Fred Wunpound, who was pressed into service in 1966 in return for a payment of £1 to the Plymouth RSPCA – hence his name. During his service he travelled over a quarter of a million miles (402,000km), earned two good-conduct medals and one disgraceful conduct medal following an incident in Brixham fish market.

APPENDICES

I Types of Vessel

The inconsistency with which the names of different types of ship were used during the Middle Ages and indeed, long after, often makes it impossible to say with any degree of certainty that a particular name specifically implies a particular size, rig or, indeed, use. The following list includes the names of most types of ship or boat which the reader is likely to encounter and the purpose for which they were generally used. For descriptions of those vessels which are covered more fully in the main text the reader is referred to the appropriate page.

Actuaire: an open French troop transport, with sails and oars, used in the 18th and early 19th centuries.

Actuairole: a small French galley used as a troop transporter in the 18th and early 19th centuries.

Argosy: large medieval trading vessel, used principally in the Mediterranean. Some say the name is derived from the port of Ragusa (now Dubrovnik), others from the *Argo*, the legendary ship which carried Jason on his quest for the Golden Fleece.

Badan: small sailing vessel used in Southern Arabia, particularly, in former times, by smugglers and slave-traders.

Baghla: large, two-masted, lateen-rigged sailing vessel used to this day in the Indian Ocean. The design of its stern was clearly influenced by the ships of early European traders.

Balam: used in the marshy areas at the mouth of the Tigris and the Euphrates. 'Very roomy, with high sides, about 30ft (9m) long, and with a covered

stern and prow . . . carried a crew of three who propelled the boat slowly forward by setting their poles in the water and then moving step by step along the gunwale, from bow to stern' (WILFRID THESIGER, *The Marsh Arabs*).

Balinger: a vessel of about 40 tons, usually with two masts and auxiliary oars, used in the 15th and 16th centuries both for fishing and cargo, sometimes as troop transport. They probably originated in the Bay of Biscay and because the name is derived from *balena* (L. Whale) it is assumed that they were used as whalers, but it has also been suggested that the name derives, not from their use, but from their shape, which, being high and broad at the bows and relatively narrow at the stern, resembles that of a whale.

Barca-Longa: large Spanish fishing boat of the 17th to 19th centuries, with two or three masts each carrying a single lugsail. Common in the Mediterranean.

Barge: at various times used to describe several different types of vessel. 1) a small sea-going ship with sails, next up in size to a balinger. 2) a large flat-bottomed freight boat used chiefly for river and canal navigation, either with or without sails. 3) a ceremonial oared vessel, usually much ornamented, used on state occasions. 4) the second boat of a man-of-war, a long narrow boat, generally with not less than 10 oars.

Barque: originally a general term for any small sailing ship, by the 18th century applied specifically to a three-masted sailing vessel with fore-

and mainmast square-rigged and mizen mast fore-and-aft rigged. Until the mid-19th century barques were quite small, but, with the growth of the grain and nitrate trades, four and five-masted barques of up to 5000 tons were built. In America the word is spelt bark.

Barquentine: a vessel similar to a barque, but having only the foremast square-rigged, the main and mizen being fore-and-aft rigged.

Bateira: A general-purpose sailing boat from Central Portugal with standing lugsails and leeboards which are roped to the mast but not fixed to the side of the boat in any way.

Bateloe: large wooden vessel used on the River Madeira in Brazil to carry latex.

Bawley: a small cutter-rigged fishing vessel or oyster dredger used in the Thames Estuary.

Beancod: English name for a small single-masted Portuguese fishing boat used on rivers and estuaries.

Bellum: a canoe-like boat propelled by pole or paddle used in and around the mouth of the Tigris and Euphrates.

Bergantina: small Mediterranean vessel of the 14th to 16th centuries equipped with oars and sails; fulfilling the same role as the English pinnace.

Bezan: a small yacht of the 17th century, from the Dutch word *bezaan* = mizen sail.

Bilander: a two-masted merchant ship, lateen-rigged on the mainmast, used in the Mediterranean and in Holland for coastal and canal traffic in the 17th and 18th centuries. From the Dutch *bij* = close to: *lander* = the land.

Billy-boy: bluff-bowed, single-masted trading vessel of river-barge build used along the East Coast of England during the 19th century. It has been suggested that the word is a corruption of bilander.

Bireme: see p. 9.

Boat: the basic rule which divides the boats from the ships is that the latter are open craft without decking and are propelled by oars, sails or an outboard engine. There are, of course, exceptions to this rule: Submarines are usually called boats and fishing boats are generally referred to as such, irrespective of size. Though boat trains take travellers to board passenger steamers, the latter are ships not boats.

Boeier or **Boier** or **Boejer**: during the 16th century the boeier was a Dutch seagoing merchant vessel of up to 65ft (20m) in length with a mainsail rigged on a standing gaff, and sometimes a square topsail and a small lateen mizen. A similar vessel was found in Norway, where it was called a *bojort*. In the 19th century the name boeier came to be applied to smaller craft used on inland waterways, with a single mast carrying a boomed mainsail which could be lowered when passing under bridges. They were much used as pleasure craft.

Botter: flat-bottomed Dutch fishing boat with a long, narrow stem and a high curved stern. The catch was kept alive in a free-flooding well amidships. Many botters were adapted for use as pleasure craft.

Brig: originally identical with the brigantine, the colloquial abbreviation came to be applied exclusively to a modified rig – a two-masted vessel square-rigged on both fore and mainmasts, carrying also on her main mast a lower fore-and-aft sail with a gaff and boom. Originally used as coastal traders, brigs later became popular as training ships for boy seamen.

Brigantine: a two-masted vessel square-rigged on the foremast and fore-and-aft rigged on the mainmast. The name comes from the same root as 'brigand' since the original brigantine was a small, easily manoeuvrable vessel equipped with sails and oars and much favoured on account of its handiness by pirates in the Mediterranean. As the habit of piracy spread north the vessel changed but the name stuck.

Bumboat: a small boat used to take provisions out to ships lying in harbour, and originally, and somewhat unhygienically, to collect the refuse from those ships.

Buss: a two- or three-masted fishing vessel, usually of from 50 to 70 tons, used particularly in the North Sea by English and Dutch herring fishermen in the 17th and 18th centuries.

Caballito: Peruvian coastal reed boat ridden through the surf as on a pony, which the word means in Spanish. They are unusual in that they are built by the fishermen themselves.

Caique: a word loosely applied to small sailing and rowing boats in the Bosphorus and the Aegean sea.

Canoe: small open boat propelled by paddles. Today the word is generally used to cover the very light craft used for sport on inland waterways but among the Pacific Islands war and ceremonial canoes had as many as 30 paddles on each side.

Caracor: East Indian carvel-built vessel fitted with outriggers on each side and paddled by several rows of men seated within the hull and on the outriggers.

Caravel: see p. 33.

Carley Float: a large life-raft made of canvas stuffed with kapok able to carry up to 50 men.

Carrack: see p. 18.

Carvel: a small, light, two-masted, lateen-rigged cargo vessel used in Spain and Portugal in the late Middle Ages, thought by some to be synonymous with the caravel.

Catamaran: originally a sort of raft comprising two logs lashed together, getting its name from the Tamil words *katta*, to tie, and *marana*, wood. Now normally applied to twin-hulled racing and cruising yachts.

Cat: stoutly built sailing collier used along the north-east coast of England until the mid-19th century. The ships chosen by Captain James Cook (see p. 47–50) for his voyages of discovery were cats.

Cat-boat: shallow sailing boat of considerable beam used in the Cape Cod region of N. America during the mid-19th century and later adapted for racing (see *Sandbagger*).

Chasse-Marée: three-masted French inshore fishing vessel – the name means 'that which chases the tide' – the rig was refined by smugglers and privateers in the early 19th century to achieve maximum speed.

Clipper: see p. 171 *et seq*.

Coble: 1) a low, flat-bottomed, clinkerbuilt fishing boat, rowed with three pairs of oars and fitted with a lug-sail, used particularly by cod and turbot fishermen off the north-east coast of England. It was in a coble that Grace Darling (see pp. 231–2) earned her place in the Hall of Fame.
2) the name is also applied to a smaller rowing boat used for netting salmon in estuaries and for crossing rivers or lakes.

Cog: see p. 152.

Collier: any vessel carrying a cargo of coal. 17th and 18th century colliers, many of them cats, carried about 300–400 tons of coal, but the advent of steam propulsion and the establishment of world-wide bunkering depots gave rise to the construction of colliers capable of carrying up to 6000 tons. The introduction of oil-fired engines killed this trade but bulk transport of coal is still a necessity and modern colliers are built to carry in excess of 25,000 tons.

Container ship: a vessel specially designed to carry cargo in standardized containers, each containing 18 tons, thus greatly facilitating handling and stowage and eliminating the danger of the cargo shifting in heavy weather.

Coracle: small boat constructed of wickerwork covered with hide or oiled cloth and propelled by a paddle. Julius Caesar describes the coracles used by the Britons of his day and they are still in use on certain rivers in Wales.

Corbita: the merchant ship of Imperial Rome, a solidly-built vessel capable of carrying 400 tons of cargo. The name comes from the Latin *corbis*, a basket.

Corvette: originally a three-masted, square-rigged warship with a single tier of guns under a covered deck. The name, which derives from *corbita*, was applied during the Second World War to small, fast escort vessels equipped with anti-submarine and anti-aircraft weapons.

Crayer: a small sailing vessel of 30–50 tons used in coastal trade.

Cruiser: see p. 100.

Curragh or Currach: a small boat of similar construction to the coracle, still used on the west coast of Ireland, particularly in the Arran Islands. Formerly almost round, they are now built in the shape of a conventional boat.

Cutter: 1) in the 18th century a small, single-masted, gaff-rigged, decked vessel used for dispatch and patrol purposes. Cutters carried anything up to twelve 4-pounder guns. They were later widely used by the Trinity House pilot service.
2) a clinker-built ship's boat, broader than a barge or pinnace, fitted for

APPENDICES

sailing and rowing by 8–14 oars.
3) any coastal patrol vessel of up to about 2000 tons used by the US Navy.

Dahabiah: originally the golden state barge of the Moslem rulers of Egypt (*Dahabiah* is Arabic for 'golden'). Now large lateen-sailed vessels used on the River Nile. Luxury motor-driven dahabiahs take passengers and tourists up and down the river.
Dghaisa: the taxi-boat of Grand Harbour, Valetta, Malta, propelled by one or two men with oars which they stand and push. Not unlike the Venetian gondola.
Dhow: a name used by Europeans to describe virtually any lateen-rigged trading vessel found in the Red Sea, Persian Gulf or Indian Ocean. Most of them now have diesel engines. There is no vessel which the Arabs themselves call a dhow.
Dinghy: name taken from *dengi*, Hindu word for a small boat used on rivers in India. Now 1) small open clinker-built rowing boat with one pair of oars
2) popular form of sailing boat used for racing
3) small collapsible boats used in emergency by airmen.
Doble: single-masted sprit-rigged fishing boat used on the River Medway.
Dogger: takes its name from the Dogger Bank, famous fishing ground in the North Sea, which, in turn, takes its name from *dogge*, Dutch for cod. A two-masted fishing vessel of about 80 tons, square-rigged on the mainmast with a lugsail on the mizen and two jibs on a long bowsprit.
Dory: small flat-bottomed boat used for line fishing on the Grand Banks off the coast of Newfoundland. The thwarts could be removed so that they could easily be stacked on board the schooners taking them to and from the Grand Banks.
Drakar or **Drakkar**: name given to the largest of the Danish longships.
Drifter: a fishing vessel using drift nets to catch fish, such as herring, which live near the surface of the sea. Fish living deeper in the sea are caught in a trawl.
Drogher: originally a ship which caught and dried herring and mackerel, from the Dutch word for 'to dry'; by extension any slow, heavy coaster.
Dromon: Mediterranean vessel of the 9th to 15th centuries with many oars and a large square sail, used both as troop-transporters and for carrying cargo.

Dugout: primitive form of canoe made by hollowing out a single tree-trunk either with stone implements or fire.

Felucca: sailing boat used in the Mediterranean and on the Nile with one or two lateen-rigged masts, occasionally a mizen mast, a high bow and raking sternpost.
Flatboat: name given to large flat-bottomed boat used for transporting men and horses during amphibious operations in the 18th and 19th centuries.
Freighter: generic name for any cargo-carrying vessel.
Frigate: originally an oared sailing ship of the Mediterranean; later a three-masted ship, fully rigged on each mast, armed with 24–38 guns on a single gundeck. In the Second World War the name was given to a special type of ship of 1600 tons designed for convoy escort duty and equipped for anti-submarine work. In the Royal Navy frigates are smaller than destroyers but the reverse is the case in the US Navy.

Gaiassa: long, shallow-draught cargo-barge used on the Nile, with one or two lateen-rigged masts.
Galleass: see pp. 22–3.
Galleon: see pp. 19–20.
Galley: see pp. 21–2.
Galliot or **Galiot**: 1) a small galley with 16–20 oars and a single mast used in the 17th and 18th centuries to chase and capture enemy ships.
2) small Dutch trading vessel of the 18th century with one or two masts, a barge-like hull and leeboards.
Gig: 1) a narrow, light, clinker-built ship's boat with oars and sail generally used by the commanding officer.
2) a modified form of (1) used on the Thames as a rowing boat, chiefly for racing.
Gondola: 1) long, narrow, flat-bottomed boat used for the conveyance of people on the canals of Venice since the 11th century. The gondola is propelled by one man standing in the stern plying a single oar, so the sides are deliberately built to a different length and curve, thus causing the starboard side to sink lower in the water than port, which in turn induces increased drag on the starboard side to counterbalance the thrust of the single blade, which would otherwise continually force the boat to turn to port. Gondolas measure about 30ft (9.1m) in length by 4 or 5ft (1.2–1.5m) in width.

2) some river gunboats used in the American War of Independence were referred to as gondolas.
Guarda-Costa: Spanish vessels used in the 17th–18th centuries as revenue cutters in the West Indies and notorious for the barbaric cruelty of the excisemen who manned them.
Gufah or **Guffa**: a circular cargo-and-passenger-carrying coracle used on the River Tigris and made of pomegranate stalks, twine, straw and a covering of pitch.
Gundelo or **Gundalow**: obsolete type of N. American river barge.

Hermaphrodite Brig: a two-masted sailing ship with square sails on the foremast, and a square topsail set above a fore-and-aft sail on the mainmast.
Hooker: 1) a two-masted Dutch coasting or shipping vessel, mainly used, as the name implies, for line fishing.
2) a single-masted fishing smack, similar in construction to a hoy, once used off the coasts of Ireland and South-West England.
Hoy: small coastal sailing vessel of up to about 60 tons usually with a single fore-and-aft sail, but the word was loosely used to denote a variety of Dutch and English coastal vessels and does not imply a specific rig.
Hulk or **Hulc**: word used in late medieval times to describe any large unwieldly merchant ship of rude build; also the body of a dismantled ship retained in use for some other purpose, such as a prison.

Jackass-Barque: a four-masted sailing ship square-rigged on the two foremost masts and fore-and-aft rigged on the two after-masts.
Jaegt or **Jagt**: Norwegian sailing boat used from the 14th to the 19th century and a direct descendant of the Viking longship, with a high stem and stern and a single mast carrying a large square sail. They were used to carry fish caught off the Lofoten Islands down to Bergen.
Jalibot: name given to a certain type of Arab dhow; the word is probably a corruption of Jollyboat.
Jigger: a small fishing sloop fitted with a 'jigger' sail, a small sail rigged out on a mast and boom from the stern.
Jollyboat; a clinker-built ship's boat, smaller than a cutter, propelled by oars and usually hoisted on a davit at the stern of the ship.
Junk: generic term used to describe a

240

high-sterned, flat-bottomed Chinese or Japanese trading vessel with two or three masts carrying lugsails stiffened with battens. Though of clumsy appearance to Western eyes, the junk is a practical craft designed not only as a means of transport but also as a family home.

Kayak: canoe-like boat made of sealskin stretched and stitched over a wooden frame and used for fishing by Eskimos from Greenland to Alaska; now used for pleasure on inland waters in many countries. A kayak must be paddled by a man: if it carries a woman it is called a umiak.

Keel: a flat-bottomed boat used for loading colliers on the East coast of England before the introduction of mechanical coal-handling.

Ketch: strongly-built, two-masted, fore-and-aft rigged sailing vessel, usually from 100 to 250 tons, formerly used on account of their rig as bomb-vessels, later as yachts.

Klipper: Dutch barge used for carrying cargo, formerly ketch-rigged, now diesel-powered.

Koff: ungainly two-masted Dutch sailing vessel.

Lakatoi: craft found in New Guinea, usually 50–60ft (15.2–18.3m) long, comprising three dug-out hulls joined by through-beams and supporting a bamboo platform; two masts carry claw-shaped sails.

Launch: 1) the largest ship's boat of a sailing man-of-war, also known as a longboat, usually sloop-rigged; in the days of steam battleships the launch was 42ft (12.8m) long and had 18 oars, later paraffin engines.
2) generic term used to describe any small powered boat used for transporting passengers or as a pleasure craft.

Liberty-ship: name given to cargo vessels of 7100 gross tonnage with all-welded hulls built by the US Marine Commission between 1941 and 1945 to replace Allied tonnage sunk by U-boats. In all 2708 were built, and 414 of an improved version known as Victory ships.

Lifeboat: see p. 231.

Lighter: large, open, flat-bottomed craft used for conveyance of cargo from ship to shore and vice-versa. A lighter is classified as a 'dumb' vessel in that it lacks its own means of propulsion.

Longboat: the largest boat carried on board a sailing vessel. The word

belongs mainly to the 18th century; thereafter it was called a launch.

Longship: Norse or Viking seagoing warship with up to 80 oars and a single mast carrying a single square sail (see p. 14).

Lorcha: a vessel with a hull of European shape but rigged as a Chinese junk. They were fast, armed, and used as pirate-hunters in the 19th century.

Lugger: a small, fast sailing vessel with two masts and, occasionally, a mizen stepped right aft. They were much favoured by smugglers and privateers.

Luzzu: small, inshore, spritsail-rigged Maltese fishing boat.

Mashwa: ship's boat carried on dhows in the Indian Ocean.

Mast ship: a vessel which carried a store of masts, usually from the Baltic to South and Western Europe. They had ports cut in the bows and stern to accommodate long timbers.

Moliciero: single-masted Portuguese sailing boat used for collecting seaweed.

Monkey: small, single-masted coastal trading vessel of 16th–17th centuries.

Pallar: small sailing craft used for cargo and passengers on the River Ganges.

Pareja: Iberian fishing vessel, like a trawler, used on the Atlantic coast.

Patile: large transport barge used on the River Ganges, remarkable for the fact that it is clinker-built.

Pink: originally a name applied to small, flat-bottomed Dutch coasting and sailing vessels with bulging sides and narrow stern; in the 17th and 18th centuries applied to Mediterranean warships of greater size but having the same narrow stern.

Pinky: schooner-rigged New England fishing vessel.

Pinnace: 1) small two-masted sailing vessel of about 20 tons, formerly square-rigged, later schooner-rigged, used in both commerce and warfare.
2) a ship's boat of eight and, later, 16 oars.

Pirogue: 1) long, narrow, seagoing canoe used in the Gulf of Mexico and on the west coast of South America in the 16th and 17th centuries, fashioned from two hollowed-out tree trunks fastened together; sometimes spelt *Piragua*.
2) open, flat-bottomed, two-masted sailing barge used in America and the West Indies.

Polacre or **Polacca:** Mediterranean trading vessel used during the 17th and

18th centuries, with two or three masts each made in one piece, usually square-rigged on the mainmast and lateen-rigged on the fore and mizen.

Pram or **Praam:** 1) a flat-bottomed boat used in the Baltic and the Netherlands for shipping cargo.
2) two- or three-masted ship of shallow draught used during the Napoleonic wars as floating batteries.
3) a small ship's boat of the 16th–18th centuries.
4) a dinghy used as a tender to a yacht, often with a blunted bow.

Proa or **Prau** or **Prahu:** Malayan sailing boat with triangular lateen sail and an outrigger.

Punt: name formerly applied to a floating platform from which maintenance work was carried out on the side of a ship; now either a flat-bottomed square-ended pleasure boat used on rivers and propelled with a pole or a small boat used by wildfowlers.

Sacoleva or **Sackalever:** small lateen-rigged sailing vessel used in the Aegean.

Sambuk: flat-sterned, two-masted variety of the dhow, found in the Red Sea.

Sampan: name loosely applied by Europeans to any small, light boat of Far Eastern waters. Harbour sampans have an awning amidships and are propelled by a single scull over the stern; coastal sampans have a single mast and junk-type sail and now, usually, a diesel engine.

Sandbagger: type of sailing boat used for racing in North America in the latter half of the 19th century which carried an immense spread of canvas and a muscular crew of eight or more who shifted the ballast of sandbags on to the weather deck every time the boat tacked.

Scampavia: small Mediterranean warship used during the Napoleonic wars with 20 oarsmen on each side, a single lateen-rigged mast and a long 6-pounder gun sited forward of the mast.

Schooner: originally a small two-masted vessel rigged fore-and-aft with the aftermast not shorter than the forward. If she carried square topsails on either mast she was called a 'topsail schooner'. Later, schooners were built with three, four, and five masts. One, the *Thomas W. Lawson*, had seven (see p. 178).

Scow: large, flat-bottomed lighter or

punt, either towed or rowed.

Sculler: originally a water-taxi, especially on the River Thames in London, propelled by one man using two oars; now a light racing craft for one or two oarsmen.

Settee: two-masted lateen-rigged ship used in the Mediterranean from the 16th to mid-19th century, sometimes as a merchant ship, sometimes as a transport for spare galley crews.

Shahoof: fishing boat with oars and a lateen sail found all along the coast of south-east Arabia.

Shallop: 1) from the 17th to 19th century a large, heavy, undecked boat with one or more masts, fore-and-aft rigged, sometimes carrying guns.
2) a schooner-rigged vessel of 25 tons used for fishing.
3) a word used over the years, with statesman-like disregard for exactitude, to describe a number of vessels of varying shapes and sizes.

Shasha: fishing raft made from date palm used on the Batinah Coast, Arabia.

Sharpie: 1) a long 30–60ft (9.14m–18.28m), flat-bottomed sailing boat used for oyster dredging in Chesapeake Bay, USA.
2) a flat-bottomed cruising yacht.
3) small racing boat with a Bermudan sloop rig.

Skiff: 1) a small clinker-built ship's boat with one or two pairs of oars used for transport, communication, etc. when in harbour.
2) a clinker-built sculler used in rowing races.

Sloop: 1) name applied to a small single-masted fore-and-aft rigged vessel differing from a cutter in having a jib-stay and standing bowsprit.
2) in the 17th–19th century a two- or three-masted square-rigged warship

carrying guns on the upper deck only.
3) small unarmoured convoy escort vessel used during World War II.

Smack: single-masted, fore-and-aft rigged sailing vessel used for fishing or coastal passenger transport. Today the word is loosely applied to any small fishing craft.

Snow: European merchant ship of the 16th–19th century, the largest two-masted vessel of her period, square-rigged on both masts but having a small additional mast, called the snow-mast, stepped immediately abaft the mainmast on which a trysail was set.

Speronara: large, single-masted lateen-rigged boat of southern Italy and Malta.

Surfboat: open boat used mainly off the coasts of India and Africa for landing passengers and cargo where there is no deepwater port. Modern dredging techniques have rendered them largely obsolete except for sport.

Tarada: carvel-built, flat-bottomed canoe some 36ft (11m) in length and propelled by four men with poles, found in Southern Iraq.

Tartane: single-masted vessel with large lateen sail and foresail once used throughout the Mediterranean. Dampier speaks (1697) of a Spanish tartane carrying 30 armed men.

Tjalk: large Dutch barge used on inland waterways since the 17th century.

Tjotter: small inshore Dutch sailing craft with large fan-shaped leeboards.

Trabacolo: one or two-masted vessel found in the Adriatic in the 17th–19th centuries.

Tramp: a merchant vessel which plies no regular route but takes any available cargo wherever and whenever the

opportunity arises.

Trawler: a vessel, of any size, designed to catch the fish which live at the bottom of the sea by means of trawl nets.

Trireme: see p. 9.

Tug: small, powerful vessel designed and built for towing other larger ships or for assisting them in berthing. River and harbour tugs seldom exceed 300 tons but ocean-going tugs can be as much as 2000 tons.

Umiak: see *Kayak*.

Wherry: 1) a decked sailing barge of shallow draught with a single large mainsail used for carrying freight on the Norfolk Broads.
2) a light rowing boat used chiefly for passenger transport on inland waters.

Xavega: four-oared sea-going rowing boat used in the Aveiro area of Portugal.

Xebec: small, three-masted vessel much favoured by pirates in the Mediterranean from the 16th to 19th centuries.

Yawl: 1) small two-masted fore-and-aft rigged sailing vessel, similar to a ketch.
2) a ship's boat with four or six oars, smaller than a pinnace.

Zaima: coracle made of reeds and coated with bitumen used on the Euphrates.

Zaruk: small, single-masted fishing boat from the south end of the Red Sea.

Zulu: two-masted fishing vessel once found on the north-east coast of Scotland. The name derives from the fact that they were introduced during the Zulu War (1879) by a boat-builder called Cameron.

II Glossary of Nautical Terms

Aback: a ship is said to be taken aback when the wind brings her sails back against the mast, either inadvertently, due to a sudden change of the wind, or purposely, to assist in tacking or to lose way.

Abaft: on or towards the rearmost or stern part of a ship, but only used in relation to something on board, e.g. abaft the gangway.

Abeam: at right angles to the line of the keel; usually applied to objects outside the vessel. Variations: abreast, on the beam.

About: a sailing vessel is said to go about when she tacks across the wind to bring the wind from one side of the ship to the other.

A-cockbill: an anchor is a-cockbill when it hangs at the cathead ready to be let go. The 'ck' is not pronounced.

Aft: at or towards the stern, used in the general sense, e.g. to go aft *but* abaft the beam. The adjective of aft is after, as in 'the after gangway'.

A-lee: the position of the helm of a vessel when it has been pushed down to leeward in order to bring her bows into

the wind.

'Andrew': sailors' slang name for the Royal Navy, said to derive from an 18th century press-gang officer named Andrew Miller.

Apostles: two large bollards near the bows on the main deck of square-rigged sailing ships round which hawsers or cables were secured.

Apron: a piece of curved timber above the forward end of the keel of a wooden ship.

Artemon: small square sail set over the bows of Roman merchant ships used mainly as a steering aid.

Astern: the backward movement of a ship – to go astern; the hinder part of a ship – he's gone astern; behind and outside a ship – land fell away astern.

Back and Fill: to fill a vessel's sails and let them be taken aback alternately; formerly used when handling a sailing ship in a narrow tideway.

Backstays: long ropes running back from all mastheads above the lower mast to sides or stern of the ship, intended to give additional support to the shrouds when the wind is abaft the beam.

Bare Poles: a ship is said to be riding under bare poles when all her sails have been taken in, usually because of bad weather.

Battens: thin, flat pieces of wood or plastic used to stiffen a sail.

Batten down the hatches: securing the hatches by means of gratings and tarpaulins, which are kept in place by battens being secured over them.

Beakhead: the space in a sailing ship of war immediately forward of the forecastle, used as the seamen's lavatory and known as the heads. The term is still used in the Royal Navy.

Beam: 1) the measurement of a ship at her widest part; hence 'abaft the beam' means anywhere astern of an imaginary line drawn across the vessel amidships. 'On the starboard beam' means anywhere away to the right, 'on the port beam' away to the left.
2) that part of a ship's side which lies between the bow and the quarter.
3) a transverse piece of timber joining the ribs and supporting the deck.

Bear away, to: to change course so that the vessel is heading further away from the direction from which the wind is blowing.

Beat: to beat is to sail as nearly as possible into the wind by a series of tacks.

Belay, to: to secure a rope on a cleat or belaying-pin.

Bend, to: to join two ropes to each other, one rope to another object or two objects by means of a rope, as when sails are 'bent' to the yards.

Bermuda rig: standard rig on most modern yachts consisting of mainsail, headsail and no bowsprit. There is no space between mast and sail, the latter being attached to the former by slides fitted into metal grooves.

Berth: 1) a place in which to sleep on board ship.
2) a place in harbour where a ship is moored.
3) a measure of safety as in 'to give a wide berth' to a source of danger.

Bilboes: shackles by which the legs of prisoners were secured.

Bilge: the bottom of a ship's hull, or that part on either side of a ship's keel which has more a horizontal than a vertical direction and upon which the ship would rest if aground. Hence the lowest part of the ship inside the hull is called the bilges, into which the bilge-water drains. This, being foul and noxious, explains the commoner use of the word.

Binnacle: the case or box containing the ship's compass.

Bitts: strong upright timbers coming through the decks to which the ends of ropes and cables could be fastened. The end of the rope fastened to the bitts was called the bitter end, hence the common expression.

Blackbirder: ship employed in the slave trade.

Black Ship: sailing ship built in India of Burmese teak.

Block: a pulley fitted with sheaves to increase the purchase on a rope, and for leading it in a desired direction.

Board: each tack when a ship is sailing against the wind; thus, when tacking across the wind, a ship may be said to make long or short boards. Also in such self-explanatory uses as 'to board', 'to go on board', 'overboard', 'shipboard'.

Bobstay: a chain or rope running from the bowsprit to the stem of a ship to counteract the upward pull of the forestays and headsails of the foremast.

Bollard: large post of wood or metal sunk in the quay to which a ship's mooring lines are made fast.

Bolt-rope: rope sewn round the edge of a sail to prevent fraying.

Bonaventure: an extra mizen sail, obsolete since the 17th century.

Bonnet: an extra strip of canvas laced to the foot of a sail.

Boom: 1) in a square-rigged ship a spar used to extend the foot of a sail.
2) in a fore-and-aft rig a permanent spar at the foot of the mainsail, foresail or mizen, depending on the rig.
3) a floating barrier across the entrance to a harbour.

Bow or Bows: the foremost end or front area of a ship; pronounced to rhyme with cow.

Bowline: 1) a knot used to make a loop at the end of a rope.
2) a rope used to keep the weather edge of a square sail taut when sailing close-hauled to the wind.

Bowsprit: spar projecting over the bows of a vessel and carrying its own sail or sails.

Brace, to: to move the yards of a square-rigged ship so as to present the optimum sail surface to the wind for whatever manoeuvre is desired. The ropes by which the yards are swung are called braces.

Break: a change in the level of the deck.

Bridge: raised superstructure in a steam or motor vessel from which the captain or officer of the watch exercises his command.

Bring-to, to: to take the way off a sailing vessel while her sails are still set.

Bulkhead: a vertical partition dividing a ship into separate compartments.

Bulwarks: the sides of a ship above the upper deck, for protection against heavy seas and to prevent people being washed overboard.

Bunk: built-in wooden bed, often in tiers.

Bunkers: the spaces in a ship in which fuel is stored.

Bunt: the middle part of a square sail cut to form a bag or cavity in order to gather more wind.

Buntlines: ropes attached to the foot ropes of square sails which, when hauled up, spilled the wind out of the sails prior to reefing or furling.

Buoy: anchored floating body used as a guide to navigation or for mooring ships.

Burgee: small triangular or swallow-tailed flag flown by yachts at the masthead for identification and as a wind-vane. Racing burgees are square.

Burgoo: a thick oatmeal gruel or porridge formerly eaten by seamen.

Burthen: term once used as the measure of a ship's carrying capacity, based on the number of tuns of wine she could carry.

Cabin: small room in a ship normally used as a sleeping compartment.

Cable: 1) heavy rope or iron chain attached to the anchor.
2) a measurement of distance at sea, one-tenth of a nautical mile or 200yd (183m), often expressed as 'a cable's length'.

Cap: the wooden piece which connects the top of one mast with the foot of the mast above.

Capstan: cylindrical barrel with concave waist used for hauling in a cable, especially the anchor cable. Formerly worked by hand, now mechanically operated by steam or electricity.

Careen, to: strictly, to lay a ship over on one side so as to get at her bottom for cleaning, repairs or inspection; by extension the act of cleaning itself, also used of a vessel lying over when sailing on the wind: 'she went careening down the harbour'.

Carronade: a very short light carriage gun using a small charge to fire a heavy shot a short distance.

Carvel-built: a wooden vessel in which the side planks are laid flush, as opposed to *clinker-built* in which each plank overlaps the next.

Castles: fighting platforms erected at each end of medieval merchant ships when adapted for war. The names forecastle and aftercastle outlived their original application, the former being still with us, as are the abbreviations 'Fx' and 'Ax', the latter being the quarterdeck.

Cast off, to: to release a rope or cable in order that a ship may proceed to sea.

Cathead: heavy timber projecting from the bow of a ship for securing the anchor when hoisted.

Caulk, to: to make a ship watertight by forcing oakum between the planks and then covering the seams with pitch.

Cavitation: a phenomenon whereby water is forced away from the surface of the propellor with resultant loss of thrust.

Centreboard: a flat board or plate in the hull of a small sailing boat which can be lowered through a slot to reduce sideways movement.

Chains: small platform on either side of the hull to which the shrouds were attached by chains and on which the leadsman stood to take the depth when sailing in shallow water.

Chart: marine map showing coasts, depths, lighthouses, lightships, currents, etc.

Chronometer: highly accurate marine watch formerly essential for ascertaining the degree of longitude.

Claw off, to: to beat to windward to avoid being driven on to a lee shore.

Cleat: small twin-horned metal fitting round which a rope may be hitched.

Clew: the lower aftermost corner of a fore-and-aft sail or either lower corner of a square sail.

Clew up, to: to haul a sail up to the yard, by means of *clew-lines*, ready for furling.

Clews: cords from which a hammock is slung.

Clinker-built: see *carvel-built*.

Close-hauled: said of a vessel with her sails trimmed so that she sails as nearly as possible in the direction from which the wind is blowing.

Coamings: raised edges of any opening in the deck to prevent water running below.

Cockpit: 1) the well of a small sailing vessel where the tiller is located. 2) in old sailing warships a space aft below the lower gundeck which served as quarters for midshipmen and was used as the operating theatre in battle.

Companion Way: stairs leading down from the deck to the cabins or public rooms in a merchant ship.

Conning Tower: originally the armoured control centre of a major warship in time of battle; now used to describe that part of a submarine between the bridge and the hull.

Counter: that part of the stern of a vessel which projects aft above the waterline.

Course: 1) the direction in which a ship proceeds expressed as a measurement in degrees of the variation from north. Hence due east is 090°, due south 180°, etc; also expressed in points of the compass in vessels having only a magnetic compass, e.g. 'a course of East-North-East by East'. 2) the lowest sail on any mast of a square-rigged ship.

Coxswain: (pronounced coxun). 1) helmsman and senior member of a ship's boat, all of which were once known as cockboats, hence the name. 2) the senior petty officer in smaller warships, such as destroyers.

CQR: type of anchor with no stock much favoured by yachtsmen and so called because the letters make much the same sound as 'secure'.

Crank: a ship which lists or heels too easily is said to be crank.

Crimp: one who decoyed men into naval service for so much a head.

Crossing the line: a mock ceremony in which crew or passengers crossing the equator for the first time are ducked in a canvas bath full of sea water before the court of King Neptune.

Crossing the T: naval battle manoeuvre in which one fleet in line ahead formation crosses the line of the enemy fleet, thereby enabling him to bring the full weight of his broadside to bear while the enemy can only fire the bow guns of his leading ships.

Cross-jack: (pronounced crojeck) a sail set on the lower yards of the mizen mast; a mizen course.

Crow's nest: a look-out station on the foremast, originally made from a barrel.

Cutwater: the foremost part of a ship where she meets the water.

Danforth Anchor: American-designed anchor, used by yachtsmen, with the stock across the crown instead of at the end of the shank.

Davits: (pronounced dayvits) small cranes from which a ship's lifeboats are slung.

Dead-eye: a round, laterally-flattened wooden block pierced with three holes used for securing the lower rigging in old ships and so named on account of its resemblance to the human skull.

Dead Reckoning: obtaining the position of a ship without astronomical observation, from the course steered and her speed through the water since the last fixed position, making due allowance for current, tide, wind and leeway.

Deadweight: see *Tonnage*.

Decks: different horizontal levels in a ship, corresponding to storeys in a house.

Deck-house: a small cabin or hut on the upper deck.

Departure: a ship takes her departure not when she leaves port but from the last fixing of her position by sightings of points ashore.

Derelict: any vessel abandoned at sea is legally termed a derelict and can be claimed by whoever brings her into port.

Deviation: the extent to which a ship's compass is deflected from magnetic north by magnetism in the hull and fittings.

Displacement: see *Tonnage*.

Dog Watches: the two two-hour watches between 4pm and 8pm, the other watches being of four hours. The day is thus divided into seven watches which ensures that watchkeepers do not keep the same watches every day. They are known as 'First Dog' and 'Last Dog', *never* 'Second Dog'.

Doldrums: areas close to the equator notable for calms or light and inconsistent winds, hence the expression 'in the doldrums' meaning listless or depressed.

Draught: the depth at which a ship floats in the water, varying, naturally, according to the load carried. See also *Plimsoll Line*.

Draw, to: 1) a sail is said to be drawing when it is full of wind.

2) an indication of *draught* – a ship may be said to draw 20ft (6m), meaning that the vertical distance between the keel and the waterline is 20ft (6m).

Drive, to: a ship is said to drive before the wind when her engines are not powerful enough to hold her against the wind. In the case of a sailing vessel a ship is said to be driven when forced by wind and sea to leeward.

Drogue: a canvas device, shaped like a bucket, towed behind a sailing vessel to reduce her speed, or streamed ahead to keep the bows into the wind when hove to.

Dunnage: timber used in the hold of a merchant ship to keep the cargo in place.

Ensign: 1) the flag flown on the ensign staff of a vessel indicating its nationality.
2) a rank in some navies equivalent to that of midshipman in the Royal Navy.

Entry Port: a hole cut in the side of a ship through which cargo may be loaded or passengers embarked.

Eye: 1) a loop at the end of a rope or wire, usually round a curved piece of metal called a *thimble*, and spliced into itself.
2) the eye of the wind means the exact direction from which it blows.

Fairlead: any fitting which allows a rope to run easily and in the required direction.

Fairway: the navigable channel into an estuary or harbour, usually marked by buoys.

Falls: the ropes used to hoist in or lower a lifeboat or ship's boat from the *davits*.

Fathom: once used as the standard measure of depth of water, the fathom, from the old English word *faedm*, to embrace, was based on the measurement of the outstretched arms of a man and was set at 6ft, but is rapidly being rendered obsolete by the introduction of metrication, the equivalent being 1.8256m.

Fender: anything from old motor tyres to bags of canvas filled with cork hung over the side of a vessel to prevent chafing when coming alongside another ship or a quay.

Fetch, to: to arrive, particularly after a stormy voyage: 'It was the 14 day of October before we could fetch Dartmouth (HAKLUYT).

Fife Rail: railings round the base of a sailing vessel's mast in which are inserted the belaying pins to which the halyards of the sails are secured.

Figurehead: figure, statue, bust or other device attached to a ship's prow immediately under the bowsprit.

Fish, to: 1) to repair a spar by binding on an extra piece of wood, called a fish.
2) to fish an anchor is to haul the *flukes* over the rail.

Fitting-out: the preparation of any vessel to make her ready for sea.

Flag Officer: a Naval officer with the rank of Rear-Admiral or above, entitled to fly his Flag in the ship in which he is exercising his command.

Flagship: ship carrying the admiral or commander-in-chief of a fleet or squadron. The commander of the flagship herself is called the *flag-captain*; also used of the largest or most important ship of a merchant fleet.

Flags of Convenience: device adopted by certain shipping companies of registering their ships in countries where regulations are less strict than those laid down by the major maritime nations, thereby enabling them to save money on taxes, wages, etc.

Flare: the outward curve of the bows of a ship.

Fluke: one of the flat triangular plates at the end of each arm of an anchor.

Flush Deck: a continuous deck running on the same plane from fore to aft.

Flying Jib: The foremost and smallest of the triangular sails set on the bowsprit and jib booms of vessels large enough to take it.

Foot: the bottom edge of a sail.

Footropes: the ropes set under the yards on which men stand when handling square sails.

Fore-and-Aft rig: rigged with sails that lie along the ship's length.

Forecastle: (pronounced fō'c'sle): the forward end of the upper deck; formerly loosely used to denote the crew's quarters; see also *Castle*.

Foremast: the mast nearest to the bows, but, in a two-masted ship, only if the other mast is taller.

Forward: (pronounced forrard): an unspecific way of denoting any part of a vessel nearer to the bows than where one happens to be; also used as an adjective – forward gangway, forward cargo hatch.

Frames: the ribs of a ship, set at right-angles to the keel.

Freeboard: the vertical distance between the waterline and the upper deck level.

Freight: cargo carried in a ship or the payment for such carriage.

Furl, to: to gather up the sails and make them secure to the mast or yard.

Gaff: a spar of which the lower end runs up and down the mast of a fore-and-aft rigged vessel, and which is secured to the head of a four-sided sail.

Gage or Gauge: to have the weather gauge of another ship means to be to windward of her, to have the lee gauge to be to leeward, a matter of vital importance in battles between sailing ships.

Gallery: covered platform running round the stern of a sailing warship, usually outside the admiral's or captain's cabin. Some of the earlier battleships had small galleries known as 'The Admiral's Walk'.

Galley: the ship's kitchen.

Gallows: wooden frames in which spare booms and spars were stored in square-rigged ships.

Gammoning: the lashing which secures the bowsprit to the stem.

Gangway: specifically, the moveable passageway by which passengers and crew embark or disembark; loosely, any unobstructed passageway, hence, 'Make a gangway there!'

Garboard Strake: the plank alongside the keel; in steel ships the plates next to the keel are called the garboard plates.

Gasket: short length of rope used to secure a sail when furled to a yard or boom.

Gimbals: two concentric metal rings so mounted as to hold a compass, lamp or small stove level, irrespective of the motion of the ship.

Gooseneck: a metal fitting which attaches the boom, gaff or spar of a sailing vessel to the mast, while still allowing free lateral and vertical movement.

Goosewinged: in fore-and-aft rigged sailing craft sailing down wind with the mainsail boomed out on one side and the jib on the other in order to present the maximum sail area to the wind.

Graving: cleaning the outside of a ship's hull below the waterline, hence a graving dock, now synonymous with a dry-dock.

Great Circle Sailing: charting and following the shortest distance between two points on the earth's surface. To demonstrate that this is not as simple as it sounds, one has only to draw a line between two points on an atlas, then connect the same two points with a

The Sails and Running Rigging.

THE SAILS.

▲ 1. Fore-sail.
▲ 2. Fore lower topsail.
▲ 3. Fore upper topsail.
▲ 4. Fore lower topgallant sail.
▲ 5. Fore upper topgallant sail.
▲ 6. Fore-royal.
▲ 7. Main-sail.
▲ 8. Main lower topsail.
▲ 9. Main upper topsail.
▲ 10. Main lower topgallant sail.
▲ 11. Main upper topgallant sail.
▲ 12. Main royal.
▲ 13. Crossjack.
▲ 14. Mizzen lower topsail.
▲ 15. Mizzen upper topsail.
▲ 16. Mizzen lower topgallant sail.
▲ 17. Mizzen upper topgallant sail.
▲ 18. Mizzen-royal.
▲ 19. Fore-topmast stay-sail.
▲ 20. Inner-jib.
▲ 21. Outer-jib.
▲ 22. Flying-jib.
▲ 23. Main-topmast stay-sail.
▲ 24. Main-topgallant stay-sail.
▲ 25. Main royal stay-sail.
▲ 26. Mizzen-topmast stay-sail.
▲ 27. Mizzen-topgallant stay-sail.
▲ 28. Mizzen-royal stay-sail.
▲ 29. Jigger stay-sail.
▲ 30. Jigger middle stay-sail.
▲ 31. Jigger-topmast stay-sail.
▲ 32. Jigger-topgallant stay-sail.
▲ 33. Jigger.
▲ 34. Gaff topsail.

THE RUNNING RIGGING.

1. Fore-tack.
2. Fore-sheet.
3. Fore clew-garnet.
4. Fore-braces.
5. Fore lower topsail sheet.
6. Fore lower topsail clew-lines.
7. Fore lower topsail braces.
8. Fore upper topsail sheets.
9. Fore upper topsail clew-lines.
10. Fore upper topsail braces.
11. Fore lower topgallant sheet.
12. Fore lower topgallant clew-lines.
13. Fore lower topgallant braces.
14. Fore upper topgallant sheet.
15. Fore upper topgallant clew-lines.
16. Fore upper topgallant braces.
17. Fore-royal sheet.
18. Fore royal clew-lines.
19. Fore-royal braces.
20. Fore-topsail halyards.
21. Fore-topgallant halyards.
22. Fore-royal halyards.
23. Fore-signal halyards.
24. Fore reef-tackles.
25. Fore-topsail reef-tackles.
26. Main-tack.
27. Main-sheet.
28. Main clew-garnet.
29. Main-brace.
30. Main lower topsail sheet.
31. Main lower topsail clew-lines.
32. Main lower topsail brace.
33. Main upper topsail sheet.
34. Main upper topsail clew-lines.
35. Main upper topsail braces.
36. Main lower topgallant sheet.
37. Main lower topgallant clew-lines.
38. Main lower topgallant braces.
39. Main upper topgallant sheet.
40. Main upper topgallant clew-lines.
41. Main upper topgallant brace.
42. Main-royal sheet.
43. Main-royal clew-lines.
44. Main royal braces.
45. Main-topsail halyards.
46. Main-topgallant halyards.
47. Main-royal halyards.
48. Main signal-halyards.
49. Main reef-tackles.
50. Main-topsail reef-tackles.
51. Crossjack tack.
52. Crossjack sheet.
53. Crossjack clew-garnet.
54. Crossjack braces.
55. Mizzen lower topsail clew-lines.
56. Mizzen lower topsail braces.
57. Mizzen upper topsail sheet.
58. Mizzen upper topsail clew-lines.
59. Mizzen upper topsail braces.
60. Mizzen lower topgallant sheet.
61. Mizzen lower topgallant clew-lines.
62. Mizzen lower topgallant braces.
63. Mizzen upper topgallant sheet.
64. Mizzen upper topgallant clew-lines.
65. Mizzen upper topgallant braces.
66. Mizzen-royal sheet.
67. Mizzen-royal clew-lines.
68. Mizzen-royal braces.
69. Mizzen-topsail halyards.
70. Mizzen-topgallant halyards.
71. Mizzen-royal halyards.
72. Mizzen-signal halyards.
73. Crossjack reef-tackles.
74. Mizzen-topsail reef-tackles.
75. Jigger peak-halyards.
76. Jigger brails.
77. Jigger gaff-topsail sheet.
78. Ensign halyards.
79. British ensign.
80. Gaff-topsail halyards.
81. Vangs.
82. Jigger outhaul.
83. Boom topping lift.
84. Boom guys.
85. Boom sheet.
86. Flying-jib sheet.
87. Outer-jib sheet.
88. Inner-jib sheet.
89. Fore-topmast stay-sail sheet.
90. Fore-bowline.
91. Main-topmast stay-sail sheet.
92. Main-topgallant stay-sail sheet.
93. Main-royal stay-sail sheet.
94. Mizzen-topmast stay-sail sheet.
95. Mizzen-topgallant stay-sail sheet.
96. Mizzen-royal stay-sail sheet.
97. Jigger stay-sail sheet.

The Hull, Spars, and Standing Rigging.

THE HULL.

1. Head.
2. Cutwater.
3. Bow.
4. Forecastle-deck.
5. Stern.
6. Rudder.
7. Fore-chains.
8. Main-chains.
9. Mizzen-chains.
10. Bulwarks.
11. Poop-deck.
12. Gun-ports.
13. Trail-boards.
14. Cat-head.
15. Head-rails.
16. Capstan.
17. Skylight.
18. Light-boards.
19. Foredeck-house.
20. Life-boats.
21. Gig.
22. Companion.
23. Skylight.
24. Wheel-box.
25. Poop-rails.
26. Afterdeck-house.

THE SPARS.

27. Bowsprit.
28. Inner jib-boom.
29. Outer jib-boom.
30. Flying jib-boom.
31. Martingale.
32. Fore-mast.
33. Fore-topmast.
34. Fore-topgallant mast.
35. Fore-royal mast.
36. Main-mast.
37. Main-topmast.
38. Main-topgallant mast.
39. Main-royal mast.
40. Mizzen-mast.
41. Mizzen-topmast.
42. Mizzen-topgallant mast.

43. Mizzen-royal mast.
44. Jigger-mast.
45. Jigger-topmast.
46. Jigger-topgallant mast.
47. Fore-yard.
48. Fore lower topsail yard.
49. Fore upper topsail yard.
50. Fore lower topgallant yard.
51. Fore upper topgallant yard.
52. Fore-royal yard.
53. Main-yard.
54. Main lower topsail yard.
55. Main upper topsail yard.
56. Main lower topgallant yard.
57. Main upper topgallant yard.
58. Main-royal yard.
59. Crossjack yard.
60. Mizzen lower topsail yard.
61. Mizzen upper topsail yard.
62. Mizzen lower topgallant yard.
63. Mizzen upper topgallant yard.
64. Mizzen-royal yard.
65. Jigger-gaff.
66. Jigger-boom.
67. Fore-top.
68. Main-top.
69. Mizzen-top.
70. Jigger-top.
71. Fore-doublings.
72. Fore-mast cap.
73. Fore-topmast cross-trees.
74. Fore-topmast cap.
75. Ensign.
76. Company's flag.

THE STANDING RIGGING.

A 1. Bobstay.
A 2. Bowsprit-shroud.
A 3. Martingale-stay.
A 4. Jib-boom guys.
A 5. Fore-stays.
A 6. Fore-topmast stays.
A 7. Inner-jib stay.
A 8. Outer-jib stay.
A 9. Flying-jib stay.
A 10. Fore-royal stay.
A 11. Fore-rigging.
A 12. Fore-topmast rigging.
A 13. Fore-topgallant rigging.
A 14. Fore-cap back-stay.
A 15. Fore-topmast back-stays.
A 16. Fore-topgallant back-stays.
A 17. Fore-royal back-stay.
A 18. Fore-lift.
A 19. Fore-topsail lift.
A 20. Fore-topgallant lift.
A 21. Fore-royal lift.
A 22. Main-stays.
A 23. Main-topmast stays.
A 24. Main-topgallant stays.
A 25. Main-royal stays.
A 26. Main-rigging.
A 27. Main-topmast rigging.
A 28. Main-topgallant rigging.
A 29. Main-cap back-stay.
A 30. Main-topmast back-stays.
A 31. Main-topgallant back-stays.
A 32. Main-royal back-stays.
A 33. Main-lift.
A 34. Main-topsail lift.
A 35. Main-topgallant lift.
A 36. Main-royal lift.
A 37. Mizzen-stays.
A 38. Mizzen topmast stays.
A 39. Mizzen-topgallant stay.
A 40. Mizzen-royal stay.

A 41. Mizzen-rigging.
A 42. Mizzen-topmast rigging.
A 43. Mizzen-topgallant rigging.
A 44. Mizzen-cap back-stay.
A 45. Mizzen-topmast back-stays.
A 46. Mizzen-topgallant back-stays.
A 47. Mizzen-royal back-stays.
A 48. Crossjack lift.
A 49. Mizzen-topsail lift.
A 50. Mizzen-topgallant lift.
A 51. Mizzen-royal lift.
A 52. Jigger-stays.
A 53. Jigger middle stay.
A 54. Jigger-topmast stay.
A 55. Jigger-topgallant stay.
A 56. Jigger-rigging.
A 57. Jigger-topmast rigging.
A 58. Jigger-topmast back-stays.
A 59. Jigger-topgallant back-stays.

piece of cotton on a globe and compare the results.

Gripe, to: a sailing ship which has a tendency to come up into the wind in spite of the helm is said to gripe.

Gripes: ropes or canvas bands used to hold ship's boats securely under the davits.

Gudgeon: the metal plate attached to the stern of a small boat through the eye of which the pintle of a detachable rudder is inserted.

Gunport: hole cut in the side of a wooden man-of-war through which the broadside guns were fired.

Gunroom: sub-lieutenants' and midshipmens' mess.

Gunwale: (pronounced gunnel). 1) the strength member running along the top of a ship's or boat's side.
2) loosely, and generally, applied to the top of the side, including any extension above the gunwale proper, such as coamings or washstrakes, designed to increase the angle to which the vessel can be heeled before water can come inboard.

Guy: any wire, chain or rope used to control the movement of a spar or boom.

Gybe, to: to allow the stern of a sailing vessel to pass through the wind when sailing before the wind, so that the sails in a fore-and-aft rig move from one side of the vessel to the other. This is an unintentional and potentially dangerous manoeuvre. See *Wear*, which is a controlled gybe, intentionally carried out.

Half-deck: 1) traditionally the living space allowed to apprentices in sailing ships, usually in the waist of the vessel.
2) now applied to any deck which extends over only part of a ship.

Halyard: any rope or tackle used for hoisting a sail or flag.

Hammock: a hanging bed made of canvas (see p. 20).

Hand: a member of a ship's crew, as in 'All hands on deck'.

Hatch: an opening to allow passage for goods or people either through the upper deck or from one deck to another.

Haul, to: usually to pull, as in 'haul away', or, in a different sense, to haul out of the line, meaning to pull out of a line of ships. A ship hauls her wind when she is brought closer to it.

Hawsehole – Hawsepipe: the aperture and passage in the bows of a ship through which the anchor cable passes. 'To come up through the hawse-hole'

used to be naval slang for promotion from the lower deck to commissioned rank.

Head: the top edge of a four-sided sail.

Heads: lavatory – see *Beakhead*.

Heave-to, to: to bring a sailing ship to a standstill by setting the sails in such a fashion that they counteract each other. A steamship is said to be hove to when her engines balance the force of the wind and sea and she can hold her position safely in a storm.

Heel: 1) the point where the keel joins the sternpost.
2) the lower end of a mast or upright spar; the inboard end of a boom or bowsprit.
3) the angle from the vertical to which a vessel leans when the wind pushes her over sideways. It should not be confused with a list, which is permanent, nor with a roll, which is spasmodic. Also used as a verb – 'The *Mary Rose* began to heel, that is to say to lean heavily to one side' (J. Hooker 1575).

Helm: the handle, or tiller, by which the rudder is managed: in larger ships the steering wheel.

Hogging: hogging occurs when a vessel is supported by the sea amidships, while the bow and stern hang over the trough.

Hold: the interior cavity of a ship where the cargo is stowed.

Hull: the body of a ship without her superstructure or rigging. Thus a ship is said to be 'hull down' when only her superstructure can be seen above the horizon.

In Irons: 1) a sailing ship is said to be in irons if she has been allowed to come head to the wind without sufficient momentum to carry her through on to the other tack. If at the same time way is lost and the rudder is therefore ineffective, it is difficult to cause her to fall off the wind in either direction. She is therefore helpless and drifting until special measures are taken.
2) put in shackles as a punishment. See also bilboes.

Irish Hurricane: sailors' term for a flat calm.

Jackstaff: small pole at the bow on which the national flag, or jack, is hoisted when at anchor.

Jackstay: 1) a rope or iron rod running parallel with the yard on which the head of a square sail is bent.
2) any wire or rope used to secure something.

Jamming cleat: a ridged sprung slot into which a rope can be jammed to hold it taut.

Jib: a triangular sail set before the foremast, of which there may be as many as four – from forward, flying jib, outer jib, inner jib and jib.

Jib-boom: a spar running forward from the bowsprit on which the jib is spread.

Jolly Roger: there is, in fact, no evidence that pirates ever flew a flag bearing a white skull and crossbones on a black ground.

Jury: any temporary contrivance designed to get a disabled vessel back to harbour, as in jury mast, jury rig, jury rudder.

Kedge: a small anchor laid away from the ship and used for *warping* or moving over a short distance by hauling against the anchor, usually from one harbour berth to another.

Keel: the backbone of any vessel. In wooden ships the keel is the lowest continuous longitudinal timber and runs the whole length of the vessel. In a steel or iron ship the keel is the lowest continual line of plates.

Keelson: an internal keel above the timbers, bolted down to the keel itself, to which it gives additional strength.

Kentledge: pig-iron cast as permanent ballast and laid over the keelson plates to give a ship added stability.

Kevel: a large form of *cleat*, usually on the gunwhale of a sailing ship.

Kicking Strap: a rope from the boom to the base of the mast which prevents the boom from lifting too high.

Knees: pieces of right-angled metal or timber which connect the ribs of a vessel to her beams, the stem to the keel or the thwarts to the frames.

Knot: the unit of measurement of a ship's speed, one knot being a speed of one nautical mile per hour. A nautical mile is traditionally defined as the length of a minute of the arc of a great circle of the earth, but as this length varies in different latitudes, owing to the fact that the earth is not a perfect sphere, it has been rounded off at 6080ft (1.8532km). A knot is specifically a measure of speed and cannot be used to express distance.

Lagan: goods cast overboard and marked with a buoy so that they may be recovered later; a ruse once frequently used by smugglers.

Larboard: the old word for the port or left-hand side of a ship, when looking forward.

Lateen sail: triangular sail laced to a long yard which is hoisted up the mast, so that the upper end is raised in the air and the lower brought down to form the tack. The word comes from the French *voile latine* (Latin sail) because of its wide use in the Mediterranean.

Lay days: the days allowed for the loading and unloading of the cargo of a merchant ship.

Lead: (pronounced 'led') device used for discovering the depth of water at sea. The lead weighs between 7 and 14lb (3 and 6kg), is conical in shape and has a cavity at the lower end filled with tallow which tells the leadsmen the nature of the seabed. The lead line is marked off at intervals of 2, 3, 5, 7, 10, 13, 15, 17 and 20 fathoms with standard marks (strips of leather, canvas, serge, etc.) so that the leadsman can read off the depth in the dark. The deep sea leadline can measure depths of up to about 100 fathoms.

Lee: the lee side is the side away from the wind. Thus the lee side of a vessel is the opposite side to that on which the wind is blowing. A lee shore, however, is a shore to leeward of a vessel and therefore a shore on which the wind is blowing from the sea.

Leeboards: large hinged boards fitted to the side of a flat-bottomed sailing vessel to act as a keel.

Leech: the outer edges of a square sail; the after edge of a fore-and-aft sail.

Leeway: the sideways drift from a desired course occasioned by the wind. Hence the expression 'he has a lot of leeway to make up', meaning 'he's got much to do in order to get back on course'.

Lie-to, to: a sailing ship is said to lie-to when she comes almost to a standstill nearly head to wind, just keeping steerage way with her sails full.

Lifts: ropes, later chains or wires, which reach from each masthead to the respective yardarms to steady and suspend the ends.

Line: 1) the equator is referred to as the Line.
2) line abreast – ships formed up abeam of each other.
3) line ahead – ships formed up in single file.
4) line of battle – ships formed up for battle.
5) ship of the line – a sailing warship with sufficient gunpower to take her place in the line of battle.

List: prolonged inclination of a ship to one side or the other, often caused by shifting cargo.

Lizard: a short piece of rope with an eye or thimble spliced into one end of it to enable it to run along another rope.

Lodestone: nautical term for magnetite, an oxide of iron with magnetic properties – hence, figuratively, a guide.

Log: 1) the book in which is recorded all information relating to a ship's progress, including details of weather, course, speed, behaviour of the crew, etc. The keeping of a log book is compulsory and it must be submitted to the appropriate authority at the end of a voyage.
2) any apparatus for measuring the speed of a ship. Most ships today have electro-magnetic logs but for centuries the commonest way of ascertaining a ship's speed was to unreel a logline over the stern, to the end of which was attached a floating log-ship, and relate the knots tied in the logline at specified intervals to the running time of a sandglass. For this reason a ship's speed is still expressed in knots.

Loose-footed: a fore-and-aft sail which is set without a boom.

Luff: 1) as a noun, the leading edge of a fore-and-aft sail.
2) as a verb, to alter course so that the ship is heading nearer to the wind.

Lugsail: a four-sided sail bent upon a yard which is slung at about one-third or one-fourth of its length from one end so that it hangs obliquely.

Mainsail: principal sail of a sailing vessel: in a square-rigged ship the mainsail is the lowest sail on the mainmast.

Mark: the distinguishing attachments on a leadline are called marks. Thus, if the leadsman sees a piece of white canvas on the surface when the lead touches the bottom, he will call out, 'By the mark, five'. The unmarked fathoms are called deeps. See also *lead*.

Martingale: stay under the jib-boom which counteracts the pull of the fore topgallant stay; also used, less accurately, to describe any line or wire which is used to hold a spar down.

Mast: in sailing ships, the vertical pole which supports the sails; in mechanically propelled ships the mast carries aerials, radar equipment, etc.

Master: 1) once the rank held by the officer solely responsible for the navigation of a warship, obsolete since the late 19th century.
2) the title usually given to the captain of a merchant ship.

Mate: 1) once a rank in the British Navy, first as a grade of petty officer, later to describe an officer commissioned from the lower deck.
2) in the Merchant Navy officers junior to the Master are called mates; thus the chief officer is known as the First Mate.

Midshipman: originally ratings quartered amidships whose duties included boarding and entering enemy ships, now applied to young officers still wholly or partly under training before they are commissioned.

Mizen or **Mizzen**: the aftermost mast of a three-masted vessel or of a two-masted vessel if the foremost mast is the main mast.

Muster, to: to assemble all the crew of a warship on deck and conduct a roll-call. The ship's muster means all those on board, the list of whose names is kept in the muster-book.

Navicert: a certificate issued in time of war by a belligerent power to the master of a neutral merchant vessel exempting his ship from search or seizure.

Nettings: 1) spaces on the upper deck of sailing warships enclosed with rope netting in which hammocks were stored by day.
2) nets rigged horizontally above the upper deck of a sailing warship to prevent injury to the crew from falling masts or spars shot away in battle.

Nipper: in large warships on which the anchor cable was too thick to be wound round the capstan it was hauled in by binding it to an endless rope which ran round the capstan and two blocks set forward. The short lengths of rope used for this were called nippers, as were the younger members of the crew who performed the task; hence the expression 'a smart nipper'.

Number One: colloquial name in the Royal Navy for the First Lieutenant, by which he may properly be addressed. In lower-deck parlance he is referred to, but not addressed as, Jimmy-the-One.

Offing: the safe distance between a ship and the land. 'In the offing' means that a vessel may be seen from the shore.

Ordinary: in the days of sailing warships a vessel was said to be 'in ordinary' when she was out of commission and laid up in a harbour or dockyard.

Orlop deck: the lowest deck of an old sailing warship, from the Dutch word *overloopen*, to run over (the beams).

Otter: a board attached to a line and set at an angle so that it is forced outward when towed behind a ship. It was used by minesweepers and is still used by trawlers to spread their nets. The name derives from the fact that it was originally used by salmon fishers and otters prey on salmon.

Outrigger: 1) a log or beam attached by spars and running parallel to the hull of various native craft found in the Pacific and Indian Oceans to give added stability.
2) an extension to the stays on larger sailing vessels.
3) temporary beams fitted to the sides of sailing vessels to which extra shrouds were attached to take the added strain imposed on the masts when the ship was tilted on her side to be careened.
4) a metal stay attached to the outside of a rowing boat on which the oar rests.

Overhaul, to: 1) one ship overhauls another; it does not overtake.
2) also used in the conventional sense to describe the examination and repair of machinery, equipment, etc., though the more accepted term for this procedure is 'refit'.

Painter: a short length of rope used to secure a boat to a pier or jetty.

Paravane: a device invented during the First World War for minesweeping. The paravane works on the same principle as the otter and is equipped with wirecutters which sever the mooring wire of the mine, allowing it to float to the surface where it can be exploded.

Parbuckle: an arrangement of ropes used for hoisting or lowering heavy cylindrical objects over the side of a ship.

Passage: a sea journey between two ports, hence 'to work one's passage'.

Pay, to: to apply some form of varnish, waterproofing substance or preservative to the hull or masts of a vessel.

Pay off, to: 1) to fall away to leeward when tacking.
2) to pay and discharge the crew of a merchant ship at the end of a voyage.

Pay out, to: to slacken a rope or cable so that it can run out at the speed desired.

Pendant: now more normally spelt, and always pronounced, pennant, originally the long narrow streamer flown from the masthead top or yardarm of 15th and 16th century warships, now used for signalling. A Commissioning Pendant is flown at the masthead of warships commanded by commissioned officers. In the Royal Navy it is white with a red cross.

Pennant Numbers: the letter and number painted on the sides of ships of the Royal Navy are called Pennant Numbers. The letter denotes the class of ship: S: submarine; C: cruiser; D: destroyer; F: frigate, etc. It is the custom to 'Make your pennant number' to the senior officer present when joining a Command, as a form of reporting for duty, hence the expression 'I must make my number with so-and-so'.

Petty Officer: the naval equivalent of a sergeant; the word petty derives from the French *petit*–small.

Pilot: a person, not belonging to any particular ship, licensed to conduct ships through certain rivers, roadsteads or channels or into certain ports and taken on board at a particular place for that purpose only.

Pinch, to: to sail a vessel so close to the wind that she loses speed.

Pipe down: the pipe (order) on a boatswain's call (whistle) indicating that the hands are to turn in; since this results in silence the expression has come to mean 'keep quiet' or 'stop talking'.

Pitch: a distillation of coal tar used for sealing the gaps between planks on the deck or sides of a vessel.

Pitch, to: a ship is said to pitch when a wave lifts her bows and then her stern so that she tilts successively backwards and then forwards.

Plain sailing: the earliest navigational charts were drawn on the assumption that the world was flat and were therefore drawn on a plane, of which plain in this context is a corruption. Since this simple form of navigation paid no heed to its inherent error, the expression came to mean anything easy and uncomplicated.

Plane, to: a boat is said to plane when its bows are lifted clear of the water, a phenomenon which only occurs in small, fast sailing craft and power-driven boats, of which the ultimate outcome in this respect is the hydrofoil.

Plates: name given to the steel sheets once riveted but now welded together to form the sides and deck of a ship.

Plimsoll Line: a mark, also known as the load-line, painted on the sides of all British merchant ships which indicates the six different draught levels to which a cargo ship may be loaded under varying conditions. It takes its name from Samuel Plimsoll (1824–98), who introduced the bill which resulted in the passing of the Merchant Shipping Act in 1876.

Point: a division of the 32 points into which the magnetic compass card is divided, equal to $11\frac{1}{4}°$.

Pole mast: a mast made in one piece.

Poop: 1) a vessel is said to be pooped when a wave breaks over her stern.
2) a raised deck right aft of a ship, an evolution of the aftercastle.

Port: 1) the left hand side of a vessel when looking towards the bows, formerly known as the larboard side, but changed officially in 1844 to avoid confusion with starboard.
2) a harbour offering some shelter and usually having facilities for loading and unloading passengers and cargo.
3) an opening in the side of a ship, as in gunport or porthole, though the correct nautical term for the latter is scuttle.

Post-Captain: an old rank in the Royal Navy which signified that the ship entitled the captain to carry a master who was responsible for the navigation.

Powder-Monkey: a ship's boy who carried the gunpowder from the powder magazine to the guns, a task in which he was assisted by any women who happened to be on board.

Pressgang: name given to the detachment of men commissioned to execute the impressment of men for service. Impressment, though in abeyance, is still legal.

Prize: a prize ship or enemy ship captured in time of war traditionally became the property of the Crown, though a proportion of the prize-money, the proceeds of the sale of the vessel and its cargo, were distributed to the crew, after she had undergone the legal process of being condemned in prize.

Purchase: a mechanical device whereby a rope is passed round a number of pulleys mounted in blocks in order to increase its lifting power.

Purser: the name by which paymasters were once known in the Royal Navy and still used, particularly in passenger-carrying ships, to describe the officer in charge of financial matters relating to the passengers.

Quarter: anything lying abaft the transverse centre-line of a vessel may be said to be on the port or starboard quarter.

Quarterdeck: originally the after-part of the upper deck before the poop, the name is now given to that part of the upper deck abaft the upper superstructure. In medieval British warships the quarterdeck housed a religious shrine to which the sailors doffed their caps when they passed and from this evolved the practice of saluting the quarterdeck which survives in British warships to this day.

Quartermaster: senior rating who is responsible for stowage, steering and soundings of a ship.

Quoin: wedge pushed under the breech of a cannon in sailing ships to elevate or depress the muzzle.

Raffee Sail: a small sail set above the skysails on square-rigged ships.

Rake: 1) the degree to which masts or funnels incline from the perpendicular. 2) the projection of the stem or stern beyond the length of the keel.

Randan: an arrangement of three oarsmen whereby stroke and bow each pull one oar and the centre man pulls two.

Rate: see p. 74.

Rating: 1) term loosely used to describe a seaman on a warship. Correctly the word, being the present participle of the verb 'to rate', means the classification of men into rates or grades. 2) a calculation of a yacht's performance relative to that of another, based on the yacht's specifications, not its performance.

Ratlines: the ropes which run horizontally across the shrouds forming the rungs of the ladder.

Reach: 1) a stretch of navigable water on a river or estuary. 2) a sailing term, used either as a verb or a noun, used to describe the point of sailing of a vessel when she is sailing free with the wind on or just before the beam.

Red Ensign: the flag of the British Merchant Navy, known familiarly as the Red Duster.

Reef: a narrow ridge or chain of rocks, shingle, sand or coral at or near the surface of the sea and usually a serious danger to shipping.

Reef, to: to reduce the area of a sail by gathering or rolling up part of it and securing it by reef-points, short lengths of rope set in reef-bands, which are strips of extra canvas running horizontally across a sail.

Relieving Tackle: 1) tackle used to hold a ship securely at the right angle when being careened on a beach. 2) name given to purchases rigged on either side of the tiller of a sailing ship

to ease the strain in heavy seas when steering was impossible by manpower alone.

Rig: the arrangement of a ship's masts and sails is referred to as her rig and determines what type of ship she is. By extension the clothing of both officers and men is referred to as their rig.

Rigging: a word which embraces the entire system of wires, chains and ropes used to support the masts and handle the sails. It may be divided into two kinds, standing rigging and running rigging, the former being used to support the masts and yards and fixed permanently in position, the latter being used to handle the ship.

Rowlock: (pronounced rollock) U-shaped indentation in the gunwale of a rowing boat which acts as a fulcrum for the oar. The metal fitting used in small rowing boats and shaped like a wine glass with no base is often incorrectly called a rowlock. Its correct name is a crutch.

Rudder: vertical plate fitted to the stern of a ship below the waterline. When the angle of the rudder is altered the pressure of the water causes the ship to change course.

Run: 1) the afterpart of a ship's hull below the water. If it offers little resistance to the water the ship is said to have a clean run. 2) used in a variety of other senses, mostly self-explanatory, such as a) the day's run, b) the run to Rio, c) the sea was running high, d) to run into harbour, e) to run down another vessel f) to run up a flag, g) to run out the guns, h) to smuggle, as in gun-running, i) to break out, as in running a blockade, j) to run aground. 3) a sailing vessel is said to be running free when sailing with the wind blowing from within a point or two of dead astern.

Sag: 1) a downward curve in the centre of the hull. The opposite of hogging (q.v.). 2) a ship is said to sag away to leeward or windward if she has a tendency to drift in one direction.

Sail: a piece of cloth cut to a particular shape so that when hoisted on a mast it will be best able to catch the wind and drive the vessel forward. See diagram on p. 246 for names of sails.

Samson Posts: mast-like structures on merchant ships fitted with derricks for handling cargo. They look like and are known as goalposts.

Scantlings: the relative dimensions of

all parts of a ship's hull laid down and published by Lloyd's to ensure maximum safety.

Scupper, to: deliberately to sink a ship by blowing a hole in her hull below the waterline or by opening the seacocks. To scuttle a ship means the same.

Scuppers: holes cut in the bulwarks of a ship to allow water on deck to drain away over the side.

Scuttle: correct name for the 'window' in the side of a ship familiarly known as a porthole.

Scuttle, to: same as to scupper.

Sea Anchor: anything, such as a sail or a barrel, attached to a long line and thrown overboard during a storm in order to help a vessel keep her head to the wind, and to reduce drift downwind.

Seams: the small spaces deliberately left between the planks forming the hull and deck of wooden vessels. When the planks get wet they expand and compress the oakum packed between them, thereby making the vessel more watertight.

Seize, to: to bind together with light cord, usually said of seizing one rope to another.

Set Sail, to: mechanically propelled ships are still said to set sail when they set out on a voyage.

Sextant: navigational instrument used for measuring vertical and horizontal angles in order to ascertain one's position at sea.

Shackle: 1) U-shaped piece of iron with a bolt across the open end used to secure anchor cables, rigging, etc. 2) the name given to the length of a chain cable between each joining shackle. 1 shackle = 12½ fathoms. 8 shackles = 100 fathoms or 1 cable.

Shakes: the staves of a cask after it has been taken apart; hence the expression 'no great shakes' meaning of little value or importance.

Shanghai, to: a man is said to have been shanghaied when he has been rendered insensible by means of drink or drugs and comes to to find himself part of the crew of an outward-bound ship. The origin of the word is obscure.

Shank: the main part of an anchor which connects the arms to the ring.

Sheave: the grooved metal wheel in a block round which the rope runs.

Sheer: 1) the upward curve of the deck of a ship from the lowest point amidships rising to stem and stern. If, as in some yachts, the highest point is amidships and the deck falls away to stem and stern it is called reverse sheer.

2) to sheer away means to move away from, particularly in the context of one ship turning away from another.

Sheers or **Sheerlegs**: two or three spars lashed together at the top, with a tackle secured to that point, to act as a temporary derrick.

Sheer strake: the line of plates or planks immediately below the gunwale.

Sheet: the rope securing the clew, or lower corner, of a sail. A square sail has two sheets, a fore-and-aft sail only one.

Sheet anchor: an additional anchor carried as an extra measure of security. The term has thus come to be used to imply reliability in any field.

Ship: generic term now used to describe any sea-going vessel, though in the narrowest sense it means a square-rigged sailing ship with three or more masts, which may properly be described as ship-rigged.

Ship of the line: a sailing warship carrying enough guns to enable her to take her place in the line of battle.

Ship, to: to take on board, as in 'ship the outboard motor', 'ship the rudder'.

Shrouds: the ropes running from the mastheads to the ship's sides supporting the masts.

Skysail: sail set above the Royal.

Sound: 1) a stretch of water mostly enclosed by land but with access to the open sea, as in Plymouth Sound. *The Sound* is the strait leading from the Kattegat to the Baltic Sea.
2) to measure the depth of water under a ship.
3) a whale is said to sound when it dives deep.

Sounding: the act of measuring the depth of water under a ship, formerly done with a lead and line, now with an echo sounder or sounding machine.

Spanker: fore-and-aft sail set on the mizen mast to take advantage of a following wind.

Spar Deck: originally a temporary deck, now used to describe the upper deck of a flush-decked ship.

Spinnaker: large, three-cornered sail cut to balloon out well, rigged before all headsails and used when running before the wind; mostly used on racing yachts.

Splice, to: to join two ropes or wires together by inlaying the strands and relaying them according to the nature of the splice required.

Splice the mainbrace, to: to issue an extra tot of rum, in the days when every sailor in the Royal Navy received a ration of rum daily.

Sprit: a long spar which stretches diagonally across a four-sided fore-and-aft sail from the base of the mast to the peak of the sail.

Spritsail: 1) small, square sail set on a yard beneath the bowsprit in square-rigged ships. A spritsail topsail was set on a small mast rising perpendicularly from the end of the bowsprit.
2) a four-sided fore-and-aft sail set on a sprit, as found on barges.

Square-rigged: having the principal sails extended on yards suspended at the middle horizontally from the mast.

Starboard: the right-hand side of a vessel when looking towards the bows. The word is a corruption of steer-board and goes back to the days before the invention of the hanging rudder when ships were steered with a steering oar or board which was positioned on the starboard quarter.

Staves: the component planks of a wooden pail or barrel.

Stay: 1) part of the standing rigging of a sailing vessel which supports the masts from fore-and-aft, as opposed to shrouds which support the mast from side to side. Backstays support a mast from aft, forestays from forward, and are further identified by the mast they support, as in main topmast backstay.
2) used in connection with an anchor, which is said to be at short stay if it is close under the bows and the cable is at a steep angle, or at long stay if it is well away from the bows.
3) to stay a sailing vessel is to bring her head up to the wind in order to tack or go about. At the moment she is head to the wind, she is said to be in stays; if she fails to go about and falls back on the original tack, she is said to have missed stays. See also *In Irons*.

Stay sail: triangular fore-and-aft sail set on a stay.

Steerage: large space below deck used in the 19th century to provide inferior accommodation for emigrants.

Steeve: the angle of the bowsprit from the horizontal.

Step: square socket of metal or wood fixed to the keelson, into which the heel of the mast is fitted. To step a mast is to erect it.

Stern: the after end of a vessel.

Sternpost: the principal timber or casting in the after part of a ship.

Stock: the horizontal crossbar of an anchor at the other end of the shank to the arms. Most modern anchors no longer have stocks.

Strake: a single continuous line of

planking running from stem to stern of a wooden vessel.

Strike, to: to take down or lower, as in to strike colours, once the customary gesture of surrender.

Studdingsail: (pronounced stuns'l) a quadrilateral sail set outside the leech, or perpendicular edge, of a square sail to catch light winds. They are set by extending the yards with booms.

Swifter: a specially made rope fitted to the ends of the capstan bars to hold them together, to spread the considerable bending load and to allow purchase for extra hands.

Tabernacle: a socket fixed to the deck of a sailing vessel in which a mast is set, secured by a bolt passing through its foot, which can be removed in order to lower the mast.

Tack: 1) sailor's word for food, soft tack being more edible than hard tack.
2) the lower forward corner of a fore-and-aft sail.
3) the rope with which the clew, or lower corner, of a course, the lowest square sail, was held when sailing close-hauled.

Tack, to: to change the direction in which a sailing vessel moves in order to bring the wind on to her opposite side. This zig-zag progression, known as tacking, is the only way a sailing vessel can travel in the direction from which the wind is blowing.

Tackle: (pronounced taykel) an arrangement of ropes and blocks designed to increase the power of the pull on the ropes.

Taffrail: the rail around the stern of a ship.

Tarpaulin Captain: in Tudor and Stuart times, a captain who had attained command of his ship by experience and promotion rather than by patronage.

Telltale: now used of any mechanical or electrical device which disseminates information on board a ship; originally a repeating compass kept in the captain's cabin.

Thimble: a circular or pear-shaped metal ring with a groove round the outside around which a rope runs to form an eye.

Thole pins: pins inserted in the gunwale of a rowing boat to make a pivoting point for the oars.

Thwart: the wooden board running across a rowing boat on which the oarsman sits.

Tiddley: seaman's word for neat and tidy.

Tiller: a wooden or metal bar which fits into or round the head of the rudder and by which it is moved. Until the late 17th century all ships were steered with a tiller; now tillers are only found in small craft.

Tompion: a stopper put in the mouth of a gun to prevent water going down the barrel.

Tonnage: the measure of the weight of a ship or of its carrying capacity. Until the advent of iron-built ships, the tonnage of a vessel was calculated by a method known as Builder's Old Measurement, or B.O.M. There are now, confusingly, four methods of expressing the tonnage of a ship:
1) *displacement tonnage* is the weight of water displaced by a ship when loaded, which, since a floating body displaces its own weight in water, is also the weight of the ship. It is arrived at by calculating the cubic feet of water displaced and dividing by 35, since 35 cubic feet of water weigh one ton. Warships are normally measured by their displacement tonnage.
2) *deadweight tonnage* is the measure of the exact amount of cargo, bunkers, stores, etc., that a ship can carry when floating at her load draught. It is normally expressed in metric tons, or tonnes, of 1000kg or 2205lb.
3) *gross registered tonnage* is a measure of all the space available below the upper deck for cargo, stores and accommodation.
4) *net registered tonnage* is arrived at by deducting from the gross registered tonnage any space on which freightage cannot be charged, such as that taken up by machinery, crew's quarters, etc. Merchant ships are usually quoted by their gross or their deadweight tonnage. Both the gross and the net tonnage are quoted on a vessel's Certificate of Registry and it is on the latter that dues are normally paid.

Top: a platform at the head of the lower masts of a sailing ship, thus fore, main and mizen tops. In men-of-war they were used as fighting tops and manned by soldiers with muskets.

Topgallant: the topgallant mast, on which was set the topgallant sail, was the third in ascending order from the deck.

Top Hamper: anything, whether cargo or superstructure, above the deck.

Topmast: the second mast, coming between the lower mast and the topgallant mast.

Topping Lift: a rope used for lifting the end of a swinging spar.

Topsail: sail set on the yards of the topmast in square-rigged ships, or the sail above the mainsail in a fore-and-after.

Transoms: the horizontal timbers fixed across the sternpost of a wooden-built vessel to give her a flat, or transom, stern.

Treenails: (pronounced 'trennels') cylindrical pins of hard wood used in wooden ships to fasten the planks of a ship's side and bottom to the ribs. Treenails were preferred to iron nails or bolts because they did not rust nor rot the timber.

Trim, to: 1) to distribute the weight inside a ship so that she floats level in the water. Most ships of any size have trimming tanks, or, in submarines, ballast tanks, by means of which the trim can be adjusted by pumping water in or out as required. If a vessel is down in the water aft or forward, she is said to be trimmed by the stern or trimmed by the head.
2) to trim the sails is to set them so as to make the best use of the wind.

Truck: small wooden disc at the extreme top of a mast.

True: the direction of the North Pole where all lines of longitude converge, as opposed to the magnetic pole, the direction to which the compass needle points.

Truss: once the bands of rope by which the yards were secured to the masts, made obsolete by the introduction of the metal gooseneck, now itself known as a truss.

Trysail: 1) fore-and-aft sail set on a gaff on the fore- and mainmasts of a square-rigged three-master.
2) a small triangular sail set when heaving-to in a gale.

Tumble-home: the inward inclination of the upper part of a ship's side, the opposite of which is called flare.

Under Way: a vessel is said to be under way when she is moving through the water and will answer her helm. It is frequently, though incorrectly, written under weigh.

Upper Deck: 1) the highest of the continuous decks of a ship.
2) the officers as distinct from the lower deck or seamen.

Vane: 1) a small flag or strip of bunting used on sailing ships to indicate the direction of the wind.

Variation: the angle between the bearing of the magnetic North Pole and that of the geographical North Pole at the point and date of observation.

Veer, to: 1) a variation of to wear, meaning to bring the stern rather than the bows across the wind in order to change tack.
2) the wind veers when it changes in a clockwise direction.
3) one veers the cable of an anchor when paying it out.

Voyage: the voyage of a ship includes both her outward and homeward passages.

Waist: part of the upper deck of a ship between the quarterdeck and the forecastle.

Wardroom: the mess, or dining room, of all commissioned officers in a British warship except the captain who has a separate mess.

Warp, to: to move a ship in harbour by hauling on a rope secured to an anchor or bollard.

Warp: 1) the rope used when warping.
2) the rope used to secure a ship alongside a quay or another ship.
3) the rope used to raise or lower a fishing trawl.

Watch: the seven periods into which the day is divided on board ship: Middle Watch, midnight to 4am; Morning, 4am to 8am; Forenoon, 8am to noon; Afternoon, noon to 4pm; First dog, 4pm to 6pm; Last dog, 6pm to 8pm; First, 8pm to midnight. In order to enable the crew to have regular periods of rest, although the running of the ship must continue day and night, the company is usually divided into two or three groups for duty, known as the port and starboard watches, or the red, white and blue watches.

Wear, to: 1) a ship flies her national flag or ensign but wears a personal flag, such as that of an admiral.
2) to wear ship is to bring her on to the opposite tack by bringing the wind around the stern, as opposed to round the bow. When this is done a ship is wore, not worn.

Weather: a word used in several nautical senses apart from the meteorological. To have the weather gage means to be to windward of another vessel; a weather shore is one that lies to windward; the weather side of a ship is that which faces the wind; a ship's weather decks are those exposed to the weather. A ship is said to carry weather helm if the tiller has to be held to windward to keep her on course. A ship that can sail closer to the wind than most is said to be weatherly.

Whack: an old nautical expression for

253

daily rations which has survived in the term 'a fair whack' for a correct portion.

Whip, to: to bind twine or yarn round the end of a rope to stop it fraying.

Whipstaff: a device, obsolete after the introduction of the steering wheel, whereby the rudder could be moved from an upper deck. In a small vessel the helmsman could handle the tiller and have a clear field of vision. As the size of the superstructure gradually increased, this became impossible, so a pole was attached to the end of the tiller which, fixed to a fulcrum about one-third of the distance to its base, rose to the upper deck from where the helmsman could, by moving it laterally, control the rudder.

Windlass: a rotating cylinder, formerly fitted with bars and worked by hand, now usually powered by steam or electricity, used principally for raising and lowering the anchor.

Windward: the side from which the wind blows; the opposite to leeward.

Yard: the spar fastened horizontally or diagonally to the mast from which the sail is set. A square yard is set at right angles to the mast in such a way that it can be moved horizontally by means of the braces in order to catch the wind. A lateen yard is fixed diagonally across the mast.

Yardarm: that part of the yard which extends beyond the earing, or top corner, of a square sail. In former times sailors sentenced to death by court-martial were hanged from the yardarm.

Yaw, to: to deviate from a desired course when sailing with a following wind or sea on account of the diminished effect of the rudder under such circumstances. An intelligent helmsman should be able to anticipate and counteract this tendency.

Yuloh: a long flexible oar used by the Chinese to propel sampans and small junks. By moving the inboard end of the yuloh from side to side, a movement such as that of a fish's tail is produced by the end which projects over the stern into the water.

Zenith: a term used in nautical astronomy to denote the point in the heavens immediately above the observer.

III Nautical Acronyms

ACV	Air-cushion vehicle.
ALC	Armed landing craft.
ARM	Anti-radiation missile.
ASM	Air-to-surface missile.
ASW	Anti-submarine warfare.
BPDMS	Basic point defence missile system.
CAH	Carrier aircraft, helicopter.
CBT	Clean ballast tanks.
CIWS	Close in weapon system.
CODAG CODOG COGAG COGOG COSAG	Descriptions of mixed propulsion systems – combined diesel and/or gas turbine, diesel or gas turbine, gas turbine and/or gas turbine, gas turbine or gas turbine, steam and/or gas turbine.
COW	Crude oil washing.
DC	Depth charge.
DCT	Depth charge thrower.
DDG	Destroyer, guided missile.
DLG	Frigate, guided missile.
DP	Dual purpose (gun – for surface or AA use).
DSRV	Deep submergence recovery vessel.
DWT	Deadweight tonnage – the actual lifting capability of a ship.
ECM	Electronic countermeasures (i.e. jamming).
ECCM	Electronic counter – countermeasures.
ELINT	Electronic intelligence.
ELSBM	Exposed location single buoy mooring.
FAC	Fast attack craft.
FCSS	Fast combat support ship.
FRAM	Fleet rehabilitation and modernization programme (US Navy).
GRT	Gross registered tonnage – a measure of internal volume.
GWS	Guided weapons system.
IGS	Inert gas systems.
IMCO	Inter-Governmental Maritime Consultative Organization.
LANBY	Large automatic navigation buoy.
LASH	Lighter aboard ship.
LCM	Landing craft mechanized.

LCU	Landing craft utility.
LNG	Liquid natural gas (methane).
LPG	Liquid petroleum gas (butane and propane).
LSD	Landing ship dock.
LSL	Landing ship logistic.
LSM	Landing ship medium.
LST	Landing ship tank.
MAC	Merchant aircraft carrier.
MAD	Magnetic anomaly detector (for anti-submarine detection – identifying a steel body in the earth's magnetic field).
MAP	Military aid programme (US).
MEM	Marine engineer mechanic.
MEO	Marine engineer officer.
MSC	Military sealift command (US).
NTDS	Naval tactical data system.
NS	Nuclear submarine.
OBO	Oil/bulk/ore (carrier).
PAM	Patrol hydrofoil missileship.
PCC	Pure car carrier.
PROBO	Product/oil/bulk/ore (carrier).
RAS	Replenishment at sea.
RFA	Royal Fleet Auxiliary.
RO/RO	Roll On/Roll Off (see also pp. 158–60).
SAM	Surface-to-air missile.
SAR	Search and rescue.
SBT	Segregated ballast tanks.
SEEBEE	See p. 162.
SLBM	Submarine-launched ballistic missile.
SLEP	Service life extension programme (for US aircraft carriers).
SOLAS	Safety of life-at-sea (convention).
SPM	Single point mooring.
SSBN	Nuclear-powered ballistic missile submarine.
SSM	Surface-to-surface missile.
TEU	Twenty equivalent units (containerization measure).
ULCC	Ultra-large crude carrier.
VDS	Variable depth sonar.
VLCC	Very large crude carrier.

Bibliography

In many instances, particularly where the only point in altering the wording of what was already clearly expressed would have been to try and pass off someone else's research as my own, the source of information is given in the text. I have, therefore, listed here only the more general works upon which I have relied in the compilation of this work:

Annual Register, The, Longman Harlow, Essex.

BASSETT-LOWKE, W. J. and HOLLAND, GEORGE *Ships and Men* Harrap London 1946.

BLAKE, GEORGE *Lloyd's Register of Shipping 1760–1960* Crawley, Sussex.

BONSOR, N. R. P. *North Atlantic Seaway* T. Stephenson & Sons Prescot, Lancashire 1955.

Britannica Book of the Year.

BURGESS, MICHAEL *Aircraft Carriers and Aircraft-Carrying Cruisers* Burgess Media Services Wellington, New Zealand 1980.

BURGESS, MICHAEL *Battleships and Battle Cruisers* Burgess Media Services Wellington, New Zealand 1981.

CABLE, BOYD *A Hundred Year History of the P. & O.* Ivor Nicholson & Watson London 1937.

COMPTON-HALL, RICHARD *The Underwater War 1939–45* Blandford Press Poole, Dorset 1982.

CORLETT, EWAN *The Revolution in Merchant Shipping 1950–80* HMSO London 1981.

CORNWELL, E. L. (Editor) *An Illustrated History of Ships* New English Library Holborn, London 1979.

CRAIG, ROBIN *Steam Tramps and Cargo Liners* HMSO London 1980.

CRITCHLEY, MIKE *British Warships Since 1945* Maritime Books Liskeard, Cornwall 1981.

CRITCHLEY, MIKE *British Warships and Auxiliaries* Maritime Books Liskeard, Cornwall 1982.

DAVIS, RALPH *The Rise of the English Shipping Industry* David & Charles Newton Abbot, Devon 1972.

DUPUY, R. E. and DUPUY, T. N. *The Encyclopaedia of Military History* Macdonald and Jane's London 1970.

FRERE-COOK, GERVIS and MACKSEY, KENNETH *The Guinness History of*

Sea Warfare Guinness Superlatives Enfield, Middlesex 1975.

GRAY, EDWYN *A Damned Un-English Weapon* Seeley Service London 1971.

GRAY, EDWYN *The Killing Time* Seeley Service London 1972.

HAWKS, ELLISON *The Romance of the Merchant Ship* Harrap London 1936.

HOCKING, CHARLES *Dictionary of Disasters at Sea during the Age of Steam 1824–1962,* Lloyd's Register of Shipping London 1969.

Keesing's Contemporary Archives.

KEMP, PETER *The British Sailor* J. M. Dent & Sons Ltd London 1970.

KEMP, PETER (Editor) *The Oxford Companion to Ships and the Sea* Oxford University Press 1976.

LANDSTROM, BJORN *The Ship* George Allen & Unwin London 1961.

LEWIS, MICHAEL *The Navy of Britain* George Allen & Unwin London 1949.

LLOYD, CHRISTOPHER *The British Seaman* William Collins London 1968.

LYON, DAVID *Steam, Steel and Torpedoes* HMSO London 1980.

MABER, JOHN M. *Channel Packets and Ocean Liners* HMSO London 1980.

MARDER, ARTHUR *From Dreadnought to Scapa Flow* Oxford 1966.

McGOWAN, ALAN *The Century before Steam* HMSO London 1980.

McGOWAN, ALAN *Tiller and Whipstaff* HMSO London 1981.

McLEAVY, ROY *Naval Fast Strike Craft and Patrol Boats* Blandford Press Poole, Dorset 1979.

MIDDLETON, E. W. *Lifeboats of the World* Blandford Press Poole, Dorset 1977.

MOORE, J. (Editor) *Jane's Fighting Ships* Jane's Publishing Co London.

NEWELL, GORDON *Ocean Liners of the 20th Century* Bonanza Books New York 1973.

OUTHWAITE, LEONARD *The Atlantic*

Coward, McCann Inc New York 1957.

PHILLIPS-BIRT, DOUGLAS *A History of Seamanship* George Allen & Unwin London 1971.

PLUMRIDGE, JOHN H. *Hospital Ships and Ambulance Trains* Seeley Service London 1975.

PRESTON, ANTONY *Dreadnought to Nuclear Submarine* HMSO London 1980.

'Q' (Editor) *The Story of the Sea* Cassell 1895.

SPROULE, ANNA *Port Out, Starboard Home* Blandford Press Poole, Dorset 1978.

TØNNESSEN, J. N. and JOHNSEN, A. O. *The History of Modern Whaling* C. Hurst & Co London 1982.

UDEN, GRANT and COOPER, RICHARD *A Dictionary of British Ships and Seamen* Allen Lane/Kestrel Books Harmondsworth, Middlesex 1980.

VILLIERS, ALAN *The Way of a Ship* Hodder & Stoughton London 1954.

WARNER, OLIVER *Great Sea Battles* Weidenfeld and Nicolson London 1963.

WINCHESTER, CLARENCE (Editor) *Shipping Wonders of the World* 2 Vols, Amalgamated Press London 1939.

Index of Ship's Names

Index of Proper Names

General Index

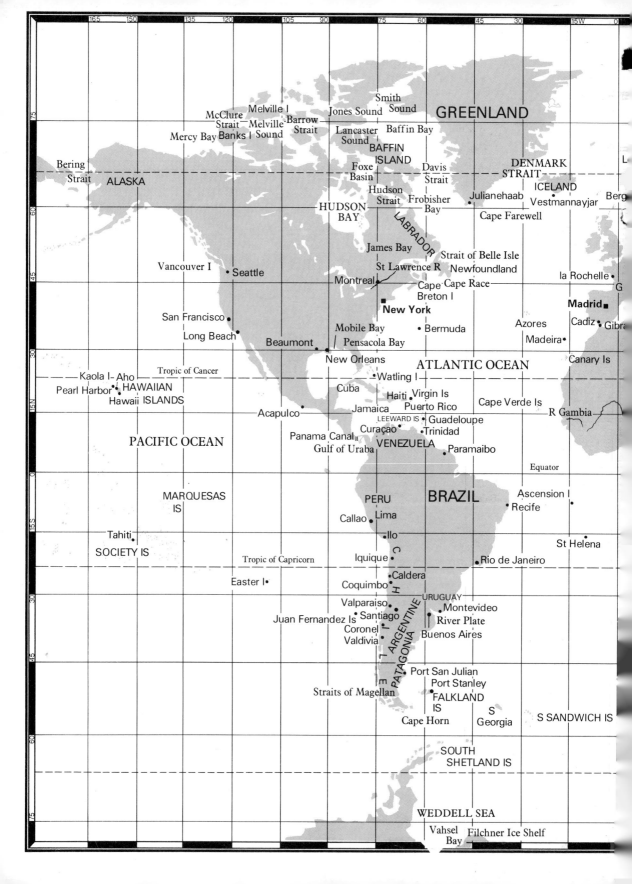